U.S. Television Network News

U.S. Television Network News
A Guide to Sources in English

compiled by Myron J. Smith, Jr.

Foreword by John Chancellor

McFarland & Company, Inc. Publishers
Jefferson, North Carolina, and London, 1984

Library of Congress Cataloging in Publication Data

Smith, Myron J.
  U.S. television network news.

  Bibliography: p.
  Includes index.
  1. Television broadcasting of news — United States —
Bibliography. 2. Documentary television programs — United
States — Bibliography. I. Title.
Z6951.S57 1983   [PN4888.T4]   016.0701'9   82-42885
ISBN 0-89950-080-3

Manufactured in the United States of America

McFarland Box 611 Jefferson NC 28640

bK 12-21-84

for Dennie

FOREWORD

Some day, archeologists will begin to put together the shards and fragments of our 20th century civilization. They will find some big pieces missing, I'm afraid.

Television, and television news, has had an incalculable effect on American life. Yet, among all the means of communication, it is the most ephemeral. When national television began around 1950, only about 9 per cent of American homes had receiving sets. By 1960, over 90 per cent had televisions. But the television industry was scandalously inept at keeping track of its own product. Those early programs, priceless historical records, were thrown carelessly on shelves, where they slowly crumbled to dust.

Things are better today. Programs are recorded on tape; the networks now take more care; a few universities have assumed the task of record-keeper. But much has been lost, and, alas, much more will be lost.

That is why I endorse, indeed, applaud, Myron J. Smith's bibliography of television network news. He has used his professional skill to a high purpose; historians and scholars will have an additional means of understanding television because of his work.

I find it ironic, but not totally surprising, that the best record of this immensely influential medium of television will be found in the printed word.

John Chancellor

ACKNOWLEDGMENTS

For their advice, assistance, or encouragement in the formulation, research, and completion of this endeavor, the following persons and libraries are gratefully acknowledged. Their involvement of course does not constitute endorsement.

John Chancellor, NBC, New York
Vera Mayer, vice president, Information and Archives, NBC, New York
Eric Sevareid, Washington, D.C.
Ray White, *Washington Journalism Review*, Washington, D.C.
Walter Cronkite, CBS News, New York
Douglas F. Gibbons, The Museum of Broadcasting, New York
James B. Poteat, Research Services, Television Information Office, New York
Pieter Visser and Robert Fulton, News Department, WBOY-TV, Clarksburg, W.V.

Special appreciation is reserved for my colleagues at Salem College without whose backing and aid this project would not have been completed. Dean Gary S. McAllister continuously supported and encouraged me to proceed. The Communications-Broadcasting Department, chaired by Rick Banks and including Al Greule and Brad Nason, provided stimulation, insight, and resources. Sara A. Casey, Margaret Allen, Jacqueline Isaacs, and Janet Underwood of the Benedum Learning Resources Center staff, and Stuart C. Godfrey, director of media, gave bibliographic and interlibrary loan assistance, in the process learning more about network television news than they may have cared to.

Finally, warmest remembrances of the many hours my wife Dennie tolerated and helped me in the preparation of this book.

Myron J. Smith, Jr.
Salem, West Virginia
1982–1983

TABLE OF CONTENTS

Table of Contents   xii

LIST OF JOURNALS CITED

Each of the titles listed below contributed at least one citation to this bibliography.

AAUW Journal
Academy of Political Science
  Proceedings
Across the Board
Advertising Age
Aerospace Historian
AFTRA
Air Force and Space Digest
Air University Review
America
American Federationist
American Film
American Film Institute Report
American Heritage
American Home
American Journal of Sociology
American Legion Magazine
American Political Quarterly
American Political Science Review
American Scholar
American Society of Newspaper
  Editors (ASNE) Bulletin
American University Law Review
Annals of the American Academy of
  Political and Social Science
Annual Review of Psychology
Armed Forces and Society
Armed Forces Journal International
Armor
Army
Army Digest
Atlanta
Atlantic
Atlas
Audubon
Aviation Week and Space Technology

Biographical News
Book Digest
Broadcast Engineering
Broadcasting
Brookings Bulletin
Bulletin of Bibliography
Business Week

California Law Review
Capitol Studies
Center Magazine
Central States Speech Journal
  Channels
Chitty's Law Journal
Choice
Christianity and Crisis
Cincinnati Law Review
City
Civil Liberties Review
Cleveland State Law Review
College and University Journal
College English
Colorado Quarterly
Columbia Journal of Law and
  Social Problems
Columbia Journalism Review
Columbia Law Review
Commentary
Commonweal
Communication Monograph
Communication Quarterly
Communication Research
Computers and Automation and
  People
Congressional Quarterly Weekly
  Report

Congressional Record
Contemporary Review
Cornell Law Review
Coronet
Cosmopolitan
Crawdaddy
Current

D Magazine
Defense '80
Democracy
DePaul Law Review
Dial

Editor and Publisher
Editorial Research Reports
Education Digest
Education Broadcasting Review
Elementary English
Emmy
Encore
Encounter
English Journal

FBI Law Enforcement Bulletin
Family Circle
Family Weekly
Federal Communications Bar Journal
Federal Register
Fifty Plus
Film Comment
Flying
Forbes
Foreign Affairs
Foreign Service Journal
Fortune
Freedom at Issue

Geo
George Washington Law Review
Georgetown Law Journal
Glamour
Good Housekeeping

Harper's
Harper's Bazaar
Harrangue, A Political and Social
   Review (Belfast)
Harvard Civil Rights–Civil Liberties
   Law Review
Harvard Journal on Legislation
Harvard Law Review
Hastings Law Journal

Holiday
Horizon
Houston
Human Behavior
Human Events

Illinois Issues
Imprimis
Indiana Law Journal
Industry Week
Inquiry
Instructor
Intellect
Interface
International Problems
International Security Review
International Social Science Journal
Issues

Johns Hopkins Magazine
Journal of Applied Psychology
Journal of Broadcasting
Journal of Communications
Journal of Instructional Media
Journal of International Affairs
Journal of Peace Research
Journal of Politics
Journal of Popular Culture
Journal of Psychology
Journal of Public Law
Journal of Social Issues
Journal of the Bar Association of the
   District of Columbia
Journalism Education
Journalism History
Journalism Monographs
Journalism Quarterly

Ladies Home Journal
Law and Contemporary Problems
Law Library Journal
Life
Lithopinion
Look
Los Angeles

McCalls
Maryland Law Review
Mass Communications Review
Matrix
Middle East Journal
Midwest Journal of Political Science
Midwest Quarterly

Military Review
Minnesota Law Review
Minority of One
Missouri Life
Modern Maturity
More
Ms.

NAEB Journal
Nation
National Journal
National Review
National Wildlife
Naval War College Review
Navy
Negro History Bulletin
New England Law Review
New Guard
New Leader
New Republic
New Statesman and Nation
New York
New York Law Forum
New York Review of Books
New York State Bar Journal
New York Times Magazine
New York University International
    Law Review
New York University Law Review
New Yorker
News Media and the Law
Newsweek
Nieman Reports
North Carolina Historical Review
Nuclear Safety

Objectivist
Officer
Oklahoma Observer

Panorama
Parents Magazine
Parliamentary Affairs (Great Britain)
Penthouse
People
Personality and Social Psychology
Personnel
Playboy
Political Communication and
    Persuasion
Political Quarterly
Political Science Quarterly
Political Studies

Politicks
Presidential Studies Quarterly
Proceedings of the American Philo-
    sophical Society
Progressive
Psychology Today
Public Administration Review
Public Interest
Public Opinion
Public Opinion Quarterly
Public Relations Journal
Public Relations Review
Public Utilities
Publishers Weekly

Quarterly Journal of Speech
Quest 81
Qui
Quill

RQ
Rackham Reports
Ramparts
Reader's Digest
Record of the Bar of the City of New
    York
Redbook
Reporter
Review
Review of Politics
The Review of Southern California
    Journalism
Rolling Stone
Rutgers-Camden Law Journal

Saturday Evening Post
Saturday Review
Saturday Review of Literature
School Review
School Science and Mathematics
Seminar
Senior Scholastic
Social Forces
Social Indicators Research
Social Policy
Social Text
Society
Sociological and Social Research
Soldiers
Southern Speech Communications
    Journal
Sponsor
Strategic Review

Television
Television Quarterly
Television-Radio Age
Temple Law Quarterly
Texas Monthly
Time
Today's Health
Today's Speech
Trans-Action
Travel and Leisure
TV Age
TV Guide
Twin Cities Journalism Review

U.S.
U.S. Naval Institute Proceedings
U.S. News and World Report
USA Today
University of Colorado Law Review
University of Pennsylvania Law
  Review
University of West Los Angeles Law
  Review

Villanova Law Review
Virginia Law Review
Vital Speeches
Viva
Vogue

W
War/Peace Report
Washington Journalism Review
Washington Monthly
Washingtonian
West Virginia History
Western Journal of Speech Com-
  munication
Western Political Quarterly
Western Speech
Wilson Library Bulletin
Wilson Quarterly
Wisconsin Journal of Education
Women's Wear Daily
Working Woman
Worldview

INTRODUCTION

According to a November 1968 *Huntley-Brinkley Field Study*, "network news is national news" focused upon "national themes."[1] As such, electronic journalism on network television is a relatively recent craft, less than a half century old, which "is still in many cases groping to determine its own role in broadcasting."[2]

Few people may have imagined when the radio broadcast networks, led by CBS, began making an organized effort to gather and report national and international news in the 1930's that a new age in information delivery was dawning, just as some suggest that another new age in communications has arrived in the 1980's due to cable and satellites. As correspondents like Edward R. Murrow and Eric Sevareid reported the actions of World War II, listeners realized that the actual sounds, as well as descriptions, of events provided "an intimacy to news reporting that the print media lacked."[3]

Broadcast news continued to develop after V-J Day, but now pictures were added with the coming of television into American homes. By 1953, difficulties with film were being ironed out and both NBC and CBS had nightly news broadcasts. As the network news departments mastered public service programming (the radio show "Meet the Press" was an early transfer to television; knowledge of Murrow's "See It Now" series is basic to every broadcasting student) and documentaries appeared more and more frequently, broadcast industry executives began to appreciate that news could provide both profit and stature.[4]

By the time NBC and CBS introduced the half-hour evening news program in 1963 (followed by ABC in 1967), network television news was widely accepted by its viewing audience as a premier source of data on the day's events. "Polls demonstrate that over-the-air broadcasting is this nation's most trusted medium," commented National Association of Broadcasters President Vincent Wasilewski in an April 1982 speech; "64% of those polled said that they receive most of their news from television."[5]

Wars and revolutions, presidents and politicians, riots and space shots, foreign affairs, economics, and defense are among the many items to have come under the scrutiny of the electronic eye. This coverage has not been limited to evening news programming, but was carried over into such documentary series as CBS's "CBS Reports" and NBC's "NBC White Paper," into public service interview programs like the aforementioned

"Meet the Press," "Face the Nation" and "Issues and Answers," and now, magazine-like series such as "20/20" and "60 Minutes." Elections, moon shots, Senate hearings, presidential press conferences, and assassination reports provide Americans with almost living documents on events of our times.

Despite the scope of its journalistic enterprise, the institution of network news, part of what is sometimes called the "fifth estate," has been the subject of controversy since the start. Author/commentators like Edward J. Epstein, Les Brown, and Bob Teague (to name only three) have pointed out the relationship between corporate policy, procedures, and profits, and the manner in which news programming is handled. Questions concerning network news "bias" and "power" to influence public opinion have been debated for years. Edward R. Murrow and Joseph R. McCarthy sparred mightily in the early 1950's, well before former Vice President Spiro T. Agnew's famous 1969 Des Moines attack. Because the networks are licensed to use the public airwaves, the Federal Communications Commission (itself often under assault) has filled thousands of pages of documents concerning actual or alleged improprieties or disputed practices, many involving network news. Concerns for First Amendment rights occupy the thoughts of broadcasters today as much or more so than they do print media executives. Echoes of Spiro Agnew are heard these days, Walter Cronkite recently warned; "a 'pattern of restriction' is becoming detectable in today's Washington."[6]

Long-standing worries over managed news by news subjects or the staging or editing of events or remarks out of context by journalists have been widely noted and discussed. The whole idea of investigative journalism on television has come under fire, both from within and without the industry, as by a recent examination by David Shaw shows.[7]

Some critics, including certain network journalists like David Brinkley, have wondered about the attention, or "star status," lavished upon on-camera network news personnel. Others have debated personnel assignments such as teaming and flashy graphics in a ratings war that is officially denied. The ideas of instant access and topicality bother many who have witnessed the ease of technology in covering—sometimes with direct journalist intervention in—distant happenings like the Iran crisis of 1979–1981 or the pre-camp David diplomacy between Egypt's Sadat and Israel's Begin.

Despite all the many advances in news programming and technology, critics, viewers, and news people alike seem to be asking, most of all, "whether or not viewers" are, as Don Pember puts it, "really getting much more than John Cameron Swayze offered in the fifties on his fifteen minute Camel News Caravan?"[8] What should be the role of network news in the information gathering marketplace of the American home? Are the 64% of those whom Mr. Wasilewski noted as receiving most of their data from television really receiving a full picture?

In a recent speech at Syracuse University, ABC Nightline host Ted

Koppel touched on these questions in parts of his address: "Modern American journalism is tailor made for the quick thrill and the easy kill.... All too rarely do we as journalists or you as an electorate, ask ourselves why something is important. We have become so obsessed with facts that we have lost touch with the truth."[9] After noting that "you can't do it in 22 minutes," pioneer Fred W. Friendly says this of people who rely on network news exclusively for information: "they're convinced they've had a picture of reality. What they've had is 22 minutes of reality. And that's a national tragedy."[10] Suggesting that people seek additional information from other sources, especially newspapers, Walter Cronkite concludes that network television news is "only the first step in being informed. It's a great guide to the day's news, but we cannot cover in depth in a half hour many of the stories required to get a good understanding of the world."[11]

This bibliography is intended to serve as a "working" guide to English-language sources (99% U.S.) concerning network television news during the period from the late 1940's through 1982 (an Addenda section brings the coverage forward through fall 1983). While aimed primarily at scholars and especially graduate and undergraduate students, it should also prove useful to librarians, general readers, teachers, and journalists. It may also be interesting to specialized students known as "news buffs."

This guide is not definitive, but it attempts comprehensiveness in that virtually all factors concerning network television news are covered. As a reference tool, it will permit users to quickly determine what material is available and help them establish a basis for further research. In general, items are cited which the user might reasonably expect to find in large university, public, or government libraries. In practice, students should be able to find many of the more recent book titles, at least, in even small- or medium-sized college or public library collections. Should you be unable to turn up a given reference locally, keep in mind that some special libraries exist, such as that of the Television Information Office, which may be visited by appointment. Many items can be obtained from other libraries via interlibrary loan, details of which service can be obtained at your nearest library.

The criteria for selection in this guide is the same as that employed in the author's twenty or so other bibliographies. The following types of published material are represented: books and monographs, scholarly papers, periodical and journal articles, government documents, doctoral dissertations, and masters' theses. Although much has been included, it was necessary to draw a line somewhere and omit certain kinds of information. Excluded materials include fiction, children's works, newspaper articles (unless reprinted in other works), poetry, and book reviews.

The nine main sections of the Table of Contents form, with their subsections, a highly simplified topical guide to the book's organization. Each alphabetically-arranged section includes an introduction to the topic(s) covered. Brief annotations are provided for book titles and certain periodical articles.

Each entry is serial numbered. The detailed author and subject indexes cite these entry numbers.

Notes

1. Quoted in Edward J. Epstein, *News from Nowhere* (New York: Vintage Books, 1974), p. 58.

2. Don R. Pember, *Mass Media in America*, 3d ed. (Chicago: Science Research Associates, 1981), p. 139.

3. Pember, *loc. cit.*

4. Epstein, *op. cit.*, pp. 58–59; Sydney W. Head, *Broadcasting in America: A Survey of Radio and Television*, 3d ed. (Boston: Houghton, Mifflin, 1976), p. 171.

5. *Broadcasting*, CII (April 12, 1982), 33.

6. *Ibid.*, 31.

7. "The Trouble with TV Muckraking," *TV Guide*, XXIX (October 10, 1981), 6–10.

8. Pember, *op. cit.*, p. 140.

9. *Broadcasting*, CII (May 17, 1982), 58.

10. Fred W. Friendly, "Network News? 'A National Tragedy'—Local News? 'It's Putrid'—Million Dollar Journalists? 'Obscene.'" *TV Guide*, XXIX (August 1, 1981), 25.

11. "What's Right, Wrong with Television News," *U.S. News and World Report*, XC (March 16, 1981), 46.

No journalistic age was ever given a weapon for truth with quite the scope of this fledgling television. — *Edward R. Murrow, "See It Now" premier, 1951*

I. REFERENCE WORKS

The purpose of this section is to provide the user with a wide variety of sources for additional research into the complexities of network television news, both as an "institution" and in its dealings with various events since the late 1940's. In addition, it cites some titles which have a general impact on the topic.

Current and retrospective English-language sources relative to this book can be located in the bibliographies and in the abstracts and indexes cited. Recent information, some of it background, and terminology useful in interpreting language or concepts in some of the works cited in this guide can be found by consulting the sources in the annuals and dictionaries subsection. Users should also be certain to check the footnotes and bibliographies (where provided) in the books, scholarly journal articles, dissertations, and documents borrowed as the result of viewing titles in sections II through VII.

BIBLIOGRAPHIES

1   ABS Guide to Recent Publications in the Social and Behav-
      ioral Sciences. New York: American Behavioral Scientist,
      1965.

2   _____: Supplements. Beverly Hills, Calif.: Sage Publi-
      cations, 1966--.

3   American Book Publishing Record. New York: R. R. Bow-
      ker, 1960--, v. 1--.

4   American Historical Association. Writings on American His-
      tory. Washington, D.C.: U.S. Government Printing Office,
1948-1961. Writings were begun in the years after World War I,
but these volumes come within our time frame.

5   _____. _____. Milwood, N.Y.: Kraus Reprint, 1962--.
      After the Writings project was removed from the GPO, the
Kraus company issued a multi-volume set covering the years
from 1962-1972 with annual volumes thereafter. From a historical perspective, this effort is quite worthwhile for students of
journalism and network television news.

6   Anderson, David A., and Brandon C. Janes, eds. Priva-
      cy and Public Disclosures under the Freedom of Information
Act. Tarleton Law Library Legal Bibliography Series, no. 11.
Austin, TX.: Tarleton Law Library, University of Texas,
1976. 173p. A useful guide to the literature on the FDA with
references to its use by journalists and editors.

1

7 Bibliographic Index. New York: H. W. Wilson Co., 1947--,
    v. 3--. A valuable source to bibliographies relative to our
    topic, both free-standing and as parts of other works.
8 Bibliography of Asian Studies. Ann Arbor, Mich.: Asso-
    ciations for Asian Studies, 1957--. v. 1--. Useful infor-
mation on coverage of events in Asia, especially the Vietnam
War.
9 Blum, Eleanor. Basic Books in the Mass Media: An Anno-
    tated, Selected Booklist Covering General Communications,
Book Publishing, Broadcasting, Films, Magazines, Newspapers,
Advertising, Indexes, and Scholarly and Professional Periodicals.
Urbana: University of Illinois Press, 1972. 252p. Set in
typescript, this first edition of the basic general media bibliography devotes approximately a fifth of its citations to radio
and television.
10 _____. _____. 2d ed. Urbana: University of
    Illinois Press, 1980. 426p. A continuance and revision of
the excellence noted in the previous entry; neither edition lists
periodical articles.
11 _____. Reference Books in the Mass Media. Urbana:
    University of Illinois Press, 1962. 103p. Formerly a
useful starting place, this work has been largely superseded by
the previous citation.
12 Books on Demand Subject Guide: 84,000 Selected Books
    Available as On-Demand Reprints. Ann Arbor, Mich.:
University Microfilms International, 1977. 786p. A catalogue
containing a few titles relative to this work.
13 Boston. Public Library. The Public Interest and the
    Right to Know--Access to Government Information and the
Role of the Press: A Selected Bibliographical Guide. Boston,
1971. 59p. Contains many useful citations but in need of
updating.
14 Broderick, Gertrude (Golden). Radio and Television Bibli-
    ography. Washington, D.C.: Office of Education Bulletin
(No. 2), U.S. Department of Health, Education and Welfare,
1956. 46p. Emphasis on the historical and sociological aspects
of media.
15 Browne, Donald R. "Broadcasting in Industrially-Devel-
    oped Nations: An Annotated Bibliography." Journal of
Broadcasting, XIX (Summer 1975), 341-355. One of a series of
around-the-world broadcasting guides printed by the Journal
of Broadcasting, this one is useful for comparison purposes.
16 Cassata, Mary, and Thomas Skill. "The Literature of
    Television: Directions." Choice, XVIII (April 1982), 1027-
    1036.
17 Clotfelter, James. Communications Theory in the Study
    of Politics: A Review of the Literature. Studies in
Journalism and Communications, no. 7. Chapel Hill, N.C.:
School of Journalism, University of North Carolina, 1968. 19p.
A brief, pioneering guide now in need of updating.
18 Comstock, George A., and Marilyn Fisher. Television
    and Human Behavior: A Guide to the Pertinent Scientific
Literature. RAND Report R-1746-CF. Santa Monica, Calif.:
RAND Corporation, 1975. 344p. Quite valuable for those
studying the effects of television in its various aspects upon
audiences.

19 Cooling, B. Franklin, 3d, and Alan Millett. Doctoral Dissertations in Military Affairs: A Bibliography. Bibliography Series, no. 10. Manhattan: Kansas State University Library, 1972. 153p. The basic source for those seeking references to dissertations on television network news relations with the military and such military events as the Vietnam War; updated in the April and then the February issues of the journal Military-Affairs.

20 Council on Foreign Affairs. Foreign Affairs 50-Year Bibliography: New Evaluations of Significant Books on International Relations, 1920-1970. New York: R. R. Bowker, 1970. Includes titles relevant to this study; the book review and other materials received sections of the journal Foreign Affairs continue to be a valuable source for those studying the relationship of international news to network television news.

21 The Cumulative Book Index. New York: H. W. Wilson Co., 1948--. Valuable for publishing information on new titles as they appear.

22 Dick, B. "Researcher's Guide to the Watergate Affair." Law Library Journal, LXXI (February-August 1978), 77-82, 266-269, 420-424. Reviews all of the pertinent references, including those related to network television news coverage.

23 Draughon, Donnie W. The Central Intelligence Agency's Reference Aid Series: A List. Washington, D.C.: Document Expediting Service, , Exchange and Gifts Division, Library of Congress, 1979. 6p. Contains 194 citations covering the period from January 1976 to December 1978; many of the documents are useful as background for those studying the international relations aspects of television network news.

24 Drazan, Joseph G. Three Mile Island: A Preliminary Checklist. P-748. Monticello, Ill.; Vance Bibliographies, 1981. 18p. The most complete listing of titles available.

25 Forthcoming Books. New York: R. R. Bowker Co., 1966--. v. 1--. This tool, with its companion Subject Guide to Forthcoming Books, will give the user advance information on new titles soon to be available on television network news.

26 Freedom of Information Center. Annotated Bibliography. Report 344. Columbia: (FDI Center) School of Journalism, University of Missouri, 1975. 17p.

27 Freidel, Frank, ed. Harvard Guide to American History, rev. ed. 2 vols. Cambridge, Mass.: Harvard University Press, 1974. Includes a few citations of a relevant background nature.

28 Friedman, Leslie J. Sex Role Stereotyping in the Mass Media: An Annotated Bibliography. New York: Garland, 1977. 324p. The most complete work of its kind; includes a variety of references relative to this work.

29 Gandy, Oscar H., Jr., et al. Media and the Government: An Annotated Bibliography. Stanford, Calif.: Institute for Communications Research, Stanford University, 1975. 93p. Although slight in size, this little tome is invaluable for those who would locate works relevant to its topic. Needs revision.

30 Genthner, Fred L. Guide to News and Information Sources for Journalists. San Luis Obispo: Robert F. Kennedy

Library, California Polytechnic State University, 1981. 58p.
Designed for the working journalist (print and media) who
desires quick reference to organizations and publications.
   31 Gitter, A. George. Communication: A Guide to Information
       Sources: Psychology Information Guide Series, no. 3.
Detroit: Gale Research, 1980. 157p. A bibliography on all
aspects of the general subject of communication.
   32 Gompertz, Kenneth. "A Bibliography of Articles About
       Broadcasting in Law Periodicals, 1956-1968." Journal of
Broadcasting, XIV (Winter 1969-1970), 83-134.
   33 Gordon, Thomas F., and Mary E. Verna. Effects and
       Processes of Mass Communications: A Comprehensive Biblio-
graphy, 1950-1975. Beverley Hills, Calif.: Sage Publications,
1978. 224p. Includes citations relative to the hows and whys
of network television news.
   34 _____. Mass Media and Socialization: A Selected Biblio-
       graphy. Philadelphia: School of Communications and
Theater, Temple University, 1973. 47p.
   35 Greenstein, Fred I., Larry Berman, and Alvin S. Felzen-
       berg. Evolution of the Modern Presidency: A Bibliography
Survey. Washington, D.C.: American Enterprise Institute for
Public Policy Research, 1977. Unpaged. Especially valuable
for citations concerning presidential press relations of Eisenhower, Kennedy, Johnson, Nixon, and Ford.
   36 Harrell, Karen F. The Role of Television in U.S. Politics
       and Government: A Bibliography, 1961-1981. Public
Administration Series, Bibliography P-814. Monticello, Ill.:
Vance Bibliographies, 1981. 12p. A slim and inexpensive
starting place for those interested in this aspect of our subject.
   37 Heath, C. Louis. Mutiny Does Not Happen Lightly: The
       Literature of the American Resistance to the Vietnam War.
Metuchen, N.J.: Scarecrow Press, 1976. 571p. Comprehensive with a number of citations relative to the role of network
television news organizations.
   38 Holler, Frderick L., comp. The Information Sources of
       Political Science. 6 vols. Santa Barbara, Calif.: ABC/
Clio Press, 1975. Comprehensive with some entries on political
communications and the role of the press, including network
television news.
   39 International Bibliography of Political Science. Chicago:
       Aldine, 1952--. v. 1--. While international in scope, this
annual guide does contain citations to political communications in
America.
   40 International Information Service: A Quarterly Annotated
       Index of Selected Materials on Current International Affairs,
1963--. v.--1. Very useful for those examining the foreign
news coverage of the American television networks.
   41 Kaid, Lynda L., Keith R. Sanders, and Robert O. Hirsch.
       Political Campaign Communications: A Bibliography and
Guide to the Literature. Metuchen, N.J.: Scarecrow Press,
1974. 211p. Especially useful for those studying the presidential campaigns of 1952-1972.
   42 Kittross, John M., comp. Theses and Dissertations in
       Broadcasting, 1920-1972. Philadelphia: Broadcast Educa-
tion Association, 1977. 250p. Traces all related to broadcasting, including network television news.

43   Liebert, Robert M., and Neala S. Schwartzberg. "Mass
     Communications." Annual Review of Psychology, 28 (1977),
141-173. Examines the general literature produced in 1970-1976.
44   McCavitt, William E. Radio and Television: A Selected,
     Annotated Bibliography. Metuchen, N.J.: Scarecrow
Press, 1978. 229p. A useful general study which concentrates
on books and reports.
45   McCoy, Ralph E. Freedom of the Press: An Annotated
     Bibliography. Carbondale: Southern Illinois University
Press, 1968. 526p.
46   _____. Freedm of the Press: A Bibliocyclopedia, Ten
     Year Supplement (1967-1977). Carbondale: Southern
Illinois University Press, 1979. 544p. McCoy's work is the
most comprehensive available on the subject, which includes
massive coverage of the government's relationship with television network news.
47   McKerns, Joseph P., et al. "Mass Media Criticism: An
     Annotated Bibliography." Mass Communications Review, III
(Winter 1975-1976), 9-18.
48   Morrison, L. D. "The Modern Presidency: A Selected
     Bibliography.: Bulletin of Bibliography, XXX (January
1973), 14-15. A quick review of books; useful for background
material.
49   Paperbound Books in Print. New York: R. R. Bowker
     Co., 1955--. v. 1--. Provides listings for paperbacks,
including originals and reprints dealing with television network
news.
50   Price, Warren G., and Calder M. Pickett. An Annotated
     Journalism Bibliography, 1958-1968. Minneapolis: Univer-
sity of Minnesota Press, 1970. 285p. Arranged alphabetically
by author, this guide covers 2,200 books with between two and
five lines of description.
51   Rosenberg, Kenyon, and Judith K. Rosenberg. Watergate:
     An Annotated Bibliography. Littleton, Colo.: Libraries
Unlimited, 1975. 141p. Books, periodical articles, and government reports are covered in this the only book-length bibliography on the subject.
52   Schramm, Wilbur. "Mass Communications." Annual Review
     of Psychology, XIII (1962), 251-284. Examines the litera-
ture of the 1950's.
53   Smith, Bruce L., and Chitra M. International Communica-
     tions and Political Opinion: A Guide to the Literature.
Princeton, N.J.: Published for the Bureau of Social Science
Research by Princeton University Press, 1956. 325p. Last in
three pioneering bibliographies on the subject, this guide
describes 2,500 titles with numerous references to broadcasting
in the years 1943-1955. Sadly in need of updating, this work
is of only limited value today, except as a historical bibliography.
54   Smith, Craig R. "Television News as Rhetoric." Western
     Journal of Speech Communications, XLI (1977), 147-149.
     A brief guide to the literature of news distortion.
55   Smith, Dwight L., and Lloyd W. Garrison, eds. The
     American Political Process: Selected Abstracts of Periodical
Literature (1954-1971). Santa Barbara, Calif.: ABC/Clio Press,

1972. 630p. A massive annotated guide to the literature which covers its subject since the founding of the Republic; includes a few citations relative to network television news since 1948.

56 Smith, Myron, J. , Jr. Intelligence, Propaganda, and Psychological Warfare, Covert Operations, 1945-1980. Vol. II of The Secret Wars: A Guide to Sources in English. War/ Peace Bibliography Series, no. 13. Santa Barbara, Calif.: ABC/Clio Press, 1981. 389p. Useful for the relationship of the CIA to the press.

57 _____. International Terrorism, 1968-1980. Vol. III of The Secret Wars: A Guide to Sources in English. War/ Peace Bibliography Series, no. 14. Santa Barbara, Calif.: ABC/Clio Press, 1980. 237p. See especially "Terrorism and the News Media," pp. 106-109.

58 Sources: A Guide to Print and Non-Print Materials Available from Organizations, Industry, Government Agencies, and Specialized Publishers. Syracuse, N.Y.: Gaylord Professional Publications, 1977--. v. 1--.

59 Stapleton, M. L. The Truman and Eisenhower Years: A Selective Bibliography. Metuchen, N.J.: Scarecrow Press, 1973. 221p. Includes a few citations to the mass media.

60 Sterling, Christopher H. The Media Sourcebook: Comparative Reviews and Listings of Textbooks in Mass Communications. Washington, D.C.: National Association of Educational Broadcasters, 1974. 53p. Evaluates some 350 titles published 1960-1973; updated in the February and later issues of Public Telecommunications Review. See also this author's "Mass Communications Tests and Readers: An Overview for 1974/75," Mass Communication Review. II (December 1974), 24-40.

61 _____. "Television as a Cultural Force: A Selected Reading List." In: Richard Adler and Douglass Cater, eds. Television as a Cultural Force. New York: Praeger, 1976. pp. 175-184. A useful brief survey with annotated entries.

62 Subject Guide to Books in Print. New York: R. R. Bowker, 1957--. v. 1--. Together with the C.B.I., this list (actually an index to the Books in Print main volumes) provides an annual comprehensive list of titles available for purchase in the English language, mostly from U.S. sources. Users should check various headings, e.g., journalism, in addition to the ones under television.

63 Sutton, Othe K. Choosing the President. USAF Academy Special Bibliography Series.no. 18. Colorado Springs, Colo.: U.S.A.F. Academy Library, 1974. 39p. A brief but useful introduction and source guide with a few references to media influences.

64 Swerdlow, Joel. "Is All the News Fit to Save?" American Film, IV (May 1979), 8-9. Not a bibliography, but a discussion of the value of placing network television news tapes into archives.

65 Tannenbaum, Percy, and Bradley Greenberg. "Mass Communications." Annual Review of Psychology, XIX (1968), 351-386. Examines the literature of 1961-1966.

66 Television in Government and Politics: A Bibliography. New York: Television Information Office, 1964. 62p. Still useful for the period prior to Lyndon Johnson.

67   United States, Library of Congress. Library of Congress
      Catalog, Books-Subjects: A Cumulative List of Works Repre-
sented by Library of Congress Printed Cards. Washington, D.C.:
U.S. Government Printing Office, 1950--. v. 1--. Users should
look under the headings journalism and television.
68   . President's Commission on Communication Policy.
      Bibliography. Springfield, Va.: National Technical Infor-
mation Service, Department of Commerce, 1969. 172p. Examines
the full range of communications policy and the Federal government's relationship to it.
69   Verticle File Index. New York: H. W. Wilson Co., 1948--.
      v. 17--. Useful for locating pamphlets issued by organiza-
tions related to television industry as well as the networks and
U.S. government.
70   Weiss, Walter. "Mass Communications." Annual Review
      of Psychology, XXII (1971), 309-336. Looks at literature
of the years 1967-1970.
71   Whitlatch, J. B. "Government Information." RQ, XVIII
      (Summer 1979), 391-397. A brief bibliography of titles,
some of which shed further light upon our subject.
72   Wright, J. L. "Television and Television Criticism: A
      Select Bibliography." Journal of Popular Culture, VII
(Spring 1974), 892-894. A brief bibliographic review of the
subject, including aspects related to network news.

ABSTRACTS AND INDEXES

73   Access: The Supplementary Index to Periodicals. Syracuse,
      N.Y.: Gaylord Professional Publications, 1975--. v. 1--.
Provides citations to magazines not usually found in Reader's
Guide.
74   America: History and Life--a Guide to Periodical Literature.
      Santa Barbara, Calif.: ABC/Clio Press, 1964--. v. 1--.
Coverage of literature on contemporary events as well as historical; journalism is covered as is the press relationship to presidents and politics.
75   Berman Associates. Checklist of Congressional Hearings
      and Reports. Washington, D.C., 1958--. v. 1--. A listing
of Congressional hearings, including several on network television news held over the years.
76   Bibliographic Index to Current U.S. Joint Publications Re-
      search Service Translations. New York: C.C.M. Infor-
mation Corp., 1962--. v. 1--. Useful in providing access to
foreign press and periodical articles relative to some of the
events touched upon by network television reports.
77   Business Periodical Index. New York: H. W. Wilson Co.,
      1958--. v. 1--. Extremely useful for citations to journals
in the press industry, e.g., Broadcasting, Editor and Publisher,
etc.
78   CBS News Index: Key to the Television News Broadcasts.
      Sanford, N.C.: Microfilming Corp. of America, 1975--.
v. 1--. Provides access to the content and location of the
topics covered in the CBS News Television Broadcasts microfilm
series, which now consists of a basic 1963-1974 set with annual
supplements.

79   CBS News Public Affairs Broadcasts Cumulative Subject
      Index.   Sanford, N.C.:   Microfilming Corp. of America,
1980--. v. 1--.   Provides access to the various dialogues
covered on the verbatim transcripts of such CBS programs as
60 Minutes, CBS Reports, and Face the Nation which are provided by this service in microfilm copy.
80   California News Index.   Claremont, Calif.:   Center for Cali-
      fornia Public Affairs, 1970--. v. 1--.   Indexes a variety
of California newspapers, many of which run stories related to
network television news.
81   The Christian Science Monitor Index. Corvallis, Ore.: Helen
      M. Cropsey, 1960--. v. 1--.   Indexes the noted newspaper,
which like others has carried stories about network television
news.
82   Congressional Information Service.   CIS Annual: Abstracts
      of Congressional Publications and Legislative Histories.
Washington, D.C.:   1969--.   v. 1--.   Especially useful for
dissecting those publications of Congressional committees looking
into television news and documentaries.
83   Communications Abstracts: An International Information Ser-
      vice.   Beverley Hills, Calif.:   Sage Publications, 1978--.
v. 1--.   Wide-ranging quarterly devoted to all aspects of communications;   editors are all from Temple University, Philadelphia.
84   Current Contents: Social and Behavioral Science.   Philadel-
      phia: Institute for Scientific Information, 1968--.   v.1--.
Reproduces journal contents pages, including those from periodicals relative to this topic.
85   Dissertation Abstracts.   Ann Arbor, Mich.:   University
      Microfilms, 1945-1968.
86   Dissertation Abstracts International: "A" Schedule.   Ann
      Arbor, Mich.:   University Microfilms, 1969--.   v. 1--.   A
continuation of Dissertations Abstract's original coverage of the
humanities and social sciences; users should examine the headings journalism and mass media.
87   Editorials on File.   New York: Facts on File, 1970--.
      v. 1--.   Gives users a handy reference to press editorials
about various network television news shows, especially public
affairs.
88   Educational Resources Information Center.   Resources in
      Education.   Washington, D.C.:   U.S. Government Printing
Office, 1965--.   v. 1--.   An index to those papers and reports
reprinted on microfiche as ERIC documents; look in the subject
index under television.
89   Garrison, Lloyd W., ed.   ABC PoliSci: Advance Bibliog-
      raphy of Contents, Political Science and Government. Santa
Barbara, Calif.:   ABC/Clio Press, 1969--.   v. 1--.   Reproduces
content pages of politically-oriented journals, including those
likely to have articles relative to our subject.
90   Historical Abstracts: Schedule B, 20th Century Abstracts
      (1914 to the Present).   Santa Barbara, Calif.:   ABC/ Clio
Press, 1955--.   v. 1--.   Should be used in conjunction with the
later guide, America: History and Life, cited below.
91   Humanities Index.   New York: H. W. Wilson Co., 1975--.
      v. 1--.   Broken off from the old Social Sciences and

Humanities Index; users can find articles of value by checking
the heading television.
92 Index to Legal Periodicals. New York: H. W. Wilson Co.,
     1948--. v. 41--. Especially useful for citations to articles
dealing with government and the press, First Amendment, etc.
93   Index to U.S. Government Periodicals. Chicago: Infor-
     data International, 1975--. v. 1--. Particularly helpful in
finding articles on television and network news from the more
obscure government journals.
94   Johnson, Catherine, ed. TV Guide 25 Year Index, 1953-
     1977. New York: Triangle Publications, 1979. 506p. A
guide to the articles appearing in the popular weekly magazine.
95   Journalism Abstracts. Los Angeles: Association for Edu-
     cation in Journalism, 1962--. v. 1--. Now published by
the University of Minnesota, this tool is a guide to PhD and
MA/MS papers with subject/author listings.
96   Masters Abstracts. Ann Arbor, Mich.: University Micro-
     films, 1962--. v. 1--. A continuing guide to MA/MS level
study in all areas; examine the headings journalism and mass
communications.
97   Newspaper Index. Webster, Ohio: Bell & Howell, 1972--.
     v. 1--. Indexes the Chicago Tribune, Washington Post,
Los Angeles Times, and New Orleans Times-Picayune, the
former three being noted over the years for their coverage of
network news.
98   New York Times Index. New York: New York Times
     Company, 1945--. A massive index which includes all
stories related to our topic.
99   PAIS Bulletin. New York: Public Affairs Information
     Service, 1948--. v. 33--. An extremely useful guide to
books, periodical articles, and documents/reports relative to our
subject among many.
100   Political Science Abstracts: Political Science, Government,
     and Public Policy Series. Edited by Samuel L. Long. New
York: Plenum, 1966. Covers politically oriented material
printed by more than 3,000 publishers in Europe and the Western Hemisphere; the 10-volume set has been supplemented by
annual updates since 1967.
101   Psychology Abstracts. Lancaster, Pa.: American Psycho-
     logical Association, 1948--. v. 21--.
102   RAND Corporation. Selected RAND Abstracts. Santa Moni-
     ca, Calif.: RAND Corporation, 1962--. v. 1--. Details
reports generated at this California "think tank," including
those devoted to television.
103   Reader's Guide to Periodical Literature. New York: H.
     W. Wilson Co., 1948--. Begun in 1900, this is the most
famous and basic of periodical indexes, a first step for those
who would seek information on general coverage of network
television news.
104   Social Sciences and Humanities Index. New York: H. W.
     Wilson Co., 1948-1974. Discontinued and broken up in
1974, this famous guide lists articles in journals a bit-too-spe-
cialized for inclusion in the Reader's Guide to Periodical
Literature.
105   Social Sciences Index. New York: H. W. Wilson Co.,
     1975--. v. 1--. Broken down from the previous citation,

this tool provides articles coverage in those journals of a special science bent, but like its companion, Humanities Index
(q.v.), contains useful network televisions news coverage.
106 Sociological Abstracts. New York: 1953--. v. 1--.
Both of the above services provide coverage of mass
communications, although the citations in the latter are a bit
broader in scope.
107 Topicator. Littleton, Colo.: Thompson Bureau, 1965--.
     v. 1--. A monthly classified guide to the advertising/
broadcasting trade press, cumulated quarterly and annually.
Probably the single most important index available to our topic.
108 United States. Air Force. Air University Library. Air
     University Library Index to Military Affairs.   Maxwell
AFB, Ala.: Air University Library, 1948--. v. 1--. Provides
coverage not found elsewhere of military periodicals; especially
useful for the relationship between network news and the mili-
tary-industrial complex.
109   Department of Commerce. National Technical Information
     Service.   Government Reports Announcements.   Spring-
field, Va.: 1948--. v. 3--. Notes various government and
government-sponsored reports prepared on a host of subjects
including those relating to communications.
110   . Superintendent of Documents. Monthly Catalog
     of U.S. Government Publications.   Washington,   D.C.:
U.S. Government Printing Office, 1948--. v. 53--. Useful for
seeking Congressional hearings related to network news; it is
suggested that users employ the subject index and look under
the heading television.
111 Vanderbilt University Television News Archives. Television
     News Index and Abstracts: A Guide to the Videotape Collec-
tion of the Network Evening News Programs in the Vanderbilt
Television News Archive. Nashville, Tenn.: Joint University
Libraries, 1974--. v. 1--. A monthly guide to the various
evening news reports carried by the major networks.
112 The Wall Street Journal Index. New York: Dow Jones,
     1958--. v. 1--. Indexes the noted economic newspaper
     which often carries reports on the television networks.

ANNUALS AND DICTIONARIES

113 Banks, Arthur S., ed. Political Handbook of the World,
     19--: Governments, Regional Issues, and Intergovernmental
Organizations. New York: McGraw Hill, 1948--. v. 20--.
Useful background summaries to events covered by network
news.
114 Bones, R. A. Dictionary of Telecommunications. New
     York: Philosophical Library, 1970. 200p. A guide to the
language as of that period, including that of network news.
115 Brown, Les. The New York Times Encyclopedia of Tele-
     vision. New York: Times Books, 1977. 492p. Not
exactly a dictionary, but rather a guide to the various facets of
television, presented in articles.
116 Cassata, Mary B., and Molefi K. Asante. "Glossary of
     Mass Communications Concepts." In: their Mass Communi-

cations: Principles and Practices. New York: Macmillan, 1979.
pp. 339-342. A brief but useful textbook glossary with con-
cise definitions of various media-related terms.
117 Clift, Charles, and Archie Greer, eds. Broadcast Program-
      ming: The Current Perspective. Washington, D.C.: Uni-
versity Press of America, 1976--. v. 1--. An anthology of
articles drawn from various broadcast trade journals and divided
by topic.
118   Diamant, Lincoln, ed. The Broadcast Communications
      Dictionary, rev. and enl. ed. New York: Hastings House,
1978. 201p. A valuable tool with many references to technical
terms.
119 Facts on File Yearbook: The Indexed Record of World Events.
      New York: Facts on File, 1948--. v. 7--. Rapidly-appear-
ing loose-leaf supplements easily keep the user abreast of developments in a variety of fields, including network television
news.
120   Gleason, William A. A Glossary of Radio and Television
      Terms. New York: Catholic Communications Foundation,
1971. 51p. A bit dated, but still useful.
121 Hudson's Washington News Media Contacts Directory. North
      Arlington, Va.: 1967--. v. 1--. A guide to news sources
in the District of Columbia.
122   Information Please Almanac. New York: Viking Press,
      1948--. v. 2--. A valuable annual review of various
events with some mention of the media.
123   International Television Almanac. New York: Quigley
      Pub. Co., 1956--. v. 1--. An annual review of develop-
ments in the television industry, including network news, which
features a biographical section.
124 McMahon, Michael, ed. 1981-1982 TV News. New York:
      Laramie Commuications, 1981. A new annual designed
specifically for those interested in our subject.
125 Miller, Carolyn H. Illustrated TV Dictionary. New York:
      Harvey House, 1980. 135p. Similar in vein to Les Brown's
work cited above with many illustrations of personalities.
126 Murray, John. Media Law Dictionary. Washington, D.C.:
      University Press of America, 1978. 152p. The only work
of its kind, this tool contains not only media terms but terms
for legal ideas, e.g. First Amendment, related to the media.
127 Norback, Craig T., and Peter G. Norback, eds. TV
      Guide Almanac. New York: Ballantine Books, 1980.
680p. Not exactly a true almanac, but a fine review of developments throughout the television industry, including network
news.
128   Plano, Jack C., and Milton Greenberg. The American
      Political Dictionary, 5th ed. New York: Holt, 1979.
488p. Useful for those who would understand American politics
while studying television network news' interaction with it.
129   Ruben, Brent D., ed. Communication Yearbook. New
      Brunswick, N.J.: Transaction Books, 1977--. v. 1--.
Covers the entire communications field, with some attention to
developments in network news.
130 Safire, William. Safire's Political Dictionary. New York:
      Random House, 1979. 845p. Similar to but more spirited

than Plano/Greenberg, by a writer long associated with politics
and journalism.
131   United States.   National Archives and Records Service.
     Weekly Compilation of Presidential Documents.   Washington,
D.C.:   U.S. Government Printing Office, 1965--.   v. 1--.
Definitely a weekly and not an annual; however, this remains
the best source for recent presidential press conference texts
outside of the pages of the New York Times.
132   Weiner, Richard, ed.   News Bureaus in the U.S., 6th ed.
     New York: Public Relations, 1981.   189p.   A guide to
those maintained in various American cities.   Revised at various
intervals, the last being in 1977 with the 3d edition in 1974.
133   World Almanac and Book of Facts.   Garden City, N.Y.:
     Doubleday, 1948--.   v. 80--.   One of the most famous
American almanacs, this tool annual reviews events of significance and provides pages of statistical figures.

II. TELEVISION NETWORK NEWS:
GENERAL WORKS, HISTORIES, AUDIENCES

From its pioneer days, television has often been considered to be an outgrowth of radio. Students of the electronic medium suggest that the same people who operated radio on a network basis were instrumental in the early development and commercial success of television, both as an entertainment and information vehicle. Much of the financial base remains identical (e.g., CBS Radio Network) while many of the programming concepts are not unlike those that listeners heard in the 1930's and 1940's. Throughout their intertwined histories, both network radio and television news and public affairs programming have been credited with being in the forefront of social change, although critics, as noted in Section IV below, have long debated whether the role of the audiovisual medium has always been positive or free of bias.

The tastes and desires of television audiences, as well as the impact made by news and public affairs programming upon them, has been a subject of research for decades. This research has varied in its objectives and methods from simple fact collection to the formulation of assorted hypotheses and their testing. Not only has this sort of activity played a role in the determination of entertainment programming, where it has received the most widespread publicity, but has now proven conspicuous in the development of news formats and newscaster assignments on a network, as well as local, level. Users doubtless recall the spurt of competition that began in the mid seventies among the netwoks concerning morning programming in news and information and the shift toward flashy graphics on the evening news programs--to a point where Dan Rather's sweaters seemed to make a difference. All of this is due in some respect to examinations of the viewer's desires and the effects programming elicit from them.

The first set of references in this section examines those general works and histories which can provide the user with insight into the background and workings of network television news. The items in the second half, especially when coupled with those beginning with entry 1676, "Network News & Voters," will give the user some idea of the complexities of broadcasting research as they relate to the specific topic of this guide.

GENERAL WORKS AND HISTORIES--Books

134   Adams, William, and Jay Schreibman, etc. Television
       Network News: Issues in Content Research.   Washington,
D.C.:   School of Public and International Affairs, George
Washington University, 1978. 231p. An anthology.
135   Arlen, Michael J. Living Room War. New York: Viking
       Press, 1969. 242p. A collection of the author's mid-1960's
New Yorker magazine pieces, several of which revolve around
network television news coverage of the Vietnam War.
136   . The View from Highway 1: Essays on Television.
       New York: Farrar, Straus & Giroux, 1976.   293p.   The
author's New Yorker pieces of September 1974-December 1975.
137   Aronson, James.   Packaging the News: A Critical Survey
       of Press, Radio, and TV. New York: International Pub-
       lishers, 1971. 112p.
138   Bagdikian, Ben H. The Information Machine: Their Impact
       on Men and the Media. New York: Harper & Row, 1971.
359p.   Treats the technological changes in communications and
conveys some of the challenges and fears arising from them.
139   Barnouw, Erik.   The Golden Web: A History of Broadcast-
       ing in the United States, 1933-1953.   New York: Oxford
University Press, 1968.   391p.   The second in the author's
monumental history, this volume traces the rise of the radio and
television networks, their growth, programming, and relationship
with the Federal government.
140   .   The Image Empire: A History of Broadcasting
       in the United States from 1953. New York: Oxford Univer-
sity Press, 1970, 396p.   The final in Barnouw's trilogy, this is
perhaps the best history of television's first two decades, when
the "box" grew from something of a toy into a nation shaker.
141   . Tube of Plenty: The Evolution of American Tele-
       vision. New York: Oxford University Press, 1975. 518p.
A one-volume summation with some revision of the material in
the author's trilogy.
142   Brown, Les.   Television: The Business Behind the Box.
       New York: Harcourt Brace Jovanovich, 1971.   374p.
Focusing on selected individuals in decision-making slots, the
author reviews network practices in 1970 to show the battles
between profit-making and programming; one chapter is devoted
to the problems of network news.
143   Cole, Barry, ed.   Television Today: A Close-up View.
       London: Oxford University Press, 1981.   448p.   An
anthology of 80 selections from TV Guide, some bearing on
network news.
144   Diamond, Edwin.   Good News, Bad News.   Cambridge,
       Mass.: MIT Press, 1978. 263p. A collection of essays on
the problems and possibilities involved in network news coverage of various events in the early- to mid-1970's.
145   .   Sign Off: The Last Days of Television.   Cam-
       bridge, Mass.: MIT Press, 1982. 280p. An examination
of television today with glimpses of the possible future are the
theme behind this essay collection; interesting chapters examine
network news coverage of the Three-Mile Island nuclear accident, Nelson Rockefeller's death, Ted Turner's CNN, and the
Iran hostage crisis.

146   Doig, Ivan, and Carol Doig. News: A Consumer's Guide.
      Englewood   Cliffs,   N.J.:   Prentice-Hall, 1972.   230p.
Attempts to convince its readers concerning methods of match-
ing network news and reading newspapers to gain the maximum
of unslanted information.
147   Epstein, Edward J.   News from Nowhere: Television and
      the News. New York: Random House, 1973. 321p. In a
detailed examination of the evening news program on the three
networks, the author suggests that internal corporate policies,
rather than outside events, shape the direction of daily coverage.
148   Fang, Irving E.   Television News, Radio News, 3d ed.
      St. Paul, Minn.: Rads Press, 1980.   414p.   A noted
textbook which examines the various skills needed of a broadcast journalist from writing to on-camera reporting.
149   Gordon, George N.   The Communications Revolution: A
      History of Mass Media in the United States.   New   York:
Hastings House, 1977.   352p.   Examines the past and contemporary history of the media--newspapers, periodicals, radio and
television--presenting the highlights and famous people.
150   _____, and Irving A. Falk.   TV Covers the Action.
      New York: Messner, 1968. 189p. A look at television's
past, present, and future designed for a juvenile audience; the
foreword is by Walter Cronkite.
151   Head, Sydney W., and Christopher N. Sterling. Broad-
      casting in America: A Survey of Television, Radio, and
New Technologies, 4th ed. Boston: Houghton, Mifflin, 1981.
624p.   Some consider this to be the best single textbook on the
subject and judging on the number of revisions in a single decade (three), they may be correct.   This edition, more than its
predecessors, focuses on such new technology as cable and
satellite.   Its bibliography is well over 100 pages.
152   Hunter, Julian K., and Lynne S. Gross. Broadcast News:
      The Inside Out. St. Louis: C. V. Mosby Co., 1980.
363p.   A college level textbook on the production, gathering,
and writing-airing of television news programs.
153   Kahn, Frank J., ed.   Documents of American Broadcasting,
      3d ed.   Englewood Cliffs, N.J.: Prentice-Hall, 1978.
638p.   A valuable history in that Kahn here provides the texts
of legal documents on broadcasting from 1910 to 1977.
154   Keirstead, Phillip.   Journalist's Notebook of Life Radio-
      TV News. Washington, D.C.: Book Division, Broadcasting
Magazine, 1981.   252p.   A survey text designed to acquaint
students with the various methods of gathering, writing, and
editing of news stories and how to put them on the air.
155   LeRoy, David J., and Christopher H. Sterling, etc. Mass
      News: Practices, Controversies, and Alternatives.   Engle-
wood Cliffs, N.J.: Prentice-Hall, 1973. 334p. An anthology
built around the problem of creative production in network news
and documentaries.
156   Lichty, Laurence W., and Malachi C. Topping, eds. Amer-
      ican Broadcasting: A Source Book on the History of Radio
and Television. New York: Hastings House, 1975. 745p. An
anthology containing 93 articles on various topics.
157   Mayer, Martin.   About Television. New York: Harper &
      Row, 1972. 434p. A fourteen-chapter review of television

in the early 1970's with three chapters of value here, including one each on network news, politics and TV, and documentaries.

158   Opotowsky, Stan. TV: The Big Picture. New York: Collier Books, 1961. 285p. A survey of television at the time when John Kennedy became president, this paperback includes chapters on broadcast journalism and public service programming.

159   Reel, A. Frank. Networks: How They Stole the Show. New York: Scribner's, 1979. 224p. A general history of the three networks, including their news division.

160   Settel, Irving, and William Laas. A Pictorial History of Television. New York: Grosset & Dunlap, 1969. 209p. One of the better illustrated TV histories so popular in discount bookstores; includes news and news correspondents.

161   Siller, Robert C., Hal Terkel, and Ted White. Television and Radio News. New York; Macmillan, 1962. 227p. An analysis of the practices of various networks; author Siller was associated with ABC while co-author Terkel worked for CBS.

162   Small, William J. To Kill a Messenger: Television News and the Real World. New York: Hastings House, 1970. 320p. The then-CBS Bureau Chief in Washington thoughtfully examines the role of network television news in American society.

163   Smith, Howard K., Osborn Elliott, and Merriman Smith. The News Media: A Service and a Force.   Memphis: Memphis State University Press, 1970. 44p. Three noted print and broadcast journalists comment on the role of those who report the news and their effect on politics and society at large.

164   Stanley, Robert H., ed. The Broadcast Industry: An Examination of Major Issues. New York: Hastings House, 1975. 256p. Important broadcasters and journalism teachers give their views on those problems facing braodcasters in the mid-1970's, including news management.

165   Teague, Bob. Live and Off-Color: News Biz. Reading, Mass.: Addison-Wesley, 1982. 288p. A down-to-earth indictment of network and local news as "infotainment"; suggests broadcasting executives are turning hard news reporting--"the news biz"--into entertainmnt--"show biz"--in pursuit of ratings and earnings. The author advocates a series of reforms.

166   Television Factbook. 2 vols. Washington, D.C.: Television Digest, Inc., 1982. A compendium of statistics and other data on the television industry.

167   Thompson, Tom. Organizational TV News. Philadelphia: Media Concepts Press, 1980. 217p. Another college-level textbook in which the author explains how news is gathered, written, edited, and reported on air.

168   Wolf, Frank. Television Programming for News and Public Affairs: A Quantitative Analysis of Networks and Stations. New York: Praeger, 1972. 203p. Looks into those factors which account of the amount and quality of news and public affairs programs shown on the national and local levels.

GENERAL WORKS AND HISTORIES--Articles

169   Arlen, Michael J.   "News."   New Yorker, LIII (October 31, 1977), 119-127.
170   Arundel, Arthur W.   "A View of News Broadcasting: An Address."   Congressional Record, CXXIII (November 29, 1977), 37911-37912.
171   Bergreen, Laurence.   "News: Television's Bargain Basement."   American Film.   V (July-August 1980), 37+.
172   Carter, Bill.   "The Brave News World of the 1980's: The Future is Now in Network News."   Washington Journalism Series, II (December 1980), 20-25.
173   Clevenger, Theodore, Jr.   "Communication and the Survival of Democracy: An Address, December 30, 1972."   Vital Speeches, XXXIX (February 1, 1973), 239-241.
174   Cronkite, Walter.   "The State of the Press."   In: Michael C. Emery and Ted C. Smythe, eds.   Readings in Mass Communication: Concepts and Issues in the Mass Media.   2d ed. Dubuque, Ia.:   William C. Brown, 1974.   pp. 488-495.
175   _____.   "What's Right, Wrong With Television News: An Interview."   U.S. News and World Report, XC (March 16, 1981), 45-46.
176   Crosland, C. A. R.   "The Mass Media."   Encounter, XIX (November 1962), 3-14.
177   Diamond, Edwin.   "All the News That Isn't News."   American Film, VI (October 1980), 74+.
178   Friendly, Fred W.   "Network News? 'A National Tragedy'-- Local News? 'It's Putrid'--Million Dollar Journalists? 'Obscene.'"   TV Guide, XXIX (August 1, 1981), 24-29.
179   _____.   "The State of Broadcast Journalism."   Current, CXIV (January 1970), 49-54.
180   Geyelin, Philip.   "The Role of the Press in an Open Society."   Naval War College Review, XXVII (March-April 1975), 3-7.
181   Gibson, William.   "Network News: Elements of a Theory."   Social Text, III (Fall 1980), 88-111.
182   "'Good Evening':   Inside the Network's Nightly News Operations."   Broadcasting, LXXXVI (February 11, 1974), 40-45.
183   Graber, Doris A.   "Media Giants in the Information Marketplace."   Illinois Issues, VII (November 1981), 19-22.
184   Grafton, Samuel.   "Television's Front Page."   TV Guide, XIII (October 2-16, 1965), 6-9, 9-11, 15-19.
185   Haley, William.   "News and Documentaries on U.S. Television: Some Notes."   In: Marvin Barrett, ed.   The Alfred I. Dupont-Columbia University Survey of Broadcast Journalism, 1968-1969.   New York: Grosset & Dunlap, 1969.   pp. 59-63.   Remarks by the Director General of B.B.C.
186   "Has Television News Lived Up to Its Early Promise: A Symposium?"   Sponsor, XII (July 19,1958), 44-45+.
187   Hiebert, Ray E., Donald F. Ungarait, and Thomas W. Bohn.   "News and Information."   In: their Mass Media II.   New York: Longman, 1979.   pp 351-367.
188   Hilts, Philip.   "The Theater of News."   American Film, I (March-April 1976), 16-21, 70-73.

189 Huntley, Chet. "The News in 1959." In: Harry J. Skornia
     and Jack W. Kitson, eds. Problems and Controversies in
Radio and Television: Basic Readings. Palo Alto, Calif.: Pacific Books, 1968. pp. 358-363.
190 Isaacs, Jeremy. "The Failure of Television Journalism."
     Encounter, XXX (March 1968), 84-90.
191 Jankowski, Gene. "Better News Shows Can Be Good
     Business: An Interview." U.S. News and World Report,
     LXXXVIII (June 9, 1980), 61.
192 Kintner, R. E. "Broadcasting and the News." Harper's,
     CCXXX (April 1965), 49-55.
193 _____. "Televising the Real World." Harper's, CCXXX
     (June 1965), 94-96+.
194 Kroeger, Albert R. "News, News, News." Television,
     XXII (February 1965), 27-33, 50-64.
195 Lange, David, Robert K. Baker, and Sandra J. Ball.
     "The News Media." In: their Mass Media and Violence:
A Report to the National Commission on the Causes and Prevention of Violence. Washington, D.C.: U.S. Government Printing
Office, 1969. pp. 33-164. A survey of the media without
emphasis on its connection to violence.
196 Lindlof, T. R. "Network News Coverage of the Broadcast
     Media." Journalism Quarterly, LVII (Summer 1980), 333-338.
197 Lyle, Jack, and Walter Wilcox. "Television News--an In-
     terim Report." Journal of Broadcasting, VII (Spring 1963),
     157-166.
198 "The March of Time for Broadcast Journalism--It's Come a
     Long Way from the Harding-Cox Election Returns: A
     Chronology." Broadcasting, XC (January 5, 1976), 52+.
199 "The More It Changes: A Decade of Broadcast Journalism."
     In: Marvin Barrett and Zachary Sklar, eds. The Eye of
the Storm: The Alfred I. Dupont-Columbia University Survey of
Broadcast Journalism. New York: Lippincott-Crowell, 1980.
pp. 11-104.
200 Nessen, Ron. "Saving the Worst for Last." TV Guide,
     XXVIII (February 16, 1980), 5-9.
201 "Network Evening News: Showcase of Electronic Journalism."
     Broadcasting, XC (January 5, 1976), 70+.
202 "News on the Spot: A Special Report on Television Journa-
     lism." TV Age, XIII (October 11, 1965), 27-74.
203 "News via TV." Newsweek, XXXI (February 2, 1965), 51.
204 "1931-1981 Chronology of Broadcasting." Broadcasting,
     CI (October 12, 1981), 143-204.
205 Ostrow, J. "And Now the News: A Special Report."
     Broadcasting, LXXXIX (August 25, 1975), 33-50.
206 Pearce, Alan. "The TV Networks: A Primer." Journal of
     Communications, XXVI (Autumn 1976), 54-60.
207 Salant, Richard S. "Salant's Views on Network News."
     Broadcasting, XCVI (January 22, 1979), 59.
208 Sarnoff, Robert W. "Television Journalism: The Shackled
     Giant." In: Gerald Cross, ed. The Responsibility of the
     Press. New York: Fleet Publications, 1966. pp. 276-286.
209 Schorr, Daniel. "The Established Press." Center Magazine,
     XII (July 1979), 2-8.

210 Severeid, Eric. "What's Right with Sight and Sound Jour-
     nalism: Excerpt from an Address." Saturday Review,
     IV (October 2, 1976), 18-21
211 _____, Harry Reasoner, and Harrison Salisbury. "Jour-
     nalism's Future: Progress and Problems." Washington
     Journalism Review, II (March 1980), 10-11.
212 Small, William J. "The State of Broadcast Journalism."
     Quill, LIV (October 1966), 30-31.
213 Sperry, Sharon L. "Television News as Narrative." In:
     Richard Adler and Douglass Cater, eds. Television as a
     Cultural Force. New York: Praeger, 1976. pp. 129-146.
214 "State of the Art: Journalism." Broadcasting, XCIX
     (December 1, 1980), 43-92.
215 Stritch, Thomas. "The Blurred Image: Some Reflections
     on the Mass Media in the 60's." Review of Politics, XXXIV
     (October 1972), 206-219.
216 "The Trials of Telenews." Newsweek, XXIV (August 8,
     1949), 41.
217 Trubo, Richard, and Michael Tracy. "Tuning in on Tele-
     vision: From 1925 to 1975." In: David Wallechinsky and
Irving Wallace, eds. The People's Almanac. Garden City,
N.Y.: Doubleday, 1975. pp. 816-823.
218 "TV Journalism: More Meaning, Wider Ranger, Harder
     Work, Bigger Budgets." Broadcasting, LXXXV (August
     20, 1973), 17-19+.
219 Williams, Roger M. "No News is Not Good News." Dial,
     1 (December 1980), 344.
220 Zalaznick, Sheldon. "The Rich, Risky Business of TV
     News." Fortune, LXXIX (May1, 1969), 92-97+.
221 Zorthian, Barry. "The Role of the News Media in a
     Democratic Society." Naval War College Review, XXIV
     (February 1972), 1-7.

AUDIENCES AND EFFECTS--Books

222 Adler, Richard, Ed. Understanding Television: Essays
     on Television as a Social and Cultural Force. New York:
Praeger, 1981. 438p. Published in cooperation with the Aspen
Institute for Humanistic Studies, this work seeks to provide an
understanding of the significance of television and includes a
chapter of analysis on the input and potential of network news.
223 Bower, Robert T. Television and the Public. New York:
     Holt, Rinehart & Winston, 1973. 205p. The results of a
national survey of audience preferences, which are compared
with a similar study undertaken a decade earlier.
224 Frank, Robert S. Message Dimensions of Television News.
     Lexington, Mass.: Lexington Books, 1973. 120p. By
examining the message content of network newscasts, the author
attempts to present an accurate reflection on the characteristics
of news and new audiences.
225 Goodhardt, G. J., A.S.C. Ehrenberg, and M. A. Collins.
     The Television Audience: Patterns of Viewing. Lexington,
Mass.: Lexington Books, 1975. 157p. A British study which
compares its results to American findings.

226   Klapper, Joseph T.   The Effects of Mass Communication.
      New York: Free Press, 1960.   302p.   A pioneering study
now dated; a long secton on television's ability to persuade may
still be useful.
227   Trenaman, J. M.   Communication and Comprehension.   New
      York: Humanities Press, 1968.   212p.   Looks into the
question of print and radio/television effects upon a users ability to understand various ideas and issues.

AUDIENCE AND EFFECTS--Articles, Documents, etc.

228   Atkins, Paul A., and Harry Elwood.   "TV News is First
      Choice in Survey of High Schools."   Journalism Quarterly,
      LV (Autumn 1978), 596-599.
229   Balon, R. E., et al.   "How Sex and Race Affect Percep-
      tions of Newscasters."   Journalism Quarterly, LV (Spring
      1978), 160-164.
230   Bassford, G. B.   "The Tube vs. the Pencil Press."   Public
      Relations Journal, XXXV (May 1979), 16+.
231   Bergreen, Laurence.   "The Coattail Effect."   TV Guide,
      XXVIII (October 18, 1980), 6-8.
232   Bresnahan, Don.   "Is TV News All You Want?"   Newsweek,
      XCIX (April 19, 1982), 23.
233   Callum, Myles. "What Viewers Love/Hate About Television."
      TV Guide, XXIX (May 12, 1979), 6-10.
234   Carter, Richard F., and Bradley S. Greenberg.   "News-
      papers or Television: Which Do You Believe?" Journalism
      Quarterly, XLII (Winter 1965), 29-34.
235   Cathcart, William L.   "Viewers Needs and Desires in Tele-
      vision Newscasters."   Journal of Broadcasting, XIV (Winter
      1969-1970), 55-62.
236   Dahlgreen, Peter G.   "Network TV News and the Corporate
      State: The Subordinate Consciousness of the Viewer-Citi-
zen."   Unpublished PhD Dissertation, City University of New
York, 1977.
237   Drew, D. C.   "Children and Television News."   Journalism
      Quarterly, LVII (Spring, 1980), 45-54.
238   Dyas, Ronald D.   "Television News Viewing Behavior: A
      Case Study."   Unpublished PhD Dissertation, Ohio State
      University, 1977.
239   Frank, Ronald E., and Marshall G. Greenberg.   "Zooming
      in on   TV Audiences."   Psychology Today, XII (October
      1979), 92-103, 114.
240   Haley, William.   "Where TV News Fails."   Columbia Journa-
      lism Review, IX (Spring 1970) 7-11.   Its inability to pro-
vide the depth of coverage available in newspapers and magazines.
241   Hutchinson, Kevin L.   "Newscaster Appearance: Does it
      Really Make a Difference?"   Interface, II (Fall-Winter 1978-
      1979), 1-10.
242   Jacobsen, Harvey K.   "Mass Media Believability: A Study
      of   Receiver   Judgments."   Journalism Quarterly, XLVI
      (Spring 1969), 20-28.

243 Klein, Andy. "How a Telecast's Organization Affects Viewer Retention." Journalism Quarterly, LV (Summer 1978), 356-359+.

244 Kowett, Don. "Whose Truth Can You Believe?" TV Guide, XXVII (September 22, 1979), 6-10.

245 Levy, Mark R. "The Audience Experience with Television News." Journalism Monographs, LV (1978), 1-29.

246 _____. "The Audience for Television News Interview Programs." Journal of Broadcasting, XXII (Summer 1978), 339-348.

247 _____. "Opinion Leadership and Television News Use." Public Opinion Quarterly, XLII (Fall 1978), 402-406.

248 _____. "The Uses and Gratifications of Television News." Unpublished PhD Dissertation, Columbia University, 1977.

249 _____. "Watching TV News as Para-Social Interaction." Journal of Broadcasting, XXIII (Winter 1979), 69-80.

250 Markham, David H. "The Dimensions of Source Credibility of Television Newscasters." Unpublished PhD Dissertation, University of Oklahoma, 1965.

251 O'Keefe, Garrett J., Jr., and H. T. Spetnagel. "Patterns of College Undergraduate Use of Selected News Media." Journalism Quarterly, L (Autumn 1973), 543-548.

252 Prisuta, Robert H. "The Adolescent and Television News: A Viewer Profile." Journalism Quarterly, LVI (Summer 1979), 77-82.

253 Reasoner, Harry. "Citizenship and Cynicism." Wisconsin Journal of Education, XCVIII (January 1966), 22-25.

254 Robinson, J. P. "The Audience for National TV News Programs." Public Opinion Quarterly, XXXV (Fall 1971), 403-405.

255 Roper Organization. Public Perceptions of Television and Other Mass Media: A Twenty-Year Review, 1959-1978. New York: Television Information Office, 1978. 23p.

256 Sanders, Keith P., and Michael Pritchett. "Some Influences of Appearance on Television Newscaster Appeal." Journal of Broadcasting, XV (Summer 1971), 293-302.

257 Sevareid, Eric. "Journalism--The Relationship Between the Print and Electronic Media: An Address, June 3, 1976." Vital Speeches, XLII (July 1, 1976), 562-567.

258 Shafer, Byron, and Richard Larson. "Did TV Create the 'Social Issue'?: The Network Evening News is Now a Social Institution." Columbia Journalism Review, IX (Septembr-October 1972), 10-17.

259 Shostack, Herschel. "Factors Influencing the Appeal of TV News Personalities." Journal of Broadcasting, XVIII (Winter 1973-1974), 63-72.

260 Skelton, Keith. "Timeliness in the News: Television vs. Newspapers." Journalism Quarterly, LV (Summer 1978), 348-350.

261 Smith, James R., et al. "Television News and Audience Viewing Intentions." Unpublished paper presented to the Annual Meeting of the Association for Education in Journalism, 1981. Available as ERIC document ED 204 753.

262 "TV Now Top Source for News." Wilson Library Bulletin, XXXVIII (April 1964), 608-609.

263 Weaver, Paul H. "Newspaper News and Television News."
In: Douglass Cater, ed. Television as a Social Force:
New Approaches to TV Criticism. New York: Praeger, 1975.
pp. 81-94.
264 Whittaker, Susan, and Ron Whittaker. "The Relative Effec-
tiveness of Male and Female Newscasters." Journal of
Broadcasting, XX (Spring 1976), 177-184.
265 Zucker, Harold G. "The Influence of Network Television
News on Public Opinion." Unpublished PhD Dissertation,
University of California at Irvine, 1978.

III. THE TELEVISION NETWORKS:
NEWS REPORTING AND PROGRAMMING

Television network news is an outgrowth of news programming on radio and in some instances, still resembles it. As many of those who have practiced and observed network news over the years have noted, one of the largest problems facing news broadcasting is the length of time available for airing, especially on evening news programs. (Fred W. Friendly, "Network News? 'A National Tragedy'--Local News? 'It's Putrid'--Million Dollar Journalism? 'Obscene,'" TV Guide 29 [Aug. 1, '81], 27-28). Even the "hard news" segments on the morning programs, such as "Today" or "Good Morning America," are restricted while documentaries and public affairs interview programs have rarely ever run longer than one hour. Ted Turner's Cable News Network, particularly CNN2, has made some impact on this problem, although not all U.S. homes are yet equipped to handle cable ("Turner's Gutsy New News Service," Business Week [Jan. 11, '82], 42).

Competition has increased over the past few years between the network news departments. This factor had been noticeable, at least for NBC and CBS, since the days of radio, but now with television seems to have accelerated in the half decade since Roone Arledge assumed the helm at ABC News. Despite the increase of graphics and various personnel changes, one wonders if any more information is imparted now than in the days John Cameron Swayze hosted the Camel News Caravan.

The simple fact remains that television news, local or network, cannot provide the same quantity of data as newspapers. "National news on television," observed Edward J. Epstein, "cannot be adequately explained by resorting to the newspaper analogy," (News from nowhere [New York: Vintage, 1973], p.40). It is, in fact, little more than a headline service, as Walter Cronkite has so often indicated (e.g., "What's Right, Wrong with Television News: An Interview, "U.S. News & World Report 40 [March 16, '81], 46), requiring viewers to seek additional information from their newspapers and weekly newsmagazines if they really want to be informed. "A television news program." noted Reuven Frank of NBC News, "must be put together with the assumption that each item will be of some interest to everyone that watches," (Epstein, News from Nowhere). The level of generality on network news dwarfs that on local news or in community newspapers. Despite this, surveys taken each year over the past decade indicate that more Americans obtain their news from television than any other national source (see Friendly, "Network News?").

23

It was Edward R. Murrow who led the way in the development of television documentaries and public affairs interview programs. His noteworthy, trendsetting series "See It Now," produced with Fred W. Friendly, appeared over CBS from 1951 to 1958 and seemed to parallel his interview program. "Person-to-Person." A Murrow colleague and noted documentary producer, the late Fred Freed, commented on an early "See It Now" episode: "It was journalism, not art. That turned out to be crucial. It settled the way we would make news documentaries or television for the next twenty years. They would be in the hands of journalists. The important decisions would be journalistic. Ideas would come first" ("The Rise and Fall of the Television Documentary," Television Quarterly 10 [Fall '72], 56).

Although viewers may see fewer documentaries on network television these days, an offshoot appears to be alive and well. Magazine-style programs, such as "60 Minutes" and "20/20," provide weekly reports on a variety of subjects, and on many an occasion, are just as hardhitting, controversial, and popular as such earlier efforts as "Hunger in America" or "The Selling of the Pentagon."

The manner in which news and information is reported and presented over the network airwaves is as controversial today as it was when radio was king. Perhaps the most ire-raising features of electronic journalism since Murrow's day have been the commentaries/analysis and investigative reporting, the latter usually associated with something the size of the Watergate scandal, but actually applied to many other topics in a fashion sometimes identified with "new" or "advocacy journalism, (see e.g. David Shaw, "The Trouble with TV Muckraking," TV Guide 29 [Oct. 10,'81], 67). "Network news people, their employers, and various associations have adopted ethics code and standards in an effort to eliminate even an appearance of impropriety.

Women as a group have not always fared well as employees in broadcasting, just as they have done poorly in other professions. The story of the increase in women broadcast journalists in recent (see e.g. Katherine Krupp, "Update-Women in TV News: Just How Far Have We Come?" Glamour '79 [Sept. '81], 249). Careers in electronic journalism and television news are especially attractive and additional technological developments suggest that personnel recruitment for network news departments will remain steady (Radio-Television News Directors' Association, Careers in Broadcast News [Washington, D.C., 1980], pp. 1-2).

The citations in III-A, provide materials on five networks while the entries in III-B, demonstrate the competition among network news efforts. The citations in III-C provide data on eight specific news programs while those in III-D look at the documentary, both generally and with respect to a number of specific programs. Reporting and the presentation of network news is the topic of III-E, including ethics and codes, commentators, commentary, and analysis. Entries on the roll of women in network news can be found in III-F while careers are coveed in III-G.

III-A. THE TELEVISION NETWORKS

AMERICAN BROADCASTING COMPANY--Book

266   Quinlan, Sterling.   Inside ABC: The American Broadcasting Company's Rise to Power.   New York: Hastings House, 1979. 290p. Concerns the total network effort to become a major entertainment-sports-news enterprise.

AMERICAN BROADCASTING COMPANY--Articles, Documents, etc.

267   ABC News.   Correspondent's Handbook: A Guide to the Operating Practices of ABC News.   New York: American Broadcasting Company, News Division, 1966.
268   "ABC News, Closeup." US, II (January 23, 1979), 62-64.
269   "ABC Tops Networks in News Emmys." Broadcasting, CII (April 14, 1982), 73-74.
270   Bedell, Sally.   "Can Roone [Arledge] Make the Double-Play at ABC?" TV Guide, XXVI (June 10, 1978), 7-10.
271   Bryan, John.   "Inside the TV Networks: ABC." In: David Wallechinsky and Irving Wallace, eds.   The People's Almanac 2.   Garden City, N.Y.: Doubleday, 1978. pp. 740-741.
272   Christopher, M. "ABC Vows All-Out News Effort." Advertising Age, XLVIII (May 16, 1977), 2+.
273   "Roone Arledge and the Sherpas of ABC News: Out to Climb the Everest of TV Journalism." Broadcasting, XCIII (August 15,1977), 23-28.
274   "Roone Arledge Sounds Out His New Term." Broadcasting, XCII (May 23, 1977), 55-56.
275   Rowan, Roy.   "ABC Covers Itself." Fortune, CII (November 17, 1980), 45-48.
276   Stahl, Bob.   "The Men Who Run ABC." TV Guide, VII (August 1, 1959), 4-7.
277   Thomas, Lynn E.   "ABC News: The Reorganization in 1961." Unpublished M.A. thesis, Boston University, 1964.
278   "Visiting ABC News." Broadcasting, CI (November 9, 1981), 31-35.
279   Waters, Harry F.   "ABC News Marches On." Newsweek, XCIV (August 20, 1979), 45.

COLUMBIA BROADCASTING SYSTEM--Books

280   Gates, Gary P.   Air Time: The Inside Story of CBS News.   New York: Harper & Row, 1978. 440p. A history which focuses not only on the famous correspondents but on the corporate background and the role of the organization in influencing American society.
281   Halberstam, David.   The Powers That Be.   New York: Alfred A. Knopf, 1979. 771p. In addition to three print giants, Halberstam concentrates on providing an inside look at the CBS of William S. Paley; provocative and readable.
282   Metz, Robert.   CBS: Reflections in a Bloodshot Eye.   Chicago: Playboy Press, 1975. 428p. With fascinating

behind-the-scenes episodes, this corporate history stresses personnel and programming, including news and public affairs.

COLUMBIA BROADCASTING SYSTEM--Articles

283 "As Time Marched On, CBS News Reported the Cadence." Broadcasting, XCIII (September 19,1977), 110-115.
284 Bedell, Sally. "The House of Murrow--Under Siege." TV Guide, XXIX (January 24, 1981),4-8.
285 "CBS: Documenting 38 Years of Exciting History--A Special Issue." Sponsor, XIX (September 13, 1965). 1+.
286 Collier, J. L. "Behind the Scenes at CBS News." Reader's Digest, CXVI (June 1980), 116-120.
287 Elwood, Ann. "Inside the TV Networks: CBS." In: David Wallechinsky and Irving Wallace, eds. The People's Almanac 2. Garden City, N.Y.: Doubleday, 1978. pp. 736-738.
288 Halberstam, David. "CBS: The Power and the Profits." Atlantic, CCXXXVII (January-February 1976), 33-48+, 54-56.
289 _____. "Power Failure." Playboy, XXVI (January 1979), 169+.
290 Hilts, Philip J. "CBS: The Fiefdom and the Power in Washington." Washington Post Potomac. (April 21, 1974), passim.
291 Landry, R. J. "Behind the Scenes at CBS." Saturday Review of Literature, L (April 1, 1967), 30-31.
292 Roche, John P. "Has CBS News Failed in Its Duty to America?" TV Guide, XXIV (October 19, 1974), A5-A6. Views of a noted Conservative commentator.
293 Stahl, Bob. "The Men Who Run CBS." TV Guide, VII (September 5, 1959). 8-11.

CABLE NEWS NETWORK

294 Allen, George N. "Cable News Network: The Prodigal's Prescription." Washington Journalism Review, II (May 1980), 22-24.
295 _____. "Ted Turner's Dream." Washington Journalism Review, 1 (September-October 1979), 30-37.
296 Banker, Stephen. "The Cable News Network Sets Sail." Panorama, 1 (April 1980), 44+.
297 "CNN: Bringing the Blue Sky Down to Earth." Broadcasting, XCVII (December 3, 1979), 44+.
298 "CNN's [President Reese] Schonfeld quits." Broadcasting, CII (May 24, 1982), 62-63.
299 "Cable News Network: Poised for the Unknown." Broadcasting, XCVIII (May 5, 1980), 72-77.
300 "Can Ted Turner's Cable News Hang On?" Business Week, (November 3, 1980), 91-92.
301 Diamond, Edwin. "All Day and All Night the Upstart Challenges the Establishment." Panorama, 1 (September 1980), 68-73.
302 Fischer, R. L. "Ted Turner's Cable News Network-- an Impossible Dream?" USA Today, CIX (November 1980), 60-62.

303 Green, Alan. "Ted Turner's Dream One Year Later."
     Washington Journalism Review, III (June 1981), 40-43.
304 Klepper, M. "Electronic Media: Cable News Network."
     Public Relations Journal, XXXVI (July 1980), 2+.
305 Shaw, David. "Ted Turner: Making Money and Enemies."
     TV Guide, XXIX (August 22, 1981), 26-34.
306 Shister, Neil. "Cable News Network." Atlanta, XX (July
     1980), 47+.
307 "Star-Spangled Start for CNN." Broadcasting, XCVIII
     (June 9, 1980), 48-54
308 "Turner"s Gutsy New News Service." Business Week,
     (January 11, 1982), 42+

NATIONAL BROADCASTING COMPANY

309 Bryan, John. "Inside the TV Networks: NBC." In:
     David Wallechinsky and Irving Wallace, eds. The People's
     Almanac 2. Garden City, NY: Doubleday, 1978. pp. 738-740.
310 Gelman, M.J. "One Day." Television, XX (March 1936),
     52-65.
311 NBC News. Stand By: NBC News. New York: National
     Broadcasting Company, News Division [1962?]. Unpaged.
312 "NBC-TV Concocts New Ingredients to Spice-Up News."
     Broadcasting, XCII (May 23, 1977), 54-55.
313 "News Areas in for Hard Look at NBC." Broadcasting,
     XXII (January 24, 1977), 54-55.
314 Pearce, Alan. "NBC News Division: A Study of the Costs,
     the Revenues, and the Benefits of Broadcasting News."
     Unpublished PhD Dissertation, Indiana University, 1968.
315 Smith, Desmond. "The Small World of NBC News."
     New York, XIV (June 29, 1981), 24-28.
316 Stahl, Bob. "The Men Who Run NBC." TV Guide, VII
     (October 10, 1959), 8-11.
317 Waters, Harry F. "NBC: In Search of News Direction."
     Newsweek, XCIV (September 3, 1979), 62.

PUBLIC BROADCASTING CORPORATION

318 Powers, Ron. "For Public Television: Hard News = Hard
     Times." TV Guide, XXIX (March 24, 1979), 2-5.

III-B. COMPETITION IN TELEVISION NETWORK NEWS

319 Atkinson, Jim. "Unhappy Medium." D Magazine, V (April
     1978), 52-58.
320 Bedell, Sally. "Escalating the War on the News Front."
     TV Guide, XXVI (June 17, 1978), 27-34.
321 _____. "Network News: The Imminent Showdown." TV
     Guide, XXX (February 6, 1982), 4-8.
322 "CBS and NBC: Walter vs. Chet and Dave." Newsweek,
     LXII (September 23, 1962), 62-65.
323 Castro, Janice. "The Battle in Network News: CBS and
     NBC Get New Chiefs as the Rating War Escalates." Time,
     CXIX (March 15, 1982), 52-53.

324 Christopher, M. "[Barbara] Walter's High-Priced ABC Shift Presages News Show Battles." Advertising Age, XLVII (April 26, 1976), 2+.

325 Clarke, George, et al. "The Battle for the Morning: 'Today,' 'Good Morning America,' and 'Morning' Fight to be First." Time, CXVI (December 1, 1980), 62-66.

326 "Early Morning TV: The Breakfast Battleground." Broadcasting, XCVI (June 11, 1979), 47-48.

327 Holder, Dennis. "Television News Enters the Redi-Whip Era: The News is Getting Softer and Sweeter" Washington Journalism Review, IV (January-February 1982), 20-24.

328 Josephson, Sanford. "TV News Competition Fueled by New Players." Television/Radio Age, XXIX (May 17, 1982), 43-45, 80-82.

329 Lemert, James B. "Content Duplication by the Networks in Competing Evening Newscasts." Journalism Quarterly, LI (Summer 1974), 238-244.

330 Pearce, Alan. "How the Networks Have Turned News Into Dollars." TV Guide, XXVIII (August 23, 1980), 7-11.

331 Pollan, Michael. "Good News?" Channels, 1 (December 1981-January 1982), 14.

332 Powers, Ron. "How the Networks Wage War for Breakfast-Time Viewers." TV Guide, XXVIII (January 12, 1980), 2-6.

333 "Sprucing Up the Evening News in Rating Race Everyone Denies." Broadcasting, LXXXIX (November 10, 1975), 56.

334 "Sunrise Sweepstakes." Time, CVIII (September 13, 1976), 70.

335 "Telling the News vs. Tapping the Cornea: ABC's Roone Arledge vs. NBC's Richard Salant." Time, CXIV (October 1, 1979), 83.

336 "TV"s Hot Global News War." TV Guide, X (February 3, 1962), 8-10.

337 Waters, Harry F. "That's the Way It is Now." Newsweek, XCVIII (August 31, 1981), 46.

338 _____. "Star Wars in TV News." Newsweek, XCIX (April 12, 1982), 72,75.

339 _____. "TV's War After Cronkite." Newsweek, XCVII (March 9, 1981), 52-56.

III-C.   SPECIFIC NEWS PROGRAMS

ABC EVENING NEWS/WORLD NEWS TONIGHT

340 Banker, Stephen. "The ABC's of News." Washington Journalism Review, 1 (September-October 1978), 74-75.

341 Bantz, Charles R. "The Critic and the Computer: A Multiple Technique Analysis of the ABC Evening News." Communication Monograph, XLVI (March 1979), 27-39.

342 Bedell, Sally. "ABC Evening News Overhauled." TV Guide, XXV (July 30, 1977), A-1.

343 Greenfield, Jeff. "Showdown at ABC News." New York Times Magazine, (February 13,1977), 32-34+.

344 Smith, Desmond. "Is This the Future of TV News?" New York, XV (February 22, 1982), 31-34.

345 "Together, for the First Time on Any Stage." Broadcasting, XC (May 31, 1976), 58. Harry Reasoner and Barbara
Walters.
346 "Two Men [Harry Reasoner and Howard K. Smith], One
Mission: Making ABC News a Contender in the Early Evening Sweepstakes." Broadcasting, LXXXIV (May 21, 1973),
72-73.

ABC NEWS BRIEF

347 Levin, Eric. "High-Profit Newscasts." TV Guide, XXV
(October 15, 1977), 35-39.

CBS EVENING NEWS WITH DAN RATHER

348 "The New Face of TV News." Time, CXV (February 25,
1980), 64-66.
349 "New Times Ahead for CBS News." Broadcasting, C (February 9, 1981), 56+.
350 Rather, Dan. "So Far, So Good, Says Dan Rather."
Broadcasting, C (May 11, 1981), 29-30.
351 Smith, Desmond. "Dan Rather in the Hot Seat." New York,
XIV (November 2, 1981), 33-36.
352 Sobran, John. "Rather Aweful." National Review, XXXIV
(February 19, 1982), 182.

CBS EVENING NEWS WITH WALTER CRONKITE

353 "CBS Evening News Feels Hot Breath on Cronkite's Neck."
Broadcasting, LXXXVII (December 2, 1974), 40-41.
354 Cronkite, Walter. "What Its Like to Broadcast the News:
Excerpt from an Address." Saturday Review of Literature,
LIII (December 12, 1970) 53-55.

CBS NEWS MORNING

355 Bergreen, Laurence. "CBS's Sunday Morning Hideaway
Remains a Big Secret." TV Guide, XXVIII (May 24, 1980,
22-27.
356 "[Bill] Kurtis to Replace Kuralt on 'Morning.'" Broadcasting, CI (December 21, 1981), 29-30.
357 "Bouncing Back at Sunrise." Broadcasting, CII (March
15, 1982), 184.
358 "CBS Rebuilding Morning News Show." Broadcasting,
XCV (December 4, 1978), 49+.
359 Kitman, Michael. "Morning Mistakes at CBS." New Leader,
LXIV (November 2, 1981), 21-22.
360 "Long Row to Hoe for Quinn and Rudd." Broadcasting,
LXXXV (August 13, 1973), 34-35.
361 Piantadosi, Roger. "Top of the Morning at CBS." Washington Journalism Review, III (September 1981),
33-37.

362   "Rudd and Quinn Talk Themselves Up." Broadcasting,
      LXXXV (July 30, 1973), 38+.

THE HUNTLEY/BRINKLEY REPORT (NBC)

363   Alpert, H.   "TV's Unique Tandem: Huntley-Brinkley."
      Coronet, LII (February 1961), 162-168.
364   Barthel, Joan.   "Huntley and Brinkley Ten Years Later."
      TV Guide, XV (July 1, 1967), 15-19.
365   "Chet-David, Reunion in Chicago." Broadcasting, LXXII
      (April 10, 1967), 74-75.
366   Ewald, B.   "The First Team." Newsweek, LVII (March
      13, 1961), 53-57.
367   Fixx, James F.   "An Anniversary Talk with Huntley and
      Brinkley." McCall's, XCIV (October 1966), 56+.
368   Greene, Daniel St. A.   "Making a Television News Show."
      Seminar 1970, XV (March 1970), 27-31.
369   Johnson, V. S.   "Two Golden Keys." Elementary English,
      XLI (May 1964), 554-557.
370   Lissit, Robert.   "Huntley and Brinkley, Plus Four." Quill,
      LV (November 1968), 32-34.
371   Schwartz, K.   "Both Sides of the Hyphen." Television,
      XVIII (January 1961), 90-93.
372   Whitworth, William.   "Accident of Casting." New Yorker,
      XLIV (August 3, 1968), 34-42.

THE MACNEIL/LEHRER REPORT (PBS)

373   Cook, Bruce.   "Going Deeper with MacNeil and Lehrer."
      American Film, II (June 1977), 56-60.
374   Kopkind, Andrew.   "MacNeil/Lehrer's Class Act." Colum-
      bia Journalism Review, XVIII (September 1979), 31-38.
375   MacNeil, Robert.   "MacNeil/Lehrer: A Better Method of
      News Reporting?" TV Guide, XXIX (March 14, 1981), 4-9.
376   The MacNeil/Lehrer Report. Sanford, N.C.: Microfilming
      Corp. of America, 1976--.   Microform copies of the tran-
      scripts of the PBS show.
377   Nadel, Gerry.   "Just About All Talk and No Action."
      TV Guide, XXV (October 8, 1977), 22-24,

NBC NIGHTLY NEWS

378   "Curtain Goes Up on 'NBC Nightly News' Mudd-Brokaw
      Anchor Team." Broadcasting, CII (April 5, 1982), 150.
379   Levin, Eric.   "Anatomy of a Newscast." TV Guide, XXIV
      (February 28, 1976), 4-8.
380   _____.   "Are Two Heads Better Than One?: Chancellor
      and Brinkley, NBC's New News Team." TV Guide, XXIV
      December 18, 1976), 6-9.
381   NBC's Brokaw and Mudd: Complementary Contrasts."
      Broadcasting, CII (May 17, 1982), 94-95.
382   Waters, Harry F.   "The New Look of TV News." Newsweek,
      LXXXVIII (October 11, 1976), 68-75.

III-D. DOCUMENTARY AND PUBLIC AFFAIRS PROGRAMMING

GENERAL WORKS--Books

383 Bailey, Robert L.   An Examination of Prime-Time Network
     Television Special Programming, 1948-1966.   New   York:
Arno Press, 1979. 339p.   The author's 1967 PhD dissertation
at the University of Wisconsin, This study looks at both public
affairs and entertainment programming for the decade and a
half.
384 Bluem, A. William.   Documentary in American Television:
     Form, Function, Method.   New York: Hastings House,
1965. 311p. A critical examination of the history, production,
shapers, successes and failure, problems and prospects of the
documentary movement.
385 Botein, Michael, and David Rice, eds. Network Television
     and the Public Interest: A Preliminary Inquiry.   Boston:
Lexington Books, 1980. 320p.   A series of essays on public
affairs programming and its value in present-day American
society.
386 Hammond, Charles M., Jr.   The Image Decade: The Tele-
     vision Documentary, 1965-1975. New York: Hastings House,
1981. 288p.   A study of the production and controversy surrounding some of the leading network television documentaries
of the covered ten-year period.
387 Yellin, David G.   Special: Fred Freed and the Television
     Documentary.   New York: MacMillian, 1972. 289p.   A
history of network documentaries from the late forties to the
early seventies chronicled through the life of a pioneer in their
production.

GENERAL WORKS--Articles

388 Bauer, Douglas. "Are Those Powerful Documentaries Gone
     Forever?"   TV Guide,   XXVII   (July 28, 1979), 2-6.
389 Davis, L.K.   "Controversy and the Network Documentary:
     A Critical Analysis of Form." Communication Quarterly,
     XXVI (Fall 1978), 45-52.
390 Diamond, Edwin. "The Myth of the Dying Documentary."
     TV Guide, XXIX (April 25, 1981), 8-13.
391 "Documentaries Make Waves at PBS." Broadcasting, CII
     (April 19, 1982), 57.
392 Hickey, Neil.   "Documentaries--Why Bother?:   Expose--
     Overrated, Foreign News--Excessive." TV Guide, XXVII
     (December 15, 1979), 4-9.
393 _____ .   "Documentary-Maker Av Westin." TV Guide,
     XXIII (May 24, 1975), 20-23.
394 _____ . "A Look at Television's Instant Specials." TV
     Guide, XXII (June 15, 1974), 30-32.
395 Murrow, Edward R. "How TV Can Help Us Survive."
     TV Guide, VI (December 13, 1958), 22-27.
396 Ostrow, J. "Documentaries." Broadcasting, LXXXIX
     (August 25, 1975), 34-36.
397 Paley, William S. "Bill Paley on Public Affairs Broadcast-
     ing." TV Guide, II (July 24, 1954), 3.

398 "Prime-Time Information Shows." TV Guide, IX (April
     22, 1961), 5-7.
399 Smith, Desmond. "Making a Documentary in Russia." TV
     Guide, XVIII (February 17, 1968), 8-11.
400 Smith, Howard K. "The Deadly Balance." Columbia Journa-
     lism Review, IV (Fall 1965), 13.
401 _____. "Television in the Nation's Service: An Address,
     October 13, 1965." Vital Speeches, XXXII (November 15,
     1965), 79-81.
402 Weeks, Edward A. "Saving the World Every Week: 'See
     It Now' Series and "CBS Reports.'" Atlantic, CCXIX (May
     1967). 124-126.

DOCUMENTARIES AND SPECIAL REPORTS--Miscellaneous

403 Arlen, Michael J. "CBS Reports: What About Ronald Rea-
     gan?" New Yorker, XLIII (December 30, 1967), 59-60.
404 Bedell, Sally, "CBS Reports: Simulating a Nuclear Attack."
     TV Guide, XXIX (June 13, 1981), 28-34.
405 Braestrup, Peter. "Mike Wallace and General Westmoreland."
     Washington Journalism Review, IV (April 1982), 46-49.
406 CBS News. "Hunger in America: Transcript of Broadcast,
     May 21, 1968." Congressional Record, CXIV (May 29,
     1968), 15568-15572.
407 Citizen's Board of Inquiry Into Hunger and Malnutrition
     in the United States. "Exhaustive Study Fails to Uncover
Hunger   Conditions: Reprinted from   the   Lewistown   (P2.)
Sentinel, July 22, 1968." Congressional Record, CXIV (July
22, 1968), 22739-22740.
408 Diehl, Kemper. "Father Disputes TV Hunger Charge:
     Reprinted from an Anonymous San Antonio (Texas) News-
paper." Congressional Record, CXIV (July 22, 1968), 22738-
22739.
409 "Documentary on Hunger: Reprinted from the Chicago
     Tribune, June 25, 1968." Congressional Record, CXIV
     (June 27, 1968), 19173.
410 Efron, Edith. "ABC News Special: A Day with Mrs.
     Johnson." TV Guide, XVI (December 21, 1968), 6-10.
411 Gould, Jack. "TV--A Study of Hunger Amid Plenty: Re-
     printed from the New York Times, May 23, 1968." Con-
     gressional Record, CXIV (May 29, 1968), 15650-15651.
412 Kowet, Don and Sally Bedell. "Anatomy of a Smear: How
     CBS 'Got' General Westmoreland." TV Guide, XXX (May 29,
     1982), 2-15.
413 Martin, Ernest F., Jr. "The 'Hunger in America' Contro-
     versy." Journal of Broadcasting, XVI (Spring 1972),
     185-195.
414 "Mrs. Kennedy's White House Tour." TV Guide, IX (Au-
     gust 19, 1961), 14-15.
415 Muravchik, Joshua, and John E. Haynes. "CBS vs. De-
     fense." Commentary, LXXII (September 1981), 44-55.
416 NBC News. "Say Goodbye: Transcript of TV Documen-
     tary [on Migrant Workers]." In: United States. Congress
House Committee on Interstate and Foreign Commerce. Special
Subcommittee on Investigations. Subpoenaed Material Re: Cer-

tain TV News Documentary Prgrams: Hearings.   92nd   Cong.,
1st sess. Washington, D.C.: U.S. Government Printing Office,
1971. pp. 152-189.
417 "Replaying an Old War Game." Newsweek, XCIX (February 8, 1982), 93-94.
418 Smith, F. Leslie. "'Hunger in America' Controversy:
Another View." Journal of Broadcasting, XVIII (Winter
1973-1974), 79-83.
419 United States. Congress. House. Committee on Interstate
and Foreign Commerce, Subcommittee on Investigations.
Network News Documentary Practices--CBS "Project Peacock":
Hearings. 91st Cong., 1st sess. Washington, D.C.: U.S.Govern-
ment Printing Office, 1970. 487p.
420 _____ . _____ . _____ . _____ . _____ . Report.
91st Cong., 1st sess. Washington, D.C.: U.S. Government Printing Office, 1970. 154p. A documentary on a group
supposedly planning to invade Haiti.
421 "Westmoreland Denial." Broadcasting, CII (February 1,
1982), 66-68.
422 Wolff, Perry. A Tour of the White House with Mrs. John
F. Kennedy. Garden City, N.Y.: Doubleday, 1962. 258p.

DOCUMENTARIES AND SPECIAL REPORTS-- The Selling of the
Pentagon

423 "CBS and Congress: 'The Selling of the Pentagon'-- A
Special Issue." Educational Broadcasting Review, VIII
(Winter 1972), 1+.
424 Columbia Broadcasting System. News Division Staff. "Memo-
randum: Criticism of 'The Selling of the Pentagon.'" Congressional Record, CXVII (December 15, and 17, 1971), 47268-
47273, 47717-47722.
425 _____ . "'CBS Reports--The Selling of the
Pentagon': Transcript of the Broadcast, February 23,
1971." Congressional Record, CXVII (February 26, 1971),
4103-4107, 4126-4130.
426 Crater, Robert. "What the Shooting Was All About." Broadcasting, LXXXI (July 19, 1971), 20-22.
427 Doan, Richard K. "Embattled 'Pentagon' Program Wins
Peabody Award." TV Guide, XIX (April 24, 1971), A1.
428 Foote, Edward; Veda Gilp, and George L. Hall, eds.
CBS and Congress: "The Selling of the Pentagon" Papers.
Washington, D.C.: National Association of Educational Broadcasters, 1971. 144p.
429 Ginzberg, Benjamin. "Critique of 'The Selling of the
Pentagon.'" Congressional Record, CXVII (April 1, 1971),
9418-9421. By the Executive Secretary of the group Accuracy
in Media.
430 Gould, Jack. "CBS Explains Pentagon Propaganda Costs:
Reprinted from the New York Times, February 24, 1971."
Congressional Record, CXVII (February 26, 1971), 4099-4100.
431 Hart, Jeffrey. "CBS Cons the Public: Reprinted from the
Augusta (Ga.) Chronicle, August 31, 1971," Congressional Record, CXVII (September 15, 1971.), 32018.

432 Hayakawa, S. I. "Brainwashing by the Networks: Re-
     printed from the Washington Daily News, November 18,
1971." Congressional Record, CXVII (November 22, 1971),
42733.
433 Kelly, Orr. "CBS Missed the Pentagon Mark: Reprinted
     from the Washington Evening Star, March 30, 1971."
Congressional Record, CXVII (April 15, 1971), 10479-10480.
434 Laird, Melvin, and Daniel Z. Henkin. "Answers to Ques-
     tions About the TV Program 'The Selling of the Pentagon.'"
     Congressional Record, CXVII (March 8, 1971), 5401-5407.
435 Marshall, Samuel L.A. "In Defense of the Pentagon."
     TV Guide, XIX (May 22, 1971), 8-10.
436 Mayer, Martin. "Freedom of the Press Can Be a Matter of
     Self-Interested Definition: The CBS Documentary 'The
Selling of the Pentagon.'" Harper's, CCXLIII (December 1971),
43+.
437 "Mr. Agnew vs. CBS vs the Department of Defense:
     Reprinted from the Washington Post, March 26, 1971."
Congressional Record, CXVII (April 15, 1971), 10475-10476.
See the reply by Richard S. Salant below.
438 Robinson, Michael J. "The Impact of Instant Analysis:
     'The Selling of the Pentagon.'" Journal of Communications,
     XXVII (Spring 1977), 17-23.
439 _____ . "Public Affairs Television and the Growth of
     Political Malaise: The Case of 'The Selling of the Penta-
gon.'" American Political Science Review, LXX (June 1976),
409-432. Based on next entry.
440 _____ . "Public Affairs Television and the Growth of
     Political Malaise: The Case of 'The Case of 'The Selling of
the Pentagon.'" Unpublished PhD Dissertation, University of
Michigan, 1972.
441 Rogers, Jimmie N. and Theodore Clevenger, Jr. "' The
     Selling of the Pentagon': Was CBS the Fulbright Propa-
ganda Machine?" Quarterly Journal of Speech, LVII (October
1971), 266-273.
442 Ross, Nancy L. "A Peabody for CBS and 'Pentagon':
     Reprinted from the Washington Post, April 14, 1971."
     Congressional Record, CXVII (May 17, 1971), 15334.
443 Salant, Richard S. "CBS Replies to Editorial on 'Pentagon'
     Documentary: Reprinted from the Washington Post, March
30, 1971." Congressional Record, CXVII (April 15, 1971), 10476-
10477.
444 Shain, Percy. "CBS News Chief [Richard S. Salant] Sees
     Peril for Journalism: Reprinted from the Boston Globe,
April 29, 1971." Congressional Record, CXVII (May 17, 1971),
15335.
445 Sherrill, Robert. "Happy Ending (Maybe) of 'The Selling
     of the Pentagon.'" New York Times Magazine, May 16,
     1971, 25-27+.
446 Small, William J. Political Power and the Press. New York:
     W. W. Norton, 1972. 423p. A general history with much
insight into the controversy generated by this most famous--
or infamous--of all documentaries.
447 Smith, F. Leslie. "CBS Reports: The Selling of the Penta-
     gon." In: David J. LeRoy and Christopher H. Sterling,

eds.   Mass News: Practices, Controversies, and Alternatives. Englewood Cliffs, N. J.: Prentice-Hall, 1973. pp. 220-210.
448 United States. Congress. House. Committee on Inter-state and Foreign Commerce, Special Subcommittee on Investigations. Subpoenaed Material Re: TV News Documentary Programs. 92nd Cong., 1st sess. Washington, D.C.: U.S. Government Printing Office, 1971. 373p.
449   .   .   .   . Proceeding Against Frank Stanton and the Columbia Broadcasting System, Inc.: Report. 92nd Cong., 1st sess. Washington, D.C.: U.S. Government Printing Office, 1971. 272p.
450 Witze, Claude. "The Wayward Press (Tube Division): Reprinted from Air Force Magazine, April 1971." Con-gressional Record, CXVII (April 15 and May 10, 1971), 10477-10479, 14280-14281.
451 Woods, William C. "The Selling of the Pentagon: Reprinted from the Washington Post, February 26, 1971." Congres-sional Record, CXVII (February 26, 1971), 4100.

PUBLIC AFFAIRS PROGRAMMING--General

452 Abrams, Burton A., and Paul H. Ferber. "Television Interview Shows: The Politics of Visibility." Journal of Broadcasting, XXI (Spring 1977), 141-152.
453 Buckley, William F., Jr. "What Makes Those Discussion Shows Click?" TV Guide, XIV (June 10, 1967), 7-11.
454 Hickey, Neil. "Bigwig-Hunting in Washington." TVGuide, XVIII (May 9, 1970), 6-12.
455 Hilton, Jack, and Mary Knoblauch. On Television: A Survival Guide for Media Interviews. New York: Amacom, 1980. 185p. Designed for those who might find themselves being interviewed on camera for such shows as 60 Minutes; explains how to avoid offering potentially embarrassing com-ments.
456 Izard, Ralph S. Reporting the Citizen's News: Public Affairs Reporting in Modern Society. New York: Holt, Rinehart & Winston, 1982. 352p. Concerned with all aspects of the media, not just television.
457 Massing, Michael. "Should Public Affairs Be the Networks' Private Domain?" Columbia Journalism Review, XIX (May-June 1980), 34-37.
458 Stout, Richart T. "Sunday Morning Quarterbacks: 'Meet the Press,' 'Face the Nation,' and 'Issues and Answers' are Having a Mid-Life Crisis." Washington Journalism Review, II (December 1980), 34-37.

PUBLIC AFFAIRS--"See It Now": General

459 Baughman, James L. "'See It Now' and Television's Golden Age, 1951-1958." Journal of Popular Culture, XV (Fall 1981), 106-115.
460 Doan, Richard K. "When Ed Murrow Paid a Visit to Harry Truman." TV Guide, XXI (January 6, 1973), Al.
461 "Edward R. Murrow of CBS: 'See It Now.'" Newsweek, XLI (March 9, 1953), 40-41.

462 "Eyes of Conscience: 'See It Now.'" Newsweek, XLII
     (December 7, 1953), 65-66.
463 Hamburger, Philip. "Edward R. Murrow's 'See It Now.'"
     New Yorker, XXVII (December 8, 1951), 147-149.
464 Murrow, Edward R., and Fred W. Friendly. See It Now.
     New York: Simon & Schuster, 1955. 210p. A number of
     illustrated transcripts of various shows.
465 "Murrow on TV: 'See It Now.'" Newsweek, XXXIX (May
     12, 1952), 88-89.
466 "'See It Now.'" Time, LVIII (November 26, 1951), 73.
467 "'See It Now.'" Newsweek, LXXIX (January 17, 1972),
     83-84.
468 Smith, L. "'See It Now.'" Newsweek, LXXIV (October 6,
     1969), 114.
469 "Top of the News: 'See It Now.'" Newsweek, XXXVIII
     (December 3, 1951), 58.

PUBLIC AFFAIRS--"See It Now": Murrow vs. McCarthy

470 Bayley, Edwin R. Joe McCarthy and the Press. Madison,
     Wis.: University of Wisconsin Press, 1981. 254p. The
latest examination of the Wisconsin senator's relationship to the
print and broadcast media, including his famous "See It Now"
duel with Edward R. Murrow.
471 "Behind the Scenes at the Army-McCarthy Hearings."
     TV Guide, II (April 30, 1954), A1.
472 Buckley, William F., Jr., and L. Brent Bozell. McCarthy
     and His Enemies: The Record and Its Meaning.   Chicago,
     Ill.: Regnery, 1954. 413p. A pro-McCarthy examination.
473 Caute, David. The Great Fear: The Anti-Communist Purge
     Under Truman and Eisenhower. New York: Simon & Schus-
ter, 1978. 697p. A political treatise with some reference to the
Murrow-McCarthy altercation.
474 Cook, Fred J. The Nightmare Decade: The Life and Times
     of Senator Joe McCarthy.   New York: Random House,
1971. 626p. A general history of McCarthyism and its effects
on American society with coverage of the senator's conflict with
Murrow.
475 Deaver, Jean F. "A Study of Senator Joseph R. McCarthy
     and 'McCarthyism' as Influences Upon the Mass Media and
the Evolution of Reportorial Method." Unpublished PhD Dissertation, University of Texas at Austin, 1969.
476 Fried, Richard. Men Against McCarthy. New York:
     Columbia University Press, 1976. 428p. Includes Murrow.
477 Goldston, Robert C. The American Nightmare: Senator
     Joseph R. McCarthy and the Politics of Hate. Indianapolis,
In.: Bobbs-Merrill, 1973. 202p. A shorter account of McCarthyism concentrating on the tactics of the Wisconsin senator, especially when he found himelf opposed by men like Murrow.
478 Griffith, Robert. The Politics of Fear: Joseph R. McCarthy
     and the Senate. Lexington, Ky.: University of Kentucky
Press, 1970. 362p. How the members of the U.S. Senate feared
McCarthy and were unable to unite against him until the Army-
Murrow altercations of 1954.

479 Hamburger, Philip. "Report on McCarthy on 'See It Now' Program." New Yorker, XXX (March 20, 1954), 71-73.
480 McCarthy, Joseph. "The Inside Story of 'Person to Person.'" Look, XIX (December 13, 1955), 85-86+.
481 Murray, M. D. "The Persuasive Dimensions of 'See It Now's' Report on Senator Joseph R. McCarthy." Today's Speech, XXXIII (Fall 1975), 13-20.
482 Murrow, Edward R. "Let's Leave Each Other Alone." Coronet, XXXV (February 1954), 70-71.
483 _____, and Fred W. Friendly. "Annie Lee Moss Before the McCarthy Committee: Transcript of 'See It Now,' March 16, 1954." In: their See It Now. New York: Simon & Schuster, 1955, pp. 54-67.
484 Nizer, Louis. "Background: 'Fear on Trial.'" TV Guide, XXIII (September 27, 1975), 9-10.
485 Oshinsky, David. Senator Joe McCarthy. New York: Macmillan, 1978. 336p. A biography with some passing reference to the Morrow duel.
486 Potter, Charles E. Days of Shame. New York: Coward-McCann, 1965. 304p. Concentrates on the Army-McCarthy hearings, which were televised, with some mention of the "See It Now" shows.
487 Reeves, Thomas C. The Life and Times of Joe McCarthy: A Biography. New York: Stein & Day, 1982. 825p. The most comprehensive examination of McCarthy to date with details on his altercations with Murrow via TV.
488 Rovere, Richard H. Senator Joe McCarthy. New York: Harper & Row, 1973. 280p. A biography touching most of the familiar television events.
489 "Scorched Aid: Murrow vs. Senator McCarthy." Newsweek, XLIII (March 22, 1954), 86-87.
490 Seldes, Gilbert V. "Murrow, McCarty, and the Empty [Fairness] Formula: Giving Equal Time for Reply." Saturday Review of Literature, XXXVII (April 24, 1954), 26-27.
491 "Television in Controversy: The Debate and Defense." Newsweek, XLIII (March 29, 1954), 50-52.
492 Wallace, H. L. "The McCarthy Era, 1954." In: Vol. V of Congress Investigates: A Documented History. Edited by Arthur M. Schlesinger, Jr., and Richard Burns. New York: Chelsea House, 1975. pp. 3729-3919.
493 Wershba, Joseph. "Murrow vs. McCarthy: "See It Now.'" New York Times Magazine, (March 4, 1979), 31-38. The most useful account to date.

PUBLIC AFFAIRS--"Sixty Minutes"

494 Bergreen, Laurence. "The Strange Case of a Pain Killer." TV Guide, XXVIII (July 26, 1980), 3-7. A 60 Minutes expose.
495 Black, Jonathan. "The Stung." Channels, 1 (April-May 1981), 42-46.
496 Braun, Saul. "What Makes 60 Minutes Tick?" TV Guide, XXI (October 20, 1973), 16-19.

497 Bryski, Bruce G. "60 Minutes as Pseudo-Event: The Social Deflection of Reality." State College, Pa.: Department of Speech Communication, Pennsylvania State University, 1980. 23p. Available as ERIC document ED 193 710.
498 "CBS and Colonel [Anthony B.] Herbert: Appearance on 60 Minutes." Time, CI (February 12, 1973), 36-37.
499 Cunningham, Laura. "Behind the Scenes with 60 Minutes." Cosmopolitan, CLXXXVIII (June 1980), 244+.
500 Danzig, Fred. "'60 Minutes'--Confrontation Overkill?" Advertising Age, XLIX (March 6, 1978), 32+.
501 Diamond, Edwin. "The Power of Arrogance." Washington Journalism Review, III (December 1981), 59.
502 "Don Hewitt and Accounting for Every Second of CBS's 60 Minutes." Broadcasting, XC (April 12, 1976), 81.
503 Franklin, Marc A. "Libel Gets Tougher." More, VIII (February 1978), 26-29.
504 Good, Paul. "Why You Can't Always Trust 60 Minutes Reporting." Panorama, 1 (September 1980), 38+.
505 Kowet, Don. "Do Those 60 Minutes Crusades Pay Off?" TV Guide, XXVII (March 10, 1979), 18-22.
506 Levin, Eric. "Discovering What Makes 60 Minutes Tick." TV Guide, XXV (April 23, 1977), 24-30.
507 Media Institute. Punch, Counterpunch: 60 Minutes vs. Illinois Power Company. Washington, D.C., 1981. 50p.
508 Moore, Donavan. "60 Minutes." Rolling Stone, (January 12, 1978), 43-46.
509 "Newsmagazine of the Air: 60 Minutes." Time, XCII (October 4, 1968), 84.
510 Ognibene, Peter J. "Electronic Battlefield Coverage at CBS?: 60 Minutes Edited Segment of Cluster-Bombs Unit's Story." New Republic, CLXIX (July 21, 1973), 21-23.
511 Rubin, Alan M. "A Multivariate Analysis of 60 Minutes' Viewing Motivations." Journalism Quarterly, LVIII (Winter 1981), 529-533.
512 Schudson, Michael. "Sundays at Seven." Nation, CCXVI (September 5, 1981), 181-183.
513 Sherry, J. E. H. "Trespassing Reporters: What are the Rights of the Restauranteur?" Cornell Hotel and Restaurant Administration Quarterly, XXII (November 1981), 16-17.
514 "'60 Minutes.'" New Yorker, LIII (November 28, 1977), 166-173.
515 "'60 Minutes.'" Reader's Digest, CXI (July 1977), 155-158.
516 "'60 Minutes' Brings Back Afghan War." Broadcasting, XCVIII (March 10, 1980), 84-85.
517 Smilgis, Martha. "What Makes 60 Minutes Tick?: Rivalries, Tantrums, and a Genius Referee Named Don Hewitt." People, XI (May 28, 1979), 84-93.
518 Stein, Harry. "How 60 Minutes Makes News." New York Times Magazine, (May 6, 1979), 28-30+.
519 Zito, Stephen. "Inside 60 Minutes." American Film, II (December 1976-January 1977), 31+.

PUBLIC AFFAIRS--Other Individual Programs

520 Andrews, Peter. "How 'Good Morning America' Is Chal-
lenging 'Today.'" TV Guide, XXV (February 26, 1977),
26-29.
521 "Back to the Drawing Board for Today." Broadcasting,
XCIX (August 11, 1980), 48-99.
522 Barber, Rowland. "A Look at NBC's Tomorrow." TV
Guide, XXII (August 24, 1974), 12-14.
523 "Battling Panelists: 'Face the Nation.'" Newsweek, XLVII
(January 16, 1956), 78.
524 "Bill Moyer's Journal." Newsweek, LXXXIII (April 15,
1974), 79-80.
525 Birmingham, Fred A. "Everything Happens in the Today
Show." Saturday Evening Post, CCXLV (September 1973),
58-63+.
526 "Brinkley's Journal." Time, LXXVIII (November 17, 1961),
80.
527 CBS News. Face the Nation: The Collected Transcripts,
1954--. Metuchen, N.J.: The Scarecrow Press, 1975--.
528 _____. _____, 1954-1978. 21 vols. (microfiche).
Sanford, N.C.: Microfilming Corp. of America, 1979.
529 Cimons, Marlene. "The Action Is All Talk." TV Guide,
XXVII (November 10, 1979), 39-42. The long-time PBS
report.
530 Coates, C. "Cheerful, Spicy 'Good Morning America' De-
presses 'Today.'" Advertising Age, LI (April 20,1980),
24+.
531 "David Brinkley's Journal Aims for the Truth." TV Guide,
IX (December 9, 1961), 20-23.
532 "'Face the Nation,' the Show That Makes Headlines." TV
Guide, XIII (November 13, 1965), 6-9.
533 Graves, Florence. "20/20's Bomb Sparks Controversy."
Washington Journalism Review, 1 (September-October
1978), 20-22. An energy expose concerning Mobil Oil.
534 Hamburger, Philip. "Today." New Yorker, XXVII (February 2, 1952), 60-61.
535 Levine, Irving R. "A Quarter-Century of 'Meet the Press.'"
TV Guide, XXI (February 17, 1973), 5-8.
536 Metz, Robert. The Today Show: An Inside Look at 25 Tumultuous Years. Chicago, Ill.: Playboy Press, 1977.
264p. An interesting celebration of this long-time NBC show's
history which does not spare the controversies.
537 Minardi, Cathleen V. "The Today Show: The First 25
Years." Unpublished PhD Dissertation, University of Michigan, 1978.
538 Morgan, Thomas B. "'Meet the Press' Likes Its News
Hot." TV Guide, IX (July 1-8, 1961), 17-19, 26-29.
539 Nelson, H. "Two Methods of Presentation of 'Meet the
Press' Compared." Journal of Broadcasting, 1 (Spring
1957), 274-277.
540 "New Competition in the Morning." Broadcasting, LXXXVIII
(January 13, 1975), 18-20.
541 Nix, Mindy. "The 'Meet the Press' Game." In: Gaye
Tuchmen, ed. The TV Establishment. Englewood Cliffs,
N.J.: Prentice-Hall, 1974. pp. 66-71.

542 Rossman, Jules. "'Meet the Press' and National Elections:
     The Candidates and the Issues, 1952-1964." Unpublished
     PhD Dissertation, Michigan State University, 1968.
543 "60 Minute Dash: Magazine Style Shows." Time, CXI (March
     27, 1978), 83-84.
544 Stahl, Bob. "'Meet the Press': The Program Presidents
     Watch." TV Guide, IV (March 17, 1956), 10-11.
545 "The Sweet Smell of Success at NBC News in the Morning."
     Broadcasting, LXXXV (December 3, 1973), 46.
546 Whedon, Peggy. Always on Sunday: 1,000 Sundays with
     "Issues and Answers." New York: W. W. Norton, 1980.
A review of some of the production difficulties, personalities
and significant broadcasts of the long-time ABC public affairs
interview show.
547 _____. "When Jack Kennedy Spilled His Daiquiri." TV
     Guide, XXVIII (November 8, 1980), 24-26.

III-E. REPORTING AND PRESENTING THE NETWORK NEWS

GENERAL WORKS--Books

548 Bagdikian, Ben H., et al., eds. Liberating the Media:
     The New Journalism. Contemporary Issues in Journalism,
v. 4. Washington, D.C.: Acropolis Books, 1974. 210p. An
anthology on investigative reporting.
549 Bliss, Edward, Jr., and John M. Patterson. Writing News
     for Broadcast. 2nd ed., rev. New York: Columbia Uni-
versity Press, 1978. 220p. Written by two former CBS personnel, this volume draws on stories from Murrow which have
served as examples and been aired over the CBS television network.
550 Broussard, E. Joseph, and Jack F. Holgate. Writing
     and Reporting Brodcast News. New York: Macmillan,
     1982. A college text which provides various examples
     of "how to do it."
551 CBS News. Television News Reporting. New York:
     McGraw-Hill, 1958. 182p. A classic text of the pre-
investigative reporting school which emphasizes dignity and
resourcefulness.
552 Dary, David. TV News Handbook. Blue Ridge Summit,
     PA.: TAB Books, 1971. 251p. Takes the user through
the definition of news, reporter's qualifications, production,
writing, and editing methods, and production.
553 Fishman, Mark. Manufacturing the News. Austin, Tx.:
     University of Texas Press, 1980. 180p. Suggests that
routine news collection, not ideology, determines the character
of the news viewers see each evening.
554 Gans, Herbert J. Deciding What's News: A Study of the
     CBS Evening News, NBC Nightly News, Newsweek, and
Time. New York: Pantheon, 1979. 393p. Somewhat similar
to David Halberstam's The Powers That Be cited in Section
II:A; this study focuses on the editorial process of the big
network and magazine leaders.

555 Haight, Timothy R. Journalism Trends: Aspen Institute
   Guide to Print and Electronic Journalism Statistics.   New
York: Praeger, 1982. 256p. Focuses on radio/television and
cable communications in an introduction providing a focused
synthesis of broadcasting trends and issues.
556 Harrison, John M., and Henry H. Stein, eds. Muckraking: Past, Present, and Future.   State College, Pa.:
Pennsylvania State University Press, 1973. 165p. Includes a
section on the suitability of TV news for the role of expose reporting.
557 Metzler, Ken. Creative Interviewing. Englewood Cliffs,
   N.J.: Prentice-Hall, 1977. 174p. Includes tips from noted
   network TV interviewers on tricks of the trade.
558 Peterson, Sheldon, ed. The Newsroom and the Newscast.
   New York: Time-Life, 1966. 112p. Report of a conference
sponsored by the Radio-Television News Directors' Association,
this volume stresses newsroom staffing and operations.
559 Shook, Frederick and Dan Lattimore. The Broadcast News
   Process. Denver, Col.: Morton Publishing Company, 1979.
369p. A handbook for radio-tv newsrooms and college students
which examines the process from every angle.
560 Siller, Robert C. Guide to Professional Radio and TV
   Newscasting. Blue Ridge Summit, Pa.: TAB Books, 1972.
223p. A useful production guide now ten years old, which
shows novices how the pros on network news prepare for a
newscast.
561 Tyrell, Robert. The Work of the Television Journalist.
   New York: Hastings House, 1972. 180p. Looks at the
team concept of news describing the job and role of each mem-
ber from writer and producer to editor, cameraman, and reporter.
562 Wood, William A. Electronic Journalism. New York: Columbia University Press, 1967. 175p. A favorable look at
   television news and those involved in it.
563 Yorke, Ivor. The Technique of Television News. New
   York: Hastings House, 1978. 214p. A valuable guide
covering the various facets of electronic journalism and
news production.

GENERAL WORKS--Articles, Reports

564 Bailey, George. "How Newsmakers Make the News." Journal
   of Communications,   XXVIII   (Fall   1978),   80-83.
565 Banker, Stephen. "Beware of TV Scoops." Panorama,
   II (January 1981), 36+.
566 Barrett, Marvin. "Broadcast Journalism Since Watergate."
   Columbia Journalism Review, XIV (March 1976), 73-83.
567 Becker, Theodore and Peter R. Meyers. "Empathy and
   Bravado: Interviewing Reluctant Bureaucrats." Public
   Opinion Quarterly, XXXVIII (Winter 1974-1975), 605-613.
568 Bliss, Edward, Jr. "There is Good Journalism on TV."
   TV Guide, XXVI (July 15, 1978), 39-40.
569 Brinkley, David. "A Question for Television Newsmen:
   Does Anyone Care?" TV Guide, XXV (March 19, 1977),
   A5.

570   "Calling the Shots as They See Them Still Credo of Network Newsmen." Broadcasting, LXXXIII (July 24, 1972), 70-71.

571   Crystal, Lester M. "Using Technology: Improve Substance, Not Just Appearance." Television-Radio Age, (October 24, 1977), 43-78.

572   Day, John F. "TV News: Reporting or Performing?" In: Louis M. Lyons, ed. Reporting the News: Selections from Nieman Reports. Cambridge, Mass.: Harvard University Press, 1965. pp. 191-197.

573   Epstein, Edward J. "The Selection of Reality." In: Elie Abel, ed. What's News. San Francisco, Calif.: Institute for Contemporary Studies, 1981. pp. 119-132.

574   _____. "The Selection of Reality on Network News." Unpublished PhD Dissertation, Harvard University, 1973.

575   Erbring, Lutz, Edie N. Goldenberg, and Arthur H. Miller. "Front-Page News and Real-World Cues: A New Look at Agenda-Setting by the Media." American Journal of Political Science, XXIV (February 1980), 16-49.

576   Fowler, Joseph S. and Stuart W. Showalter. "Evening Network News Selection: A Confirmation of News Judgment." Journalism Quarterly, LI (Winter 1974), 712-715.

577   Frank, Reuven. "TV Journalism." In: A. William Blum and Roger Manveu, eds. The Progress in Television. New York: Focac Press, 1967. p. 117.

578   Frank, Robert S. "The 'Grammar of Film' in Television News." Journalism Quarterly, LI (Summer 1974), 244-250.

579   Fromson, Michael. "The Mass Media's Role is Reporting." College and University Journal, IX (Spring 1970), 5-8.

580   Funkhouser, G. Ray. "Trends in Media Coverage of the Issues of the '60's." Journalism Quarterly, L (Autumn 1973), 53-542, 548.

581   Henry, William A., 3rd. "News as Entertainment: The Search for Dramatic Unity." In: Elie Abel, ed. What's News. San Francisco, Calif.: Institute for Contemporary Issues, 1981. pp. 133-158.

582   Hickey, Neil. "Behind TV's Cautious Pursuit of Wrongdoing." TV Guide, XXV (April 9, 1977), 43-46.

583   _____. "How Well Does Television Keep America Informed?" TV Guide, XVI (March 9-16, 1968), 10-14, 30-33.

584   _____. "Is Television Doing Its Investigative Reporting Job?" TV Guide, XXV (April 2, 1977), 2-6.

585   _____. "TV News Bulletins--Too Many and Too Soon?" TV Guide, XIII (May 8, 1965), 6-10.

586   Houlberg, Rich and John Dimmick. "Influences on TV Newscasters' On-Camera Image." Journalism Quarterly, LVII (Autumn 1980), 481-485.

587   "How Newsmen Can Open Closed Doors." Broadcasting, LXXV (November 18, 1968), 62-64.

588   "How They Do It." Newsweek, LXXIV (December 1, 1969), 56-57.

589   Jencks, Richard W. "How Less Can Be More in Television News." Broadcasting, CII (April 5, 1982), 14. Format and graphic changes.

590 Lefever, Ernest W.   "Are Network Newscasts Too Long?"
     TV Guide, XXIV (January 17, 1976), 11-13.
591 Levin, Eric. "How Networks Choose the News." TV Guide,
     XXV (July 2-9, 1977), 4-10, 28-33.
592 _____. "Sensational--but is It News?" TV Guide, XXVI
     (April 15, 1978), 30-32.
593 _____.   "The Zoo Contingent vs. the Prima Donnas."
     TV Guide, XXIV (July 17, 1976), 2-4.
594 "The Life of a News Story: A Pictorial." TV Guide,
     IX (August 19, 1961), 14-15.
595 "The Live One: Spot Coverage is TV's Biggest Advantage."
     Broadcasting, XCV (August 18, 1978), 48-66.
596 Luter, John. "Investigative Reporting, 1968-1969." In:
     Marvin   Barrett,   ed.   The Alfred I. Dupont-Columbia
     University Survey of Broadcast Journalism, 1968-1969. New York:
     Grosset & Dunlap, 1969. pp. 67-82.
597 Murrow, Edward R. "Why Should News Come in 5-Minute
     Packages?" In: Louis M. Lyons, ed. Reporting the
     News: Selections from Nieman Reports.   Cambridge,   Mass.:
     Harvard University Press, 1965. pp. 186-190.
598 National Association of Broadcasters. Broadcasting of News:
     An Operational Guide. Washington, D.C., 1975.   27p.
599 Nessen, Ron. "Too Much Trivia, Too Little Substance."
     TV Guide, XXV (March 12, 1977), 2-5.
600 "The News That Takes a Little Longer to Do." Broad-
     casting, XCV (August 28, 1978), 68-76. Investigative
     reporting.
601 "Peril, Promise in Investigative Reporting." Broadcasting,
     XCVI (June 18, 1979), 49-61.
602 Powers, Ron. "The Battle Over Hour-Long Network News."
     TV Guide, XXI (August 22, 1981), 4-10.
603 _____. "Hard News Equals Hard Times." TV Guide,
     XXVII (March 24, 1979), 2-6.
604 Reasoner, Harry. "Problems in Reporting Controversial
     Issues." Issues, XIX (Spring 1965), 20-30.
605 Rowland, H.S. "Journalism vs. the Mass Media: Unit
     on Radio and Television News Reporting." English Journ-
     al, LIII (May 1964), 345-348.
606 Rule, Elton H. "Television and the Presentation of News--
     No Room for the Electronic Ostrich: Remarks at an ABC
     Luncheon, May 3, 1971." Congressional Record, CXVII (May
     24, 1971), 16625-16626.
607 Saltman, David. "Newscasters' Verbless Language." TV
     Guide, XXIX (December 12, 1981), 27-28.
608 Saltzman, Joe. "It's Live and It's Terrifying." TV Guide,
     XXIII (March 15, 1975), 6-10.
609 Shaw, David. "The Trouble with TV Muckraking." TV
     Guide, XXIX (October 10, 1981), 6-10.
610 Smith J. R. "Patterns of Graphic Presentation in Network
     Nightly News." Journal of Instructional Media, VII (Winter
     1979-1980), 13-23.
611 Townley, Richard. "The New Checkbook Journalism."
     TV Guide, XXIV (October 9, 1976), 5-10.

612 Weaver, Paul H. "The New Journalism vs the Old: Thoughts
     After Watergate." Public Interest, (Spring 1974), 67-88.
613 Wilkerson, Jim. "You Be the News Director." Atlanta,
     XX (May 1980), 108+.
614 Wolff, Adele. "Performing the News." Human Behavior,
     V (October 1976), 64-68.
615 Zeidenberg, L. "Push Has Come to Shove in Broadcast
     Journalism." Broadcasting, LXXXIV (January 1, 1973),
     35-38.

ETHICS AND CODES--Books

616 Epstein, Edward J. Between Fact and Fiction: The Problem
     of Journalism. New York: Vintage, 1975. 232p. Questions
the ethics of reporting by some and the presentation of news by
others.
617 Hohenberg, John. The Professional Journalist: A Guide
     to the Practices and Principles of the News Media. 2nd ed.
New York: Holt, Rinehard and Winston, 1969. 532p. A far
ranging treatise which examines ethics and codes among other
topics of concern to reporters, editors, and newscasters.
618 Hulteng, John L. The Messenger's Motives: Ethical Prob-
     lems of the News Media. Englewood Cliffs, N.J.: Prentice-
Hall, 1976. 262p. Looks at how the news is presented and examines the ethical concerns of those who edit, write, report,
and produce it.
619 Merrill, John C. and Ralph D. Barney, eds. Ethics and
     the Press: Readings in Mass Media Morality. New York:
Hastings House, 1981. 352p. A new anthology designed to
give the reader a glimpse of differing opinions concerning both
the print and electronic media and their handling of the news.
620 Rubin, Bernard, ed. Questioning Media Ethics. New
     York: Praeger, 1978. 250p. Practitioning critics-media
people appraise such practical issues as professional standards,
minority discrimination, Third World coverage and call for more
workable codes and standards.

ETHICS AND CODES--Articles, Reports

621 Cronkite, Walter. "Cronkite Calls for Truth-in-Packaging
     for TV Journalism." Broadcasting, CI (September 21,
     1981), 46-47.
622 "Do's and Don'ts of Television News: CBS Code." Time,
     CX (December 5, 1977), 114.
623 Epstein, Edward J. "The Values of Newsmen." Television
     Quarterly, (Winter 1973), 9-20.
624 Friendly, Fred W. "The Responsibility of TV Journalism:
     Fred W. Friendly's Letter of Resignation as President of
CBS News." In: Gerald Gross, ed. The Responsibility of the
Press. New York: Fleet Publication Co., 1966. pp. 309-313.
625 Hagerty, James C. "A Creed for Television Newsmen."
     TV Guide, XIX (February 25, 1961), 17-19.

626 Hart, John. "On News Responsibilities and Cosmetics." Broadcasting, XCIII (September 19, 1977), 124.
627 Idsvoog, Karl A., and James Hoyt. "Professionalism and Performance of Television Journalists." Journal of Broadcasting, XXI (Winter 1977), 97-110.
628 Johnstone, John W. C., Edward J. Slawski, and William W. Bowman. "The Professional Values of American Newsmen." Public Opionion Quarterly, XXXVI (Winter 1972-1973), 522-540.
629 Menaker, Daniel. "Art and Artifice in Network News." Harper's, CCXLV (October 1972), 40-42+.
630 Radio-Television News Directors' Association. "Code of Broadcast Ethics, as Amended October 13, 1971." In: Mary B. Cassata and Molefi K. Asante, eds. Mass Communication: Principles and Practices. New York: Macmillan, 1979. pp. 292-294.
631 The Society of Professional Journalists, Sigma Delta Chi. "Code of Ethics, 1973." In: Mary B. Cassata and Molefi K. Asante, eds. Mass Communications: Principles and Practices. New York: Macmillan, 1979. pp. 263-265.
632 Swertlow, Frank. "The Policy." TV Guide, XXIII (November 15, 1975), 6-9.
633 United States. Congress. Senate. Committee on Commerce, Science and Transportation, Subcommittee on Communications. Television Broadcast Policies: Hearings. 95th Cong., 1st sess. Washington, D.C.: U.S. Government Printing Office, 1978. 512p.

COMMENTATORS, COMMENTARY

634 Back, Gunnar. "The Role of the Commentator as Censor of the News." In: Harry J. Skornia and Jack W. Kitson, eds. Problems and Controversies in Radio and Television: Basic Readings. Palo Alto, Calif.: Pacific Books, 1968. pp. 339-346.
635 Bland, Brian. "Changing Aspects of Broadcast News Commentary and Analysis." Unpublished MA thesis, University of Illinois, 1964
636 Breiner, Richard M. "David Brinkley, Harry Reasoner, Eric Sevareid, and Howard K. Smith: An Examination of Apparent Role Fulfillment of TV Network News Commentators During Crisis Periods of 1973-1975." Unpublished PhD Dissertation, Kent State University, 1980.
637 "Deferred Analysis: End of CBS's Instant Analysis After Presidential TV Addresses." Time, CI (June 18, 1973), 72.
638 "Delayed Reaction: No More Commentaries Immediately After Presidential Speeches on CBS." Newsweek, LXXXI (June 18, 1973), 74-75. Analysis was later reinstated.
639 Emerson, Gloria. "Why I Won't Miss Eric Sevareid" New York, X (December 5, 1977), 56-57.
640 Feuer, L.S. "Why Not a Commentary on Sevareid?: The Power of Reporters and Commentators." National Review, XXVII (August 15, 1975), 874-876.

641   Griffith, Thomas.   "'Don't Tell Us What to Think.'" Time,
      CXIX (May 24, 1982), 71.   On the evening news com-
mentaries of John Chancellor (NBC) and Bill Moyers (CBS).
642   Henthoff, Nat.   "Howard K. Smith: How Far Can a News-
      man Go?" TV Guide, X (June 23, 1962), 6-9.
643   Hiebert, Ray E., Donald F. Lengurait, and Thomas W.
      Bohn.   "Analysis and Interpretation."   In: their Mass
      Media II. New York: Longmans, 1979. pp. 368-381.
644   "Instant Analysis: CBS and Instant Analysis." New Repub-
      lic, CLXVIII (June 20, 1973), 8-9.
645   Jaffe, Louis L. "The Editorial Responsibility of the Broad-
      caster: A Reflection on Fairness and Access." Harvard
      Law Review, LXXXV (February 1972), 768-792.
646   Just, Ward S.   "Politics, Are We the Hostages?"   Atlantic,
      CCXLV (April 1980), 99-101. Candidates and com-
      mentators.
647   Kilpatrick, James J.   "TV Opinion has a Place--as TV
      Opinion." TV Guide, XXIII (June 21, 1975), A3-A4.
648   Klein, Herbert.   "Analytical-Interpretive Journalism."
      In: R. Gordon Hoxie, ed. The White House--Organization
and Operations: Proceedings of the United States.   New York:
Center for the Study of the Presidency, 1971.   pp. 21-23.
649   Klose, Albert P.   "Howard K. Smith Comments on the
      News: A Comparative Analysis of the Use of Television and
Print."   Unpublished PhD Dissertation, Northwestern University, 1970.
650   Paletz, David L. and Michael J. Vinegar. "Presidents on
      Television: The Effects of Instant Analysis." Public Opinion
      Quarterly, XLI (Winter 1977-1978), 488-497.
651   Phillips, Kevin.   "Replacing Eric Sevareid: The Larger
      Questions." TV Guide, XXV (November 12, 1977), A5-A6.
652   Powers, Ron.   "Where Have the News Analysts Gone?"
      TV Guide, XXVIII (October 4, 1980), 4-9.
653   Selph, Barbara J.   "A Descriptive Analysis of the Network
      Television News Commentary Program 'Howard K. Smith,
News and Comment.'"   Unpublished MA thesis, Ohio State
University, 1963.
654   Sevareid, Eric, Martin Agronsky, and Louis Lyons.   "The
      Television News Commentator." In: Harry J. Skornia and
Jack W. Kitson, eds.   Problems and Controversies in Radio and
Television: Basic Readings.   Palo Alto, Calif.: Pacific Books,
1968. pp. 364-376.
655   Shayon, R. L.   "Two and a Half Minute Storm: Howard
      K. Smith's News and Comment Program." Saturday Review
      of Literature, XLV (December 1, 1962), 28-30.
656   Smith, R. Franklin.   "The Nature and Development of
      Commentary." Journal of Broadcasting, VI (Winter 1961-
      1962), 11-22.
657   Stahl, Bob. "Howard K. Smith: Analyze, Don't Editorial-
      ize." TV Guide, VIII (April 16, 1960), 10-11.
658   Sullivan, John P.   "Editorials and Controversy: The
      Broadcaster's Dilemma."   George Washington Law Review,
      XXXII (April 1964), 719-768.
659   "Tough Mind, Clear Talk: Howard K. Smith--News and
      Comment." Newsweek, LX (October 19, 1962), 82.

660 Vanocur, Sander and John Carmody. "TV News Judgment
     Assailed: Reprinted from the Washington Post, January 18,
1976." Congressional Record, CXXII (January 28, 1976), 1378.
661 Von Hoffman, Nicholas. "The Art of Commenting Sagely,
     While Saying as Little as Possible." TV Guide, XXIV
     (May 1, 1976), A5-A6.
662   . "TV Commentators: Burbles from Olympus."
     Columbia Journalism Review, XIV (January 1976), 9-13.
663 "When Nixon Goes on TV: New Rule on the Right to Re-
     ply." U.S. News and World Report, LXIX (August 31,
     1970), 26-27.

THE ROLE OF WOMEN--Books

664 Baehr, Helen, ed. Women and the Media. Oxford, N.Y.:
     Pergamon Press, 1980. 137 p. An anthology containing
articles pertaining to women in both the print and broadcast
media.
665 Beasley, Maurine H. and Sheila Silver. Women in Media:
     A Documentary Source Book. Washington, D.C.: Women's
Institute for Freedom of the Press, 1977. 198p. Chronicles the
sexism problems of women in the male-dominated print and
broadcast media.
666 Epstein, Laurily K., ed. Women and the News. New
     York: Hastings House, 1978. 192p. Another series of
articles focusing on the distaff difficulties of functioning in a
male-oriented medium.
667 Gelfman, Judith S. Women in Television News. New York:
     Columbia University Press, 1976. 186p. Like the other
titles noted above, this title examines the difficulties of and
expansion of women's roles in television news's various facets.

THE ROLE OF WOMEN--Articles, Reports

668 Allen, Jennifer. "The Women Who Make the News." Life,
     V (June 1982), 100-106.
669 Bowan, William W. "Distaff Journalists: Women as a Minor-
     ity Group in the News Media." Unpublished PhD Disserta-
     tion, University of Illinois at Chicago Circle, 1974.
670 "CPB Study Finds Women Underused and Underserved."
     Broadcasting, LXXXIX (October 13, 1975), 36-37.
671 Day, Nancy L. "Women Journalists: Professional/Personal
     Conflicts." Nieman Reports, XXXIII (Summer 1979), 34-40.
672 Eddings, Barbara M. "Women in Broadcasting: De Jure,
     De Facto." In: Marvin Barrett, ed. Rich News, Poor
News: The Alfred I. Dupont-Columbia University Survey of
Broadcast Journalism. New York: T.Y. Crowell, 1978. pp.
151-167.
673 "Fashion Newsmakers [Women Newscasters]." Ladies Home
     Journal, XCIX (April 1982), 72-75.
674 Gottlieb, P.G. "Newswomen on the Air." Working Woman,
     VI (February 1981), 66-69.

675 Hennessee, Judith A. "Some News is Good News: The Television Newswoman." Ms., III (July 1974), 25-29.

676 _____. "What Progress Women at CBS?" Personnel, LII (July 1975), 33-44.

677 Krupp, Katherine. "Update--Women in TV News: Just How Far have We Come?" Glamour, LXXIX (September 1981), 249+.

678 Madden, K. "New Image of Success--Women in Television News: A Symposium." Vogue, CLXIX (October 1979), 296-297+.

679 Mannes, Marya. "Should Women Only be Seen and Not Heard?" TV Guide, XVI (November 23, 1968), 6-10.

680 Marzolf, Marion. "Newswoman on Camera." In: her Up from the Footnote: A History of Women Journalists. New York: Hastings House, 1977. pp. 157-198.

681 "The New Breed." Newsweek, LXXXVIII (August 30, 1971), 62.

682 Otte, Mary L. "Sexism in Local and Network Television News." Unpublished PhD Dissertation, Georgia State University, 1978.

683 "Prime Time for TV Newswomen." Time, CIX (March 21, 1977), 85-86.

684 Singleton, Loy A. and Stephanie L. Cook. "Television Network News Reporting by Female Correspondents: An Update." Journal of Broadcasting, XXVI (Winter 1982), 487-492.

685 Smith, Don C. and Kenneth Harwood. "Women in Broadcasting." Journal of Broadcasting, X (Fall 1966), 339-355.

686 Stone, Vernon A. "Attitudes Toward Television Newswomen." Journal of Broadcasting, XVIII (Winter 1973-1974), 49-62.

687 Warga, Wayne. "Focus on TV Anchorwomen." Cosmopolitan, CXC (June 1981), 262-267.

CAREERS IN NETWORK NEWS

688 Allosso, Michael. Exploring Theater and Media Careers: A Student Guide. Washington, D.C.: U.S. Government Printing Office, 1976. 138p.

689 Fisher, H. A. "Broadcast Journalists' Perceptions of Appropriate Career Preparation." Journalism Quarterly, LV (Spring 1978), 140-144.

690 Freeman, Ira H. and Beatrice O. "Broadcast Journalism." In: their Careers and Opportunities in Journalism. New York: E.P. Dutton, 1966. pp. 129-156.

691 Kienzle, Kathleen. "A Study of Employment Opportunities for Women in Broadcast News." Unpublished MA thesis, Ohio State University, 1965.

692 Radio-Television News Directors' Association. Careers in Broadcast News. Washington, D.C., 1980. Unpaged. Probably the most worthwhile item cited in this subsection.

693 Reed, Maxine K. and Robert M. Career Opportunities in Television and Video. New York: Facts on File, Inc., 1982. 224 p. Description of position, salary possibilities, employment prospects, and chances for advancement.

IV. NETWORK TELEVISION
NEWS IN CONTROVERSY

Television network news has long been controversial. Questions about the work of certain journalists, the purpose of various documentaries, and the political philosophies of producers and network chiefs have been raised. The perceived ability of electronic journalism to guide or set the agenda in such areas as foreign affairs and national elections through an ability to deal with principals or influence public opinion, has proven troubling for some, as was so well noted in Max M. Kampelman's recent study ("The Power of the Press: A Problem for Our Democracy," Congressional Record, 125 [Dec. 12, 1979], H11889-H11896).

Government control of information sources and censorship have always faced journalists. Such government maneuvers have included not only classification, but deliberate misinformation, often through selected "leaks." Morton Halperin and Daniel Hoffman report that the public's "right to know" and the reporter's ability to ferret out information are often in direct conflict, from a government viewpoint, especially with regard to those secrets seen to have some bearing on national security (Top Secret: National Security and the Right to Know [New York: Simon & Schuster, 1977]).

In Lyndon B. Johnson's administration, the way information was handled, especially such touchy issues as the Vietnam War, led to the coining of such terms as "credibility gap" and "managed news" (William McGaffin and Ewin Knoll, Anything But the Truth: The Credibility Gap--How the News Is Managed in Washington [New York: G.P. Putnam, 1969], pp. 1-2). New concerns in this direction have evolved just as this guide was being compiled: the Reagan administration's drive to tighten the provisions of the Freedom of Information Act, reversal of document declassification schedules and procedures, and the feud over network coverage of the events in El Salvador. Perhaps Walter Cronkite summed up these concerns best while accepting the National Association of Broadcasters (NAB) Distinguished Service Award for 1982: "It is all the 'ifs' and 'buts' so many people want to place between their own interests and the freedom of the press...all the little restrictions and constrictions enacted and proposed on the people's right to know" ("Cronkite Warns of Growing Trend of Censorship," Broadcasting, 102 [April 12, 1982], 32).

About two hundred years ago, the First Amendment to the U.S. Constitution was adopted. "Congress," the ruling stated, "shall make no law abridging the freedom of speech or of the press." Later, the Supreme Court interpreted another amend-

49

ment, the Fourteenth, as extending those First Amendment
prohibitions to the states.

The new era of broadcasting, ushered in with the introduction of commercial radio in the 1920's, brought with it the
need for some controls, because of the finite reaches of the
electromagnetic spectrum. In 1934, Congress, reworking legislation from 1927, passed the Communications Act, which established the Federal Communications Commission (FCC), gave that
new body regulatory power through the granting of licenses for
broadcasters who employed the public airwaves on an exclusive
basis. In the years since, through court decisions and FCC
rules and regulations, the electronic medium has been brought
under some conformity.

Among the more noteworthy standards brought about
through government regulation and license control are the
requirements of fairness and equal time. These are still often
confused, writes former FCC Chairman Charles D. Ferris, who
offers these definitions: "Equal time applies only to political
candidates. When one candidate gets time from a television or
radio station, the same opportunity must be provided to an
opponent. The fairness doctrine applies to issues, not people"
("The Fairness Doctrine Is Fair," Washington Post [March 20,
1981], K22). It was the suspension of the equal time clause
which allowed the various presidential debates.

Due to licensing requirements, the possibilities of government censorship, and various court decisions and FCC rulings,
a vigorous discussion has taken place since the 1934 Communications Act concerning the relationship of electronic journalism to the First Amendment. Although broadcasters have
sometimes felt a bit inferior to their print colleagues, whose
media are free of licensing restrictions, most would agree with a
fact noted in President Reagan's recent letter to the NAB:
"Radio and television comprise an important part of the American press and provide much of the news and information received by the American people" ("Reagan Supports First Amendment Rights for Broadcasters," Broadcasting 102 [April 12,
'82], 31). Today, as recently-retired CBS News President Bill
Leonard has noted, "Changing technology is bringing the different media together so fast that old arguments advocating
control of broadcast news are disappearing" ("Tug-of-War over
First Amendment for Fifth Estate," Broadcasting 102 [April 12,
'82], 32). In an April 1982 address, NAB President Vincent
Wasilewski suggested that communications technologies have
begun to "blend," signalling the 1980's as "the threshold decade
of the communications age." "Broadcasters," he said, "must
have the freedom to seek out and report information without
government oversight, which could easily become government
censure" ("Wasilewski Urges Stepped Up Fight for Protection
of First Amendment," Broadcasting 102 [April 12, '82], 33).
These sentiments echo the long held belief of television pioneer
Fred W. Friendly, who was quoted in a 1981 TV Guide interview: "My view [is] that broadcast journalism, like all journalism, ought to be free..." ("Network News? 'A National Tragedy'--Local News? 'It's Putrid'--Million Dollar Journalists?

'Obscene,'" TV Guide 29 [Aug. 1, '81], 27), and of Walter
Cronkite: "If we vote for democracy, then we have to defend
at every quarter the sine qua non of popular rule, the free and
independent flow of public information, free and vigorously
active news media and their access to information a democratic
public needs to know" ("Cronkite Warns...," loc. cit.).
   The concern with government interference and attack on
the part of broadcasters and others is not just communications
theory. Various administrations have, over the past fifty
years, had their differences with the electronic media and have
demonstrated their displeasure in different ways. Both presidents Kennedy and Eisenhower were angered by various news
programming, while Lyndon B. Johnson often personally tele-
phoned network news executives and reporters to express his
ire in plain and sometimes earthy terms. It is the administration of Richard Nixon, however, that is usually pointed to
as an example of what might happen when a government becomes unfriendly towards electronic journalism. In addition to a
planned, concentrated harrassment effort, usually covert,
against the media through such agencies as the FBI, Nixon's
vice president, Spiro T. Agnew, beginning in 1969, actively
campaigned against network television news. The perception of
Fred W. Friendly here is informative: "If Spiro Agnew had
been smarter, if he had done his homework better, if he hadn't
been such a bully about it all, it would have been clear that
everything he was saying about the press wasn't wrong. He
just let it get politicized" ("Network News?" loc. cit.).
   These various attacks on network programming, policies,
and procedures, some of which may have been justified, did
have an effect on network news production and dissemination
and have certainly contributed to the First Amendment concerns
of broadcasters and politicians alike ("The Packwood Amendment: Going for Broke." Broadcasting 102 [April 12, '82], 30).
   The citations in this section all deal with the controversies
and rulings which have surrounded network television news
since the early 1950's. Part IV-A provides sources on the
question of media bias and power while IV-B includes entries
relative to government control of information sources and censorship. The materials in IV-C are aimed at the relationship of
the First Amendment to the Fifth Estate, the Fairness Doctrine
(also see Chapter V under Presidential Debates) and the relatively new practice of media law. Government attacks on the
electronic media are the subject of the entries in IV-D, which
should be employed with the other part in this section as well
as those in Chapter V under Presidents.

IV-A. MEDIA BIAS AND POWER

BOOKS

694 Altheide, David L. Creating Reality: How TV News Distorts
     Events. Sage Library of Social Research, v. 33. Los
     Angeles, Calif.: Sage Professional Publications, 1976. 221p.

Examines the various aspects of the "bias question," including the impact of media technology, geography and time-zones, reporting styles and commentary.
695 Brown, Lee. Reluctant Revolution: On Criticizing the Press in America. New York: David McKay, 1974. 242p. Looks at press criticism (print and broadcast) in America and examines the motives and inclinations of those involved as well as the targets of criticism and why they are perceived to be in need of criticism.
696 Cirino, Robert. Don't Blame the People. New York: Vintage Books, 1972. 339p. A documented account of how the print and broadcast media employed distortion, bias, and in-house censorship to manipulate public opinion.
697 _____. Power to Persuade: Mass Media and the News. New York: Bantam Books, 1974. 246p. A slightly revised and retitled version of the above study.
698 Efron, Edith. How CBS Tried to Kill a Book. New York: Manor Books, 1972. 187p. Explains how CBS, considering itself the main target of the author's The News Twisters (next entry), employed a variety of tactics to have the publication and distribution of the book halted.
699 _____. The News Twisters. Los Angeles, Calif.: Nash Publishing, 1971. 355p. Employing statistics and other data, the author, a noted TV Guide columnist, sets out to prove that the television networks, especially CBS, employ distortion, in-house censorship, selected coverage, commentary and instant analysis, and political bias to manipulate public opinion. This title, perhaps the most virulent ever penned about network news, provided critics with a gold mine and left defenders gasping at a time when they were already under attack by the Nixon White House.
700 Epstein, Edward J. Between Fact and Fiction: The Problem of Journalism. New York: Vintage Books, 1975. 232p. A series of eleven studies on such subjects as Vietnam, Watergate, the Bernie Cornfeld Scandal, drawn from the author's pieces in TV Guide, Commentary, and the New Yorker. After analyzing the process by which the informtion in each case was gathered, edited, and presented to the public, the writer suggests that the story was a selective manipulation of the data at hand.
701 Herschensohn, Bruce. The Gods of Antenna. New Rochelle, N.Y.: Arlington House, 1975. 155p. Written by a deputy special assistant to President Nixon, this slim volume identifies a variety of methods whereby network news can be presented to accomplish planned results.
702 Hulteng, John L. and Roy P. Nelson. The Fourth Estate: An Informal Appraisal of the News and Opinion Media. New York: Harper & Row, 1971. 356p. Examines the motives and methods employed by both the print and broadcast media to influence public opinion; tame in comparison to the Efron study (above) published the same year.
703 Johnson, Nicholas. How to Talk Back to Your Television Set. Boston: Little, Brown, 1970. 228p. The FCC Commissioner at the time of Nixon's presidency suggests that more creativity is needed to deal with the national policy questions

involving broadcasting, especially the bias in network news. The author presents several "tips" on how viewers can avoid being manipulated by the networks which, he suggests as an example, always censor news injurious to sponsors.

704 Keely, Joseph. The Left-Leaning Antenna: Political Bias in Television. New Rochelle, N.Y.: Arlington House, 1971. 320p. Suggests that those involved with network news are all liberals bent on manipulating the public to that political persuasion.

705 Mankiewicz, Frank, and Joel Swerdlow. Remote Control: Television and the Manipulation of American Life. New York: Times Books, 1978. 308p. Not so much a critique of bias in network news as an examination of the role of television upon the daily lives of Americans, commerically, politically, and socially.

706 Skornia, Harry J. Television and the News: A Critical Appraisal. Palo Alto, Calif.: Pacific Books, 1968. 343p. Suggests that American decision-making on various issues is hampered by non-receipt of properly diverse and clear news from radio and television sources. After examining certain reasons for these weaknessesses and failures, the author presents some ideas for improvements which might be considered by the public and media industry.

707 Stein, Robert. Media Power: Who Is Shaping Your Picture of the World. Boston: Houghton-Mifflin, 1972. 265p. An examination of media power, how it came about and who controls it, suggesting that broadcast industry leaders have failed to recognize the nature of their new problems and potentials and that additional standards are required.

708 Tuchman, Gaye, ed. The TV Establishment: Programming for Power and Profit. Englewood Cliffs, N.J.: Prentice-Hall, 1974. 186p. An anthology of very anti-establishment views on the three commercial networks, all of which concentrate on the impact of economics on programming, including news and public affairs.

709 United States. Congress. House. Committee on Interstate and Foreign Commerce. Special Subcommittee on Investigations. Inquiry Into Alleged Rigging of Television News Programs: Hearings. 92nd Cong., 2nd sess. Washington, D.C.: U.S. Government Printing Office, 1972. 216p.

ARTICLES

710 "America's News Industry: Responsible or Reckless?" U.S. News and World Report, LXXVI (April 29, 1974), 32-36.

711 Arnston, Paul H., and Craig R. Smith. "News Distortion as a Function of Organizational Communication." Communication Monographs, XLV (November 1978), 371-381. Emphasis on CBS.

712 Barber, J.D. "Not the New York Times: What Network News Should Be." Washington Monthly, XI (September 1979), 14-16+.

713 Birt, John. "There is a Bias in Television Journalism,
It is Not Against Any Particular Party or Point-of-View--It
is a Bias Against Understanding." TV Guide, XXIII (August 9,
1975), 3-7.
714 Bleiberg, Robert. "'Slanted' Journalism--Henceforth the
Fox Will Be Guarding the Chickens: Remarks." Congressional Record, CXXI (August 24, 1976), 27571-27572. Views on
CBS by the editor of Baron's.
715 "Both Sides of Debate Over Television News." U.S. News
and World Report, LXXIV (February 19, 1973), 48-52.
716 Breen, Myles P. Television News as Drama: An International Perspective. DeKalb, Ill.: Department of Speech
Communications, Northern Illinois University, 1981. 21p.
Available as ERIC document ED 198-574.
717 Buchanan, Patrick. "Why the War Wages Over Network
News." TV Guide, XXII (February 23, 1974), A3-A4.
718 Chancellor, John. "Television and the News Realities."
TV Quarterly, VI (Fall 1968), 87-91.
719 Cronkite, Walter. "Cronkite Defends TV's Objectivity."
Broadcasting, LXXXV (October 7, 1968), 47-48.
720 _____. "The Media and the News: An Interview." Current, CCXXIII (June 1980), 14-18.
721 Diamond, Edwin, and Stephen Bates. "Special Report:
How Accurate is the Network News?" TV Guide, XXX
(Februay 27, 1982), 2-12.
722 Dominick, Joseph R. "Geographic Bias in National TV
News." Journal of Communications, XXVII (Fall 1977),
94-99.
723 Efron, Edith. "Bias in Broadcast News: Testimony before
Subcommittee on Constitutional Rights, February 2, 1972."
Congressional Record, CXVIII (March 22, 1972), 9514-9517.
724 _____. "The Bias Issue is Still Alive in News Coverage." TV Guide, XXII (September 21, 1974), A3-A4.
725 _____. "Debate Over Bias, Power of TV News Still
Continues." TV Guide, XXIII (March 15, 1975), A3-A4.
726 _____. "The Real Problem Behind the Bias of TV's Hard
News." TV Guide, XXIV (February 7, 1976), A5-A6.
727 _____. "The 'Silent American' Comes Into Focus." TV
Guide, XVII (September 27, 1969), 6-9.
728 _____. "There Is--Is Not a Network News Bias: Interviews with Howard K. Smith [yes] and Eric Sevareid
[no]." TV Guide, XVIII (February 28 and March 14, 1970),
6-11, 6-11.
729 Elliott, Bill. "Network TV News Lacks Balance: Reprinted
from the Dallas White Rocker, March 1, 1974." Congressional Record, CXX (March 5, 1974), 5423-5424.
730 Epstein, Edward J. "The Strange, Tilted World of TV
Network News." Reader's Digest, CIV (February 1974),
142-146.
731 Fairlie, Henry. "Can You Believe Your Eyes?" Horizon,
IX (Spring 1967), 24-27. Abridged in Reader's Digest,
XCI (August 1967), 127-130, under the title, "The Unreal World
of Television News."

732   Furlong, William B. "The Misleading of America." TV Guide, XXV (June 18, 1977), 4-7.
733   _____. "The Tactical Gamesmanship in Manipulating the News." TV Guide, XXVI (June 11, 1977), 4-8.
734   Haley, William. "Where Television News Fails." Columbia Journalism Review, IX (Spring 1970), 7-11.
735   Hentoff, Nat. "How 'Fair' Should TV Be?" Lithopinion, IX (Summer 1974), 25-31.
736   Herschensohn, Bruce. "How the TV Networks Manipulate You: Reprinted from the Conservative Digest, February 1976." Congressional Record, CXXII (January 28, 1976), 1403-1404.
737   Hofstetter, C. Richard, and Terry F. Buss. "Bias in Television News Coverage of Political Events: A Methodological Analysis." Journal of Broadcasting, XII (Fall 1978), 517-530.
738   Horowitz, Andrew R. "Playing Monopoly with the News." More, V (March 1975), 16+.
739   Howard, Robert. "Bias in Television News: A Content Analysis." Unpublished PhD Dissertation, Florida State University, 1972.
740   Hulteng, John L. "Holding the Media Accountable." In: Elie Abel, ed. What's News. San Francisco, Calif.: Institute for Contemporary Studies, 1981. pp. 211-232.
741   International Broadcast Institute Panel. "How Influential is TV News?" Columbia Journalism Review, IX (Summer 1970), 19-30. Conclusion: very influential.
742   Johnson, Nicholas. "Is there a Slant in TV News: Address, International Conference of Radio/Television News Directors, September 26, 1969." Congressional Record, CXV (December 1, 1969), 36298-36302.
743   Kampelman, Max. "The Power of the Press: A Problem for Our Democracy." Congressional Record, CXXV (December 12, 1979), H11889-H11896.
744   Kraft, Joseph. "The Imperial Media." Commentary, LXXI (May 1981), 36-47.
745   Lee, R.S.H. "The Credibility of Newspaper and TV News." Journalism Quarterly, LV (Summer 1978), 282-287.
746   Levinsohn, F.H. "TV's Deadly Inadvertent Bias." School Review, LXXXIV (May 1976), 390-400.
747   Lower, Elmer. "Fairness and Balance in Television News Reporting." Quill, LVIII (February 1970), 12-15.
748   Ludel, Susan. "Who Programs the Programmers?" Objectivist, IX (March-April 1970), 11-16, 8-12.
749   Panitt, Merrill. "Network Power: Is It Absolute?" TV Guide, XXV (February 26, 1977), 34-37.
750   Phillips, Kevin. "The Changing Public Perception of Newscaster Bias." TV Guide, XXII (July 13, 1974), A3-A4.
751   Reagan, Ronald. "Do the Networks Always Shortchange the Loyal Opposition?" TV Guide, XXVI (March 11, 1978), 4-8.
752   Sanoff, Alvin P. "TV News Growing Too Powerful?" U.S. News and World Report, LXXXVIII (June 9, 1980), 59-60.

753 Schrag, Peter. "The Powers That Be." _More_, VI (Jan-
     uary 1976), 26+.
754 Sevareid, Eric. "A Harsh Word for TV Critics." _Report-
     er_, XIX (July 10, 1958), 35-36.
755 _____. _The Quest for Objectivity_. Elmer Davis Memorial
     Lecture, no. 4. New York: Television Information Office,
     1970. 11p.
756 Shaw, Eugene F. "Media Credibility: Taking the Measure
     of a Measure." _Journalism Quarterly_, L (Summer 1973),
     306-311.
757 Smith, Howard K., and Eric Sevareid. "Is There a Net-
     work Bias?" In: Michael C. Emergy and Ted C. Smythe,
eds. _Readings in Mass Communications: Concepts and Issues in
the Mass Media_. 2nd ed. Dubuque, Ia.: William C. Brown, 1974.
pp. 456-467.
758 Smith, Robert R. _Beyond the Wasteland: The Criticism
     of Broadcasting_. Annandale, VA.: Speech Communications
     Association, 1976.
759 Stanley, R. H. "Television News: Format as a Form of
     Censorship." _ETC_, XXXV (Winter 1978), 433-441.
760 Stevensen, R. L., et al. "Untwisting the News Twisters:
     A Replication of Efron's Study." _Journalism Quarterly_,
     L (Summer 1973), 211-219.
761 "Symposium on TV News: Is That the Way It Is?" _Journal
     of Communications_, XXVII (Autumn 1977), 94-117.
762 "Television Comes Under Fire." _U.S. News and World
     Report_, LXV (July 15, 1968), 36-39.
763 Weaver, Paul H. "Is Television News Biased?" _The Public
     Interest_, XXVI (Winter 1972), 57-74.
764 Williams, Alden. "Unbiased Study of Television News
     Bias." _Journal of Communications_, XXV (Autumn 1975),
     190-199.
765 Wilson, C. Edward, and Douglas M. Howard. "Public
     Perception of Media Accuracy." _Journalism Quarterly_,
     LV (Spring 1978), 73-76.

IV-B. GOVERNMENT CONTROL AND CENSORSHIP

BOOKS

766 Archer, Jules. _Superspys: The Secret Side of Govern-
     ment_. New York: Delacorte Press, 1977. 252p. Examines
overt and covert methods of controlling government information
and those who would handle it.
767 Ashmore, Harry S., ed. _The William O. Douglas Inquiry
     into the State of Individual Freedom_. Boulder, Col.:
Westview Press, 1979. 250p. A series of articles built around
the theme of liberty and knowledge.
768 Blum, Richard H. _Deceivers and Deceived_. Stanford
     University Institute of Public Policy Analysis Publications.
Springfield, Ill.: CC Thomas, 1971. 328p. A look at government misinformation and its effects upon the public.

769 Cox, Arthur M. The Myth of National Security: The Peril
     of Secret Government. Boston, Mass.: Beacon Press,
1975. 231 p. Suggests that the inability of the public to
receive data on what is happening inside government circles has
in some cases led to tyranny and misuse of Federal power.
770 Dorsen, Norman and Stephen Gillers, eds. None of Your
     Business: Government Secrecy in America. New York:
Viking Press, 1974. 362p.
771 Galnoor, Itzhak, ed. Government Secrecy in Democracies.
     New York: Harper & Row, 1977. 313p. A series of
articles contrasting government control of information in such
democracies as Great Britain, West Germany, Israel, and the
United States.
772 Goulding, Phil G. Confirm or Deny: Informing the People
     on National Security. New York: Harper & Row, 1970.
361p. Suggests that the government is ill-prepared to admit
certain things until after reporters have stumbled upon them
and even then often give the reply "neither confirmed or denied."
773 Halperin, Morton and Daniel Hoffman. Top Secret: National
     Security and the Right to Know. New York: Simon and
Schuster, 1977. 158p. The public's "right to know" and
reporter's ability to ferret out information are in conflict with
the Federal government's desire to classify assorted information,
much of it not related to important national security requirements.
774 Hiebert, Ray E. and Carlton E. Spitzer. The Voice of
     Government. New York: John Wiley, 1968. 354p. Re-
views the process of government informing the American public.
775 Johnson, M. B. The Government Secrecy Controversy: A
     Dispute Involving the Government and the Press in the
Eisenhower, Kennedy, and Johnson Administrations. New York:
Vantage, 1967. 136p. A brief review of the growth of the
controversy from 1952 to 1966 with emphasis on defense-foreign
policy activities.
776 McGaffin, William and Erwin Knoll. Anything But the Truth:
     The Credibility Gap--How the News is Managed in Washing-
ton. New York: G. P. Putnam, 1969. 250p. The manner in
which government information was made available to the public,
especially on such issues as Vietnam during Lyndon Johnson's
administration, led to operational terms "credibility gap" and
"managed news" as this title outlines with a variety of examples.
777 The Public's Right to Know. Washington, D.C.: Editorial
     Research Reports, Congressional Quarterly, Inc., 1980.
196p. An extremely useful little handbook; topics covered include: the Supreme Court and the Press, Atomic Secrecy, and
the Freedom of Information Act.
778 Rourke, Francis E. Secrecy and Publicity: Dilemma of
     Democracy. Baltimore, Md.: Johns Hopkins University
Press, 1961. 336p. Examines the inherent philosophical conflict
between secrecy and openness in the American democracy.
779 Shils, Edward A. The Torment of Secrecy: The Back-
     ground and Consequences of American Security Policies.

Carbondale, Ill.:   Southern Illinois University Press, 1974.
238p.   Traces the government's history of misinformation and
censorship and suggests that heavy-handed application led to
many of the problems of the Watergate era.
780 Steinberg, Charles S. The Information Establishment: Our
     Government and the Media. New York: Hastings House,
1980,   366p. Reviews the growth of big media and big government's relationship to it, often in terms of the cloak-and-dagger
games played between the two.
781 United States. Commission on Freedom of the Press.
     Government and Mass Communications: A Report. Hamden,
     Conn.: Archon Books, 1965. 823p.
782 Wise, David. The Policies of Lying: Government Deception,
     Secrecy, and Power. New York: Random House, 1973.
415p.   A fascinating and pointed anti-government report on the
managed news policies of the Federal government by an author
well known for his examinations of intelligence activities.

ARTICLES AND GOVERNMENT DOCUMENTS

783 Austin, D. V. "Government Censorship in Radio and
     Television Broadcasting." Public Utilities, LXVI (August
     19, 1965), 27-42.
784 Baldwin, Hanson, W. "Managed News: Our Peacetime
     Censorship." Atlantic, CCXI (April 1963), 53-59.
785 Berg, Don. "Communicating with People: The Relation-
     ship Between Government and the Press." Quarterly
     Journal of Speech, LVII (October 1971), 340-357.
786 Bernstein, Barton J. "The Road to Watergate and Beyond:
     The Growth and Abuse of Executive Authority Since 1940."
     Law and Contemporary Problems, XL (Spring 1976), 58-86.
787 Blankenship, William B. "The Adversaries and the News
     Ethic: Tensions Between Press and Government are His-
toric and Continuing." Public Relations Journal, XIV (Fall
1970), 30-37.
788 Borosage, Robert. "Secrecy vs. the Constitution." Society,
     XII (March-April 1975), 71-75.
789 Brown, David H. "Information Officers and Reporters:
     Friends or Foes?" Public Relations Review, II (Summer
     1976), 29-38.
790 Cater, Douglass. "Secrets, Scoops, and Leaks." In:
     Alan A. Altshuler, ed. The Politics of the Federal Bureau-
     cracy. New York; Dodd, Mead, 1973. pp. 395-408.
791 Colby, William E. "Intelligence Secrecy and Security in a
     Free Society." International Security Review, I (Fall
     1976), 3-14.
792 Cotler, Richard D. "Notes Toward a Definition of National
     Security." Washington Monthly, VII (December 1975),
     4-16.
793 Cronkite, Walter. "Cronkite Warns of Growing Trend of
     [Government] Censorship: Speech to the National Associ-
ation of Broadcasters, April 7, 1982." CII (April 12, 1982),
31-32.

794 Cutlip, Scott M. "Public Relations in Government." Public Relations Review, II (Summer 1976), 5-28.
795 Edgar, Harold, and Benno C. Schmidt, Jr. "The Espionage Statutes and Publication of Defense Information." Columbia Law Review, LXIII (May 1973), 929-1087.
796 Futterman, Stanley N. "Controlling Secrecy in Foreign Affairs." In: Francis C. Wilcox and Richard A. Frank, eds. The Constitution and the Conduct of Foreign Policy: An Inquiry by a Panel of the American Society of International Law. New York: Praeger, 1976. pp. 6-58.
797 Galnoor, Itzhak. "Government Secrecy: Exchanges, Inter- mediaries, and Middlemen." Public Administration Review, XXXV (January-February 1975), 32-42.
798 "The Hottest TV News Controversies." TV Guide, XXVII (January 13, 1979), 16-18.
799 "Lid on Leaks." Time, CXIX (January 25, 1982), 25.
800 Lyford, Joseph. "The Pacification of the Press." In: Michael C. Emery and Ted C. Smythe, eds. Readings in Mass Communications: Concepts and Issues in the Mass Media. 2nd ed. Dubuque, IA.: William G. Brown, 1974. pp. 41-423.
801 McCartney, James. "What Should Be Secret?" Columbia Journalism Review. X (September-October 1971), 40-44.
802 MacNeil, Robert. "News on TV and How It is Unmade." Harper's, CCXXXVII (October 1968), 72-80.
803 Maxa, Rudy. "Dealing in Sweet Secrets: News Leaks as a Way of Doing Business." Quill, LXI (September 1974), 18-21.
804 "Media Manipulation by the President?" Broadcasting, LXXXVII (October 21, 1974), 42-43.
805 Merrill, John C. "The 'People's Right to Know' Myth." New York State Bar Journal, XLV (November 1973), 461- 466.
806 Mollenhoff, Clark R. "Managing the News." Nieman Reports, XV (December 1962), 3-6.
807 _____. "The Security Dilemma." Nieman Reports, XV (April 1962), 2, 35-37.
808 Nathan, James. "Did Kissinger Leak the Big One?" Wash- ington Monthly, VI (June 1974), 25-27.
809 Nesson, Charles R. "Aspects of the Executive's Power Over National Security Matters: Secrecy Classifications and Foreign Intelligence Wiretaps." Indiana Law Journal, XLIX (Spring 1974), 399-421.
810 Nesson, Ron. "National Security: Should TV News Always Tell All?" TV Guide XXIX (June 27, 1981), 4-15.
811 Powers, Ron. "News Leaks: Should There Be Any Limits?" TV Guide, XXVII (November 17, 1979), 4-9.
812 Relyea, H. C. "Freedom of Information, Privacy, and Official Secrecy: The Evolution of Federal Government Information Policy Concepts." Social Indicators Research. VII (January 1980), 154-156.
813 Robertson, K. G. "The American Government and Secrecy" [and] "Secrecy, the Law and Civil Service in America." In: his Public Secrets: A Study in the Development of Govern- ment Secrecy. New York: St. Martin's Press, 1982. Chpts. 5 and 6.

814 Rol, David. "U.S. Agencies Violate Information Act: Re-
     printed from the Los Angeles Times, August 27, 1969." In:
Theodore L. Becker and Vernon C. Murray, eds. Government
Lawlessness in America. New York: Oxford University Press,
1971. pp. 244-245.
815 Sarnoff, Robert W. "Television Journalism, the Shackled
     Giant: An Address, December 7, 1964." Vital Speeches,
     XXXI (January 1, 1965), 174-177.
816 Smith, Robert D. "The 1966 Freedom of Information Act:
     The Executive, the Congress, and the Press." Unpublished
     MA thesis, University of Washington, 1977.
817 Stanton, Frank. "The Responsibility of the Press." In:
     Gerald Cross, ed. The Responsibility of the Press. New
     York: Fleet Publications, 1966. pp. 287-308.
818 United States. Congress. House. Committee on Govern-
     ment Operations. Subcommittee on Foreign Operations and
Government Information. Security Classification Reform: Hearings. 93rd Cong., 2nd sess. Washington, D.C.: U.S. Government Printing Office, 1974. 756p.
819   .   .   .   . Government
     Information and Individual Rights Subcommittee. Freedom
of Information Act Oversight: Hearings.   97th   Cong.,   1st
sess. Washington, D.C.:   U.S. Government Printing Office,
1980. 1,022p.
820   .   . Senate. Committee on Armed Ser-
     vices. Unauthorized Disclosures and Transmittal of Classi-
fied Documents: Report. 93rd Cong., 2nd sess. Washington,
D.C.: U.S. Government Printing Office, 1974. 11p.
821   .   .   . Select Committee on
     Intelligence. Intelligence Reform Act of 1981: Hearings.
97th Cong., 1st sess. Washington, D.C.: U.S. Government
Printing Office, 1981. 90p. Much on the Freedom of Information Act and media disclosure of intelligence information.
822 Wicker, Tom. "The Greening of the Press: Are the News
     Media too Oriented Toward 'Official Sources'?" Columbia
     Journalism Review, X (May-June 1971), 7-12.

IV-C. FIRST AMENDMENT, FAIRNESS DOCTRINE, MEDIA LAW

BOOKS

823 Agee, Vernon K., ed.   Mass Media in a Free Society.
     Lawrence: University Press of Kansas, 1969. 96p. Six
spokesmen discuss the problems and challenges facing the print
and electronic media, including those relative to the subject of
this subsection.
824 Ashmore, Harry S.   Fear in the Air: Broadcasting and
     the First Amendment--The Anatomy of a Constitutional
Crisis. New York: W. W. Norton, 1973. 180p. An examination of the changes in First Amendment theory and issues
arising out of the Nixon Administration's challenge as well as
the populist demand for right of access to communication channels, spelling out in both the inadequacies of formal regulation
by the Federal Communications Commission.

825 Bittner, John R. Broadcast Law and Regulation. Engle-
     wood Cliffs, N.J.: Prentice-Hall, 1982. 441p. The latest
survey which includes chapters on the fairness doctrine, priv-
acy-libel-access issues, and self-regulation and ethics difficulties.
826 Botein, Michael, and David M. Rice, eds. Network Tele-
     vision and the Public Interest: A Preliminary Inquiry. Bos-
ton, Mass.: D. C. Heath, 1980. Presents 22 papers from a
1978 New York Law School conference, including several on regulation and access.
827 Cullen, Maurice R., Jr. Mass Media and the First Amend-
     ment: An Introduction to the Issues, Problems, and Prac-
tices. Dubuque, Ia.: William C. Brown, 1981. 452p. An excellent new summary designed for use as a college-level text; details are presented on a variety of First Amendment topics, including most of those covered by the citations here.
828 Emery, Walter B. Broadcasting and Government: Respon-
     sibilities and Regulations. East Lansing, Mich.: Michigan
State University Press, 1961. 492p. Divided into sections
dealing with such diverse ideas as the history of broadcasting,
creation of the FCC, and regulation, this title has as its theme
the government's control of broadcasting.
829 Francois, William E. Mass Media Law and Regulation.
     Columbus, Ohio: Grid, 1975. 470p. A variety of authori-
tatively documented pieces are contained on those major print-
electronic media regions confronting the law, e.g., the Fairness
Doctrine.
830 Franklin, Marc A. The First Amendment and the Fourth
     Estate. 2nd ed. Mineola, N.Y.: Foundation Press, 1981.
715p. First published in 1977, this is a legal textbook designed
for the law students and faculty; many cases are noted and
considered in light of the legal literature on them.
831 Friendly, Fred W. The Good Guys, the Bad Guys, and
     the First Amendment: Free Speech vs. Fairness in Broad-
casting. New York: Random House, 1976. 268 p. An intriguing and fascinating account by the former CBS News official,
now of Columbia University, which weaves its way between the
political and legal aspects of the issues, stopping to consider
interesting personalities along the way.
832 Georgetown Law Journal, Editors of. Media and the First
     Amendment in a Free Society. Amherst, Mass.: Univer-
sity of Massachusetts Press, 1973. 229p. An anthology of
writings from the Georgetown Law Journal, some of which are
cited with the articles noted below.
833 Gillmer, Donald H., and Jerome A. Barron. Mass Communi-
     cation Law: Cases and Comment. 2nd ed. St. Paul, Mn.:
West Publishing Company, 1974. A collection of cases, materials,
and notes for legal students which is overshadowed by the next
citation.
834 Ginsburg, Douglas H. Regulation of Broadcasting: Law
     and Policy Towards Radio, Television, and Cable Communi-
cations. American Casebook Series. St. Paul, Mn.: West
Publishing Company, 1979. 741p. A fine collection of cases
which includes some dealing with that new form of television
transmission--cable; extensive notes and citation to the legal
literature.

835 Gora, Joel M. The Rights of Reporters: The Basic ACLU
     Guide to a Reporter's Rights. New York: Avon, 1974,
254p. As they were seen at the time of this paperback's publication; touches on, but does not resolve practically, such
problems as sources and shields which became big issues in the
late 1970's.

836 Hohenberg, John. Free Press/Free People: The Best
     Cause. New York: Columbia University Press, 1971.
514p. Traces the regulation and attacks on the print-broadcast
media and suggests that, for democracy to survive, the idea of
a free press had best be maintained.

837 Jones, William K. Cases and Materials on Electronic Mass
     Media: Radio, Television, and Cable. Mineola, N.Y.:
Foundation Press, 1976. 474p. Zeroes in on the regulation of
the electronic media by the FCC, the legislation which allows
that watchdog agency to do its job, and the review of cases by
the judiciary in which the FCC and a petitioner/plaintiff/ defen-
dant are in conflict.

838 Kohlmeier, Louis M., Jr. The Regulations: Watchdog
     Agencies and the Public interest. New York: Harper &
Row, 1969. 339p. Looks at a variety of Congressionally-cre-
ated agencies, including the FCC, and their relationship to the
law, Federal programs, and the industries they were created to
"watch."

839 Kranow, Erwin G., and Lawrence D. Longley. The Politics
     of Broadcast Regulation. 2nd ed. New York: St. Martin's
Press, 1978. 213p. By examining actual cases, the authors
attempt to show how the process works, how decisions are made,
and how politics often influence outcomes. Useful footnotes and
bibliography.

840 Krislov, Samuel and Lloyd Musolf. The Politics of Regula-
     tion: A Reader. Boston, Mass.: Houghton-Mifflin, 1964.
261p. An outdated discussion on an intellectual-professional
scale, vis-a-vis the rubrics of legal textbooks.

841 Labunski, Richard E. The First Amendment Under Siege:
     The Politics of Broadcast Regulations. Contributions in
Political Science, no. 62. Westport, Conn.: Greenwood Press,
1981. 184p. In this review, the author contends throughout
that broadcasters have not fought strongly enough for their
First Amendment rights, especially that of parity with the print
media.

842 LeDuc, Don R., ed. Issues in Broadcast Regulation.
     Broadcast Education Association Monographs, no. 1.
Washington, D.C.: Broadcast Education Association, National
Association of Broadcasters, 1974. 151p. An anthology contain-
ing over two dozen brief essays which outline arguments and
illustrate issues on a number of topics, including access, the
Fairness Doctrine, and FCC involvement with network news.

843 Minow, Newton N. Equal Time: The Private Broadcaster
     and the Public Interest. New York: Atheneum, 1964.
316p. Written to explain the motives and actions of President
Kennedy's FCC chairman; Minow once called television "a great
wasteland."

844 Nelson, Harold L. and Dwight L. Teeter. Law of Mass
     Communications: Freedom and Control of the Print and

Broadcast Media. 3rd ed. Mineola, N.Y.: Foundation Press,
1978. 722p. In the 1973 first edition published by the same
firm, the authors concentrated on such topics as libel law,
privacy, and access; in this second edition, the emphasis is on
the public interest in communications law.
845 Noll, Roger G., Meron J. Peck, and John McGowan. Eco-
     nomic Aspects of Television Regulation. Washington, D.C.:
Brookings Institution, 1973. 342p. Explores the often-complex
relationships between technology, politics, and economics in
regulation; relatively little on such ideas as access or the Fairness Doctrine.
846 Overback, Wayne and Rick D. Pullen. Major Principles of
     Media Law. New York: Holt, Rinehart, and Winston,
1982. 353p. An overview of the issues confronting the print
and electronic media on the legal front, including regulation,
access, and First Amendment problems.
847 Owen, Bruce M. Economics and Freedom of Expression:
     Media Structure and the First Amendment. Cambridge,
Mass.: Ballinger, 1975. 202p. Contends that Federal policy
towards the communications industry is based on erroneous
technical and economic assumptions which are ostensively based
on the First Amendment.
848 Pember, Don R. Mass Media Law. Dubuque, Ia.: William
     C. Brown, 1977. 484p. Another college-level text de-
signed to review, via case studies, the complex legal issues
facing print-broadcast media.
849 _____. Privacy and the Press: The Law, the Mass Media,
     and the First Amendment. Seattle, Wash.: University of
Washington Press, 1972. 298p. Follows the history of the privacy issue in America as it relates to the press and broadcast
media.
850 Pennybacker, John H. and Waldo W. Branden, eds. Broad-
     casting and the Public Interest. New York: Random House,
1969. 176p. The text is divided into four sections: 1) the
makeup of the FCC; 2) programming on commercial television;
3) the Fairness Doctrine and Section 315; and 4) a review of
the portents of the communications revolution.
851 Rivers, William I., and Michael J. Nyhan. Aspen Notebook
     on Government and the Media. New York: Praeger, 1973.
208p. A series of essays and dialogue from three seminars held
by the Aspen Program on Communications and Society; among
the provocative chapter titles: "Adversaries or Cronies?,"
"Meanings of the First Amendment," and "Citizens Access to the
Media."
852 Ruckelshaus, William, and Elie Abel, eds. Freedom of the
     Press. Washington, D.C.: American Enterprise Institute
for Public Policy Research, 1976. 101p. Part I is "First Amendment Protections" while Part II is "Regulation of the Media."
853 Schmidt, Benno C., Jr. Freedom of the Press vs. Public
     Access. New York: Praeger, 1976. 296p. A general
review of broadcast regulation and print/media problems relating
to access obligations and their constitutional ramifications.
854 Shapiro, Andrew O. Media Access: Your Right to Ex-
     press Your Views on Radio and Television. Boston, Mass.:
Little, Brown, 1976. 297p. The ultimate populist primer on

the subject of how-to-do it, spiked with valuable background data on the status of broadcast regulation.

855 Simmons, Steven J. The Fairness Doctrine and the Media. Berkeley, Calif.: University of California Press, 1978. Examines the development of the doctrine and provides broadcasters with practical compliance information; be sure to see the author's articles cited below.

856 Simons, Howard, and Joseph A. Califano, Jr., eds. The Media and the Law. New York: Praeger, 1976. 225p. In a March 1975 weekend discussion sponsored by the Washington Post and the Ford Foundation and moderated by three Harvard professors, representatives of the legal community and the media examine a trio of hypothetical situations involving media release of government information; joint editor Califano was HEW Secretary under President Jimmy Carter.

857 Van Gerpen, Maurice. Privileged Communication and the Press: The Citizen's Right to Know versus the Law's Right to Confidential News Source Evidence. Westport, Conn.: Greenwood Press, 1979. 239p. An examination of the law's right to obtain such items as reporter's notes and television outtakes; most readers may remember hearing of such cases in connection with the CBS program 60 Minutes.

ARTICLES AND GOVERNMENT DOCUMENTS

858 Access to the Air: A Conference on the Public Responsibility of Broadcast Licensees and the Ethical and Legal Consideration of Equal Time, Editorializing, Personal Attacks, Balanced Programming, and the Fairness Doctrine.   New   York: Graduate School of Journalism, Columbia University, 1969. 46p.

859 "All's Love and War on Fairness." Broadcasting, LXXXVIII (May 12, 1975), 30-31.

860 American Bar Association. Communications Law Committee. "Electronic Journalism and First Amendment Problems." Federal Communications Bar Journal,   XXIX   (Spring   1976), 1-62.

861 Bagdikian, Ben H. "The [First Amendment] Child in Jeopardy." In: Francis H. and Ludmila A. Voelker, eds. News Media: Forces in Our Society.   New   York: Harcourt, Brace, 1978. pp. 263-268.

862 Baker, Charles R. How to Combat Air Pollution: A Manual on the FCC's Fairness Doctrine. Washington, D.C.: Institute for American Democracy, 1969. Unpaged.

863 Barnett, S. R. "Televising the President: Equal Time and the Nixon Style." Nation, CCXIV (June 26, 1972), 807+.

864 Barron, Jerome A. "An Emerging First Amendment Right of Access to the Media." George Washington Law Review, XXXVII (March 1969), 487-509.

865 _____ . "The FCC's Fairness Doctrine: An Examination." George Washington Law Review, XXX (October 1961), 1-62.

866 _____ . "In Defense of Fairness: A First Amendment Rationale for Broadcasting's Fairness Doctrine." University of Colorado Law Review, XXXVII (Fall 1964), 31+.

867 Barrow, Roscoe. "The Equal Opportunities and Fairness Doctrines in Broadcasting." Cincinnati Law Review, XXXVII (1968), 447-493.
868 _____. "The Fairness Doctrine: A Double Standard for Electronics and Print Media." Hastings Law Journal, XXVI (1975), 659-677.
869 Berns, Walter. "The Constitution and a Responsible Press." In: H. M. Clor, ed. The Mass Media and Modern Democracy. Chicago, Ill.: Rand McNally, 1974. pp. 113-136.
870 "[Benjamin, L.] Hooks Wants FCC off the Fence on Section 315," Broadcasting, XIII (May 16, 1977), 36-38.
871 Blaine, Harry B. "Equality, Fairness, and 315: The Frustrations of Democratic Politics." Maryland Law Review, XXIV (Spring 1964), 166+.
872 Branscomb, Anna W. "Should Political Broadcasting Be Fair or Equal?: A Reappraisal of Section 315 of the Federal Communications Act." George Washington Law Review, XXX (October 1961), 63+.
873 "The Broadcast Media and the First Amendment: A Redefinition." American University Law Review, XXII (Fall 1972), 180+.
874 Burch, Dean. "Fairness Doctrine No Hunting Ground for FCC--Burch." Broadcasting, LXXXV (July 2, 1973), 36-38.
875 Cahill, Robert V. "'Fairness' and the FCC." Federal Communications Bar Journal, XXI (1967), 17+.
876 Cannon, Bradley G. "The FCC's Fairness Doctrine: Its Substance, Enforcement, and Impact." Unpublished PhD Dissertation, University of Wisconsin, 1967.
877 Cohn, D. S. "Access to Television to Rebut the President of the United States: An Analysis and Proposal." Temple Law Quarterly, XLV (Winter 1971), 141+.
878 "Concepts of the Broadcast Media Under the First Amendment: A Reevaluation and a Proposal." New York University Law Review, XLVII (April 1972), 83+.
879 "Court Spikes Blunderbuss Fairness Case Against CBS." Broadcasting, XLVII (July 9, 1979), 47-50.
880 Crapton, Charles S., Jr. "Appearances on News Programs Excluded from Equal Time Act." Virginia Law Review, XLV (April 1960), 564+.
881 Cronkite, Walter. "Privilege--Broadcast News and the First Amendment: An Address, May 2, 1973." Vital Speeches, XXXIX (June 15, 1973), 521-524.
882 Crowley, Juanita A., and David F. B. Smith. "Constitutional Ramifications of a Repeal of the Fairness Doctrine." Georgetown Law Journal, LXIV (July 1976), 1293-1321.
883 Dean, John W. "Political Broadcasting: The Communications Act of 1934 Revised." Federal Communications Bar Journal, XX (1966), 16+.
884 Derby, E. Stephen. "Section 315: Analysis and Proposal." Harvard Journal on Legislation, III (February 1966), 25+.
885 Diamond, Edwin. "The First Amendment Dilemma." TV Guide, XXV (October 29-November 5, 1977), 4-8, 41-46.

886   Douglas, Cathleen H. "The First Amendment and the Electronic Press." University of West Los Angeles Law Review, X (Summer 1979), 123-140.

887   Dunham, Corydon B. "Fairness Doctrine Repeal Held Vital to Free Speech Amidst Communications Explosion." Television/Radio Age, XIX (April 19, 1982), 36-37.

888   Epstein, Edward J. "Television News Regulations." New Yorker, XLIX (March 3, 1973), 64-68.

889   Ernest, G. Lane. "The 'Equal Time' Provisions: Has Broadcasting Come of Age?" University of Colorado Law Review, XXXVI (Winter 1964), 257+.

890   "Evaluation of Basis for and Effect of Broadcasting's Fairness Doctrine." Rutgers-Camden Law Journal, V (Fall 1973), 167+.

891   "The FCC and the Fairness Doctrine." Cleveland State Law Review, XIV (September 1970), 579+.

892   "The FCC Fairness Doctrine and Informed Social Choice." Harvard Journal of Legislation, VIII (January 1971), 333+.

893   "The FCC Moves Further Into Judgments of Broadcast News." Broadcasting, LXXXV (December 3, 1973), 42-44.

894   "The FCC Proposes Easing of 315." Broadcasting, XCII (May 9, 1977), 28-30.

895   "The FCC says Public Stations Must Give Reasonable Amount of Access to Candidates." Broadcasting, XCI (November 1, 1976), 53-54.

896   "The FCC Sees Flaws in Proxmire's Reform Ideas." Broadcasting, LXXXIV (June 11, 1973), 23-24.

897   "FCC 315 Stance Holds Up Against Protests from Minor Candidates." Broadcasting, XCI (October 11, 1976), 41-42.

898   "FCC Told to Take Another Look at Proposed Fairness Plans." Broadcasting, XCIII (November 21, 1977), 29-30.

899   "The FCC's Fairness Doctrine and the First Amendment." Journal of Public Law, XIV (1970), 129+.

900   "The FCC's Fairness Doctrine is Constitutional." Villanova Law Review, XIII (Winter 1968), 343+.

901   "The FCC's Fairness Regulation: A First Step Towards Creation of Access to the Mass Media." Cornell Law Review. LIV (January 1969), 294+.

902   "The Fairness Doctrine and Presidential Appearances." New York Law Forum, XIX (Fall 1973), 398+.

903   "The First Amendment." Quill, LXIV (September 1976), 16-45.

904   "The First Amendment and Regulation of Television News." Columbia Law Review, LXXII (April 1977), 746-771.

905   "The First Amendment and the Fifth Estate." Broadcasting, XC (January 5, 1976), 45-101.

906   "The First [Amendment] Comes First at Dallas [60th Convention of the National Association of Broadcasters]." Broadcasting, CII (April 12 1982), 29.

907   Foley, Joseph M. "Broadcast Regulation Research: A Primer for Non-Lawyers." Journal of Broadcasting, XVII (Spring 1973), 131-157.

908   Frank, Reuven. "The First Amendment: An Address, June 22, 1972." Vital Speeches, XXXVIII (August 1, 1972), 629-632.

909 _____ . "The Freedom of the Broadcast Press: An
Address, February 17, 1970." Vital Speeches, XXXVI
(March 15, 1970), 332-336.
910 "Free Speech and the Mass Media." Virginia Law Review,
LVII (May 1971), 636+.
911 Friedenthal, Jack H., and Richard J. Medalie. "Impact of
Federal Regulation of Political Broadcasting: Section 315 of
the Communications Act." Harvard Law Review, LXXII (January
1959), 445+.
912 Friendly, Fred W. "Television and the First Amendment."
Saturday Review of Literature, LV (January 8, 1972),
46-47+.
913 _____ . "What's Fair on the Air." New York Times
Magazine, (March 30, 1975), 11-12, 37-48. Reprinted in
the United States, Congress, Senate, Committee on Commerce,
Subcommittee on Communications, Fairness Doctrine: Hearings
(94th Cong., 1st sess.: Washington, D.C.: U.S. Government
Printing Office, 1975), pp. 177-186.
914 Geller, Henry. The Fairness Doctrine in Broadcasting:
Problems and Suggested Courses of Action. RAND Report
R-1412-FF. Santa Monica, Calif.: RAND Corporation, 1977.
56p.
915 Goldberg, Henry, and Michael Couzens. "Peculiar Characteristics: An Analysis of the First Amendment Implications
of Broadcast Regulation." Federal Communications Bar Journal,
XXXI (Winter 1978), 1-50.
916 Goodman, Julian. "It's Everybody's Freedom." Television
Quarterly, XI (Summer 1974), 55-58.
917 Graham, Fred P., and Jack C. Landau. "The Federal
Shield Law We Need." In: Michael C. Emery and Ted C.
Smythe, eds. Readings in Mass Communications: Concepts and
Issues in the Mass Media. 2nd ed. Dubuque, Ia.: William C.
Brown, 1974. pp. 89-107.
918 Green, Frances M., and Warren L. Lewis. "A Fair Break
for Controversial Speakers: Limitations of the Fairness
Doctrine and the Need for Individual Access." George Washington Law Review, XXXIX (March 1971), 532-569.
919 Harding, Ronald. "'Freedom of Speech--One Step Back-
ward': Columbia Broadcasting System, Inc., vs. Democratic National Committee." New England Law Review, IX
(Winter 1974), 321-331.
920 Hentoff, Nat. "The Deepening Chill: Print and Broadcast
Journalists and the First Amendment." Commonweal, XCV
(February 1972), 486-488.
921 Hickey, Neil. "Someone's Bound to Holler for Equal Time."
TV Guide, XXIV (May 22, 1976), 12-15.
922 Hill, Alfred. "Defamation and Privacy Under the First
Amendment." Columbia Law Review, LXXVI (December
1976), 1205-1212.
923 Jaffe, Louis L. "The Editorial Responsibility of the Broadcaster: Reflections on Fairness and Access." Harvard
Law Review, LXXXV (February 1972), 768-792.
924 Jencks, Richard, and Robert L. Shayon. "A Fairness
Doctrine Debate Before the National Association of Educa-

tional Broadcasters, November 20, 1974." Congressional Record, CXX (December 16, 1974), S4007-S40012.

925 King, David. "Equal Time for Political Candidates." New York University International Law Review, XXIII (May 1968), 266+.

926 Knoll, Steven. "Can TV Call a Spade a Spade?" New Republic, (August 31, 1974), 16-18.

927 Krasnow, Erwin, and Bill Pearl. "TV's Other Season: The Fall Lineup of First Amendment Cases." Washington Journalism Review, I (October 1977), 7-8.

928 Kuralt, Charles. "Journalism is Crisis-Ridden--The Country is Not." American Society of Newspaper Editor's Bulletin, no. 592 (January 1976), 13-15.

929 Lashner, Marilyn A. "Broadcasting and the Separate Traditions of First Amendment Theory: Temple University Prize Essay." Congressional Record, CXXIII (July 29, 1977), 25757-25758.

930 Lefever, Ernest W. "Study of CBS-TV Evening News Demonstrates Need for the Fairness Doctrine." In: United States. Congress. Senate. Committee on Commerce, Subcommittee on Communications. Fairness Doctrine: Hearings. 94th Cong., 1st sess., Washington, D.C.: U.S. Government Printing Office, 1975. pp. 361-371.

931 Litwak, Thomas R. "The Doctrine of Prior Restraint." Harvard Civil Rights-Civil Liberties Law Review, XII (Summer 1977), 519-558.

932 Loevinger, Lee. "Free Speech, Fairness, and Fiduciary Duty in Broadcasting." Law and Contemporary Problems, XXXIV (Spring 1969), 278+.

933 Loucks, Philip G. "Section 315 (of the Communication Act of 1934)." Federal Communications Bar Journal, XVIII (1963), 33+.

934 Lower, Elmer W. "Freedom of the Press and Our Right to Know." Nieman Reports, XXVIII (Spring-Summer 1974), 32-37.

935 McCranery, H. C. "Exemption from the Section 315 Equal Time Standard: A Proposal for Presidential Elections." Federal Communications Bar Journal, XXIV (Winter 1970-1971), 177+.

936 Malmgren, Lynn C. "The First Amendment: Freedom of the Press to Gather News." Villanova Law Review, XX (1974), 189+.

937 Marks, Richard D. "Broadcasting and Censorship: First Amendment Theory After 'Red Lion.'" George Washington Law Review, XXXVIII (July 1970), 974-1005.

938 Matthews, Donald G. "Potomac Fever: Deregulating Telecommunications." America, CXLI (July 14, 1979), 6-8.

939 Mayer, Martin. "In All Fairness." TV Guide, XVIII (October 10, 1970), 6-10.

940 _____. "It's Like Walking on Water." TV Guide, XVIII (October 17, 1971), 36-40.

941 _____. "You Can't Impose Fairness." TV Guide, XVIII (October 24, 1970), 36-40.

942 "Media and the First Amendment in a Free Society." Georgetown Law Review, XL (March 1972), 863-1099.

943 Meeske, Milan D., and Roger Handberg, Jr. "News Directors' Attitudes Toward the Fairness Doctrine." Journalism
Quarterly, LIII (Spring 1976), 126-129.
944 "Militant Support for 'Fairness' Fast Fading." Broadcasting,
LXXXV (July 9, 1979), 17-19.
945 Monroe, Bill. "Captive Media: TV and the First Amend-
ment--An Address." Vital Speeches, XXXVII (February
15, 1971), 267-269.
946 "More on 'Fairness.'" Broadcasting, XCV (October 2,
1978), 46-47.
947 Morse, Leon. "Attitudes are Changing on Fairness Doctrine." Television/Radio Age, (October 13, 1975), 39-41+.
948 Mullally, D. P. "The Fairness Doctrine: Benefits and
Costs." Public Opinion Quarterly, XXXIII (Winter 1969),
577+.
949 National Association of Broadcasters. Legal Guide to FCC
Broadcast Rules, Regulations, and Policies. Washington,
D.C., 1977. Unpaged.
950 National Citizen's Committee for Broadcasting. A Citizen's
Primer on the Fairness Doctrine. Washington, D.C., 1982.
Unpaged.
951 Packwood, Bob. "The Packwood Amendment: Going for
Broke." Broadcasting, CII (April 12, 1982), 30. First
Amendment.
952 . "Packwood Won't Fight Alone." Broadcasting,
CII (June 28,1982), 52-53.
953 Paley, William S. "Broadcast Journalism--At the Crossroads
of Freedom: An Address, May 31, 1974." Vital Speeches,
XL (July 15, 1974), 581-584.
954 . "Paley Declares It's Time to End Fairness Threat
to News Media." Broadcasting, LXXXVI (June 3, 1974),
31-32.
955 "Pastore Sticks to His Guns as CBS, NBC Fire on Fairness." Broadcasting, LXXXVIII (May 5, 1974), 14-16.
956 "Proxmire Takes Up the Flag Against the Fairness Doctrine." Broadcasting, LXXXVII (July 15, 1974), 48-49.
957 Reagan, Ronald. "Reagan Supports First Amendment Rights
for Broadcasters." Broadcasting, CII (April 12, 1982), 31.
958 "The Regulation of Competing First Amendment Rights: A
New Fairness Doctrine Balance After 'CBS [v. DNC].'"
University of Pennsylvania Law Review, CXXII (1974), 1283-1293.
959 Robbins, J. C. "Deciding First Amendment Cases." Journalism Quarterly, XLIX (Summer-Autumn 1972), 263-270,
569-578.
960 Robinson, Glenn O. "The FCC and the First Amendment:
Observations on Forty Years of Radio and Television
Regulation." Minnesota Law Review, LIII (June 1969), 1179+.
961 Roper, Robert T. "The Gag Order: Asphyxiating the
First Amendment." Western Political Quarterly, XXXIV
(September 1981), 372-388.
962 Salant, Richard S. "Broadcasting Industry and the First
Amendment: Remarks Upon Acceptance of the Boston
University School of Public Communications Special Award, April
1971." Congressional Record, CXVII (May 6, 1971), 13943-13945.

963 Schmidt, Benno C., Jr. "The First Amendment and the Press." In: Ele Abel, ed. What's News: The Media in American Society. San Francisco, Calif.: Institute for Contemporary Studies, 1981. Chpt. 3.

964 Schorr, Daniel. "A Point of Privilege." Washington Journalism Review, I April-May 1970), 26-27.

965 Sevareid, Eric. "First Amendment Confrontation: An Address before the National Association of Broadcasters Convention." Congressional Record, CXXIII (May 26, 1977), 16996-16997.

966 Shayron, Robert L. "Defending the Doctrine: Fairness to be Reviewed by the Supreme Court." Saturday Review of Literature, II (October 26, 1968), 56-58.

967 _____. "Nicholas Johnson vs. Broadcasting." Saturday Review of Literature, III (April 12, 1969), 82+.

968 Simmons, Steven J. "The FCC's Personal Attack and Political Editorial Rules Reconsidered." University of Pennsylvania Law Review, CXXV (May 1977), 990-1022.

969 _____. "The Problems of 'Issue' in the Administration of the Fairness Doctrine." California Law Review, LXV (May 1977), 546-596.

970 Singer, Richard G. "The FCC and Equal Time: Never-Never Land Revisited." Maryland Law Review, XXVII (Summer 1967), 227+.

971 Small, William. "Treated Like Distant Cousins." Quill, LXIV (September 1976), 30-32. This review of broadcasters and the First Amendment was reprinted in Francis H. and Ludmila A. Voelker (eds.), Mass Media: Forces in Our Society (3rd ed.: New York: Harcourt, Brace, 1978), pp. 243-247.

972 Smith, Fred L. "The 'Selling of the Pentagon' and the First Amendment." Journalism History, II (Spring 1975), 2-5+. Based on the next entry.

973 _____. "The Selling of the First Amendment: An Analysis of Congressional Investigations of Four CBS Television Documentary Projects." Unpublished PhD Dissertation. Florida State University.

974 Stanton, Frank. "Broadcasting and the Law--An Address, September 14, 1979." Vital Speeches, XLVI (November 15, 1979), 75-78.

975 Stone, Marvin. "TV and the First Amendment." U.S. News and World Report, XCII (April 12, 1982), 76.

976 "Supreme Court Hears Debate Over Candidate Access to the Air." Broadcasting, C (March 9, 1981), 110+.

977 "The Surprising Support for Easing of Section 315." Broadcasting, XCVIII (February 11, 1980), 37-38.

978 "Television Presidential Addresses and the FCC's Fairness Doctrine." Columbia Journal of Law and Social Problems, VII (Winter 1971), 75+.

979 "Tightening the Reins on 'Fairness.'" Broadcasting, LXXXVII (July 8, 1974), 17-19.

980 "Tug-of-War Over First Amendment for the Fifth Estate." Broadcasting, CII (April 12, 1982), 32-33.

981 "Turnabout is 'Fairness' Play." Broadcasting, XCIII (August 15, 1977), 44-45.

982 Tyler, John. The Government Regulation of Broadcasting.
Freedom of Information Center Report, pp. 368. Columbia,
Mo.: (FOI) School of Journalism, University of Missouri, 1977,
10p.
983 United States. Congress. House. Committee on Interstate
and Foreign Commerce. Broadcasting: Hearings. 4 pts.
88th Cong., 1st and 2nd sess., Washington, D.C.: U.S.
Govenment Printing Office, 1965.
984   .   .   .   . Fairness
Doctrine and Related Issues: Report. 91st Cong., 1st
sess. Washington, D.C.: U.S. Government Printing Office,
1969.
985   .   .   .   . Legislative
History of the Fairness Doctrine: A Staff Study.   90th
Cong., 2nd sess. Washington, D.C.: U.S. Government Printing Office, 1968.
986   .   .   .   . Political
Broadcasting, 1970: Hearings. 91st Cong., 2nd sess.
Washington, D.C.: U.S. Government Printing Office, 1970.
987   .   . Senate. Committee on Commerce.
Fairness Doctrine: Hearings. 90th Cong., 2nd sess.
Washington, D.C.: U.S. Government Printing Office,
1968.
988   .   .   .   . Subcommittee
on Communications. Fairness Doctrine: Hearings. 94th
Cong., 1st sess. Washington, D.C.: U.S. Government Printing
Office, 1975. 451p.
989   .   .   .   .   .
Federal Election Campaign Act of 1971: Hearings.   92nd
Cong., 1st sess. Washington, D.C.: U.S. Government Printing
Office, 1971. 204p.
990   .   .   .   .   :
Report. 92nd Cong., 1st sess. Washington, D.C.: U.S.
Government Printing Office, 1971. 97p.
991   .   .   .   . Federal
Election Campaign Act of 1973: Hearings to Relieve Broad-
casters of the Equal Time Requirement of Section 315.   93rd
Cong., 1st sess. Washington, D.C.: U.S. Government
Printing Office, 1973.
992   .   .   .   .   . Review
of Section 315 of the Communications Act: Report.   82nd
Cong., 1st sess. Washington, D.C.: U.S. Government
Printing Office, 1961. 117p.
993   .   .   . Committee on Commerce,
Science, and Transportation, Subcommittee on Communica-
tions. The First Amendment Clarification Act of 1977: Hearings.
95th Cong., 2nd sess. Washington, D.C.: U.S. Government
Printing Office, 1978. 123p.
994   . Federal Communications Commission. Annual
Report. Washington, D.C.: U.S. Government Printing
Office, 1948--. v. 12--.
995   .   . "Fairness Doctrine and Public Interest
Standards: Report Regarding the Handling of Public
Issues." Federal Register, XXXIX (July 18, 1974), 26372-
26390.

996 _____ . _____ . "The Law of Political Broadcasting and Cablecasting (The Political Broadcast Primer)." Federal Register, XLIII (August 16-24, 1978). 36341+, 37977+.
997 _____ . _____ . Survey of Political Broadcasting: Primary and General Election Campaign of 1968. Washington, D.C.: 1969.
998 _____ . General Accounting Office. Selected FCC Regulatory Policies--Their Purpose and Consequences for Commercial Radio and Television: A Report to Congress. Washington, D.C.: U.S. Government Printing Office, 1979. 231p. See Section VI: "Equal Opportunity/Fairness Doctrine."
999 _____ . Library of Congress. Congressional Research Service. Should the Federal Government Significantly Strengthen the Regulation of Mass Media Communications in the United States: Intercollegiate Debate Topic, 1979-1980. Washington, D.C.: U.S. Government Printing Office, 1979. 425p.
1000 Welles, Chris. "The Pros and Cons of the Fairness Doctrine." TV Guide, XXV (August 30, 1975), 4-9.
1001 Wick, M. D. "The Federal Election Campaign Act of 1971 and Political Broadcast Reform." DePaul Law Review, XXII (Spring 1973), 582+.
1002 Ziedenberg, Leonard. "The Struggle Over Broadcast Access: A Special Report." Broadcasting. LXXXIII (September 20-27, 1971), 32-43, 24-29.

IV-D. GOVERNMENT ATTACKS ON THE MEDIA

BOOKS

1003 Agnew, Spiro T. The Collected Speeches of Spiro Agnew. New York: Audubon Books, 1971. 319p. Includes the Vice President's now famous Des Moines "assault" on the effete Eastern television establishment, as well as several other speeches concerning network news.
1004 _____ . Frankly Speaking: A Collection of Extraordinary Speeches. Washington, D.C.: Public Affairs Press, 1970. 108p. Another source for the Des Moines speech.
1005 _____ . Go Quietly--Or Else! New York: William Morrow, 190. 288p. Mr. Agnew's reminiscences of service as Vice President, including the manner of his resignation and his relations with the media.
1006 Barrett, Marvin, ed. The Alfred I. DuPont-Columbia University Survey of Broadcast Journalism, 1970-1971: A State of Siege. New York: Grosset & Dunlap, 191. 183p. A series of articles built around the concern over the Nixon administration's apparently orchestrated attack on network news.
1007 Coyne, John R. The Impudent Snobs: Agnew vs. the Intellectual Establishment. New Rochelle, N.Y.: Arlington House, 1972. 524p. A conservative defense of the Vice President which includes transcripts of 94 speeches, ad lib and prepared.
1008 Dash, Samuel, et al. The Eavesdroppers. New York: DeCapo Press, 1974. 484p. Examines the government's policy of domestic spying by telephone bugs (wiretap) upon

various groups in society, including reporters and television newsmen such as Daniel Schorr.
1009   Knappman, Edward W., ed. Government and the Press in Conflict 1970-1974. New York: Facts on File, Inc., 1974. 204p. Using the Facts on File chronological daily digest films, the editor here presents a report with no analysis of the continual battle between the press and the Nixon administration.
1010   Krieghbaum, William. Pressures on the Press. New York: T. Y. Crowell, 1972. 248p. An examination of the difficulties facing newsmen, which ranged from simple harassment to FBI surveillance and an organized "blitz" by the Nixon White House.
1011   Lucas, Jim C. Agnew: Profile in Conflict. New York: Scribners, 1970. 160p. A sympathetic profile of the Vice President drawn by a former Marine Corps war correspondent.
1012   Miller, Arthur R. The Assault on Privacy: Computers, Data Banks, and Dossiers. Ann Arbor, Mich.: University of Michigan Press, 1971. 333p. An assessment on the government's campaign to obtain information on its potential opponents and critics, both real and imagined.
1013   Perkus, Cathy, ed. Cointelpro: The FBI's Secret War on Political Freedom. New York: Monad Press, 1976. 190p. Contains a series of articles depicting the illegal operations of J. Edgar Hoover's organization against those elements, including some in the media, believed to be in opposition to the government.
1014   Peterson, R. W., ed. Agnew: The Coining of a Household Word. New York: Facts on File, Inc., 1972. 181p. Follows the career of the Vice President while he occupied that office, including his running conflict with the press.
1015   Porter, William E. Assault on the Media: The Nixon Years. Ann Arbor, Mich.: University of Michigan Press, 1976. 320p. A chronological review of the Nixon administration's efforts against the media, including the harassment of newsmen, legal actions against the networks, and the unleashing of Spiro Agnew in an effort to turn public opinion against television news. A selection of key documents is appended.
1016   Red Channels: The Report of Communist Influence in Radio and Television. New York: Counterattack: The Newsletter of Facts to Combat Communism, 1950. 215p. One of the many witch-hunting publications published around the time of Joseph McCarthy; names 151 distinguished Americans as communists, including journalists Howard K. Smith and William L. Shirer.
1017   Theoharis, Athan. Spying on Americans: Political Surveillance from Hoover to the Houston Plan. Philadelphia, Pa.: Temple University Press, 1978. 360p. A well-known critic of FBI procedures under Hoover here takes aim at that organization's illegal efforts to wage a covert legal-harassing war against perceived White House enemies, a conflict joined in by such other agencies as the CIA.
1018   Wise, David. The American Police State: The Government Against the People. New York. Random House, 1976. 437p. Domestic counterintelligence operations aimed at U.S. citizens in Johnson-Nixon years, especially reporters.

1019 Witcover, Jules. White Knight: The Rise of Spiro Agnew.
      New York: Random House,   1972.   465p.   The noted
journalist's biography of the Vice President includes an interesting study of the Marylander's conflict with the electronic
media.

ARTICLES AND GOVERNMENT DOCUMENTS

1020 "ABC casts a Dragnet to Prove White House was Out to
      Get Networks." Broadcasting, LXXXVI (January 14, 1974)
      13-14.
1021 "The Administration [Nixon's] vs. the Critics." Time,
      XCIV (November 28, 1969), 19-20.
1022 Agnew, Spiro. "Address on TV News--Des Moines: Re-
      printed from the Washington Evening Star, November 14,
1969." Congressional Record, CXV (November 19, 1969), 35005-
35007.
1023 _____. "Agnew: Let Newsmen Face the Nation."
      Broadcasting, LXXIX (October 26, 1970), 23-24.
1024 _____. "Agnew Reviews His Views on News." Broad-
      casting, LXXX (June 7, 1971), 25-26.
1025 _____. "Another Challenge to the Television Industry."
      TV Guide, XVIII (May 16, 1970), 6-10.
1026 _____. "News Media Prejudices Views: Address,
      Montgomery [Alabama] Chamber of Commerce, November
20, 1969." Congressional Record, CXV (November 20, 1969),
35315-35316.
1027 _____. "Television News Coverage: An Address,
      November 13, 1969." Vital Speeches, XXXVI (December 1,
1969), 98-101. Excerpted in U.S. News and World Report,
LXVII (November 24, 1969), 10.
1028 "Agnew and the Networks: Reprinted from the New York
      Dispatch, November 15, 1969." Congressional Record,
      CXV (November 26, 1969), 36037.
1029 "Agnew Demands Equal Time." Time, XCIV (November
      21, 1969), 18-19.
1030 "Agnew Views Television News: Comment and Reply."
      Educational Broadcasting Review, VI (February 1970),
      12-22.
1031 "Agnew's Attacks on Television and Newpapers." New
      Yorker, XLV (December 6, 1969), 51-53.
1032 "Agnew's Complaint: The Trouble with TV." Newsweek,
      LXXIV (November 24, 1969), 88-90.
1033 Balk, Alfred. "Beyond Agnewism." Columbia Journalism
      Review, VIII (Winter 1969-1970), 14-21.
1034 Blackstock, Paul W. "Political Surveillance and the Consti-
      tutional Order." Worldview, XIV (May 1971), 11-14.
1035 Blankenburg, William B. "Nixon vs. the Network: Madi-
      son Ave. and Wall Street." Journal of Broadcasting, XXI
      (Spring 1977), 163-176.
1036 Blum, Richard H., ed. Surveillance and Espionage in a
      Free Society: A Report by the Planning Group to the

Policy Council of the Democratic National Committee. New York:
Praeger, 1972. 319p.
1037 Buckley, William F., Jr. "Calling TV to Account Applaud-
      ed: Reprinted from the Washington Star, November 19,
1969." Congressional Record, CXIX (November 20, 1969),
35091.
1038 Burlingham, Bo. "Paranoia in Power: [Tom C.] Huston's
      Domestic Spy Plan." Harper's, CCXLIX (October 1974),
      26+.
1039 "Can the Administration Cow TV Journalists?" Broad-
      casting, LXXVII (November 24, 1969), 54-57.
1040 Childs, Marquis. "Agnew's Diatribes are Eroding Confi-
      dence in the Press: Reprinted from the Baltimore Sun,
March 29, 1971." Congressional Record, CXVII (May 17, 1971,
15334-15335.
1041 Civil Liberties Review, Editors of. "Rx for Surveillance:
      Special Feature." Civil Liberties Review, I (Summer 1974),
      7-78.
1042 Crewdson, John M. "FBI Checking of Radicals Went on
      Beyond Deadline." In: Grant S. McClellan, ed. The
Right of Privacy. Reference Shelf, . 48, n. 1. New York:
H. W. Wilson Co., 1976. pp. 106-109.
1043 Cronkite, Walter. "'Conspiracy' Against a Free Press."
      Seminar, (December 1971), 21-22.
1044 _____ . "Cronkite Hits Washington Harassment." Broad-
      casting, LXXVI (March 31, 1969), 86-87.
1045 _____ . "Cronkite Indicts the Administration." Broad-
      casting, LXXX (May 24, 1971), 42-43.
1046 _____ . "Is the Free Press in America Under Attack?:
      An Address, January 23, 1979." Vital Speeches, XLV
      (March 15, 1979), 331-334.
1047 Crown, John. "That Inaugural Address--Spiro Agnew
      Had the Courage to Speak Out: Reprinted from the Atlanta
Journal, November 20, 1969." Congressional Record, CXV
(November 24, 1969), 35595.
1048 Dershowitz, A. M. "Unchecked Wiretapping: Before
      Watergate and After." New Republic, CLXXII (May 31,
      1975) 13-17.
1049 Doan, Richard K. "Many Back Agnew's Attack on Net-
      work News: TV Chiefs Deny Bias." TV Guide, XVII
      (November 22, 1969), A1.
1050 _____ . "Networks Strike Back at Agnew's Charges of
      News Bias." TV Guide, XVII (November 29, 1969), A1.
1051 "Does TV News Present an Accurate Picture?: Four
      Different Viewpoints." Senior Scholastic, XCVII (September
      14, 1970), 9-11.
1052 Donner, Frank. "Domestic Political Intelligence." In:
      Howard Frazier, ed. Uncloaking the CIA. New York:
      Free Press, 1978. pp. 165-173.
1053 _____ . "Electronic Surveillance: The National Security
      Game." Civil Liberties Review, II (Summer 1975), 15-47.
1054 _____ . "Memos to the Chairman: The Issue, of Course
      is Power." Nation, CCXVII (February 22, 1975), 200-204.
1055 _____ . "Political Intelligence: Cameras, Informers, and
      Files." Civil Liberties Review, 1 (Summer 1974), 8-25.

1056   Efron, Edith. "Anchormen Not Intimidated by Spiro Agnew." TV Guide, XVIII (February 14, 1970), A1.
1057   Evans, Gordon H. "Is the Press too Powerful?" Columbia Journalism Review. X (January-February 1972), 8-16.
1058   Feldman, Samuel and Joseph Webb. "How TV Networks
Covered Agnew's 'Day of Infamy.'" The Review of Southern
California Journalism, (Winter 1974), 8-9.
1059   Frank, Reuven. "If Benjamin Franklin Had Invented
Television: An Address to the Conference on Electronic
Journalism, June 22, 1972." Congressional Record, CXVIII
(Spetember 12, 1972), 30385-30387.
1060   _____. "Let Television News Alone." In: Michael C.
Emery and Ted C. Smythe, eds. Readings in Mass Com-
munications: Concepts and Issues in the Mass Media.   2nd ed.
Dubuque, Ia.: William C. Brown, 1974. pp. 481-487.
1061   "Freedom to Cheer: Vice President Agnew's Des Moines
Speech." Nation, CCIX (December 1, 1969), 586-587.
1062   Friendly, Fred W. "The Assault on Broadcast Journalism."
In: Britannica Book of the Year, 1972.   Chicago, Ill.:
Encyclopedia Britannica, Inc., 1972. pp. 664-666.
1063   _____. "The Campaign to Politicize Broadcasting."
Columbia Journalism Review, XI (March-April 1973), 9-18.
1064   _____. "Government Plan--Chilling: An Interview."
U.S. News and World Report, LXXIV (February 19, 1973),
51-52.
1065   _____. "Some Sober Second Thoughts on Vice President Agnew." Saturday Review of Literature, LII (December 13, 1969), 61-62+.
1066   _____. "TV at the Turning Point." In: Bernard
Rosenberg and David M. White, eds. Mass Culture Revisited. Princeton, N.J.: Van Nostrand, 1971. pp. 196-206.
1067   _____. "Will Broadcasting Be Politicized?" Current,
CLI (May 1973), 19-31.
1068   Gans, Herbert J. "How Well Does TV Present the News?"
New York Times Magazine, (January 11, 1970), 30-31+.
1069   Goralski, Robert. "Agnew and the Networks Revisited."
Johns Hopkins Magazine, XXII (Spring 1971), 19-22.
1070   "The Government Campaign Against the News Media."
New Yorker, XLVI (February 28, 1970), 29-30.
1071   Graham, Fred P. Press Freedoms Under Pressure: Report and Background Paper. New York: Twentieth Century Fund, Task Force on the Government and the Press, 1972,
193p.
1072   Hickey, Neil. "TV Newsmen Should Not Be Hindered."
TV Guide, XVII (April 4, 1969), 6-9.
1073   _____. "Television in Turmoil." TV Guide, XVII
(February 8-March 1, 1969), 6-11, 34-40, 14-18, 38-41.
1074   Johnson, Nicholas. "Comments on the Vice President's
Speech: An Address at the University of Iowa, November
17, 1969." Congressional Record, CXV (November 25, 1969),
35872-35873.
1075   Katz, Harvey. "Big Brother is Listening: The Wiretap-
pers are Loose in the Land and 1984 May be Closer Than
You Think." Washingtonian, V (June 1970), 44-45, 73-78.

1076 Kelly, Clarence M. "The FBI's Illegal Activities." In:
      Robert A. Diamond, ed. Historic Documents of 1976.
Washington, D.C.: Congressional Quarterly, Inc., 1977. pp.
321-331.
1077 Knoll, Erwin. "Shaping Up CBS: A Case Study in Intimi-
      dation." Progressive, XXXIV (July 1970), 18-22. Examines
the reported relationship between an attack by the Des Moines
Register on CBS's Vietnam coverage and White House advisor
Clark Mollenhoff.
1078 Lowenstein, Ralph L. Why Network TV News is Criticized.
      Freedom of Information Center Report, no. 12. Columbia,
Mo.: (FOI) School of Journalism, University of Missouri, 1971.
30p.
1079 Lowry, Dennis T. "Agnew and the Network TV News:
      A Before/After Content Analysis." Journalism Quarterly,
      XLVIII (Summer 1971), 205-210.
1080 Macy, John W., Jr. "Broadcasting and Government: An
      Essay for the Center for the Study of Democratic Institu-
tions, February 16, 1973." Congressional Record, CXIX (May
29, 1973), 17210-17213.
1081 Mudd, Roger. "Equal Time for the Closed Fraternity:
      Excerpt from an Address." Life, LX (March 13, 1970), 4.
1082 "Network News: Alone in the Target Zone." Broadcast-
      ing, LXXX (April 5, 1971), 21-23.
1083 "Newsmen Answer Agnew on CBS and NET." Broadcasting,
      LXXVII (December 1, 1969), 58-61.
1084 "Nixon Men Hit Again at TV News." Broadcasting, LXXVIII
      (March 2, 1970), 44-45.
1085 "'Operation Chaos': Reprinted from the New York Times,
      June 11, 1975." Congressional Record, CXXI (June 11,
1975), 18284-18285. CIA domestic spying.
1086 Osborne, John. "Agnew's Effect." New Republic, CLXII
      (February 28, 1970), 13-15.
1087 Owen, Stephen T. "Eavesdropping at the Government's
      Discretion: First Amendment Implications of the National
Security Eavesdropping Power." Cornell Law Review, LVI
(November 1970), 161-170.
1088 Pyle, Christopher H. "Military Surveillance of Civilian
      Politics, 1967-1970." Unpublished PhD Dissertation, Colum-
bia University, 1974.
1089 _____. "Spies Without Masters: The Army Still Watches
Civilian Politics." Civil Liberties Review, I (Summer 1974),
38-40. Based on previous entry.
1090 Rosko, Bernard. "The Phony Issue of News Management
      [by the Networks]." Interplay, III (April 1970), 19-23.
1091 Rule, Philip C. "CBS, the White House, and the Myth of
      Objectivity." American, CXXIV (May 22, 1971), 541-542.
1092 Salant, Richard S. "The Challenge to Broadcasters."
      Public Relations Journal, XXVI (October 1970), 58-60.
1093 Schwartz, Hermann. "Six Years of Tapping and Bugging."
      Civil Liberties Review, I (Summer 1974), 26-37.
1094 Seamans, Andrew. "Developing the Internal Security
      Mission." In: Richard O. Wright, ed. Whose FBI? LaSalle,
      Ill.: Open Court Publishers, 1974. pp. 139-172.

1095   Sessions, Charles.   "Agnew's Attack on the Media: Intimidation or a Plea for 'Self-Examination?'" National Journal, I
(December 1969), 183-193.
1096   Spiers, Al.   "Let's Talk Politics--What Did Agnew Say?:
Reprinted from the Peru, [Indiana] Tribune, November 18,
1969."   Congressional Record,   CXV   (November   20,   1969),
35283.
1097   Spievack, Edwin B.   "The Presidential Assault on Communications."   Federal Communications Bar Journal,   XXIII
(1969), 157+.
1098   Stanton, Frank.   "Pressures on the Press."   Nieman
Reports,   XXII (December 1968), 3-6.
1099   _____.   "Stanton Plays News Intimidation."   Broadcasting, LXXVII (December 1, 1969), 56-58.
1100   _____., and Dan Rather.   "Stanton [and] Rather Say
White House Made Open Threats."   Broadcasting, LXXXVI
(May 6, 1974), 32-33.
1101   Stein, Benjamin.   "PBS Under Fire."   TV Guide, XXV
(December 13-27, 1975), 4-7, 24-27, 28-33.
1102   Stein, M. L.   "First Round to Agnew."   Nation, CCXI
(September 7, 1970), 178-181.
1103   "That Liberal Cabel: Questioning the 'Eastern Establishment Media.'"   Time XCV (June 8, 1970), 41.
1104   Theoharis, Athan C. "Bureaucrats Above the Law: Double-
Entry Intelligence Files."   Nation, CCXXV (October 22,
1977), 393-397.
1105   _____.   "From the Cold War to Watergate: National
Security and Civil Liberties."   Intellect.   CIII (October
1974), 20-26.
1106   Ungar, Sanford J.   "Counterintelligence and Internal
Security."   In: his FBI: An Uncensored Look Behind the
Walls.   Boston, Mass.:   Little, Brown, 1976.   pp. 111-146.
1107   United States. Congress. House.   Committee on Internal
Security.   Domestic Intelligence Operations for Internal Security Purposes: Hearings. 93rd Cong., 2nd sess. Washington,
D.C.:   U.S. Government Printing Office, 1974.   590p.
1108   _____.   _____.   _____. Committee on the Judiciary,
Subcommittee on Civil Rights and Constitutional Rights.
FBI Counterintelligence Programs: Report.   93rd Cong., 2nd
sess.   Washington, D.C.:   U.S. Government Printing Office,
1974.   47p.
1109   _____.   _____.   _____.   _____. FBI Oversight:
Hearings.   95th Cong., 1st sess.   Washington, D.C.:
U.S. Government Printing Office, 1978.   391p.
1110   _____.   _____.   _____.   _____. Surveillance:
Hearings on the Matter of Wiretapping, Electronic Eavesdropping, and Other Surveillance.   94th Cong., 1st sess.   2
pts.   Washington, D.C.:   U.S. Government Printing Office,
1975.
1111   _____.   _____.   _____. Select Committee on Intelligence.   U.S. Intelligence Agenices and Activities--Domestic
Intelligence Programs: Hearings.   94th Cong., 1st sess.   2 pts.
Washington, D.C.:   U.S. Government Printing Office, 1975.
175p.

1112 _____ . _____ . Senate. Committee on the Judiciary,
Subcommittee on Administrative Practice and Procedures.
FBI Statutory Charter: Hearings. 95th Cong., 2nd sess. 2
pts. Washington, D.C.: U.S. Government Printing Office,
1978.
1113 _____ . _____ . _____ . _____ . Warrantless
Wiretapping: Hearings. 92nd Cong., 2nd sess. Washington, D.C.: U.S. Government Printing Office, 1973. 221p.
1114 _____ . _____ . _____ . _____ . Warrantless
Wiretapping, 1974: Hearings. 93rd Cong., 2nd sess.
Washington, D.C.: U.S. Government Printing Office, 1974.
519p.
1115 _____ . _____ . _____ . _____ . Subcommittee
on Constitutional Rights. Military Surveillance: Hearings.
93rd Cong., 2nd sess. Washington, D.C.: U.S. Government
Printing Office, 1974. 397p.
1116 _____ . _____ . _____ . _____ . _____ . Military
Surveillance of Civilian Politics: A Report. 93rd Cong.,
1st sess. Washington, D.C.: U.S. Government Printing Office,
1973. 150p.
1117 _____ . _____ . _____ . Select Committee to Study
Government Operations with Respect to Intelligence Activities. The Federal Bureau of Investigation: Hearings. 94th
Cong., 1st sess. Washington, D.C.: U.S. Government Printing Office, 1976. 1,000p.
1118 _____ . _____ . _____ . _____ . The Huston Plan.
94th Cong., 1st sess. Washington, D.C.: U.S. Government Printing Office, 1976. 403p.
1119 _____ . _____ . _____ . _____ . Domestic Intelligence Programs: Hearings. 94th Cong., 1st sess. Washington, D.C.: U.S. Government Printing Office, 1976. 285p.
1120 _____ . _____ . _____ . _____ . Intelligence
Activities and the Rights of Americans: Hearings. 94th
Cong., 2nd sess. Washington, D.C.: U.S. Government Printing Office, 1976. 396p.
1121 "Widening Attacks on Network News." Broadcasting, LXXX
(March 29, 1971), 35-37.
1122 Wilson, Richard. "Move Against Mass Media Bold and
Calculated: Reprinted from the Washington Star, November
19, 1969." Congressional Record, CXV (November 19, 1969.),
35091.
1123 Witcover, Jules. "Washington: The News Explosion."
Columbia Journalism Review, VIII (Spring 1969), 23-27.

V. NETWORK TELEVISION NEWS
AND DOMESTIC AFFAIRS

V-A. BLACK AMERICANS AND CIVIL RIGHTS

As might be expected, a large body of literature has
grown up around the experiences of blacks in the United States
since 1948, especially as they relate to the civil rights movements of the late 1950's and 1960's. Unfortunately, relatively
little of this literature has concerned itself with the relationship
of either blacks or civil rights to the presentation of these
persons, ideas, or events by television network news--which
had, however, provided wide coverage prior to the end of the
Lyndon Johnson presidency.

1124   Colle, Royal D.   "Negro Image in the Mass Media: A
       Case   Study in Social Change." Journalism Quarterly,
       XLV (Spring 1968), 55-60.
1125   Diamond, Edwin.   "School Busing: A Story in Two Acts."
       Columbia Journalism Review, XIV (November-December 1975),
       35-37.
1126   Efron, Edith.   "Why Has TV News Forgotten the Black
       Civil Rights Cause?"   TV Guide,   XXII (November 30,
       1974), A3-A4.
1127   Fisher, Paul and Ralph L. Lowentein, eds.   Race and the
       News Media.   New York: Praeger, 1968.   158p.   The
       proceedings of the Eighth Annual Conference of the Freedom of
       Information Center (School of Journalism, University of Missouri)
       revolve around the theme of "The Racial Crisis and the News
       Media" and consist of the remarks of 21 newsmen.
1128   Frady, Marshall.   "It was TV's First Jab at the Nation's
       Conscience."   Panorama, I (November 1980), 42+.
1129   Good, Paul.   "Is Network News Slighting the Minorities?"
       TV Guide, XXV (March 5, 1977), 4-8.
1130   Monroe, Will.   "TV's Hard Road on Race News."   Broad-
       casting, LXIX (November 22, 1965), 77-78.
1131   "The Press and the N.A.A.C.P."   Nieman Reports, XXVII
       (Fall 1973), 18-21.
1132   Pride, Richard A. and Daniel M. Clarke.   "Race Relations
       in Television News: A Content Analysis of the Networks."
       Journalism Quarterly, L (Summer 1973), 319-328.
1133   Roberts, Churchill.   "The Presentation of Blacks in Tele-
       vision Network Newscasts."   Journalism Quarterly,   LII
       (Spring 1975), 50-55.
1134   Rubin, Bernard, ed.   Small Voices and Great Trumpets:
       Minorities and the Media.   New   York: Praeger,   1980,

308p. A well-received anthology of writings which analyze the uneven news coverage of all minorities, including Black Americans, pinpointing deficiencies in a number of key areas, and providing the results of innovative research. Dwight M. Ellis of the National Association of Broadcasters has labeled this book "essential reading . . . ."

1135   Tan, Alexis and Percy Vaughn. "Mass Media Exposure, Public Affairs Knowledge, and Black Militancy." Journalism Quarterly, LIII (Summer 1976), 271-279.
1136   Wells, Elmer E. "The Mass Media and the Negro Community." Negro History Bulletin, XXXVI (December 1973), 180-189.
1137   Wilkins, Roger. "From Silence to Silence." More, V (July 1975), 27+.

V-B. BUSINESS AND INDUSTRY

The network news relationship to business, industry, labor, and goverment economic policy has, for the most part, been marked by controversy and misunderstanding; reporters, editors, and viewers have often found the economic story extremely difficult to present and absorb, while business leaders, government officials, and labor leaders accused the media of other sensational or dull coverage. Many users can recall the frequent reports of such veterans as Irving R. Levine, while others mostly remember the exposes of 20/20 or 60 Minutes. The material available for research on the business "connection" is almost as limited as that for black Americans and civil rights, although one suspects that many corporate offices now maintain folders thicker than this book which explains how to deal with the potential problems posed by representatives of "the tube."

1138   Adoni, Hanna, and Akiba A. Cohen. "Television Economic News and the Social Construction of Economic Reality." Journal of Communications, XXVIII (Autumn 1978), 61-70.
1139   Bartley, Robert . "The News Business and Business News." In: Elie Abel, ed. What's News. San Francisco, Calif.: Institute for Contemporary Studies, 1981. pp. 187-210.
1140   Bethell, Tom. Television Evening News Covers Inflation, 1978-1979: An Analysis. Washington, D.C.: Media Institute, 1980. 51p.
1141   Buchanan, Patrick. "Journalism and Business: Scorpions in a Bottle." TV Guide, XXV (August 13, 1977), A5-A6.
1142   "Business and Broadcast News." In: Marvin Barrett, ed. Rich News, Poor News: The Alfred I. DuPont-Columbia University Survey of Broadcast Journalism. New York: T. Y. Crowell, 1978. pp. 39-77.
1143   "Business Starts to Play a Starring Role." Business Week, (November 30, 1981), 54-55.
1144   Dominick, Joseph R. "Business Coverage in Network News." Journalism Quartely, LVIII (Summer 1981), 179-185.
1145   Efron, Edith. "Before Businessmen 'Meet the Press.'" TV Guide, XIX (November 20, 1971), 8-11.

1146 "The Failing of Business and Journalism." Time, CXVII (February 9, 1976), 78-79.

1147 "Labor and the Press." American Federationist, (December 1975), 1-8.

1148 Levine, Irving R. "Covering the Economy on TV." TV Guide, XXIV (February 7, 1976), 6-8.

1149 Lichter, S. Robert and Stanley Rothman. "Media and Business Elites.' Public Opinion, IV (October-November 1981), 42-46.

1150 MacDougall, A. Kent. 90 Seconds to Tell It All: Big Business and the News Media. New York: Dow-Jones, Irwin, 1981. 154p.

1151 "Media Coverage of Business and Labor: Who Serves?" Twin Cities Journalism Review, (August 1975), 3-54.

1152 Meese, Edwin 3rd. "Meese Critiques Economic Reporting." Broadcasting, CII (March 22, 1982), 83.

1153 Mosettig, Michael D. "Ninety Seconds Over the Economy." Channels, I (December 1981-January 1982), 30-35.

1154 Phillips, Kevin. "Why Coverage of Business News is Sensationalized." TV Guide, XXIV (September 25, 1976), A5-A6.

1155 Roper, Burns W. The Growing Importance of Television News and the Medium's Emerging Role in Corporate Public Relations. New York: Elmo Roper and Associates, 1966. 6p.

1156 Simons, Howard, and Joseph A. Califano, Jr., eds. The Media and Business. New York: Vintage Books, 1979. 227p. A transcript of a 1977 seminar which saw an exchange between media leaders and business executives.

1157 "'60 Minutes' Still Panned: TV Losing Image as Business Bully." Industry Week, CCXI (November 16, 1981), 103-104+.

1158 White, Ray and Peter Claudy. "Reporting on Reaganomics." Washington Journalism Review, III (July-August 1961), 26-31.

V-C. CONGRESS

Works relating to network news coverage of Congress, which has been extensive at times, are entirely inadequate. Outside of the few citations noted here, much of what is available is buried in the general histories of the various networks, political science texts, and in reviews of special topics such as those noted in connection with the previous section on Business and Industry, and Section V-G, Politics, below.

1159 Bagdikian, Ben H. "Congress and the Media: Partners in Propaganda." Columbia Journalism Review, XIII (January-February 1974), 3-10.

1160 Blanchard, Robert O., comp. Congress and the News Media. New York: Hastings House, 1974. 506p. An anthology containing the most extensive survey of the topic available, much of it devoted to the manner of coverage by representatives of the print and broadcast media and the effect of such coverage on events and elections.

1161   _____. "A Profile of Congressional Correspondents."
Capitol Studies, III (Fall 1975), 53-67.

1162   Dodd, Lawrence C. and Bruce I. Oppenheimer. Congress
Reconsidered. 2nd ed. Washington, D.C. Congressional
Quarterly, Inc., 1981. 440p. A collection of essays in which
the authors discuss key institutional and operational changes in
Congress and the effect of these changes on the legislative
body; contains some mention of the media.

1163   Endess, Kathleen L. "Capitol Hill Newswomen: A Descriptive Study." Journalism Quarterly, LIII (Spring 1976),
135-137.

1164   Garay, Ron. "Television and the 1951 Senate Crime Committee Hearings." Journal of Broadcasting, XXII (Fall
1978), 469-490.

1165   Lewis, Carolyn. "The Battle of Capitol Hill." TV Guide,
XXIV (July 27, 1974), 24-26.

1166   MacCann, Richard D. "Televising Congress." American
Scholar, XLIV (Summer 1975), 466-472.

1167   Robinson, Michael J. "Three Faces of Congressional Media."
In: Thomas E. Mann and Norman J. Ornstein, eds. The
New Congress. Washington, D.C.:   American Enterprise Insti-
tute for Public Policy Research, 1981. Chpt. 3.

1168   _____. and Kevin R. Appel. "Network News Coverage
of Congress." Political Science Quarterly, XCIV (Fall
1979), 407-418.

1169   "Special Report: Congress and the News." Washington
Journalism Review, III (June 1981), 23-35.

1170   Tannenbaum, Percy H. "What Effect When TV Covers a
Congressional   Hearing?"   Journalism Quarterly,   XXXII
(1955), 434-450.

1171   Taylor, Adrian C. "The Flacks on the Hill." Washington
Journalism Review, I (June-July 1979), 36-45.

1172   "TV and Congress: Reprinted from the Washington Star,
January 26, 1976." Congressional Record, CXXII (January
28, 1976), 1378-1379.

V-D.   THE SUPREME COURT

Reporters for the television networks have often found
that covering the Supreme Court can be a most frustrating
experience; maybe, even the most difficult beat in Washington.
Not only is the judicial unlike the legislative or executive bran-
ches in our checks-and-balances system, the people connected
with it, namely nine justices, are not as a rule influenced by
media coverage of their work or opinions.   Nevertheless, the
Supreme Court, with its ability to rule on laws and legal cases,
remains an important source of power, one which must be
covered.   Little has been written about the relationship of the
Supreme Court to the coverage provided it by the media; however, the work of the court has had vast impact upon the
American scene and thus coverage in the press (especially television) has been substantial.

1173   Devol, Kenneth S., comp. Mass Media and the Supreme
    Court: The Legacy of the Warren Years.   2nd ed., rev.
New York: Hastings House, 1976. 200p.   Cases and reprints
from legal journals impacting on the First Amendment, censorship, and privacy are provided in an effort to examine the
media-related rulings of the high court during and since the
term of Chief Justice Earl Warren.
1174   Goldstein, Tom. "The Burger Court and Broadcasting:
    An Uneasy Balance." In: Marvin Barrett and Zachary
Sklar,   eds.   The Eye of the Storm: The Alfred I. DuPont-
Columbia University Survey of Broadcast Journalism.   New York:
Lippincott-Crowell, 1980. pp. 203-214.
1175   Higdon, Philip R.   The Burger Court and the Press.
    Freedom of Information Canter Report, no. 0020.   Columbia,
Mo.: (FOI) School of Journalism, University of Missouri, 1979.
7p.
1176   "News and the Supreme Court." Television-Radio Age,
    XI (August 27, 1979), 36-39+.
1177   "The Supreme Court and the Press." News Media and the
    Law, III (January 1979), 1-120.
1178   Woodward, Bob. Brethren: Inside the Supreme Court.
    New York: Simon & Schuster, 1979. 467p. A study of
the high court by one of the former Washington Post Watergate
reporters reveals that certain of its members are less than kind
in their opinion of television network news.

V-E. CRIME, RIOTS, PROTEST

    Murder, mayhem, and civil disorder has long been a staple
of the news media in the United States and when network
television news joined the ranks of newspapers, magazines, and
radio, questions concerning such coverage began to arise. It
was during the 1960's that the role of network news in civil
disturbance came under scrutiny; many concluded that certain
riots and demonstrations would not have been so violent had
television cameras not been present. Others have continuously
worried about the effects on various segments of the community
of constant coverage of such events as political assassinations,
domestic terrorism, and such non-political acts as the murder of
celebrities such as John Lennon. The citations in this subsection examine the role of network news in the arena of crime,
riots, and protests and seek answers to some of the strategies
and tactics employed in reporting and airing such events.

1179   Alexander, Shana. Anyone's Daughter: The Times and
    Trials of Patty Hearst. New York: Viking Press, 1979.
562p. Perhaps best remembered to 60 Minutes viewers as the
liberal equal of conservative James J. Kilpatrick of the "Point-
Counterpoint" segment, Alexander here details her intensive
investigation of the Hearst-CIA drama which captured the lead
on many a segment of the network evening news shows in
1973-1974.

1180   Arlen, Michael J.   "The Shooting of Martin Luther King,
       Jr."   New Yorker, XLIV (April 13, 1968), 157-159.   As
       covered by network news.
1181   Brechner, Joseph L.   "Were Broadcasters Color Blind?"
       In: Paul L. Fisher and Ralph Lowenstein, eds.   Race and
the News Media.   New York: Anti-Defamation League of B'nai
B'rith, 1967.   pp 99-106.
1182   "Broadcast Media Dominate DC Coverage of Courthouse
       Takeover."   Broadcasting, LXXXVII (July 22, 1974), 36-
       37.   Hanafi Muslims.
1183   Brownfeld, Allan G.   "Television and the Big City Riots."
       American Legion Magazine, LXXXIII (December 1967), 6-8.
1184   "CBS Gets Stung for $10,000 Hoping to Find Hoffa's Body."
       Broadcasting, LXXXIX (December 15, 1975), 51-5.
1185   Diamond, Edwin.   "The Miami Riots: Did TV Get the Real
       Story?"   TV Guide, XXVIII (August 30, 1980), 18-22.
1186   Doan, Richard K.   "How TV Saw the Assassination [of
       Robert Kennedy]."   TV Guide, XVI (June 15, 1968), A1.
1187   Dunne, J. G.   "TV's Riot Squad: Bias in News Cover-
       age."   New Republic, CLIII (September 11, 1965), 27-29.
1188   Fanning, Lawrence S.   "The Media: Observer or Partici-
       pant?"   In: Paul L. Fisher and Ralph Lowenstein, eds.
Race and the News Media.   New York: Anti-Defamation League
of B'nai B'rith, 1967.   pp. 107-108+.
1189   Gold, Victor.   "Of Fallen Trees and Wounded Knees:
       News Coverage at Wounded Knee, South Dakota."   National
       Review, XXV (April 27, 1973), 464-465.
1190   Graber, Doris A.   Crime News and the Public.   New
       York: Praeger, 1980.   239p.   In perhaps the most solid
book-length study of the topic to date, this University of
Illinois professor contrasts the coverage of crime by the media
in three types of cities and reaches these conclusions: 1) the
public's images of criminals and their mode of operation differ
substantially from the images presented by the media; 2) public
attention to crime stories does not correspond to the amount of
media emphasis; 3) the crime rate does not depend on media
attention or public concern; and 4) prospects for altering media
impact by modifying the substance, frequency, and emphasis of
media content are limited.
1191   _____.   "Is Crime News Coverage Extensive?"   Journal
       of Communications.   XXIX (Summer 1979), 81-92.
1192   Hickey, Neil.   "Detroit: Television on Trial."   TV Guide,
       XVI (June 1-8, 1968), 6-10, 16-20.
1193   _____.   "What is Television's Most Critical Failure?:
       Some Think It Could Well Be Its Coverage of the Unrest
on American College Campuses."   TV Guide, XVIII (January 23-
February 20, 1970), 7-10, 6-11, 35-36, 43, 36-38.
1194   Homer, Frederic B.   "Terror in the United States: Three
       Perspectives."   In: Michael Stohl, ed.   The Politics of
Terrorism.   New York: Marcel Dekher, Inc., 1979.   pp. 373-
406.
1195   Lang, G. E.   "Some Pertinent Questions on Collective
       Violence and the News Media."   Journal of Social Issues,
       XXVIII (Spring 1972), 93-110.

1196   Lange, David, Robert K. Baker, and Sandra J. Ball.
       "Coverage of Civil Disorders." In: their Mass Media and
Violence: A Report to the National Commission on the Causes
and Prevention of Violence.   Washington, D.C.:   U.S. Government Printing Office, 1969.   pp 103-120.
1197   Laurent, Lawrence.   "An Ethic Code [on Riot Coverage]
       for TV News?:   Reprinted from the Washington Post,
August 15, 1967."   Congressional Record, CXIII (August 16,
1967), 22871-22872.
1198   _____.   "Radio and Television--Vice President [Hubert
       H. Humphrey] Speaks Out on TV's Role in Riots: Re-
printed from the Washington Post, June 27, 1968."   Congressional Record, CXIV (July 12, 1969), 21088.
1199   Levin, Eric.   "On Wednesday, the Hanafis Struck."   TV
       Guide, XXV (July 9, 1977), 28-32.
1200   Linn, Edward.   "Do the Networks Cover Crime Adequate-
       ly?"   TV Guide, XXV (August 20, 1977), 4-9.
1201   "The Long Watch: TV Coverage of Robert F. Kennedy's
       Assassination."   Newsweek, LXXI (June 17, 1968), 102-
103.
1202   McLellan, Vin and Paul Avery.   The Voices of Guns: The
       Definitive and Dramatic Story of the 22-Month Career of the
Symbionese Liberation Army.   New York: G. P. Putnam, 1976.
544p.   An excellent review of the domestic terrorist group with
emphasis on the Patty Hearst kidnapping and reference to the
role of the media and its coverage of the spree.
1203   Mishra, Vishwa M.   "How Commercial Television Networks
       Cover News of Law Enforcement."   Journalism Quarterly,
       LVI (Autumn 1979), 611-616.
1204   _____.   Law and Disorder: Law Enforcement in Tele-
       vision Network News.   New York: Asia Publishing House,
1979.   127p.   Concentrates on the way in which the networks in
their evening news and magazine programs cover the various
aspects of crime and law enforcement in their presentations and
the effects of those programs on society's perception of who is
winning the "war on crime."
1205   NBC News.   "Guidelines for Riot Coverage." In: U.S.
       Congress, House, Committee on the Judiciary, Subcommit-
tee on Civil and Constitutional Rights.   Federal Capabilities in
Crisis Management and Terrorism: A Staff Report.   95th Cong.,
2nd sess.   Washington, D.C.:   U.S. Government Printing Office,
1978.   pp. 78-80.
1206   Newton, Dwight.   "Accessory to the Riots?:   Reprinted
       from the San Francisco Examiner, August 6, 1967."   Con-
gressional Record, CXIII (August 16, 1967.), 22872.
1207   Nizer, Louis.   "Does TV Tip the Scales of Justice?"   TV
       Guide, XI (June 22, 1963), 5-7.
1208   "Not Since Dallas: Coverage of the Assassination of Dr.
       Martin Luther King, Jr."   Newsweek, LXXI (April 15,
1968), 91-92.
1209   Pierce, Laurens.   "He [a CBS Cameraman] Carried a
       Camera--and a .38."   TV Guide, XXX (May 1, 1982),
22-24.
1210   Polskin, Howard.   "John Lennon's Murder: Did TV Go
       Too Far?"   TV Guide, XXIX (November 21, 1981), 2-9.

1211   "Press Dilemma--Media Split in Debate Over Handling of News About Racial Troubles: Reprinted from the Wall Street Journal, March 1, 1968." Congressional Record, CXIV (March 1, 1968), 4877-4878.

1212   Prugh, Jeff. "The Atlanta Murders: Did TV Show Too Much--or Too Little?" TV Guide, XXIX (October 17, 1981), 2-10.

1213   Rivers, William L. "The Negro and the News: A Case Study [of the Watts Riots]." In: Wilbur Schramm and Donald F. Roberts, eds. The Process and Effects of Mass Communications. 2nd ed. Urbana, Ill.: University of Illinois Press, 1971. pp. 151-168.

1214   Roebuck, Julian B. Political Crime in the United States: Analyzing Crimes by and Against Government. New York: Praeger, 1978. 224p. References to the media are included in this study of such political crimes as those committed under the umbrella term "Watergate."

1215   Senate Staff Observer. "A Report on Television-Radio-Press Coverage of the Racial Situation, August 2, 1967." Congressional Record, XIII (August 11, 1967),22426.

1216   Sevareid, Eric. "Dissent Within a Lawful Society: An Address, December 4, 1970." Vital Speeches, XXXVII (February 1, 1971), 251-253.

1217   Shields, Mitchell J. "The Atlanta Story." Columbia Journalism Review, XX (September-October 1981), 29-35.

1218   Singer, Benjamin D. "Journalism and the Kerner Report: The Report's Critique of Television." Columbia Journalism Review, VI (Fall 1968), 57+.

1219   _____. "Mass Media and Communication Processes in the Detroit Riot of 1967." Public Opinion Quarterly, XXXIV (Summer 1970), 236-245.

1220   Slater, John and Maxwell E. McCombs. "Some Aspects of Broadcast News Coverage and Riot Participation." Journal of Broadcasting, XIII (Fall 1969), 367-371.

1221   Smith, Desmond. "Wounded Knee: The Media Coup d'Etat." Nation, CCXVI (June 25, 1973), 806-809.

1222   "Television Comes Under Fire [for Detroit Riot Coverage]." U.S. News and World Report, LXV (July 15, 1968), 36-39.

1223   "38 Hours--Trial by Terror: Washington, D.C. Siege by Hanafi Muslems." Time, CIX (March 21, 1977), 14-20.

1224   "The Trap at Wounded Knee: Television Coverage of the Sioux Protest." Time, CI (March 26, 1973), 67.

1225   "TV's Grip on History and Vice Versa." Broadcasting, C (April 6, 1981), 35-38. The assassination attempt on President Ronald Reagan.

1226   United States. Congress. House. Committee on Internal Security. Symbionese Liberation Army: A Staff Study. 93rd Cong., 2nd sess. Washington, D.C.: U.S. Government Printing Office, 1974. 21p.

1227   _____. National Advisory Comission on Civil Disorders. "The News Media and the Disorders." In: Its Report. New York: E. P. Dutton, 1968. pp. 362-388. This commercial edition was reprinted from pages 201-204 of the Kerner Commission's GPO report published the same year.

1228 Viorst, Milton. Fire in the Streets: America in the 1960's. New York: Simon & Schuster, 1980. 384p. A valuable review of the state of American society during the covered period with emphasis on the big urban riots and protest demonstrations; comments are offered on the role of the media, especially television network news.
1229 "What was Going On: Coverage of Robert F. Kennedy's Assassination." Time, XCI (June 14, 1968), 72-73.

V-F. THE ENVIRONMENT

The references in this section concern themselves with several issues related to man and nature and how those issues were examined by the news departments of the television networks. Among the problems listed are those of science content in programming, oil spills, ecology, the energy crisis, and the nuclear power plant accident at Three Mile Island, near Harrisburg, Pennsylvania. While not receiving perhaps the mass attention it received a few years ago, issues relating to man and the environment continue to be covered by the networks in many of their current evening news segments.

1230 Arlen, Michael J. "Opening the Baseball Season: Reporting the Three Mile Island Nuclear Plant Crisis on Television News." New Yorker, LV (April 16, 1979), 153-154.
1231 Ayers, J. B. "An Analysis of the Science Content of the Evening Television News: ABC, CBS, and NBC Networks." School Science and Mathematics, LXXX (February 1980), 109-113.
1232 Bagdikian, Ben H. "How Communications May Shape Our Future Environment." AAUW Journal, LXII (March 1969), 123-126.
1233 Behr, Peter. "CBS Pulls Producer [Charles Thompson] Off [Billy Carter] Energy Story." Washington Journalism Review, I (April-May 1978), 16-17.
1234 Dangerfield, Linda A., Hunter P. McCartney, and Ann T. Starcher. "How Did Mass Commuications, as Sentry, Perform in the Gasoline 'Crunch?'" Journalism Quarterly, LII (Summer 1975), 316-320.
1235 Diamond, Edwin. "Is TV Out to Get Big Oil?" TV Guide, XXVIII (May 17, 1980), 4-9.
1236 _____. and Leigh Passman. "Three-Mile Island: How Clear Was TV's Picture?" TV Guide, XXVII (August 4, 1979), 4-12.
1237 Downs, Anthony. "Up and Down with Ecology: The 'Issue Attention' Cycle." The Public Interest, XXVIII (Summer 1972), 38-50.
1238 DuPont, Robert L. Nuclear Phobia--Phobic Thinking About Nuclear Power. Washington, D.C.: Media Institute, 1980. 29p.
1239 Efron, Edith. "Are the Arabs Duping U.S. TV and the Press?" TV Guide, XXIII (May 3, 1975), A3-A4.
1240 _____. "The Energy Crisis: Network Coverage is Weirdly Out-of-Date." TV Guide, XXV (March 5, 1977), A7-A8.

1241 Firebaugh, Morris W. "Public Attitudes and Information
     on the Nuclear Option." Nuclear Safety, II (March-April
     1981), 147-156.
1242 Hickey, Neil. "Some Hard Facts About the Energy Crisis."
     TV Guide, XXI (September 1, 1973), 6-9.
1243 Lewis, Caroline. "Three Mile Island." In: Marvin Barrett
     and Zachary Sklar, eds. The Eye of the Storm: The Alfred
I. DuPont-Columbia University Survey of Broadcast Journalism.
New York: Lippincott-Crowell, 1980. pp. 189-202.
1244 MacLeish, Rod. "Utility Communications: A Need for
     Understanding the American Character." In: Gary W.
Selnow, et al., eds. Energy Essays: A Focus on Utility Communication. Project DE-A001-80RG10347. East Lansing, Mich.:
Center for Evaluation and Assessment. Michigan State University, 1981. pp. 13-22.
1245 Media Institute. The Public's Right to Know: Communi-
     cators' Response to the Kememy Commission Report.
Washington, D.C., 1980. 33p.
1246 Molotch, Harvey and Marilyn J. Lester. "Accidental
     News: The Great Oil Spill as Local Occurrence and Nation-
al Event." American Journal of Sociology, LXXXI (September
1975), 235-260. The major example is the Santa Barbara, Calif.,
spill of 1969.
1247 Nimmo, Dan, and Jane E. Combs. "The Horror Tonight:
     Network Television News and Three Mile Island." Journal
of Broadcasting, XXV (Summer 1981), 289-294.
1248 Phillips, Kevin. "Critics Charge Bias in Network's Cover-
     age of Nuclear Issues." TV Guide, XXV (April 2, 1977),
A5-A6.
1249 Pride, Richard A. and Barbara Richards. "The Denigra-
     tion of Political Authority in TV News: The Ecology
Issue." Western Political Quarterly, XXVIII (December 1975),
635-645.
1250 Rubin, David, et al. Report of the Public's Right-to-
     Information Task Force: Staff Report to President's Com-
mission on the Accident at Three Mile Island. Washington, D.C.:
U.S. Government Printing Office, 1979. 262p.
1251 TV Coverage of the Oil Crises: How Well Is the Public
     Served? Washington, D.C.: TMI Croporation, 1982.
1252 Television Evening News Covers Nuclear Energy: A Ten-
     Year Perspective. Washington, D.C.: Media Institute,
1979. 140p.
1253 "Three-Mile Island: As Confusing as It Was Dangerous."
     Broadcasting, XCVI (April 9, 1979), 61-62.
1254 United States. Congress. Report of the President's
     Commission on the Three Mile Island Accident: Joint
Hearings. 96th Cong., 1st session. Washington, D.C.: U.S.
Government Printing Office, 1980. 154p.
1255 _____. _____. House. Committee on Science and
     Technology. Subcommittee on Energy Research and Produc-
tion. Nuclear Public Information and Rational Policy Decisions:
Hearings. 97th Cong., 1st sess. Washington, D.C.: U.S.
Government Printing Office, 1981. 270p.
1256 _____. President [Carter]. Report of the President's
     Commission on the Three Mile Island Accident. Washington,
D.C.: U.S. Government Printing Office, 1980.

1257   Weisman, John. "How TV Covered the Energy Crisis."
       TV Guide, XXX (March 6, 1982), 4-12.
1258   Wiebe, G. D. "The Mass Media and Man's Relationship to
       His Environment." Journalism Quarterly, L (Autumn
       1973), 426-432, 446.
1259   Zarb, Frank G. "The Energy Crisis: Is TV Doing Its
       Job?" TV Guide, XXV (July 16, 1977), 2-6.

V-G.   THE NEW LEFT, ROCK & ROLL, ETC.

American network television news coverage of students,
their movements and philosophies, were something of a "happening" during the 1960's and college campuses and inner cities
became hotbeds of anti-Vietnam war agitation, political activism
(later to encompass environmental issues), defiantly dressed
youngsters (called "hippies," "yippies," and other labels)
smoking marijuana, drinking beer, and listening to very loud
music.   The citations in this section look not only at those
people, but the manner in which the news people covered them.

1260   Blumberg, Nathan B. "Misrepresenting the Peace Move-
       ment."   Columbia Journalism Review, IX (Winter 1970-
       1971), 28-32.
1261   Cantor, Milton. Divided Left: American Radicalism, 1900-
       1975. New York: Hill and Wang, 1978. 248p. A review
of the growth of American radicalism with much on its student
involvement; little on news coverage, but useful for the background information provided.
1262   Gitlin, Todd. The Whole World Is Watching: Mass Media
       in the Making and Unmaking of the New Left.   Berkeley,
Calif.: University of California Press, 1980. 350p. Contends
that the New Left's various stands were misrepresented and
ultimately thwarted by media coverage.
1263   Gregory, Neal, and Janice Gregory. "The Day Elvis
       Died: A Study of TV Judgment." TV Guide, XXIX (Au-
       gust 19, 1981), 4-10.
1264   _____, and _____. When Elvis Died. Washington,
       D.C.: Communications Press, 1980. 292p. Examines the
grief of those who followed the Tennessee musician and the
manner in which network news presented details of the death
and grief to the nation.
1265   Grupp, F. W., Jr. "Newscast Avoidance Among Political
       Activists."   Public Opinion Quarterly, XXXIV (Summer
       1970), 262-266.
1266   Montgomery, Kathryn. "Gay Activists and the Networks."
       Journal of Communications, XXXI (Summer 1981), 49-57.
1267   Pride, Richard A. and Barbara Richards. "Denigration of
       Authority?: Television News Coverage of the Student
Movement." Journal of Politics, XXXVI (August 1974), 637-660.
1268   Roche, John P. "TV's Addiction to a Phony Countercul-
       ture."   TV Guide, XXIV (December 25, 1976), A5-A6.
1269   Singer, B. D. "Violence, Protest, and War in Television
       News: The U.S. and Canada Compared." Public Opinion
       Quarterly, XXXIV (Winter, 1970-1971), 611-616.

1270   Young, Nigel.   An Infantile Disorder?:   The Crisis and
    Decline of the New Left.   Boulder, Col.:   Westview Pres,
1978.   490p.   A full examination of the political activism of
students during the 1960's and early 1970's with some attention
to media portrayals.

V-H.   POLITICS

It is difficult to overemphasize the role of the print and
electronic news media in the political life of the American nation
in the late 20th century.   As the various citations in this
section demonstrate, cameramen and media journalists, or so it
is often claimed, have been instrumental in breaking up the old
political coalitions--or, at the very least, in reflecting great
changes in society.   The role of television news in shaping the
opinions of voters via campaign and issue coverage, and in
helping to create consensus through the events reported, has
been the subject of debate for some time.   The General Works
immediately below are followed by works devoted to the most
noted group of journalists involved with political coverage, the
Washington Press Corps.

GENERAL WORKS--Books

1271   Buchanan, Patrick J.   Conservative Votes, Liberal Vic-
    tories: Why the Right has Failed.   New   York: Quad-
rangle Books, 1975.   184p.   A noted conservative critic and
Nixon speechwriter contends that the media, especially CBS
News and the Washington Post, represented "the most formid-
able obstacle in the path of a conservative countereformation in
the United States."
1272   Clor, Harry M., ed.   The Mass Media and Modern Demo-
    cracy.   Chicago, Ill.:   Rand McNally, 1874.   232p.   Seven
papers from a college conference examine a variety of topics
related to democracy's maintenance, with emphasis on print and
broadcast political journalism.
1273   Diamond, Edwin.   The Tin Kazoo: Television, Politics,
    and the News.   Cambridge, Mass.:   MIT   Press,   1975.
269p.   A veteran commentator examines the dynamic medium of
television and notes the changes in its format and impact on
politics since the late 1940's to 1975, contending that electronic
journalism is neither as influential as many believed or as close
to its stories as necessary to reflect accuracy.   Although in
need of some revision, this remains required reading for anyone
interested in the topic of this section.
1274   Fixx, James F.   The Mass Media and Politics.   New York:
    Arno Press, 1972.   636p.   A collection of New York Times
articles on the subject which were penned during the years
1936-1971; many deal with the impact of network television
news, especially after 1956.
1275   Graber, Doris A.   Mass Media and American Politics.
    Washington, D.C.:   Congressional Quarterly, Inc., 1980.

304p. A short but valuable comprehensive study which thoroughly discusses the effect of the mass media on politics and political behavior; topics covered include the impact of television on election results and network news impact on individual opinion.

1276 Lang, Kurt and Gladys. Politics and Television. Chicago, Ill.: Quadrangle Books, 1968. 315p. Examines the manner in which television news, through its presentation of events, has shaped the public's image of personalities and political life during the years 1945-1968.

1277 Lee, Richard W., ed. Politics and the Press. Contemporary Issues in Journalism, no. 1. Washington, D.C.: Acropolis Books, 1972. 191p. A collection of essays built around the theme that press, including newspaper, magazine, radio, and television, coverage of political events and politicians impacts on the opinions of voters and their actions on election days.

1278 MacNeil, Robert. The People Machine: The Influence of Television on American Politics. New York: Harper & Row, 1968. 362p. The senior half of PBS's "MacNeil/Lehrer Report," gives us a very critical review of network news reporting methods, with emphasis on political journalism at election time.

1279 Mendelsohn, Harold and Irving Crespi. Polls, Television, and the New Politics. Scranton, Pa.: Chandler Publishing Co., 1970. 329p. A challenge to widely-held beliefs concerning the impact on politics of both television news and public opinion polls.

1280 Nickelson, Sig. The Electric Mirror: Politics in an Age of Television. New York: Dodd, Mead, 1972. 304p. A former head of CBS News examines the methods and insides of television news coverage of national politics, elections, and campaigns.

1281 Nimmo, Dan, ed. Watching American Politics: Articles and Commentaries About Citizens, Politicians, and the News Media. New York: Longman, 1981. 336p. An anthology devoted to coverage of each of the above subtitled elements and their interactions with one another, with emphasis on the role played by the print and electronic media on both voters and those seeking office.

1282 Paletz, David L. and Robert M. Entman. Media, Power, and Politics. New York: Macmillan, 1981. 308p. A study of the impact of the media on politics with emphasis not only on coverage but on fund-raising and image-building for candidates.

1283 Rivers, William L. The Adversaries: Politics and the Press. Boston, Mass.: Beacon Press, 1970. 273p. Looks at ways in which the print and electronic news media deal with politics and politicians from an adversarial position.

1284 Rubin, Bernard. Political Television. Belmont, Calif.: Wadsworth, 1967. 200p. An important volume which put forward the idea, based on a study of the five-year period preceding the 1964 election, that television, by bringing current events into the home, had a dramatic impact, indeed profound influence if you will, on the reshaping of both American elections and the U.S. presidency.

1285   Saldich, Anne.   Electronic Democracy: Television's Im-
    pact on the American Political Process.   New York: Prae-
ger, 1979. 142p. Focusing on the way in which TV affects
public participation in the political process, Saldich examines
the content of TV news and its social role as a major source of
information about public affairs, analyzes the assumptions and
decision-making processes of television news broadcasters,
explores the ways in which politicians and pressure-groups
have tried to manipulate the news to further their own purposes, discusses the importance of name and face recognition
conferred by TV, notes how the public's evaluation of an event's
importance or the credibility of a public figure is influenced by
TV coverage and concludes that, despite the centralization of
power within the national networks, television plays a positive
role that enhances American democracy.   The foreword is by
Bernard Rubin, author of the previous citation.
1286   Sigal, William.   Reporters and Officials: The Organization
    and Politics of Newsmaking.   Boston, Mass.:   Lexington
Books, 1973. 256p. Contends that the relationship established
between print/broadcast reporters and politicians/bureaucrats
can flavor what becomes "news" and demonstrates the manner in
which groups work to "organize" the most effective coverage
possible.
1287   Wilhelmsen, Frederick D. and Jane Bret.   Telepolitics:
    The Politics of Neuronic Man.   Plattsburg, N.Y.:   Tundra
Books, 1972. 254p. An interesting if little-reviewed title
which is concerned with the effect of media coverage of politics
on news events and which suggests that form, not content, has
created a new era of political interaction whih they call that of
the "Neuronic man."

GENERAL WORKS--Articles

1288   Alexander, Herbert E.   "Communications and Politics:
    The Media and the Message."   In: Robert Agranoff, ed.
The New Style in Election Campaigns.   Boston, Mass.:   Hol-
brook Press, 1972. pp. 371-372.
1289   Arlen, Michael J.   "Politics Inside the Rectangle."   New
    Yorker, LII (October 25, 1976), 174-176+.
1290   Bennett, W. Lance.   "Public Opinion and the News Media."
    In: his Public Opinion in American Politics.   New York.
    Harcourt, Brace, 1980. pp. 304-344.
1291   Brown, Janellen H.   "An Investigation of the Effects of
    News and Public Affairs Media Consumption on Individuals'
Issue Accuracy and Political Discussion."   Unpublished PhD
Dissertation, University of Oregon, 1978.
1292   Compton, Neil.   "Television and Politics."   Commentary,
    XLVI (December 1968), 26-30.
1293   Defleur, Melvin L.   "Mass Communications and Social
    Change."   Social Forces, (March 1966), 314-326.
1294   Efron, Edith.   "Lou Harris Teams Up with TV."   TV Guide,
    XIX (April 3, 1971), 42-47.

1295   Emery, Edwin. "The Changing Role of the Mass Media in American Politics." Annals of the American Academy of Political and Social Science, no. 427 (September 1976), 84-94.

1296   Farley, James A. "James A, Farley Discusses TV's Impact on Politics." TV Guide, IV (August 11, 1956), 17-19.

1297   Goldstein, Walter. "Network Television and Political Change." Western Political Quarterly, XX (December 1967), 875-887.

1298   Gregg, Richard B. "The Rhetoric of Political Newscasting." Central States Speech Journal, XXVIII (Winter 1977), 221-237.

1299   Huntley, Chet. "What's Happened to Spellbinders?" TV Guide, IV (October 20, 1956), 10-11.

1300   Kennedy, John F. "Television: A Force·in Politics." TV Guide, VII (November 14, 1959), 5-7.

1301   MacNeil, Robert. "Has Television Cast a Spell Over Politics?" TV Guide, XVIII (June 28, 1980), 5-12.

1302   Mendelsohn, Harold and Irving Crespi. "Television and the New Politics." In: their Polls, Television and the New Politics. San Francisco, Calif.: Chandler, 1970. pp. 297-317.

1303   Mullally, Donald F. "Broadcasting and Social Change." Quarterly Journal of Speech, LVI (February 1970), 40-44.

1304   Newman, Edwin. "Television News and Its Effect on Public Affairs." Colorado Quarterly, XX (February 1970), 149-165.

1305   Nofziger, Lyn. "The News of Politics vs. the Politics of News." Imprimis, IX (June 1980), 1-7.

1306   Pettit, Tom. "Newsmen, Too, Often Play the Politician's Shell Game." Broadcastig, XCII (April 4, 1977), 78.

1307   Reeves, Richard. "TV Forces the Issues--And That Can Be Dangerous." Panorama, I (October 1980), 6-7.

1308   Robinson, Michael J. "American Political Legitimacy in an Era of Electronic Journalism: Reflections on the Evening News." In: Douglass Cater, ed. Television as a Social Force: New Approaches to TV Criticism. New York: Praeger, 1975. pp. 97-139.

1309   _____. "A Statesman is a Dead Politician." In: Elie Abel, ed. What's News. San Francisco, Calif.: Institute for Contemporary Studies, 1981. pp. 159-186.

1310   _____. "Television and American Politics, 1956-1976." The Public Interest, no. 48 (Summer 1977), 3-39.

1311   Schlesinger, Arthur M., Jr. "Politics and TV." TV Guide, XIV (October 22, 1966), 6-10.

1312   Stanton, Frank. "20th Century Reforms in the Political Arena: Abstracts." Broadcasting, LXVII (December 14, 1964), 55+.

1313   "Television and Politics: Views of Leading Sociologists, Psychologists, and Political Analysts." Television, XVII (July 1960), 47-49+.

1314   Trenaman, Joseph and Denis McQuail. "The Effects of Television and Other Media." In: their Television and the Political Image. London: Methuen, 1961. pp. 182-206.

1315   Wamsley, G. L. "Television Network News: Rethinking the Iceberg Problems." Western Political Quarterly, XXV (September 1972), 434-450.

1316   White, William S. "Television's Role in Politics." <u>TV</u>
Guide, XII (July 11, 1964), 9-13.
1317 <u>Will,</u> George F., ed. <u>Press, Politics, and Popular Govern-</u>
<u>ment.</u> Domestic Affairs Study, no. 3. Washington, D.C.:
American Enterprise Institute for Public Policy Research, 1972.
52p.
1318   Youman, Roger J. "Television's Political Coverage--What
Does America Think, Now?" <u>TV Guide</u>, XX (September 30,
1972), A1-A4.

WASHINGTON PRESS CORPS--Books

1319   Collier, Barney. <u>Hope and Fear in Washington (the Early</u>
<u>Seventies): The Story of the Washington Press Corps.</u>
New York: Dial Press, 1975. 254p. Examines how Washington-
based reporters had to operate during the Nixon administration
in order to provide unbiased (reporters and government bias)
news to the "folks back home"; contains a variety of references
to network television news personalities as well as those who
worked in print and radio news.
1320   Hess, Stephen. <u>The Washington Reporters.</u> Washington,
D,C,: Brookings Institution, 1981. 174p. The latest
title available for review by this compiler, Hess details not only
the history of Washington reporting, but in the case of the
networks, studies the impact of government and industry pressure and advances in technology.
1321   Hiebert, Ray E., ed. <u>The Press in Washington: Sixteen</u>
<u>Top Newsmen Tell How the News is Collected, Written, and</u>
Communicated from the World's Most Important Capital. New York:
Dodd, Mead, 1966. 233p. Interviews with mostly print journalists who attempt to provide readers with insights into how journalism works in the nation's capital; not overly critical in any
direction.
1322   Hoyt, Kendall K. and Frances Spatz. <u>Drunk Before Noon:</u>
<u>The Behind-the-Scenes Story of the Washington Press Corps</u>.
Englewood Cliffs, N.J.: Prentice-Hall, 1979. 418p. A fascinating account which provides not only history but a large number of anecdotes about reporters, their sources, connections,
contacts, and habits; much of the emphasis here is on print
journalism, but the electronic media is well covered.
1323   Kraft, Joseph. <u>Profiles in Power: A Washington Insight</u>.
New York: New American Library, 1966. 192p. Thoughts
by a prominent print journalist, including comments on the
Washington Press Corps, which are also excerpted in our articles
section of this subsection.
1324   Marbut, F. B. <u>News from the Capital: The Story of</u>
<u>Washington Reporting.</u> Carbondale, Ill.: Southern Illinois
University Press, 1972. 304p. This is pure history, with some
attention paid to electronic journalism into the early days of the
Nixon administration.
1325   Rivers, William L. <u>The Opinionmakers.</u> Boston, Mass.:
Beacon Press, 1965. 207p. A study of the interplay
between politics, politicians, and the print/broadcast press in

Washington through the early years of Lyndon Johnson's presidency.

1326 _____ . The Other Government: Power and the Washington Media. New York: Universe Books, 1982. Contends that the "opinion press" (such big newspapers as the Washington Post) and the networks have reached a point where they are powerful enough to not only report but shape the news.

1327 Weinberg, Steve. Trade Secrets of Washington Journalists: How to Get the Facts About What's Going on in Washington. Washington, D.C.: Acropolis Books, 1981. 253p. Reports on sources that can be tapped and how to go about obtaining information both official and unofficial; should be compared with the comments in Dan Rather's The Camera Never Blinks cited in VII:B below. Foreword by Walter Cronkite.

WASHINGTON PRESS CORPS--Articles

1328 Alsop, Stewart. "The Press: Fashions in the News." In: his The Center: People and Power in Political Washington. New York: Harper & Row, 1968. pp. 170-212.

1329 Hess, Stephen. "Fear and Fraternity in the Washington Press Corps." Washington Journalism Review, III (January-February 1981), 73-41.

1330 _____ . "The Washington Press Corps." Across the Board, XVIII (June 1981), 48-60.

1331 _____ . "Washington Reporters and Their World." Brookings Bulletin, XVII (Winter 1981), 15-18.

1332 Kraft, Joseph. "The Politics of the Washington Press Corps." Harper's, CCXXX (June 1965), 100+.

1333 Lanouette, William J. "The Washington Press Corps: Is It All That Powerful?" National Journal, XI (June 2, 1979) 896-901.

1334 "The Washington Connection: The Big Boom in Broadcast Journalism." Broadcasting, CI (August 3, 1981), 46-50.

1335 White, Ray. "Government VIP's Rate the Washington Press." Washington Journalism Review, IV (January-February 1982), 37-40.

V-I. SPACE EXPLORATION

The news departments of the commercial television networks have been intimately involved with America's space effort since its beginnings in the late 1950's. Spurred by Russia's Sputnik of 1957, U.S. scientists attempted without success in the months following the Soviet success to place a satellite, the Vanguard, into orbit. When these failed, citizens and propagandists took comfort and commented upon the "openness" of a society which could show its failures on television. Following the success of Explorer I in 1958, the race heated up again with the idea of putting man in orbit and on the moon. Again, television was on hand to record for the world America's successes, near failures (Apollo 13), and the fatal launch pad disaster that claimed the lives of Gus Grissom and his colleagues. After a decade of space spectaculars, the crowning achievement came on July 20, 1969, when American astronauts successfully landed on the moon, an event reported live at 10:56 p.m. EDT by the American networks for a worldwide audience. In the years since 1969, space events have been rather limited and viewers have come to expect flawless coverage of successful operations. Such was the case with Apollo-Soyuz in 1975 and the U.S. Space Shuttle in 1981. Perhaps, as Edwin Diamond has observed, television and space are a perfect match of technologies which reflect American pride in an era when other news is not so pleasant or uncomplicated.

1336 Angotti, Joseph H. "A Descriptive Analysis of NBC's Radio and Television Coverage of the First U.S. Manned Orbital Flight." Unpublished MA thesis, Indiana University, 1965.

1337 "Apollo 11 Coverage is Lauded." Broadcasting, LXXVII (December 8, 1969), 67.

1338 "Apollo Revitalizes TV Space Coverage." Broadcasting, LXXV (October 21, 1968), 67.

1339 "Apollo 12: Just Another Moon Shot." Broadcasting, LXXVII (December 1, 1969), 66-67.

1340 Bergman, Jules. "Some Tales of Astronauts and Space." TV Guide, XXII (March 2, 1974), 8-13.

1341 CBS News. It Was an Unprecedented Seven Days of Television, February 14-20. New York: Columbia Broadcasting System, 1962. 36p. Both of the above citations refer to John Glenn's flight.

1342 _____. 10:56:20 PM EDT, July 20, 1969: The Historic Conquest of the Moon, as Reported to the American People by the CBS News Over the CBS Television Network. New York: Columbia Broadcasting System, 1970. 169p.

1343 Cronkite, Walter. "We are Children of the Space Age." TV Guide, XVII (July 19, 1969), 10-13.

1344 Diamond, Edwin. "A Perfect Match: TV and Space." Television, XXII (October 1965), 14.

1345 Doan, Richard K. "How TV Responded to the Crisis of Apollo 13." TV Guide, XVIII (April 25, 1970), A-1.

1346 Downs, Hugh. The Today Show Looks at Ten Years of Space Exploration. Washington, D.C.: Aerospace Association of America, 1967. Unpaged.

1347 Hickey, Neil. "Live--from the Moon!" TV Guide, XVII (July 19, 1969), 6-9.

1348 "The High Price of History." Television, XIX (April 1962), 64-69. John Glenn's orbital mission.

1349 "How Radio-TV Will Cover the First U.S. Astronaut." Broadcasting, IX (April 24, 1961), 52-53.

1350 Lachenbruch, David. "TV in the Space Age." TV Guide, X (April 28, 1962), 52-53.

1351 "Network News Chiefs Swap Snarls: CBS Announces Curtailed Gemini Coverage, NBC and ABC Say They Will Judge News on Merits." Broadcasting, LXIX (August 30, 1965), 51-52.

1352 "Networks in High Gear for Gemini-Titan 6." Broadcasting, LXIX (October 25, 1965), 78-79.

1353   "1981's TV Space Odyssey: The Flight of the Columbia."
       Broadcasting, C (April 20, 1981), 96-97.
1354   "Pad 19."   New Yorker, XLI (April 3, 1965), 38-40.   On
       Walter   Cronkite's   enthusiastic   reporting   of   space   shots.
1355   "The Remote That Broke All the Records."   Broadcasting,
       LXXVII (July 28, 1969), 28-30.
1356   "TV Coverage Soars Aloft With Apollo 11."   Broadcasting,
       LXXVII (July 21, 1969), 38-39.
1357   "TV Puts Moon Walk Before the Eyes of Millions Around
       the   World."   Aviation Week and Space Technology,   XCI
       (July 28, 1969), 38-40.
1358   Watkins, H. D.   "Surveyor Unit Permits Live TV Broad-
       cast from Ranger 9." Aviation Week and Space Technology,
       LXXXII (March 29, 1965), 26-27.
1359   "You'll Be There When Men Land on the Moon."   Broad-
       casting, LXXVII (July 14, 1969), 44-45+.

VI. NETWORK TELEVISION NEWS
AND UNITED STATES PRESIDENTS

"Perhaps," writes Don, R. Pember in the third edition of his Mass Media in America (Chicago: Science Research Associates, 1981), p. 331, "the classic American case study of press-government relationships is the manner in which the media and the president react to one another." This is more so today than ever in our past; presidents before Franklin D. Roosevelt were often not the center of news they have been since. Much of this is undoubtedly due to FDR's bold and unprecedented use of and relationship with members of the press (print and radio), which altered forever the role of information seekers and providers in this nation.

It is now widely understood and is often stated in introductory works on the presidency that the chief executive has a responsibility to communicate his ideas and programs to Americans and his media relations (now highly advanced through the office of the press secretary) and press conferences are a prime part of the process.

The press conference for U.S. presidents is an invention of the 20th century; Woodrow Wilson was the first to have them on a regular basis. Of the chief executives since Wilson, it is usually agreed that only presidents Roosevelt, Kennedy, and Reagan have had any flair with the give-and-take of these sessions.

Of the chief executives who served during the years from 1948 to 1982, only two, Kennedy and Reagan stand out, with Truman, Eisenhower, Johnson, Nixon, Ford and Carter ill at ease in answering questions before live conferences; indeed, before JFK, live television news conferences did not exist. The references in this large section treat of the interaction between presidents and the media, including press conferences, presidential coverage, and certain events (such as Watergate) connected with presidents since 1948.

A general works section (itself divided into books and articles) is followed by examinations of specific chief executives Dwight D. Eisenhower, John F. Kennedy, Lyndon B. Johnson, Richard M. Nixon, Gerald R. Ford, Jimmy Carter, and Ronald Reagan.

VI-A. GENERAL WORKS

BOOKS

1360   Bagdikian, Ben H.   The Effete Conspiracy.   New York:
Harper & Row, 1974.   159p.   Includes seven essays which
deal with various facets of presidential press relations in administrations from Kennedy through Nixon.
1361   Cornwell, Elmer E., Jr.   Presidential Leadership of Public
Opinion.   Bloomington, Ind.:   Indiana University Press,
1965.   370p.   An historical review from Washington to Johnson,
with much on the innovative manner of John Kennedy's press
relations.
1362   Grossman, Michael B. and Martha J. Kumar.   Portraying
the President: The White House and the News Media.
Baltimore, Md.:   Johns Hopkins University Press, 1981.   358p.
Details the growth of presidential image making from the White
House, the expanded role of the press secretary, and the
general relationship between presidents and network news;
provides many details and insights.
1363   Lammers, William W.   Presidential Politics: Patterns and
Prospects.   New York: Harper & Row, 1976.   310p.   A
basic college level textbook with references to the media as part
of the information provided.
1364   Minow, Newton N., John B. Martin, and Lee M. Mitchell.
Presidential Television.   New York: Basic Books, 1973.
232p.   Accompanied by much useful tabular data, this report
shows how Chief Executives from FDR through Nixon employed
their access to the electronic media as a vehicle for advancement of their goals and power; Minow, John Kennedy's FCC
chairman, and his colleagues suggest a number of reforms to
preserve the constitutional system of checks-and-balances which
they see as having been endangered because of changes in
technology.
1365   Morgan, Edward P., et al.   The Presidency and the Press
Conference.   Washington, D.C.:   American Enterprise
Institute for Public Policy Research, 1971.   56p.   A useful
assessment of the press conference as a tool of presidential
information passing before and at the time of the Nixon administration; indeed, Nixon's press secretary, Herbert G. Klein is
one of this report's several co-authors.
1366   Mullen, William F.   Presidential Power and Politics.   New
York: St. Martin's Press, 1976.   294p.   Stresses that the
office is larger than the men, especially the failures, who have
occupied it "in recent years"; includes as discussion of media
impact on the institution.
1367   Neustadt, Richard E.   Presidential Power: The Politics
of Leadership with Reflections on Johnson and Nixon.   New
York: John Wiley, 1976.   324p.   The 1960 edition of this
influential book was required reading by this author as an
undergraduate; Neustadt, one of JFK's advisors, looks at good
and poor decision-making at the White House with an analytic

discussion of how presidents can best achieve their policy aims, including their relationships with both the print and the broadcast media.

1368 Pollard, James E. The Presidents and the Press: Truman to Johnson. Washington, D.C.: Public Affairs Press, 1964. 125p. Examines the press relations of Truman, Eisenhower and Kennedy, with much more attention paid to the latter's remarkable ability to relate to the public via live television.

1369 Purvis, Hoyt, ed. The Presidency and the Press. Austin, Tx.: Lyndon B. Johnson School of Public Affairs, University of Texas, 1976. Unpaged. Report of a conference held at the Johnson Library in 1975 which featured the views of important press officials and presidential press secretaries and media advisors who served in administrations from Eisenhower to Ford.

1370 Reedy, George. The Presidency in Flux. New York: Columbia University Press, 1973. 133p. Largely a duplication of the information in the next entry.

1371 _____. The Twilight of the Presidency. Cleveland and New York: World Publishing Co., 1970. 205p. LBJ's press secretary argues that modern presidents have, for a variety of reasons which include media coverage and large staffs, developed bigger-than-life, unrealistic views both of themselves and their goals.

1372 Rossiter, Clinton L. The American Presidency. New York: Harcourt, Brace, 1960. 281p. Perhaps one of the most widely known general works on the presidency ever written, this scholar's study suggests that a Chief Executive's task is actually several distinct roles, one being the informing and education of the U.S. electorate.

1373 Rubin, Richard L. Press, Party, and Presidency. New York: W. W. Norton, 1982. 246p. Examines the role of the media in shaping the two-party system of late and its impact on the modern presidency; valuable as one of the few books now available which carry the story to the Reagan presidency.

1374 Schlesinger, Arthur M., Jr. The Imperial Presidency, With an Epilogue and Appendix: "The Vice Presidency, a Modest Proposal." New York: Popular Library, 1973. 541p. The former Kennedy aide and chronicler known as a proponent of presidential leadership here critiques the growth of autonomous presidential power, providing a number of insightful comments on media-president relations along the way.

1375 Smith, Howard E., Jr. and Louanne Norris. Newsmakers: The Press and the Presidents. Reading, Mass.: Addison-Wesley, 1974. 128p. A brief review of presidential relations with the press, including the impact of radio coverage of FDR and television coverage of John Kennedy.

1376 Sorensen, Theodore C. Decision-Making in the White House: The Olive Branch or the Arrows. New York: Columbia University Press, 1963. 94p. A brief study by one of President Kennedy's long-time associates and advisors (JFK penned the foreword) on the importance of decisive presidential leadership which "must be attuned to public opinion but not bound by it."

1377 _____. Watchmen in the Night: Presidential Accounta-
bility After Watergate. Cambridge, Mass.: MIT Press, 1975. 178p. In speaking of print and broadcast journalism, Sorensen suggests that it should provide more in-depth cover- age of presidents and their actions and dwell less on the drama and sensationalism of the office and its occupants.

1378 Spragens, William C. From Spokesman to Press Secretary: White House Media Operations. Washington, D.C.: Univer- sity Press of America, 1980. 243p. A history of the develop- ment of presidential press relations in this century and the tremendous growth in White House media operations since the time of John Kennedy; the role of press secretaries as guar- dians and information passers is stressed.

1379 Stein, Meyer L. When Presidents Meet the Press. New York: Julian Messner, 1969. 109p. A series of brief, non-scholarly sketches of presidential press relations through- out American history.

1380 Thomas, Helen. Dateline: White House. New York: Macmillan, 1975. 298p. Memoirs of a veteran UPI journa- list who began covering the White House when John Kennedy moved in and who has been at nearly every press conference since, including those dramatic television events of the Nixon years.

ARTICLES

1381 Barkan, Glenn. "The Presidency and Broadcasting: Governing Through Media." Unpublished PhD Dissertation, Claremont Graduate School, 1972.

1382 Becker, Samuel L. "Presidential Power: The Influence of Broadcasting." Quarterly Journal of Speech, XLVII (February 1961), 10-18.

1383 Boaz, John K. "The Presidential Press Conference." Unpublished PhD Dissertation, Wayne State University, 1969.

1384 Bogardus, Emery S. "The Sociology of the Presidential TV Conference." Sociological and Social Research, XLVI (January 1962), 181-185.

1385 Brown, Les. "[Speaker Carl] Albert Says TV News Favors Presidents: Reprinted from New York Times, January 18, 1976." Congressional Record, CXXII (January 28, 1976), 1378.

1386 Carter, Douglass. "The President and the Press." Annals of the American Academy of Political and Social Science, no. 307 (1956), 55-65.

1387 Chancellor, John. "The Presidency and the Media." Unpublished Frank Nelson Doubleday Lecture, Smithsonian Institution, April 1982.

1388 Cheslik, Francis E. "Presidential Influence on the Media: A Descriptive Study of the Administrations of Lyndon B. Johnson and Richard M. Nixon." Unpublished PhD Dissertation, Wayne State University, 1977.

1389   Compton, Ann. "It's a Three-Ring Circus at the White House." Washington Journalism Review, I (January-February 1978), 44-46.
1390   Cornwell, Elmer E., Jr. "The Modern Press Conference, 1953-1964." In: his Presidential Leadership of Public Opinion. Bloomington, Ind.: Indiana University Press, 1965. pp. 176-207.
1391   . "The President and the Press: Phases in the Relationship." Annals of the American Academy of Political and Social Science, no. 427 (September 1976), 53-64.
1392   . Presidential News: The Expanding Public Image." Journalism Review, XXXVI (Summer 1959), 275-285.
1393   . "The Presidential Press Conference: A Study of Institutionalization." Midwest Journal of Political Science, IV (November 1960), 370-389.
1394   Cronin, T. E. "The Presidency Public Relations Script." In: Rex G. Tugwell and T. E. Cronin, eds. The Presidency Reappraised. New York: Praeger, 1974. pp. 168-183.
1395   Diamond, Edwin. "Reagan, Carter, and the Press." Washington Journalism Review, III (March 1981), 51.
1396   "Does the Presidential News Conference Have a Future?" ASNE Bulletin, (February 1974), 12-15.
1397   Entman, Robert M. "The Imperial Media." In: Arnold J. Meltsner, ed. Politics and the Oval Office: Towards Presidential Government. San Francisco, Calif.: Institute for Contemporary Studies, 1981. Chpt. 4.
1398   Frost, David. "Why Should a Network Suffer for Putting on the President Instead of Bo Derek?: An Interview." Panorama, I (September 1980), 24+.
1399   Graber, Doris. "Personal Qualities in Presidential Images: The Contribution of the Press." Midwest Journal of Political Science , XVI (February 1972), 46-76.
1400   Grossman, Michael B. and Francis E. Rourke. "The Media and the Presidency: An Exchange Analysis." Political Science Quarterly, XCI (Fall 1976), 455-470.
1401   , and Martha J. Kumar. "The White House and the News Media: The Phases of Their Relationship." Political Science Quarterly, XCIV (Spring 1979), 37-53.
1402   Halberstam, David. "The Press and Prejudice: The White House Press Corps Relations with Richard M. Nixon, Lyndon B. Johnson, and John F. Kennedy." Esquire, LXXXI (April 1974), 109-114+.
1403   Hickey, Neil. "The White House is Their Beat." TV Guide, XIII (November 6, 1965), 18-22.
1404   Joseph, Ted. "How White House Correspondents Feel About Background Briefings." Journalism Quarterly, L (Autumn 1973), 509-516, 532.
1405   Kilpatrick, Carroll. "The Imperial Front Man." Nation, CCXVIII (February 21, 1976), 197-199. The press secretary.
1406   Klein, Herbert G. "The Press vs. White House Spokesmen." TV Guide, XXIII (August 2, 1975), 2-6. From the days of James Hagerty, Eisenhower's press secretary.

1407   Lammers, William W. "Presidential Press Conference Sche-
dules: Who Hides and When?" Political Science Quarterly,
XCVI (Summer 1981), 261-278.
1408   McGuire, Delbert. "Democracy's Confrontation: The
Presidential Press Conference." Journalism Quarterly,
XLIV (Winter 1967), 638-644; XLV (Spring 1968), 31-41, 54.
Based on next entry.
1409   _____ . "The Performance of the Presidential Press
Conference as a Medium of Communication Between the
President and the Nation Through the Mass Media." Unpub-
lished PhD Dissertation, University of Iowa, 1966.
1410   Manheim, Jarol B. "'The Honeymoon's Over': The News
Conference and the Development of Presidential Style."
Journal of Politics, XLI (February 1979), 55-74.
1411   Moore, Susan E. Presidential Press Conferences. Freedom of Information Center Report. Columbia, Mo.: (FOI)
School of Journalism, University of Missouri, 1975. 10p.
Available as ERIC document ED 140 338.
1412   Moynihan, Daniel P. "The Presidency and the Press."
Commentary, LI (March 1971), 41-53.
1413   Nessen, Ron. "Is There Enough Substance in White
House Coverage?" TV Guide, XXIII (August 2, 1975),
2-6.
1414   "Networks Deny Suggestion They Let Bars Down for
Presidents." Broadcasting, XC (January 26, 1976), 55-56.
1415   "The One-Sided Game: Presidential Press Conferences."
Newsweek, LXXIV (December 22, 1969), 90.
1416   Orr, C. Jack. "Reporters Confront the President: Sustain-
ing a Counterpoised Situation." Quarterly Journal Speech,
LXVI (February 1980), 17-32.
1417   Phillips, Glen D. "The Use of Radio and Television by
Presidents of the United States." Unpublished PhD Dissertation, University of Michigan, 1968.
1418   Plischke, Elmer. "Presidential Personal Communications."
In: his Summit Diplomacy: Personal Diplomacy of the President of the United States. College Park, Md.: College of Business and Public Administration, University of Maryland, 1960.
Chpt. 3.
1419   Pollard, James E. "The White House News Conference as a
Channel of Communication." Public Opinion Quarterly, IV
(Fall 1951), 663-678.
1420   Reedy, George E. "The President and the Press: Struggle for Dominance." Annals of the American Academy of
Political and Social Science, no. 427 (September 1976), 65-72.
1421   _____ . "We Can Improve Those Presidential Press
Conferences." TV Guide, XXVII (May 19, 1979), 10-11.
1422   Rinn, Fauneil, J. "The Presidential Press Conference."
Unpublished PhD Dissertation, University of Chicago,
1960.
1423   _____ . "The Presidential Press Conference." In: A.
Wildavsky, ed. The Presidency. Boston, Mass.: Little,
Brown, 1969. pp 327-336.
1424   Rivers, William L. "Presidents and the Press." Progressive, XXXVI (November 1972), 30-35.

1425 Robb, Lynda Johnson. "TV Coverage of the First Family."
      TV Guide, XXIX (August 17, 1981, 16-20.
1426 Roche, John P. "From Kennedy to Ford: TV and the
      Presidency." TV Guide, XXIII (May 24, 1975), A-5-A-6.
1427 Rubin, Richard E. "The Presidency in the Age of Tele-
      vision."   American Political Science Proceedings, XXXIV
      (Summer 1981), 138-152.
1428 Rutkus, Denis S. A Report on Simultaneous Television
      Network Coverage of Presidential Addresses to the Nation.
Washington, D.C.: Congressional Research Service, Library of
Congress, 1976. 20p.
1429 Scherer, Ray. "Television in the White House." TV
      Guide, X (January 13, 1962), 12-13.
1430 Schlesinger, Sarah M. "The Emerging Role of Television
      in Presidential Politics." Unpublished MA thesis, Univer-
      sity of Maryland, 1963.
1431 Seymour-Ure, Colin. "Presidential Power, Press Secretar-
      ies, and Communications." Political Studies, XXVIII (June
      1980), 253-270.
1432 Sigel, Robert S. "The Image of the American Presi-
      dency." Midwest Journal of Political Science, X (Spring
      1966), 123-137.
1433 "Television and Presidential Politics: Brainstorming the
      Possibilties." Broadcasting, CII (February 8, 1982), 90-94.
1434 Weisman, John. "Mr. Presidnt! Mr. President!" TV
      Guide, XXVI (March 18, 1978), 21-25.
1435 White, William S. "Presidents and the Press--an Adver-
      sary Relationship: Excerpts from an Address." Intellect,
      CV (November 1976), 128-129.
1436 "The White House and the Media." In: R. Gordon Hoxie,
      ed.   The White House--Organization and Operations: Pro-
ceedings of the 1970 Montauk Symposium on the Office of the
President of the United States. New York: Center for the
Study of the Presidency, 1971. pp. 19-62.
1437 Witcover, Jules. "How Well Does the White House Press
      Perform?" Columbia Journalism Review, XII (November-
      December 1973), 39-43.
1438 Wolfsen, Lewis. A Report on the State of the Presidential
      Press Conference   New   York: National   News   Council,
      1973. Unpaged.

VI-B.   DWIGHT D. EISENHOWER

1439 Adams, Sherman. First Hand Report: The Story of the
      Eisenhower Administration. New   York: Harper,   1961.
481p. Reminiscences of Eisenhower's most famous and controversial aide who constantly takes issue with the media attempt
to portray him as "assistant president."
1440 Alexander, C. C. Holding the Line: The Eisenhower Era,
      1952-1961. Bloomington, Ind.: Indiana University Press,
1975. 326p. An academic survey of Ike's presidency with some
mention of the role of the media, mostly newspapers.

1441   Donovan, Robert J.   Eisenhower: The Inside Story.   New
York: Harper, 1956.   423p.   Covers only Eisenhower's
first administration; rich in insight into the president's style
and the work of his staff.
1442   Eisenhower, Dwight D.   "Some Thoughts on the Presidency."   Reader's Digest, XCIII (November 1968), 49-55.
1443   _____.   The White House Years.   2 vols.   Garden
City, N.Y.:   Doubleday, 1963-1965.   The former president's memoirs are divided by administration into Mandate for
Change, 1953-1956 and Waging Peace, 1956-1961; they include a
few comments on his relationship with the media.
1444   Hagerty, James C.   "The President and Television: An
Interview."   TV Guide, VI (December 27, 1958), 4-7.   By
Eisenhower's press secretary.
1445   Hughes, Emmet J.   The Ordeal of Power: A Political
Memoir of the Eisenhower Years.   New York: Atheneum,
1963.   372p.   Recollections of a liberal speechwriter which
critiques Eisenhower's lack of political innovation and offers a
few comments on the role of the press.
1446   "Ike Ushered in New TV Era."   Broadcasting, LXXVI
(April 7, 1969), 105-106.
1447   Lowe, Florence.   "The President on Television."   TV
Guide, II (May 7, 1954), 5-7.
1448   Pear, P. H. "The American Presidency Under Eisenhower."
Political Quarterly, XXVIII (Spring 1957), 5-12.
1449   Pollard, James E.   "Eisenhower and the Press: The Final
Phase."   Journalism Quarterly, XXXVI (Spring 1961), 181-
186.
1450   _____.   "Eisenhower and the Press: The First Two
Years."   Journalism Quarterly, XXX (Summer 1955), 285-
300.
1451   Stein, Meyer L.   "Dwight D. Eisenhower."   In: his When
Presidents Meet the Press.   New York: Julian Messner,
1969.   pp. 111-131.
1452   United States.   National Archives.   Public Papers of the
Presidents: Dwight D. Eisenhower, 1953-1961.   8   vols.
Washington, D.C.:   U.S. Government Printing Office, 1954-1962.

VI-C.   JOHN F. KENNEDY

GENERAL WORKS

1453   Bagdikian, Ben H.   "The President Nonspeaks."   Columbia
Journalism Review, II (1963), 42-46.
1454   _____.   "Television: The President's Medium?"   Columbia Journalism Review, I (1962), 34-38.
1455   Bingham, W. and Ward Just.   "The President and the
Press."   Reporter, (April 12, 1962), 18-23.
1456   Chase, Harold W. and Allen H. Lerman, eds.   Kennedy
and the Press: The News Conferences.   New York: T.
Y. Crowell, 1965.   555p.   Selected press conference transcripts
with comment.
1457   Guback, Thomas H.   "Reporting or Distorting?:   Broadcast
Network News Treatment of a Speech by John F. Kennedy."

In: Harry J. Skornia and Jack W. Kitson, eds. Problems and
Controversies in Radio and Television: Basic Readings.   Palo
Alto, Calif.: Pacific Books, 1968. pp. 347-357.
1458 "J.F.K. and the [Press] Conference." Time, XC (March
      24, 1961), 44.
1459 The Kennedy Presidential Press Conference. New York:
      E. M. Coleman Enterprises, 1978. 640p.
1460 Kessel, John H. "Mr. Kennedy and the Manufacture of
      News." Parliamentary Affairs (Great Britain), XVI (Sum-
      mer 1963), 293-301.
1461 Knebel, Fletcher. "Kennedy vs. the Press." Look,
      XXVI (August 28, 1962), 17-21.
1462 Kyes, Elizabeth A. "President Kennedy's Press Confer-
      ence as Shapers of the News." Unpublished PhD Disserta-
      tion, University of Iowa, 1968.
1463 Lawrence, Bill. "The Presidential Press Conference."
      TV Guide, XI (May 4, 1963), 4-7.
1464 "Lights, Action, Camera: JFK." U.S. News and World
      Report, LV (November 4, 1963), 67.
1465 Manchester, William R. Portrait of a President: John F.
      Kennedy in Profile. Boston, Mass.: Little, Brown, 1962.
238p. Examines Kennedy's public comportment as president and
his impact on the Washington scene, including his relationship
with the press.
1466 NBC News. Memo to JFK from NBC News. New York:
      G. P. Putnam, 1961. 313p.
1467 New York Times, Editors of. The Kennedy Years. New
      York: Viking Press, 1964. 327p. A sympathetic view
      stressing the president's charisma.
1468 "New Under Kennedy: Reporters Analyze the First Year."
      Columbia Journalism Review. I (Spring 1962), 11-20.
1469 "1962--TV and the New Frontier Start to Hum: Year-End
      Report." Sponsor, XVI (December 24, 1962), 21-25+.
1470 Ostman, Ronald E., William A. Babcock, and J. Cecelia
      Fallery. "The Relation of Questions and Answers in
Kennedy's Press Conferences." Journalism Quarterly, LVIII
(Winter 1981), 575-581.
1471 Paper, L. J. The Promise and the Performance: The
      Leadership of John F. Kennedy. New York: Crown,
1975. 408p. The fairest scholarly balanced analysis available;
examines JFK's goals, means (including press relations), and
failures/accomplishments.
1472 Pollard, James E. "The Kennedy Adminsitration and the
      Press." Journalism Quarterly, XLI (Winter 1964), 3-14.
1473 Salinger, Pierre. With Kennedy. Garden City, N.Y.:
      Doubleday, 1966. 391p. Rich in anecdote, JFK's press
secretary also addresses the problems and delights of the first
live television news conferences.
1474 Sanders, Luther W. "A Content Analysis of President
      Kennedy's First Six Press Conferences." Journalism Quar-
      terly, XLII (Spring 1965), 114-115.
1475 Schlesinger, Arthur M., Jr. A Thousand Days: John F.
      Kennedy in the White House. Boston, Mass.: Houghton,
Mifflin, 1965. 1,087p. A partial memoir by a Harvard historian-

JFK aide, this work contains numerous references to Kennedy's press relations.

1476   Sharp, Harry W., Jr.   "The Kennedy News Conference." Unpublished PhD Dissertation, Purdue University, 1967.

1477   _____.   "Live from Washington: The Telecasting of President Kennedy's News Conferences."   Journal of Broadcasting, XIII (Winter 1968-1969), 23-32.

1478   Sidey, Hugh.   John F. Kennedy, President.   New York: Atheneum, 1964.   434p.   A sympathetic account with some references to JFK's media performances; see "The Corps,"   pp. 98-109.

1479   Sorensen, Theodore C.   Kennedy.   New York: Harper & Row, 1965.   783p.   Recollections of the White House by a top aide with many citations to the president's press relations.

1480   United States.   National Archives.   Public Papers of the Presidents: John F. Kennedy.   3   vols.   Washington, D.C.:   U.S. Government Printing Office, 1962-1964.

THE KENNEDY ASSASSINATION

1481   "America's Long Vigil."   TV Guide, XII (January 25, 1964), 19-45.

1482   Bishop, James A.   The Day Kennedy was Shot.   New York: Funk & Wagnalls, 1968.   713p.   Includes a look at the role of the press in providing the American public with details.

1483   Brinkley, David.   "President Kennedy was Shot in Dallas, Texas, Today."   TV Guide, XXVI (November 18, 1978), 20-22.

1484   Casmir, Fred L.   "Lee Harvey Oswald and Radio/Television."   NAEB Journal,   XXIV (September-October 1965), 71-83.

1485   Columbia Broadcasting System. Newsletter: The Assassination of President Kennedy--A Description, in Pictures and Words from the CBS News Broadcast.   "The Four Dark Days: From Dallas to Arlington."   New York, 1963.   19p.

1486   Dale, William.   "'The Four Dark Days':   An Analysis of the Major Television Network Coverage, from the Assassination in Dallas to the Burial in Arlington."   Unpublished MA thesis, University of Illinois, 1964.

1487   Epstein, Edward J.   Inquest: The Warren Commission and the Establishment of truth.   New York: Viking press, 1966.   224p.   Critical of the Commission's findings, including those dealing with the media.

1488   "Four Days: TV Coverage of Events Surrounding the Death of President Kennedy."   Television, XXI (January 1964), 27-33.

1489   Graves, Florence.   "The Mysterious Kennedy Out-Takes: Does CBS News Have Something to Hide?"   Washington Journalism Review,   I (September-October 1978), 24-28.

1490   Greenberg, Bradley S. "Diffusion of News of the Kennedy Assassination."   Public Opinion Quarterly, XXVIII (Summer 1964), 225-232.

1491 _____, and Edwin B. Parker, eds. The Kennedy Assassination and the American Public: Social Communication in Crisis. Stanford, Calif.: Stanford University Press, 1965. 392p. From the viewpoint of our topic, the most important book on the subject; examines, indeed, dissects news coverage of the event.

1492 Love, Ruth L. "Television and the Death of a President: Network Decisions in Covering Collective Events." Unpublished PhD Dissertation, Columbia University, 1969.

1493 Manchester, William R. The Death of a President: November 20-November 25, 1963. New York: Harper & Row, 1967. 710p. A thorough and controversial account of the four days connected with Kennedy's death and funeral.

1494 Mendelsohn, Harold. "Broadcast vs. Personal Sources of Information in Emergent Public Crisis: The Presidential Assassination." Journal of Broadcasting, VIII (Spring 1964), 147-156.

1495 National Broadcasting Company, News Division. Seventy Hours and Thiry Minutes, as Broadcast on the NBC Television Network by NBC News. New York: Random House, 1966. 152p. A pictorial and transcript review of the broadcast.

1496 Pierson, W. Theodore. "Criticism of News Media by the Warren Commission." Journal of the Bar Association of the District of Columbia, XXXII (January 1965), 16+.

1497 Rather, Dan. "Dallas: All the Doctors Were Busy." In: his The Camera Never Blinks: Adventures of a TV Journalist. New York: Ballantine Books, 1977. pp. 117-138.

1498 Sprague, R. E. "American News Media and the Assassination of President John F. Kennedy: Accessories After the Fact." Computers and Automation and People, XXII (June-July 1973), 36-40, 31-38.

1499 United States. Congress. House. Select Committee on Assassinations. Investigation of the Assassination of President John F. Kennedy: Hearings. 95th Cong., 2nd sess. 5 pts. Washington, D.C.: U.S. Government Printing Office, 1978.

1500 _____. President's Commission on the Assassination of President Kennedy. Hearings. 26 vols. Washington, D.C. U.S. Government Printing Office, 1964.

1501 _____. _____. Report of the Warren Commission. New York: McGraw-Hill, 1969. 726p.

1502 _____. _____. "The Warren Commission Report on the Role of the Press in the Assassination of President John F. Kennedy." In: Gerald Cross, ed. The Responsibility of the Press. New York; Fleet Publication Co., 1966. pp. 50-82.

1503 Winchester, J. H. "TV's Four Days of History." Reader's Digest, LXXXIV (April 1964), 204I-204J+.

1504 "The World Listened and Watched." Broadcasting, LIV (December 2, 1963), 36-61.

VI-D.   LYNDON B. JOHNSON

1505   "Back of the Uproar About LBJ Managing the News."
       U.S. News and World report, LX (January 31, 1966),
       42-43.
1506   Bagdikian, Ben H.   "Press Agent--But Still President."
       Columbia Journalism Review, IV (Summer 1965), 10-13.
1507   Brinkley, David. "Leading from Strength: LBJ in Action."
       Atlantic, CCXV (February 1965), 49-54.
1508   Cooper, Stephen L.   "A Rhetorical Assessment of Lyndon
       Johnson's Presidential Press Conferences."   Unpublished
       PhD Dissertation, Louisiana State University, 1972.
1509   Cornwell, Elmer E., Jr.   "The Johnson Press Relations
       Style." Journalism Quarterly, XLIII (Spring 1966), 3-9.
1510   Divine, Robert A., ed. Exploring the Johnson Years:
       Essays and Materials at the Lyndon Baines Johnson Library
       Presented at a Conference Held at the Library in January 1980.
       Austin, Tx.:   University of Texas Press, 1981. 280p. In-
       cludes an analysis of Johnson and the media, by David Cutbert.
1511   Evans, Rowland, and Robert Novak. Lyndon B. Johnson:
       The Exercise of Power--a Political Biography. New York:
       New American Library, 1966. 597p. Covers Johnson's career
       from Congressman to the mid-point of his presidency; examines
       his highly personal style of exercising influence, including his
       relationship to the press.
1512   Goldman, Eric F. The Tragedy of Lyndon Johnson. New
       York: Alfred A. Knopf, 1969. 531p. A Princeton Univer-
       sity historian who served on Johnson's White House staff ex-
       amines the president's unhappy relationship to the intellectual
       community, including the press and media.
1513   Goralski, Robert.   "Television and the President."   TV
       Guide, XII (July 4, 1964), 3-5.
1514   Hickey, Neil.   "When the President Speaks."   TV Guide,
       XIV (January 1, 1966), 6-7.
1515   Johnson, Claudia A.   "Lady Bird."   A White House Diary.
       New York: Holt, Rinehart, and Winston, 1970.   806p.
       The former First Lady's recollections of the Johnson presidency,
       with seveal interesting references to the broadcast media.
1516   Johnson, Lyndon B.   "LBJ's Musings About the Media."
       Time, XCIII (February 14, 1969), 68.
1517   _____. The Vantage Point: Perspectives of the
       Presidency, 1963-1969. New York: Holt, Rinehart, and
       Winston, 1971.   636p.   LBJ's presidential recollections include
       some comments on the role of broadcast journalism in covering
       his administration.
1518   The Johnson Presidential Press Conferences.   New York:
       E. M. Coleman Enterprises, 1978. 700p.
1519   Kearns, Doris. Lyndon Johnson and the American Press.
       New York: Harper & Row, 1976.   432p.   A controversial
       life-history and psychobiography which contains only limited
       reference to the press.
1520   "Lights, Cameras, Action!:   The LBJ News Conference."
       U.S. News and World Report, LIX (September 20, 1965),
       66-67.

1521 Miller, Merle. Lyndon: An Oral Biography. New York:
      G. P. Putnam, 1980.   645p.´ Similar to this author's
Truman: An Oral Biography; provides quotes from Johnson's
thoughts on a variety of subjects, including the broadcast
media.
1522 Moyers, Bill. "Bill Moyers Talks About the War and LBJ:
      An Interview."   Atlantic, CCXVIII (July 1968), 29-37.
1523 _____ . "Moyers Says TV Not LBJ's Forte." Broad-
      casting, LXXIV (May 6, 1968), 75-76.
1524 "The President and the Press: Changes in the Way the
      Country is to Get the News." U.S. News and World Report,
      LV (December 30, 1963), 34-35.
1525 Sidey, Hugh.   A Very Personal Presidency: Lyndon
      Johnson in the White House. New York: Atheneum, 1968.
305p. Filled with anecdotes and vignettes concerning Johnson's
style and relations with a variety of personalities and problems,
including those of television network news.
1526 Spragens, William C.   "The Myth of the Johnson 'Credi-
      bility Gap.'" Presidential Studies Quarterly, X (Fall 1980),
      629-635.
1527 United States. National Archives. Public Papers of the
      Presidents: Lyndon B. Johnson, 1963-1969.   8   vols.
Washington, D.C.:   U.S. Government Printing Office, 1965-
1970.
1528 Wicker, Tom.   "Bill Moyers, Johnson's Good Angel."
      Reader's Digest, LXXXVIII (January 1966), 72-77.

                 VI-E. RICHARD M. NIXON

GENERAL WORKS

1529 "Adversary Relationships." Newsweek, LXXXIII (April 1,
      1974), 66-67.
1530 Allen, Roger E. "How Nixon Changed His TV Image: An
      Interview." U.S. News and World Report, LXVIII (Febru-
      ary 2, 1970), 68-71.
1531 American University. Department of Communications. "The
      Press Covers Government: The Nixon Years from 1969 to
Watergate."   Congressional Record, CXIX (June 13, 1973),
S11058-S11071. Prepared for the National Press Club, with
conclusions and recommendations of the Professional Relations
Committee of that body.
1532 Aronson, James. Deadline for the Media: Today's Chal-
      lenge to Press, TV, and Radio. Indianapolis, Ind.: Bobbs-
Merrill, 1973. 327p. Includes an extensive discussion of the
relationship between the pre-Watergate Nixon White House and
the news media.
1533 Bonafede, Dom. "A Conversation with Ron Ziegler."
      Washington Journalism Review, I (April-May 1978), 46-49.
1534 Buscha, Julius. "The White House Watch Over TV and
      the Press."   New York Times Magazine. (August 20,
      1972), 9+.
1535 CBS News. The President and the Media: An Evaluation
      of Credibility Among the Public. New York: CBS News,
      Survey and Data Services, 1973.

1536 "Co-ordinating the Media: Dragnet Subpoenas Served on
      CBS and Other Reporters." Nation, CCX (February 16,
      1970), 163-64.
1537 Dean, John W., 3rd. Blind Ambition: The White House
      Years. New York: Simon and Schuster, 1976. 415p.
Memoirs of the counsel to the president noted for his testimony
before the Senate Watergate Committee; contains some thoughts
on the White House reaction to broadcast journalism.
1538 Diamond, Edwin. "How the White House Keeps Its Eye on
      the Network News Shows." New York, IV (May 10, 1971),
      45-49.
1539 Efron, Edith. "Is There Truth in Charges of Anti-Nixon
      Bias?" TV Guide, XXII (May 11, 1974), A3-A4.
1540 Ehrlichman, John. Witness to Power: The Nixon Years.
      New York: Simon and Schuster, 1982. 432p. Reminis-
cences of Nixon's chief domestic affairs advisor; less than
complimentary to either Nixon or the press.
1541 Evans, Rowland, and Robert Novak. Nixon in the White
      House: The Frustration of Power. New York: Random
House, 1971. 431p. Examines the first few years of the first
Nixon administration, with a variety of references to the press.
1542 "The Fairness Problem Reexamined: Has the Press Done
      a Job on Nixon?" Columbia Journalism Review, XII (Janu-
      ary-February 1974), 50-58.
1543 Guerra, David M. "Network Television News Policy and
      the Nixon Administration." Unpublished PhD Dissertation,
      New York University, 1974.
1544 Haldeman, H. R. The Ends of Power. New York: Times
      Books, 1977. 326p. Memoirs of Nixon's special assistant;
Bob Haldeman's comments about representatives of electronic
journalism's big three networks, especially CBS, are not kind.
1545 Harris, Richard. "The President and the Press." New
      Yorker, XLIX (October 1, 1973), 122-128.
1546 Keogh, James. "The President and the Press." Reader's
      Digest, C (April 1972), 237-240+.
1547 _____. President Nixon and the Press. New York:
      Funk and Wagnalls, 1972. 212p. One of Nixon's former
special assistants in the White House reports on the administration's extensive efforts to combat what it considered to be
biased journalism, especially on the part of network news, while
getting its story to the public at large.
1548 Klein, Herbert G. "Klein Offers Middle-Ground Perspec-
      tive on Nixon Wars with the Press." Broadcasting, XCIX
      (September 22, 1980), 57-59.
1549 _____. Making It Perfectly Clear. Garden City,
      N.Y.: Doubleday, 1980. 464p. Memoir's of Nixon's press
secretary; dwells extensively on the conflict between the White
House and broadcast journalists, especially Dan Rather.
1550 Littleton, Thomas B. "Serving Up News--With a Twist."
      Columbia Journalism Review, VIII (July-August 1974),
      47-48. The work of Ken Clawson.
1551 Lubell, Samuel. The Future While It Happened. New
      York: W. W. Norton, 1973. 162p. Studies the ways by
which a form of "psychological warfare" between the Nixon
presidency and a troubled electorate was hastening 1984.

1552 Naughton, J. "How the Second Best Informed Man in the White House Briefs the Second Worst Group in Washington." New York Times Magazine, (May 30, 1971), 9+. Ron Zieglar and the Washington Press Corps.

1553 Nixon, Richard M. RN: The Presidential Memoirs. New York: Grosset and Dunlap, 1978. 1,100p The former president's memoirs are more kind toward the electronic media than one would expect.

1554 "The Nixon Administration and the News Media." Congressional Quarterly Weekly Report, XXX (January 1, 1972), 3-7.

1555 "Nixon and the Media." Newsweek, LXXXI (January 15, 1973), 42-44.

1556 "Nixon and the Press--History of the Presidential News Conference." U.S. News and World Report, LXIX (December 28, 1970), 12-14.

1557 "Nixon-Media Feud Keeps Bubbling." Broadcasting, LXXV (November 12, 1973), 52-53.

1558 The Nixon Presidential Press Conference. New York: E. M. Coleman Enterprises, 1978. 419p.

1559 Osborne, John. The First Two Years of the Nixon Watch. New York: Liveright, 1971. 218p. This, and the following Osborne volumes, contain the full texts of the widely-respected "Nixon Watch" weekly columns of the New Republic, often with a few comments on how particular pieces were received. Several deal in whole or in part with the president's relationship with network news.

1560 _____. The Third Year of the Nixon Watch. New York: Liveright, 1972. 216p.

1561 _____. The Fourth Year of the Nixon Watch. New York: Liveright, 1973. 218p.

1562 _____. The Last Year of the Nixon Watch. Washington, D.C.: New Republic, 1975. 246p.

1563 _____. "President vs. Press: Views of James Keogh." New Republic, CLXVI (April 8, 1972), 11-13.

1564 Powledge, Fred. The Engineering of Restraint: The Nixon Administration and the Press, a Report of the ACLU. Washington, D.C.: Public Affairs Press, 1971. 53p.

1565 Reeves, Richard. "How Nixon Outwits the Press." New York, V (October 9, 1972), 49-52+.

1566 Safire, William. Before the Fall: An Inside View of the Pre-Watergate White House. Garden City, N.Y.: Doubleday, 1975. 704p. A noted Nixon speechwriter's candid, but sympathetic recollections, with some mention of the mass media.

1567 _____. "'The Press is the Enemy.'" New York, VIII (January 27, 1975), 41-44, 47-50.

1568 "Two Decades of Crisis Between Nixon and the Media." Broadcasting, LXXXVII (August 19, 1974), 22-23.

1569 United States. National Archives. Public Papers of the Presidents: Richard M. Nixon, 1969-1974. 6 vols. Washington, D.C.: U.S. Government Printing Office, 1970-1975.

1570 Whiteside, Thomas. "Annals of Television: The Nixon Administration and Television." New Yorker, LI (May 17, 1975), 41-48.

1571 "Will the Press Be Out to Get Nixon?" U.S. News and World Report, LXV (December 2, 1968), 39-40.
1572 Wise, David. "The President and the Press." Atlantic, CCXXXI (April 1973), 55-64.
1573 Witcover, Jules. "Salvaging the Presidential Press Conference." Columbia Journalism Review, VII (Fall 1970), 27-34.
1574 _____. "The Two Hats of Herbert Klein." Columbia Journalism Review, IX (Spring 1971), 26-30.

WATERGATE--Books

1575 Archer, Jules. Watergate: America in Crisis. New York: T. Y. Crowell, 1975. 306p. A review of the events of the crisis from the break-in to president Nixon's resignation.
1576 Barrett, Marvin, ed. Moments of Truth: The Alfred I. DuPont-Columbia University Survey of Broadcast Journalism. New York: T. Y. Crowell, 1975. 274p. Pays special attention to Nixon's relationship with the electronic media during the Watergate affair.
1577 Bernstein, Carl, and Bob Woodward. All the President's Men. New York: Simon and Schuster, 1974. 349p. The famous report by the Washington Post police reporters of their efforts to learn who ordered the Watergate break-in.
1578 _____. The Final Days. New York: Avon Books, 1976. 529p. Chronicles the events leading up to Nixon's resignation.
1579 Chester, Lewis, et al. Watergate: The Full Inside Story. New York: Ballantine Books, 1973. 280p. A fast-paced "instant history," penned originally for a British audience.
1580 Cohen, Richard M., and Jules Witcover. A Heartbeat Away: The Investigation and Resignation of Vice President Spiro T. Agnew. New York: Viking Press, 1974. 373p. Entered here primarily because the Agnew affair occurred during the course of the Watergate investigation; see also the citations in Section IV-D above.
1581 Congressional Quarterly, Inc. Watergate: Chronology of a Crisis. Washington, D.C., 1975. 1,039p. Follows the unfolding of the affair from 1972-1974, with entries for, among many other things, the press.
1582 Dash, Samuel. Chief Counsel: Inside the Ervin Committee--The Untold Story of Watergate. New York: Random House, 1976. 275p. Activities of the Senate Watergate Committee as described by its majority counsel; includes some comments on media coverage.
1583 Drew, Elizabeth. Washington Journal: The Events of 1973-1974. New York: Random House, 1975. 428p. A noted journalist's account not only of the Watergate events, but of the mood in Washington, including the Nixon administration's battles with the press.
1584 Ervin, Samuel J. Whole Truth: The Watergate Conspiracy. New York: Random House, 1980. 320p. This former North Carolina Democrat was chairman of the Senate Select Committee on Presidential Campaign Activities; includes several

thoughts on television coverage of this group's hearings.
1585   Jaworski, Leon.   The Right and the Power: The Pro-
        secution of Watergate. New York: Reader's Digest Press,
1976. 305p. In this Texan's memoirs, one can find extensive
thoughts on his role as the second Watergate Prosecutor and
the various behind-the-scenes aspects of the investigation.
1586   Knappman, Edward W., ed.   Watergate and the White
        House, June 1972-September 1974. 3 vols. New York:
Facts on File, Inc., 1975. A massive daily chronology from the
break-in to President Ford's pardon of Richard Nixon.
1587   Lukas, J. A.   Nightmare: The Underside of the Nixon
        Years. New York: Viking Press, 1976. 626p. Examines
not only the Watergate crisis, but the various administration-
sanctioned "dirty tricks" of 1969-1973, including those dealing
with the press and electronic braodcasting.
1588   Magruder, Jeb S.   An American Life: One Man's Road to
        Watergate. New York: Atheneum, 1974. 338p. Thoughts
by a participant in the illegal campaign practices which brought
on the scandal; compare with the thoughts of John Dean found
in Section V:H:2:d:1 above.
1589   Mankiewicz, Frank.   "'United States vs. Richard M.
        Nixon': The Final Crisis. New York: Times Books,
1975. 276p. Details the Supreme Court battle over possession
of the White House tapes.
1590   New York Times, The Staff of.   The End of the Presi-
        dency. New York: Bantam Books, 1974. 353p. An
example of "instant journalism," in which details of the event
were assembled, edited, and published within days of the
occurrence; useful for general details, if not insight.
1591   _____ .   The Watergate Hearings. New York: Bantam
        Books, 1973. 886p. A handy source for choice passages
from the Senate hearings.
1592   _____ .   The White House Transcipts. New York:
        Bantam Books, 1973. 877p. Paperback reprint of Nixon's
edited papers.
1593   Pynn, R. E., ed.   Watergate and the American Political
        Process. New York: Praeger, 1975. 246p. A collection
of essays and pieces by scholars and journalists, many of which
have been excerpted from other sources.
1594   Rather, Dan and Gary Paul Gates.   The Palace Guard.
        New York: Harper & Row, 1974. 326p. A study of
Nixon's entourage from the vantage point of CBS News; should
be compared with Woodward and Bernstein's All The President's
Men cited above, as well as the excerpt from Rather's The
Camera Never Blinks in the articles below.
1595   Sirica, John J.   To Set the Record Straight. New York:
        W. W. Norton, 1979. 394p. Memoirs of the Watergate case
by the hearing judge of the DC Federal Court; the judgments
on who was guilty and who ordered what and when are quite
specific.
1596   Thompson, Fred D   At That Point in Time: The Inside
        Story of the Senate Watergate Committee. New York:
Quadrangle Books, 1975. 275p. Activities of the Senate Watergate Committee as viewed by its chief minority counsel; should
be compared with the recollections of Samuel Dash cited above.

1597   White, Theodore H.   Breach of Faith: The Fall of Richard
     Nixon. New York: Atheneum, 1975. 373p.   A blow-by-blow
account of the end of the Nixon presidency, with some information   on the early days of the president's career; compare with
Woodward and Bernstein's The Final Days cited above.

WATERGATE--Articles, Government Documents

1598   Arlen, Michael J.   "Time, Memory, and News: Televising
     and Analyzing President Ford's Pardon of Richard Nixon."
New Yorker, L (September 30, 1974), 115-118.
1599   Becker, Lee B. "Two Tests of Media Gratification: Water-
     gate and the 1974 Election."   Journalism Quarterly, LIII
     (Spring 1976), 28-33, 87.
1600   Bensen, Stanley M. and Bridger M. Mitchell.   Watergate
     and Television: An Economic Analysis.   RAND   Report
R-1712-MF.   Santa Monica, Calif.:   RAND Corporation, 1975.
40p.
1601   Bonafede, Dom.   "Administration Tries Public Relations
     to Reestablish Image and Promote Its Efforts."   National
     Journal, V (June 1973), 908-912.
1602   Chaffee, Steven H.   "The Watergate Experience."   Ameri-
     can Political Quarterly, III (October 1975), 355-492.
1603   Chancellor, John.   "Did the Press Hatchet the President
     on Watergate?:   Excerpts from an Interview."   Senior
     Scholastic, CIII (November 8, 1973), 12-13.
1604   "The Coverage: Calm and Massive."   Time, CIV (August
     19, 1974), 73-74.
1605   "Covering Watergate: Success and Backlash."   Time, CIV
     (July 8, 1974), 68-73.
1606   Cox, Archibald.   "Some Reflections on Possible Abuses of
     Governmental   Power."   Record of the Bar of the City of
     New York, XXVIII (December 1973), 811-827.
1607   Daniloff, Nicholas.   "Falling."   Nieman Reports, XXVIII
     (Autumn 1974), 3-8.
1608   Dean, John W., 3rd.   "Interview."   Playboy, XXII (Janu-
     ary 1975), 68+.
1609   Diamond, Edwin. "Psychojournalism: Nixon on the Couch."
     Columbia Journalism Review, VII (March-April 1974), 7-11.
1610   _____ .   "TV and Watergate: What was What Might
     Have Been?"   In: Richard G. Emery and Ted C. Smythe,
eds.   Readings in Mass Communications: Concepts and Issues
in the Mass Media.   2nd ed.   Dubuque, Ia.:   William G. Brown,
1974. pp. 393-396.
1611   _____ . "Tape Shock: The Nixon Transcripts." Colum-
     bia Journalism Review,   XIII   (July-August   1974),   5-9.
1612   "Did Watergate Break the Ice Between White House and
     the Media?"   Broadcasting, LXXXIV (May 7, 1973), 21-22.
1613   Edelstein, A. S. and B. F. Tefft.   "Media Credibility and
     Respondent Credulity with Respect to Watergate."   Com-
     munication Research, 1 (October 1974), 426-439.
1614   Epstein, Edward J.   "Did the Press Uncover Watergate?"
     In: Between Fact and Fiction: The Problem of Journalism.
New York: Random House, 1975. pp. 19-32.

1615   Flatto, Elis.   "The Impeachment of Richard M. Nixon."
       Contemporary Review,   CCXXVI   (March   1975),   146-148.
1616   Friendly, Fred W.   "Paying the High Price of a President
       in an Isolation Booth."   New York, VI (June 11, 1973),
       61-64+.
1617   Hickey, Neil.   "Should Impeachment Be Televised?"   TV
       Guide, XXII (June 29, 1974), 29-30.
1618   "Historic Coverage for Historic Events."   Broadcasting,
       LXXXVII (July 29, 1974), 29-30.
1619   Holm, James, et al.   "Communication and Opinion Forma-
       tion: Issues Generated by Watergate."   Communication
       Research. I (October 1974), 368-390.
1620   Kamelman, M. M.   "Congress, the Media, and the Presi-
       dent."   In: H. C. Manfield, ed.   Congress Against the
       President.   New York: Praeger, 1975. pp. 85-97.
1621   Kanfer, Stefan.   "Watergate on TV: Show Biz and An-
       guished Ritual."   Time, CII (June 25, 1973), 14-15.
1622   Kraus, Sidney and Steven H. Chaffee.   "The Ervin Com-
       mittee Hearings and Communication Research."   Communica-
       tion Research, I (October 1974), 33-348.
1623   Lang, Kurt, and Gladys E.   "Televised Hearings: The
       Impact   Out   There."   Columbia Journalism Review,   XII
       (November-December 1973), 52-57.
1624   Larson, C. V.   "A Content Analysis of Media Reporting
       of the Watergate Hearings.:   Communication Research, I
       (October 1974), 440-448.
1625   Leamer, Lawrence.   "The Sam Ervin Show."   Harper's,
       CCXLIV (March 1973), 80-86.
1626   Leroy, David J., et al.   "The Public Televisin Viewer and
       the Watergate Hearings."   Communication Research, I (Octo-
       ber 197), 406-425.
1627   Lewis, F.   "Some Errors and Puzzles in Watergate Cover-
       age."   Columbia Journalism Review, XII (November-Decem-
       ber 1973), 26-32.
1628   Loory, Stuart H.   "CIA's Man in the White House."   Colum-
       bia Journalism Review, XIV (Septmeber 1975), 11-14.
1629   Magruder, Jeb S.   "Means: Watergate Reflections."   New
       York Times Magazine, (May 20, 1974), 103-104+.
1630   "More Network Coverage as Watergate Heats Up."   Broad-
       casting, LXXXV (July 30, 1973), 37-38.
1631   "More People Believe Network News Than Believe Nixon."
       Broadcasting, LXXXV (November 26, 1973), 21.
1632   "Nixon's Days in Court are TV's Too: Impeachment Cover-
       age Makes History."   Broadcasting, LXXXVII (August 5,
       1974), 18-22.
1633   Overland, Doris.   "The Great Watergate Conspiracy: A
       TV Blitzkrieg?"   Contemeporary Review, CCXXXIII (July
       1978), 29-32.
1634   Paletz, David L.   "Television Drama: The Appeals of the
       Senate Watergate Hearings."   Midwest Quarterly,   XXI
       (Autumn 1979), 63-70.
1635   Peters, C.   "Why the White House Press Didn't Get the
       Watergate Story."   Washington Monthly, V (July-August
       1973), 7-15.

1636   Porter, Laurenda W. "The White House Transcripts: Group Fantasy Events Concerning the Mass Media." Central States Speech Journal, XXVII (1976), 272-279.

1637   "The Press and the Watergate Hearings: Phase One." Columbia Journalism Review, XII (November-December 1973), 26-57.

1638   "Question Now: Will Nixon Try to Curb TV Journalism?" Broadcasting, LXXXV (November 5, 1973), 22-25.

1639   Rather, Dan. "The Unmaking of a President [and] Where Watergate Led." In: his The Camera Never Blinks: Adventures of a TV Journalist. New York: Ballantine Books, 1977. pp. 238-275.

1640   "The Reselling of the President." Time, CII (July 9, 1973), 20-21.

1641   Robinson, Michael J. "The Impact of the Televised Watergate Hearings." Journal of Communication, XXIV (Spring 1974), 23-26.

1642   Safire, William "Last Days in the Bunker." New York Times Magazine, (August 18, 1974), 6+.

1643   Salant, Richard S. "Nixon and Watergate are Gone: Now Do People Love Us--No!" Quill, LXII (November 1974), 23-26.

1644   _____. "Salant Says Media Shouldn't Wallow in Watergate." Broadcasting, LXXXVII (September 30, 1974), 35-36.

1645   Smith, Cecil. "Ratings Soar for Watergate on PBS: Reprinted from the Los Angeles Times, June 20, 1973." Congressional Record, CXIX (August 1, 1973), 27381-27382.

1646   Tillinghast, Diana S. "Information Seeking on Watergate and President Nixon's Resignation and Attitudes Toward Nixon and the Mass Media." Unpublished PhD Dissertation, Michigan State University, 1976.

1647   United States. Congress. House. Committee on the Judiciary. Statement of Information Submitted on Behalf of President Nixon: Hearings. 93rd Cong., 2nd sess. 4 vols. Washington, D.C.: U.S. Government Printing Office, 1974.

1648   _____. _____. Senate. Select Committee on Presidential Campaign Activities. Presidential Campaign Activities of 1972: Hearings. 93rd Cong., 1st sess. 26 vols. Washington, D.C.: U.S. Government Printing Office, 1973.

1649   _____. _____. _____. _____. Draft of Final Report. 93rd Cong., 2nd sess. 3 vols. Washington, D.C.: U.S. Government Printing Office, 1974.

1650   _____. _____. _____. _____. The Final Report. 93rd Cong., 2nd sess. Washington, D.C.: U.S. Government Printing Office, 1974. 1,250p. Reprinted in whole or in part in a variety of editions, including a 2-volume paperback set from Dell Publishers in 1976.

1651   _____. _____. _____. Committee on the Judiciary. Special Prosecutor: Hearings. 93rd Cong., 1st sess. 2 vols. Washington, D.C.: U.S. Gov. Printing Office, 1973.

1652   Varnado, S. L. "Watergate as Drama." National Review, XXV (August 31, 1973), 945+.

1653 Walters, R. "What Did Ziegler Say, and When Did He Say
      It?" Columbia Journalism Review, XIII (September-October
      1974), 30-35.
1654 "Watergate: A Hard Look at Presidential Impeachment."
      Congressional Quarterly Weekly Report, XXXI (October 27,
      1973), 2831-2853.
1655 "Watergate: A Historic Constitutional Confrontation."
      Congressional Quarterly Weekly Report, XXXI (July 28,
      1973), 2031-2051.
1656 "Watergate on TV: A Time Essay." Time, CI (June 25,
      1973), 14-15.
1657 Weaver, David H., Maxwell E. McCombs, and Charles
      Spellman. "Watergate and the Media: A Case Study of
Agenda-Setting."   American Political Quarterly,   III   (1975),
458-472.
1658 "Witness to Watergate: TV Brings It All Home." Broad-
      casting, LXXXIV (May 21, 1973), 20-21.
1659 Zimmer, T. A. "The Impact of Watergate on the Public's
      Trust in People and Confidence in the Mass Media." Social
      Science Quarterly, LIX (March 1979), 743-751.

                    VI-F. GERALD R. FORD

1660 Bonafede, Dom. "[Ron] Nessen Still Seeks 'Separate
      Peace' With the Press." National Journal, VII (October 11,
      1975), 109-1416. Thoughts on Ford's second press secretary.
1661 Collier, Peter. "Ford and the Media: CBS Declares a
      Honeymoon." Ramparts, XIII (October 1974), 45-50.
1662 Ford, Betty. The Times of My Life. New York: Harper
      & Row, 1978. 302p. Memoirs of the former First Lady
with several notes on her encounters with network news people.
1663 Ford, Gerald R. "How TV Influences a President's Deci-
      sions." TV Guide, XXIX (September 19, 1981), 4-10.
1664 _____. "Television and Me." TV Guide, (March 23,
      1974), 5-7.
1665 _____. A Time to Heal: An Autobiography. New York:
      Harper & Row, 1979. 384p. Presidential recollections,
including candid thoughts on encounters with and the role of
electronic journalism.
1666 "Ford Breaks Bread and Ice with Network Chiefs and
      News Executives." Broadcasting, LXXXVII (December 23,
      1974), 14-15.
1667 Gelman, David. "Nessen's Report Card." Newsweek,
      LXXXVIII (January 12, 1976), 52-53.
1668 Mahoney, Robert. "The Ford White House: A Correspon-
      dent's View." Publisher's Auxilliary, (December 10, 1974),
      15.
1669 Mollenhoff, Clark. The Man Who Pardoned Nixon. New
      York: St. Martin's Press, 1976. 312p. An unflattering
account of the Ford presidency, which makes a limited number
of references to the press.
1670 "The President vs. the Networks." Newsweek, LXXXIV
      (October 28, 1974), 91.

1671 "Push and Shove Over Coverage of the President." Broad-casting, LXXXIX (October 13, 1975), 23-25.
1672 Sevareid, Eric. "A New Kind of Leadership: An Address, April 26, 1974." Vital Speeches, XL (June 15, 1974), 532-535.
1673 Slater, William T. "The White House Press Corps During the Ford Administration." Unpublished PhD Dissertation, Stanford University, 1978.
1674 Terhorst, J. F. Gerald Ford and the Future of the Presidency. New York: The Third Press, 1975. 245p. Thoughts by the president's first press secretary and long-time journalist friend.
1675 United States. National Archives. Public Papers of the Presidents: Gerald R. Ford, 1974-1977. 6 vols. Washington, D.C.: U.S. Government Printing Office, 1975-1978.

VI-G. JIMMY CARTER

Aside from a few sympathetic biographies, little of sub-stance has yet appeared on either Carter or his presidency as a whole, although the former president's memoirs were published in the fall of 1982 National Archives' Public Papers series (see United States below).

1676 Bonafede, Dom. "[Jody] Powell and the Press: A New Mood in the White House." National Journal, IX (June 25, 1977), 980-986.
1677 "Carter Wows White House Reporters." Broadcasting, XCVI (May 7, 1979), 13-14.
1678 Diamond, Edwin. "Did the Media Get Bert Lance?" TV Guide, XXVI (February 18, 1978), 6-12.
1679 Donovan, Hedley. "How the White House Reads the Press." Fortune, CII (December 29, 1980), 44-48+.
1680 Evans, Katherine W. "Jody Powell on Press and Presidency ." Washington Journalism Review, III (April 1981), 34-38.
1681 Locander, Robert. "Carter and the Press: The First Two Years." Presidential Studies Quarterly, X (Winter 1980), 106-120.
1682 Powell, Jody. "Powell Charges Eavesdropping by Net-works." Broadcasting, CII (May 10, 1982), 104.
1683 Reedy, George E. "How President Carter Uses TV." TV Guide, XXV (December 31, 1977), 2-5.
1684 Reeves, Richard. "President Carter vs. the Press." New York, IX (December 20, 1976), 112+.
1685 United States. National Archives. Public papers of the Presidents: Jimmy Carter, 1977-1981. 6 vols. Washington, D.C.: U.S. Government Printing Office, 1978-1982.

VI-H. RONALD REAGAN

1686 Auchincloss, Kenneth. "The President vs. the Press."
Newsweek, XCIX (March 29, 1982), 77.

1687 Brown, Les. "Reagan and the Unseen Network." Channels, I (October-November 1981), passim.

1688 "CBS Documentary ["People Like Us"] a New Cause Cele-
bre." Broadcasting, CII (April 26, 1982), 24-31.

1689 Evans, Katherine W. "A Conversation with Dave Gergen."
Washington Journalism Review, IV (April 1982), 41-45.

1690 _____. "A Conversation with Lyn Nofziger." Washington Journalism Review, IV (March 1982), 24-31.

1691 Fritz, Sara. "No More Mr. Nice Guy." Washington Journalism Review, IV (April 1982), 37-40.

1692 Gergen, David. "Gergen's Respectful Words on the Press."
Broadcasting, CII (May 3, 1982), 84-85.

1693 _____. "Is Reagan Getting a Fair Shake from the
Press?: An Interview." U.S. News and World Report,
XCI (December 7, 1981), 25-26.

1694 _____. "So Far, So Good for President's Press Relations." Broadcasting, CII (March 1, 1982), 66-72.

1695 Glass, Andrew J. "The Secret Service vs. the Press."
Washington Journalism Review, III (July-August 1981),
14-17.

1696 Gold, Victor. "An Ex-Flack Looks at Reagan and the
Adversary Press." National Review, XXXIV (April 2,
1982), 346-349. The author was press secretary to Vice President Agnew.

1697 Goldman, Peter. "The Hard Times of Ronald Reagan."
Newsweek, XCIX (February 1, 1982), 16-17.

1698 Griffith, Tom. "Reagan's TV Troubles." Time, CXIX
(April 5, 1982), 57.

1699 "Healing Wounds." Broadcasting, CII (March 22, 1982),
28.

1700 Miller, Mark C. "On Television: Virtu, Inc." New
Republic, CLXXXVI (April 7, 1982), 28-31.

1701 Olson, Lynne. "The Press and Ronald Reagan." Washington Journalism Review, III (November 1981), 42-45.

1702 "Photo Opportunity Standoff: Networks vs. White House."
Broadcasting, CII (April 19, 1982), 73.

1703 "Reagan Goes Overhead to the People." Broadcasting,
CII (April 5, 1982), 37.

1704 "Reagan is Hit in His Television Debut." Broadcasting, C
(February 16, 1981), 75-76.

1705 Reese, Michael. "CBS, Reagan, and the Poor." Newsweek, XCIX (May 3, 1982), 22.

1706 Sanoff, A. F. "Press vs. President: New Battle in an
Old War." U.S. News and World Report, XCII (March 22,
1982), 55-56.

1707 Speakes, Larry. "Speakes Outlines White House Strategy
on Communications." Broadcasting, CII (April 26, 1982),
85.

1708 Weisman, John. "TV and the Presidency: A TV Guide
Interview with President Reagan." TV Guide, XXX (March
20, 1982), 4-10.

VII.   NETWORK TELEVISION AND
PRESIDENTIAL ELECTIONS

Politics and broadcasting have been linked almost from the start. In 1920, KDKA radio in Pittsburgh issued a report on the Harding-Cox election and ever since, people have been trusting to broadcast journalism, to one degree or another, for reports on what have now become almost continuous presidential election campaigns.

In the years since television first became a major force in providing information to the American public, some critics have grown concerned that the packaging and marketing aspects of covering presidential candidates far outweigh any issue of sub- stance in the campaigns. It would almost appear that, out on the presidential campaign trail, if it doesn't happen in time to make the network news at 6:30, it's not worth happening at all.

One of the most widely-hailed inventions in presidential campaigning has been the television debate. The first, said to be decisive, was between John F. Kennedy and Richard M. Nixon in 1960. Since then, candidates Ford and Carter, and Carter and Reagan have also debated, the success of such exchanges depending largely upon which critics are believed.

The effects of broadcasting on politics, especially presi- dential elections, have been studied more completely than almost any other category of media influence, save perhaps the relation- ship of the president to the press. The citations in the vari- ous subsections below all focus on this, beginning with the general relationship of television news to voters and continuing on by primaries, conventions, debates, and campaigns, and election night coverage since 1952.

VII-A.   NETWORK NEWS AND VOTERS

1709   Atkin, Charles E., John Galloway, and Ogus B. Nayman. "News Media Exposure, Political Knowledge, and Campaign Interest." Journalism Quarterly, LIII (Summer 1976), 231-236.
1710   Bone, Hugh A. and Austin Ranney. Politics and Voters. 5th ed. New York: McGraw-Hill, 1981. 136p. A brief college-level survey which considers the various factors, inclu- ding network news and polls, which assist voters in choosing their issues and candidates.
1711   Boyd, Richard W. "Popular Control of Public Policy: A Normal Vote Analysis of the 1968 Election." American Political Science Review, LXVI (Summer 1972), 429-449.

1712   Dreyer, Edward C. "Media Use and Electoral Choices:
    Some Political Consequences of Information Exposure."
Public Opinion Quarterly, XXXV (Winter 1971-1972), 544-553.
1713   Fang, Irving E. "Don't Hold Back the News." Quill, IV
    (November 1968), 24-27.
1714   Fuchs, Douglas A. "Does TV Election News Influence
    Voters?" Columbia Journalism Review, IV (Fall 1965),
    39-41.
1715   . "Election Day Radio-Television and Western
    Voting." Public Opinion Quarterly, XXX (Summer 1966),
    226-236.
1716   Glaser, William A. "Television and Voting Turnout."
    Public Opinion Quarterly, XXIX (January 1965), 71-86.
1717   Gordon, Leonard V. "The Image of Political Candidates:
    Values and Voter Preference." Journal of Applied Psycho-
    logy, LVI (1972), 382-387.
1718   Kecter, Charles S. "Television, Newspapers, and the
    Bases of Choice in American Presidential Elections."
Unpublished PhD Dissertation, University of North Carolina at
Chapel Hill, 1979.
1719   Lang, Kurt and Gladys E "The Mass Media and Voting."
    In: Eugene Burdick and Arthur J. Brodback, eds.
American Voting Behavior. New York: Free Press, 1959. pp.
229-234.
1720   , and   . Voting and Non-Voting: Implica-
    tions of Broadcasting Returns Before the Polls Are Closed.
Waltham, Mass.: Blaisdell, 1968. 172p. A noted study, which
was based in part on interviews conducted with over 350 California voters on November 3, 1964; the issue was raised again
in 1980 when President Carter conceded defeat before the
Western polls were closed.
1721   Lazaisfeid, Paul F., et al. The People's Choice: How
    a Voter Makes Up His Mind in a Presidential Campaign. New
York: Columbia University Press, 1978. 178p. Includes an
examination of the role of media, especially television, in voter
persuasion, be it network news coverage, debates, or paid political commercials.
1722   Lucas, William A. and William C. Adams. "Talking, Tele-
    vision, and Voter Indecision." Journal of Communications,
    XXVIII (Autumn 1978), 120-131.
1723   McLeod, Jack M., et al. "Issues and Images: The Influ-
    ence of Media Reliance in Voting Decisions." Unpublished
paper, Annual Meeting of the Association for Education in
Journalism, East Lansing, Michigan, 1981.
1724   Mendelsohn, Harold. "Western Voting and Broadcasts of
    Results on Election-Day: Election-Day Broadcasts and
Terminal Voting Decisions." Public Opinion Quarterly, XXX
(Summer 1966), 212-225.
1725   , and Garrett J. O'Keefe. The People Choose a
    President: Influences on Voter Decision-Making. New York:
Praeger, 1976. Includes thoughts on the roles of polls and television news on conduits of information, attitudes, and other
factors.
1726   Patterson, Thomas E. and Robert D. McClure. "Television
    and the Less-Interested Voter: The Costs of an Informed

Electorate." Annals of the American Academy of political and Social Science, no. 425 (May 1976), 88-97.

1727   Pierce, John C.   "Party, Ideology, and Public Evaluation of the Power of Television Newspeople." Journalism Quarterly, LIV (Summer 1977), 307-312.

1728   Pomper, Gerald M.   "From Confusion to Clarity: Issues and American Voters, 1956-1968." American Political Science Review, LXVI (Summer 1972), 415-428.

1729   Robinson, Michael J. and Clifford Zukin.   "Television and the Wallace Vote." Journal of Communications, XXVI (Summer 1976), 79-83.

1730   Ryan, Michael.   "Does TV Influence Presidential Elections?" TV Guide, XXIV (June 12, 1976), 6-10.

VII-B.   PRIMARIES

1731   Arterton, F. Christopher.   "The Media Politics of Presidential Campaigns: A Study of the Carter Nomination Drive." In: James D, Barber, ed.   Race for the Presidency: The Media and the Nominating Process.   Englewood Cliffs, N.J.: Prentice-Hall, 1978.   pp.   25-54.

1732   Bicker, William E.   "Network Television News and the 1976 Presidential Primaries: A Look from the Network's Side of the Camera."   In: James D. Barber, ed.   The Race for the Presidency: The Media and the Nominating Process.   Englewood Cliffs, N.J.:   Prentice Hall, 1978.   p. 104+.

1733   "Candidates are off and Running, Media in Tow." Broadcasting, XCVIII (January 14, 1980), 27-30.

1734   Davis, James W.   Presidential Primaries: Road to the White House.   2nd ed.   Contributions in Political Science, no. 41.   Westport, Conn.:   Greenwood Press, 1980, 395p.   A history of presidential primaries through 1976, with some comments on network news coverage, especially in 1976.

1735   Diamond, Edwin.   "Read the Labels." Washington Journalism Review, II (March 1980), 60-61.

1736   Doan, Richard K.   "Can TV Elect the Next President?" TV Guide, XVI (February 10, 1968), 10-14.

1737   _____.   "Television Hits the Campaign Trail." TV Guide, XVI (March 2, 1968), 6-10.

1738   Ernst, Harry W.   The Primary That Made a President: West Virginia, 1960.   Eagleton Institute Cases in Practical Politics, v. 26.   New York: McGraw-Hill, 1962.   32p.

1739   Hickey, Neil.   "Election '72:   TV and the Primaries." TV Guide, XX (May 6, 1972), 6-9.

1740   _____.   "Primaries and TV." TV Guide, XVI (May 4, 1968), 22-24.

1741   "Iowa Caucuses Send Campaign Into High Gear." Broadcasting, XCVIII (January 21, 1980), 30+.

1742   Lelyweld, Joseph.   "The Selling of a Candidate [Carter]." New York Times Magazine, (March 28, 1976), 66-68.

1743   "Media Gets Singed as Campaigns Begin Heating Up." Broadcasting, XCVIII (February 18, 1980), 48+.

1744   Meyers, R. A., et al. "Political Momentum: Television
       News Treatment." Communication Monographs, XLV (Novem-
       ber 1978), 382-388.
1745   Mullen, Jay C. "West Virginia's Image: The 1960 Presi-
       dential Primary and the National Press." West Virginia
       History, XXXII (July 1971), 215-223.
1746   Murray, Michael D. "[George] Wallace and the Media:
       The 1972 Election Primary." Southern Speech-Communica-
       tions Journal, XL (Summer 1975), 429-440.
1747   Naughton, James M. "Boys Will Be Boys on the Run."
       More, VI (April 1976), 22-23.
1748   "New Hampshire: A Movable Media Feast." Broadcasting,
       XCVIII (March 3, 1980), 60-65.
1749   Phillips, Kevin. "TV's Decisive Impact on Primary Results."
       TV Guide, XXIV (July 3, 1976), 43-44.
1750   Reeves, Richard. "Who's in Charge of the Presidential
       Campaign?: Television." Panorama, I (February 1980),
       15-16.
1751   Robinson, Michael J. "The TV Primaries." Wilson Quar-
       terly, I (Spring 1977), 80-83.
1752   _____, and Karen A. McPherson. "Television News
       Coverage Before the 1976 New Hampshire Primary: The
Focus of Network Journalism." Journal of Broadcasting,XXI
(Spring 1977), 177-186.
1753   Ryan, Michael. "Election '76: The New Hampshire Pri-
       mary." TV Guide, XXIV (February 21, 1976), 4-7.
1754   Swertlow, Frank. "Images, Issues." TV Guide, XXIV
       (April 24, 1976), 4-6.
1755   Weaver, Paul H. "Captives of Melodrama: Network Cover-
       age of the Primaries." New York Times Magazine, (August
       29, 1976), 6-7+

VII-C.   CONVENTIONS

GENERAL WORKS

1756   Barber, James D., ed. Race for the Presidency: The
       Media and the Nominating Process. New York: Columbia
University Press. 205p. A collection of essays on the role of
the media, especially network television news, in agenda-setting
and influence-creation in various past candidacies, especially
those of 1976.
1757   Cranston, Pat. "Political Convention Broadcasts: Their
       History and Influence." Journalism Quarterly, XXXVII
       (Summer 1960), 186-194.
1758   Fant, Charles H. "Televising Presidential Conventions,
       1952-1980." Journal of Communications, XXX (Autumn
       1980), 130-139.
1759   Foley, John, Dennis Britton, and Eugene B. Everett,
       Jr., eds. Nominating a President: The Process and the
Press. New York: Praeger, 1980. 168p. Another collection of
articles which examines the variety of tasks confronting the
press during the primary-convention stage of presidential elec-

tions as well as the role the media plays in presenting various facets concerning various candidates.

1760   Kimball, Penn. "Who Needs Gavel-to-Gavel Convention Coverage?" Columbia Journalism Review, XV (September 1976), 28-30.
1761   Reinach, J. Leonard. "Broadcasting the Convention." Journal of Broadcasting, XII (Summer 1968), 219-223.
1762   Ryan, Michael. "How TV Floor Reporters Cover Conventions." TV Guide, XXIV (August 14, 1976), 3-6.
1763   "TV Coverage of Past Conventions." TV Guide, IV (August 18, 1956), 26.

THE 1948, 1952, 1956, 1960, 1964 CONVENTIONS

1764   "Biggest Coverage in the History of Radio/TV Move in on Atlantic City." Broadcasting, LXVII (August 24, 1967) 62-63. Democrats.
1765   Bogardus, E. S. "Television and the Political Conventions." Sociology and Social Research, XXXVII (November 1952), 115-121.
1766   CBS News. The Blue Conventions: A Summary of the Most Recent Demonstration of Network Television's Ability to "Interrupt Its Regularly Scheduled Programs" to Bring an Event of National Interest to the American People. New York: Columbia Broadcasting System, 1956. 43p.
1767   Cronkite, Walter. "[Democrats] Party Personalities." TV Guide, VIII (July 9, 1960),17-19.
1768   Csida, Jim. "Convention: Best Radio/TV Coverage Yet." Sponsor, XIV (July 25, 1960), 12-13.
1769   DeBlois, Frank. "Chet Huntley, David Brinkley, and the Mightiest Western of All." TV Guide, VIII (July 9, 1960), 8-11.
1770   Edwards, Douglas. "Facing the Republican Convention." TV Guide, VIII (July 23, 1960), 17-19.
1771   Edwin, Ed, comp. Reference Guide: 1956 Democratic National Convention, Chicago, August 13. New York: Columbia Broadcasting System, 1956. 342p.
1772   _____, comp. Reference Guide: 1956 Republican National Convention, San Francisco, August 20. New York: Columbia Broadcasting System, 1956. 275p.
1773   "GPO Stage-Center for Radio/TV." Broadcasting, LXVII (July 13, 1964), 32-33.
1774   Gray, Gordon L. "Television and the National Nominating Conventions of 1952." Unpublished PhD Dissertation, Northwestern University, 1957.
1775   "Heavy Coverage of Conventions Planned." Broadcasting, LXVI (June 29, 1964), 66-67.
1776   Hickey, Neil. "TV and the GOP Convention." TV Guide, XII (July 11, 1964), 3-8.
1777   _____. "Television Turns to the Democrats." TV Guide, II (August 22, 1964), 2-7.
1778   Montgomery, Robert. "President's Advisor Speaks Up on TV and the Conventions." TV Guide, IV (June 23, 1956), 10-11.

1779   "Much Time Used But Little News." Broadcasting, LXVII
       (July 20, 1964), 37-40.
1780   "NBC Draws a Blank on Charge It Gave Credentials to
       FBI at 1964 Conventions." Broadcasting, LXXXIX (Decem-
       ber 1, 1975), 26-27.
1781   NBC News. 1960 Convention Handbook. New York: Davis
       Publications, 1960. 145 p.
1782   "Record Breaker in Costs, People." Broadcasting, LXVII
       (August 31, 1964), 50-53.
1783   Rider, John R. "A Viewer's Guide (Scholarly) to the Na-
       tional Political Conventions." Journal of Broadcasting,
       VIII (Summer 1964), 229-232.
1784   "Television Score on the Democratic Convention." News-
       week, XXXII (July 26, 1948), 52-53.
1785   "Television's Ten-Strike Coverage of the Republican Na-
       tional Convention." Newsweek, XXXII (July 5, 1948), 50-51.
1786   "Top Newsmen Who'll Cover the [Democratic] Convention."
       TV Guide, IV (August 11, 1956), 8-9.
1787   Waltzer, Herbert. "In the Magic Lantern: Television Co-
       verage of the 1964 National Conventions." Public Opinion
       Quarterly, XXX (January 1966), 33-53.

THE 1968 CONVENTION

1788   Arlen, Michael J. "Chicago" New Yorker, XLIV (Sep-
       tember 7, 1968), 109-113.
1789   "Beat the Press: Chicago Police and Newsmen." News-
       week. LXXII (September 9, 1968), 70-71.
1790   Brown, William R. "Television and the Democratic National
       Convention of 1968." Quarterly Journal of Speech, LV
       (October 1969), 237-246.
1791   CBS News, Special Events Unit. CBS News Campaign '68:
       The Democratic National Convention. New York, 1968.
1792   CBS News Campaign '68 : The Republican National Con-
       vention. New York: CBS, 1968. 125p.
1793   "Come On, See the Riots: Reprinted from the Titusville
       [Pennsylvania] Herald. September 4, 1968." Congression-
       al Record, CXIV (September 10, 1968), 26279.
1794   Cronkite, Walter. "Chicago and the Function of News."
       AFTRA, 1 (Winter 1969), 12-14.
1795   Field, Louis. "TV Fails Again: Reprinted from the Hominy
       [Oklahoma] News, September 5, 1968." Congressional Record,
       CXIV (September 10, 1968), 26304.
1796   Frank, Reuven. "Chicago: A Post-Mortem." TV Guide,
       XVI (December 14, 1968), 32-40. Reprinted in Jay Harris,
ed., TV Guide: The First 25 Years (New York: New American
Library, 1980), pp. 152-155.
1797   "High Marks for Riot Coverage." Broadcasting, LXXIV
       (June 24, 1968), 59-60.
1798   McCarthy, Eugene J. The Year of the People. Garden
       City, N.Y.: Doubleday, 1969. 323p. A difficult-to-
understand examination of the primaries and Chicago convention
by a leading contender for the nomination; makes some mention
of the media and its coverage.

1799   Mallory, Paul.   "Coverage of the Democratic National Con-
       vention: Reprinted from the Chicago Sun-Times, September
4,   1968."   Congressional Record,   CXIV   (September   9,   1968),
25529.
1800   "Mule Teams at Work: Chicago Convention Coverage by
       TV."   Broadcasting, LXXII (September 9, 1968), 68-69.
1801   "News and Riots: Reprinted from the Sacramento Bee,
       September 3, 1968."   Congressional Record, CXIV (Sep-
       tember 10, 1968), 26284.
1802   "Overreaction: Reprinted from the Washington Examiner,
       September 6, 1968."   Congessional Record, CXIV (Septem-
       ber 11, 1968), 26503-26504.
1803   Paletz, David L. "Delegates' Views of TV Coverage of the
       1968 Democratic Convention."   Journal of Broadcasting,
       XVI (Fall 1972), 441-451.
1804   "Peaceful Assembly, Anarchy, and TV: Reprinted from
       the Suburbanite Economist, September 8, 1968."   Congres-
       sional Record, CXIV (September 17, 1968), 27304.
1805   Pearson, Drew and Jack Anderson.   "Networks Slanted
       Chicago Coverage" Reprinted from the Washington Post,
September 6, 1968."   Congressional Record, CXIV (September 6,
1968), 25985.
1806   Royko, Mike.   Boss: Richard J. Daley of Chicago. New
       York: E.P. Dutton, 1971.   215p.   A political biography
of the Chicago mayor, including his role in the 1968 Democratic
convention.
1807   Stevens, Shane.   "The Death Watch, Chicago, August 28,
       1968."   Minority of One, X (October 1968), 8-9.
1808   Troy, Frosty.   "Why America Had to Have a Chicago: Re-
       printed from the Tulsa [Oklahoma] Tribune, August 30,
1968)" Congressional Record, CXIV (September 10, 1968), 26305.
1809   United States.   Congress.   House.   Committee on Inter-
       state and Foreign Commerce, Special Subcommittee on In-
vestigations.   Television Coverage of the Democratic National
Convention, Chicago Illinois, 1968:   Staff Report.   91st Cong.,
1st   sess.   Washington,   D.C.:   U.S.   Government   Printing
Office, 1969.   29p.
1810   Walter, Merton J.   "Voice of the People--Questions Media's
       Coverage at Convention: Reprinted from the Madison
[Wisc.] Capitol News, October 7, 1968."   Congressional Record,
CXIV (October 7, 1968), 29963-29964.
1811   "Week of Grievances: Coverage of the Democratic National
       Convention."   Time, XCII (September 6, 1968), 48-50.
1812   Whiteside, Thomas.   "The Corridor of Mirrors: The Tele-
       vision   Editorial   Process,   Chicago."   Columbia Journalism
       Review, VII (Winter 1968-1969), 35-54.

THE 1972, 1976 & 1980 CONVENTIONS

1813   Alder, Renata.   "Who's Here?   What Time is It?:   Tele-
       vision Coverage of the 1972 Conventions."   New Yorker,
       XLVIII (September 16, 1972), 114-118.

1814 Bedell, Sally. "The Convention Coverage." TV Guide, XXVIII (August 9, 1980), 28-35.

1815 "Biggest News Coverage Ever for Democrats." Broadcasting, XCI (July 19, 1976), 21-24.

1816 Brightman, Samuel C. "The Inside Story of Convention Coverage." TV Guide, XX (August 26, 1972), 23-26.

1817 Clarke, Blake. "Democratic Pageant: The Network's Flop." Nation, CCXXIII (July 31, 1976), 69-72.

1818 Doan, Richard K. and Neil Hickey. "Election '72: The Republican Convention." TV Guide, X (August 19, 1972), 6-11.

1819 "GOP's Turn in News Barrel Broadcasting Focuses on Kansas City." Broadcasting, XCI (August 16, 1976), 26-27.

1820 "Hard Work-Hard News: Televising the Republican Conventions." Newsweek, LXXXVIII (August 30, 1976), 78-79.

1821 Hickey, Neil. "Election '72" TV and the Democratic Convention." TV Guide, XX (July 8, 1972), 8-13.

1822 _____. "It's Politics' Greatest Show on Earth." TV Guide, XXIV (July 10, 1976), 4-8.

1823 _____, and Michael Ryan. "With No Suspense at Convention, TV Looked for 'Color.'" TV Guide, XXIV (July 24, 1976), A3-A4.

1824 "How They Rated: Convention Coverage." Newsweek, LXXX (August 7, 1972), 59.

1825 "The Longest Week: Television Coverage of the Democratic Convention." Time, C (July 24, 1972), 46.

1826 Mankiewicz, Frank. "Fourth Estate--Chinese Boxes: Coverage of the Democratic Convention." Harper's, CCLIII (October 1976), 101-103.

1827 "Mass Media in Detroit for GOP Gathering." Broadcasting, XCIX (July 14, 1980), 20-22.

1828 Mayer, Martin. "Televising the Conventions." Harper's, CCXLIV (May 1972), 68-71.

1829 "Networks Gird for Coverage of Conventions." Broadcasting, XCI (July 12, 1976), 35-38.

1830 "Networks Labor Behind-the-Scenes for Intensive Convention Coverage." Broadcast Engineering, XXII (November 1980), 22-29.

1831 O'Connor, John J. "TV--Lively Convention: Reprinted from the New York Times, August 18, 1976." Congressional Record, CXXII (August 24, 1976), 27347.

1832 Paletz, David L. and Martha Elson. "Television Coverage of Presidential Conventions: Now You See, Now You Don't." Political Science Quarterly, XCI (Spring 1976), 109-131.

1833 Powers, Thomas. "Covering Carter." Commonweal, (July 30, 1976), 501-503.

1834 Rather, Dan. "Is Television the Real Power at the Convention? Hogwash!: An Interview." People, XIV (August 11, 1980), 37-38.

1835 Ryan, Michael. "Where the Action Is." TV Guide, XXIV (August 14, 1976), 3-10.

1836 Schardt, Allen. "TV's Rush to Judgment." Newsweek, XCVI (July 28, 1980), 72-73.

1837 "Stop the War: Television Coverage of the Republican Convention." Time, C (September 4, 1972), 38-39.
1838 Vanocur, Sander. "The K. C. Sound: Reprinted from the Washington Post, August 20, 1976." Congressional Record, CXXII (August 24, 1976), 27347.
1839 Walters, Barbara. "Out of the Mouths of Babes: Reprinted from the Washington Post, August 20, 1976." Congressional Record, CXXII (August 24, 1976), 27348-27349.
1840 Waters, Harry F. "Quadrennial Overkill: Covering the Democratic Convention." Newsweek, LXXX (July 24, 1972), 85-86.
1841 Womack, David and Jere R. Hoar. "Treatment of Candidates in Convention Floor Interviews." Journalism Quarterly, LVIII (Summer 1981), 300-302.

VII-D. DEBATES

1842 "Actually, It Was Exactly 26 Minutes." Broadcasting, XCI (October 4, 1976), 28-30.
1843 Berquest, Goodwin F. and James L. Golden. "Media Rhetoric, Criticism, and the Public Perception of the 1980 Presidential Debates." Quarterly Journal of Speech, LXVII (May 1981), 125-137.
1844 Bishop, George F., Robert G. Meadow, and Marilyn Jackson-Beech, eds. The Presidential Debates: Media, Electoral, and Policy Perspectives. New York: Praeger, 1978. 352p. Employing historical, political, and social perspectives, these pieces examine the impact of the 1976 debates on the American electorate and on learning/voting behavior.
1845 _____, Robert W. Oldendick, and Alfred J. Tuchfarber. "Debate Watching and the Acquisition of Political Knowledge." Journal of Communications. XXVIII (Autumn 1978), 99-113.
1846 Bitzer, Lloyd and Theodore Rueter. Carter vs. Ford: The Counterfeit Debates of 1976. Madison, Wisc.: University of Wisconsin Press, 1980. 438p. Explains that a variety of factors had a larger impact on the American electorate in 1976 than the televised presidential debates.
1847 Brydon, Steven R. "The Carter-Ford Television Debates: A Study in Campaign Communication." Unpublished PhD Dissertation, University of Southern California, 1979.
1848 "Carter-Reagan Debate: Bringing It All Together for Campaign '80." Broadcasting, XCIX (November 3, 1980), 23-24.
1849 Chaffee, Steven H. "Presidential Debates: Are They Helpful to Voters?" Communication Monographs, XLV (November 1978), 330-346.
1850 Commager, Henry S. "Washington Would Have Lost a TV Debate." New York Times Magazine, (October 30, 1960), 13, 79-80.
1851 Davis, Leslie K. "Camera Eye-Contact by the Candidates in the Presidential Debates of 1976." Journalism Quarterly, LV (Summer 1978), 431-437.

1852 "Debate Score: Kennedy Up, Nixon Down." Broadcasting,
      LIX (November 7, 1960), 27-29.
1853 "The Debates: A Symposium." Newsweek, LXXXVIII
      (September 27, 1976), 24-28.
1854 Ellsworth, John W. "Rationality and Campaigning: A
      Content Analysis of the 1960 Presidential Campaign Debates."
Western Political Quarterly, XVIII (December 1965), 794-802.
1855 Friel, Charlotte. "The Influence of Television in the
      Political Career of Richard M. Nixon, 1946-1962." Unpub-
      lished PhD Dissertation, New York University, 1968.
1856 Gans, Herbert J. "Debates: Lessons 1976 Can Offer
      1980." Columbia Journalism Review, XV (January 1977),
      25+.
1857 Goodman, Julian. "Broadcast Journalism--Serving the
      Democratic Process: An Address delivered at Ithaca
College, October 22, 1976." Congressional Record, CXXIII
(January 14, 1977), 1265-1267.
1858 Graber, Doris A. and Young Yun Kim. "The 1976 Presi-
      dential Debates and Patterns of Political Leadership."
Paper presented to the Annual Meeting of the Association for
the Education of Journalists, 1977. 29p. Available as ERIC
document ED 147 830.
1859 "Great Debate Rightly Named." Broadcasting, LIX (Octo-
      ber 3, 1960), 88-91.
1860 "The Great Debates: Nixon vs. Kennedy." TV Guide,
      VIII September 17, 1960), A1-A2.
1861 Halberstam, David.   "Presidential Video: The Nixon-
      Kennedy Debates." Esquire, LXXXV (June 1976), 94-97+.
1862 Jagoda, Barry. "Whither Debates?" Washington Journalism
      Review, I (November-December 1979), 30.
1863 Kelly, Stanley, Jr. "Campaign Debates: Some Facts and
      Issues." Public Opinion Quarterly, XXVI (Fall 1962), 351-
      366.
1864 Kraus, Sidney, ed. The Great Debates: Background,
      Perspectives, Effects. Bloomington, Ind.: Indiana Univer-
sity Press, 1962. 439p. In addition to a number of articles by
network figures and social scientists, this fine volume includes
a production diary and the transcripts of the four encounters.
1865 Lang, Kurt and Gladys E. "The First Debate and the
      Coverage Gap." Journal of Communications, XXVIII (Fall
      1978), 93-98.
1866 Meadow, Robert G. and Marilyn Jackson-Beech. "Issues
      Evolution: A New Perspective on Presidential Debates."
Journal of Communications, XXVIII (Autumn 1978), 84-92.
1867 NBC News. NBC and the Great Debates. New York:
      National Broadcasting Company [19617] 16p.
1868 Newman, Edwin. "The TV Debates: A Moderator's Reflec-
      tions." TV Guide, XXIV (October 30, 1976), A3-A4.
1869 "Old Glory: Kennedy-Nixon Debates." Newsweek, LXXXVIII
      (September 27, 1976), 33-34.
1870 Ranney, Austin, ed. Past and Future of Presidential
      Debates. AEI Studies, no. 228. Washington, D.C.:
American Enterprise Institute for Public Policy Research, 1979.
226p. Examines the history of presidential debates, especially

those of 1960 and 1976, in an effort to demonstrate the manner in which they may have affected election outcomes; offers a variety of projections (some borne out in 1980) on future influence, including the role of the networks in bringng the personalities and philosophies involved into the homes of the American electorate.

1871   "Re-viewing the '60 Debates." Time, CVIII (September 13, 1976), 12-13.

1872   Rieselbach, Leroy N. and Paul R. Hagner. "The Presidential Debates in the 1976 Campaign: A Panel Study." Paper presented at the Annual Meeting of the Midwest Political Science Association, 1977.

1873   Salant, Richard S. "The Television Debates: A Revolution That Deserves a Future." Public Opinion Quarterly, XXVI (Fall 1962), 335-350.

1874   Samovar, Larry A. "Ambiguity and Unequivocation in the Kennedy-Nixon Television Debates." Quarterly Journal of Speech, XLVIII (October 1962), 277-284.

1875   Seldes, Gilbert. "The Future of National Debates." Television Quarterly, I (August 1962), 62-68.

1876   "Shootout in Cleveland." Broadcasting, XCIX (October 27, 1980), 27-28.

1877   Simon, John. "Words Fail in Dim Debates." More, VI (November 1976), 34-35.

1878   "Stage Wait of 28 Minutes Mars First Great Debate." Broadcasting, XCI (September 27, 1961), 25-27.

1879   Stanton, Frank. "The Case for Political Debates on TV." New York Times Magazine, (January 14, 1964), 16, 68-70.

1880   _____. "Views on the Great Debates." Broadcasting, LIX (December 12, 1960), 51-52.

1881   "TV Debate Backstage: Did the Cameras Lie?" Newsweek, LXXII (October 10, 1960), 25.

1882   Twentieth Century Fund. Task Force on Televised Presidential Debates. With the Nation Watching: A Report. Boston, Mass.: Lexington Books, 1979. 144p.

1883   United States. Congress. House. Committee on House Administration. The Debates. Vol. III of its: The Presidential Campaign 1976. 94th Cong., 2nd sess. Washington, D.C.: U.S. Government Printing Office, 1979. 285p.

1884   United States. Congress. Senate. Committee on Commerce, Subcommittee on Communications. The Joint Appearances of Senator John F. Kennedy and Vice President Richard M. Nixon and Other 1960 Campaign Presentations. Part 3 of its: Freedom of Communications: Final Report. 87th Cong., 1st sess. Washington, D.C.: U.S. Government Printing Office, 1962. 699p.

VII-E.   CAMPAIGNS

1885   Arterton, F. Christopher. "The Media Politics of Presidential Campaigns." In: James D. Barber, ed. The Race for the Presidency. Englewood Cliffs, N.J.: Prentice-Hall, 1978. pp. 32-33.

1886 Bantz, Charles R. "Television News: Reality and Research." Western Speech, XXIX (1975), 123-130.
1887 Barber, James D. The Pulse of Politics: Electing Presidents in the Media Age. New York: W. W. Norton, 1980. 342p. Examines the role of the broadcast media (radio/tv) on the campaigns of various candidates since the 1920's with comments on the role of the media in helping to shape voter perceptions and provide insights on issues and personalities; interesting passages on how Al Smith fared so poorly on radio, how FDR employed it with so much success, and how John F. Kennedy seemed the perfect television candidate.
1888 Bendiner, Robert. White House Favor: An Innocent's Guide to Principles and Practices, Respectable and Otherwise, Behind the Election of American Presidents. New York: Harcourt, 1960. 180p. Includes a brief section on "The Impact of Televison."
1889 Broder, David S. "Political Reporters in Presidential Politics." Washington Monthly, I (February 1969), 20-33.
1890 Buss, Terry F. and C. Richard Hofstetter. "The Logic of Televised News Coverage of Political Campaign Information." Journalism Quarterly, LIV (Summer 1977), 341-349.
1891 Carey, John. "How the Media Shape Campaigns." Journal of Communications, XXVI (Spring 1976), 52-55+.
1892 Costello, Mary. "Presidential Campaign Coverage." Editorial Research Reports, I, no. 13 (1976), 1-18.
1893 Doan, Richard K. "TV's 32 Years of Election Coverage." TV Guide, XX (February 26, 1972), 8-24.
1894 Evans, Rowland, Kenneth P. O'Donnell, and Tom Walker. "TV in the Political Campaign." Television Quarterly, V (Winter 1965-1966),13-26.
1895 Gilbert, Robert E. Television and Presidential Politics. North Quincy, Mass.: Christopher Publishing House, 1972. 335p. Provides information on the effects of television on and in the campaigns of 1952 through 1968 with details on how the media was employed, both coverage and commercial wise.
1896 Greenfield, Jeff. "Campaign Reporting: Advice from a Double-Agent." Columbia Journalism Review, XIV (July 1975), 37-39.
1897 Hess, Stephen. The Presidential Campaign: The Leadership Selection Process After Watergate--An Essay. Washington, D,C,: Brookings Institution, 1974. 121p. Examines the difficulties in past campaigns, especially those of the 1960's and 1972, offering suggestions for improvements; revised in a 123 page edition from the same firm in 1978.
1898 Hickey, Neil. "How Presidential Candidates Get Free TV Time." TV Guide, XXIV (March 27, 1976), 4-7.
1899 Jacobson, Gary C. "The Impact of Broadcast Campaigning on Electoral Outcomes." Journal of Politics, XXXVII (August 1975), 769-793. Based on next entry.
1900 _____. "The Impact of Radio and Television on American Election Campaign." Unpublished PhD Dissertation, Yale University, 1972.

1901   Katz, Elihu.   "Platforms and Windows: Broadcasting's
       Role in Election Campaigns."   Journalism Quarterly, XLVIII
       (Summer 1971), 304-314.
1902   Leubedorf, Carl F.   "The Reporter and the Presidential
       Candidate."   Annals of the American Academy of Political
       and Social Science, no. 427 (September 1976), 1-11.
1903   McCombs, Maxwell E.   "Mass Communications in Political
       Campaigns."   In: F. Gerald Kline and Phillip J. Tichenor,
eds.   Current Perspectives in Mass Communications.   Beverely
Hills, Calif.:   Sage Publications, 1972.   pp. 170-177.
1904   Mickelson, Sig.   "The Candidate in the Living Room." An-
       nals of the American Academy of Political and Social Science,
       no. 427 (September 1976), 23-32.
1905   Neustadt, Richard E. and Richard Paisner.   "How to Run
       on TV: The Role of News Programs in Political Campaign-
ing."   New York Times Magazine, (December 15, 1974), 20+.
1906   Ostoff, D. H.   "A Participant-Observer Study of TV
       Campaign Coverage."   Journalism Quarterly, LVII (Autumn
       1980),   415-419.
1907   Patterson, Thomas E. and Robert D. McClure.   "Political
       Campaigns: TV Power is a Myth."   Psychology Today, X
       (July 1976), 61-64, 88-90.
1908   Phillips, Kevin.   "Why TV Ignores Minor Candidates for
       President."   TV Guide, XXIV (August 7, 1976), A3-A4.
1909   Porter, Richard D.   "Some Values to the Broadcaster of
       Election Campaign Broadcasting."   Journal of Broadcasting,
       VIII (Summer 1964), 8-26.
1910   Rubin, Bernard.   Political Television.   Belmont, Calif.:
       Wadsworth Publishing Co., 1967.   200p.   A study of how
television has reshaped presidential campaigns by, for the most
part, taking politics out of the streets and bringing it into the
home via the "box"; examines the theme of television influence
in the context of the campaigns of 1960 and 1964.
1911   Rubin, Richard L. and Douglas Rivers.   "The Mass Media
       and Critical Elections: A First Report."   Paper presented
to the Annual Meeting of the Northeastern Political Science
Association, November 1978.
1912   "Symposium: Covering the Political Campaign."   Journal
       of Communications, XXVIII (Autumn 1978), 80-138.
1913   Townley, Rod.   "TV's Campaign Polls: How Much Can We
       Believe?"   TV Guide, XXVIII (September 6, 1980), 23-26.
1914   United States. Congress. Senate.   Committee on Commerce,
       Subcommittee on Communications.   Freedom of Communica-
tions: Final Report.   6 pts.   87th Cong., 1st sess.   Washington, D.C.:   U.S. Government Printing Office, 1962.
1915   Warren, Sidney.   The Battle for the Presidency.   Phila-
       delphia, Pa.:   Lippincott, 1969.   426p.   A study of recent
(through 1968) presidential campaigns including the effect of
television since Nixon's "Checkers" speech of 1952.
1916   Wayne, Stephen J.   "News Coverage."   In: his The Road
       to the White House: The Politics of Presidential Elections.
       New York: St. Martin's Press, 1980.   pp. 207-223.
1917   Weitzner, Jay.   "Handling the Candidate on Television."
       In: Ray Hiebert, et al., eds.   The Political Image Mer-

chants: Strategies in the New Politics. Washington, D.C.: Acropolis Books, 1971. p. 102+.

1918 Wicker, Tom. "TV in the Political Campaign." Television Quarterly, IV (Spring 1965), 14+.

1919 Witcover, Jules. Marathon: The Pursuit of the Presidency, 1972-1976. New York: Viking Press, 1977. A huge examination of the period between the election of Richard Nixon to his second term and the election of Jimmy Carter with ample attention paid to the role of network news in covering the various issues and personalities involved.

1920 Wychoff, Gene. The Image Candidates: American Politics in the Age of Television. New York: Macmillan, 1969. 274p. Provides information on the role of television in various elections between 1956 and 1968, including its effect on Richard Nixon's 1960 campaign and the primaries in New Hampshire, Oregon, and California in 1964.

THE 1952, 1956, 1960 CAMPAIGNS

1921 Alton, A. J., et al. The Influence of Television on the Election of 1952. Oxford, Ohio: Oxford Research Associates, 1954. 177p. The 1952 campaign was, perhaps, the first to see widespread use of television for coverage and the presentation of commercials.

1922 Bradley, Rulon L. "The Use of Mass Media in the 1960 Election." Unpublished PhD Dissertation, University of Utah, 1962.

1923 CBS News. Conventions and Elections 1960: A Complete Handbook. Edited by Stanford M. Mirkin. New York: Channel Press, 1960. 122p. A guide to what reader's might expect to happen, with a few comments on the possible role of the media.

1924 CBS News. Watch: The Television Guide to the 1956 Conventions, the Campaign, and the Election. New York: Maco Magazine Corp., 1956. 95p. A guide put out before the enterprise got under way.

1925 Campbell, Angus. "Has Television Reshaped Politics?" Columbia Jounalism Review, I (Fall, 1962), 10-13.

1926 Cronkite, Walter. "Campaign Conniptions." TV Guide, IV (September 29, 1956), 18-19.

1927 Hughes, Emmett J. "52 Million TV Sets: How Many Votes?" New York Times Magazine, (September 25, 1960), 23, 78-80.

1928 Markland, Ben C. "Evasiveness in Political Discussion Broadcasts During the 1952 Election." Unpublished PhD Dissertation, University of Michigan, 1955.

1929 Martin, John B. "The Campaign for President, 1952." In: his Adlai Stevenson of Illinois. Garden City, N.Y.: Doubleday, 1976. pp. 605-765.

1930 _____. "The Great Campaign of 1956." In: his Adlai Stevenson and the World. Garden City, N.Y.: Doubleday, 1977. pp 232-348.

1931 Nixon, Richard M. "The Fund." In: his Six Crises. Garden City, N.Y.: Doubleday, 1962. pp. 73-130.

1932 _____. "The Campaign of 1960." In: his Six Crises.
Garden City, N.Y.: Doubleday, 1962. pp. 293-426.
1933 Roucek, Joseph S. "The Influences of Television on
American Politics." Il Politico, XXVIII (Spring 1963),
124-147.
1934 Severeid, Eric, ed. Candidates, 1960: Behind the Headlines in the Presidential Race. New York: Basic Books,
1960. 369p. Nine correspondents describe seven candidates
active prior to the conventions.
1935 Thomson, Charles A. H. "Mass Media Activities and
Influence." In: Paul T. David, ed. The Presidential
Election and Transition, 1960-1961. Washington, D.C.: Brookings Institution, 1961. p. 90+.
1936 _____. Television and Presidential Politics: The Experience of 1952 and the Problems Ahead. Washington, D.C.:
Brookings Institution, 1956. 173p. An examination of the effects of television on voter behavior (e.g., Nixon's "Checkers"
speech) and turnout, commercials aimed at political persuasion,
and a prophecy concerning the future.
1937 _____. and Frances M. Shattuck. The 1956 Presidential
Campaign. Westport, Conn.: Greenwood Press, 1974.
382p. A detailed analysis reprinted from the 1960 first edition.
1938 United States. Congress. Senate. Committee on Commerce,
Subcommittee on Communications. The 15-Minute Radio and
Television Newscasts for the Period September 26 through November 7, 1960. Part IV of its: Freedom of Communications: Final
Report. 87th Cong., 1st session. Washington, D.C.: U.S.
Government Printing Office, 1962.
1939 White, Theodore H. The Making of the President, 1960.
New York: Atheneum, 1961. 400p. One of the most
famous histories of presidential campaigning ever written,
White's best-seller includes some comments on the role of net-
work news and television, especially the "Great Debates."

THE 1964 CAMPAIGN

1940 CBS News, Election Unit. 1964 Guide to Convention and
Elections. Edited by Stanford E. Mirkin. New York:
Dell, 1964. 256p. A preparatory handbook on candidates,
parties, and possible events, including media coverage.
1941 Cummings, Milton C., ed. The National Election of 1964.
Washington, D.C.: Brookings Institution, 1967. 245p. A
study of the various facets influencing the outcome; includes a
section on the role of television and the print press.
1942 Hess, Karl. In a Game That will Triumph: The Goldwater
Campaign and the Future of Conservation. Garden City,
N.Y.: Doubleday, 1967. 231p. Goldwater's speechwriter
examines the reasons behind the defeat of the 1964 Republican
candidate, castigating network news reporters among others.
1943 Mohr, Charles. "Requiem for a Lightweight." Esquire,
LXXIX (August 1968), 67-71, 121-122. Goldwater's 1964
press relations.
1944 Shadegg, Stephen. What Happened to Goldwater?: The
Inside Story of the 1964 Republican Campaign. New York:

Holt, 1966. 280p. Another examination of the causes of the Republican defeat; this too claims a hostile print and electronic media.
1945   Shalit, Gene, ed. Somehow It Works: A Candid Portrait of the 1964 Presidential Election, by NBC News. Garden City, N.Y.: Doubleday, 1965. 223p. A review of the Gold-water-Johnson campaign from the vantage point of correspondents of NBC News.
1946   Thomson, Charles A. H. "The Name Media." In: Milton C. Cummings, Jr., ed. The National Election of 1964. Washington, D.C.: Brookings Institution, 1966. pp. 111-157.
1947   White, Theodore H. The Making of the President, 1964. New York: Atheneum, 1965. 431p. Perhaps the fullest possible journalistic account with considerable mention of the media's influence.

THE 1968 CAMPAIGN

1948   Aiken, George B. "The Triumph of Media Over Matter: Vietnam and the '68 Elections." War/Peace Report, VIII (March 1968), 14-16.
1949   American Institute for Political Communication. "'Media Dependence and Credibility--General Public and Influentals' [and] 'Media Influence on Political Decision-Making." In: its The 1968 Campaign: Anatomy of a Critical Election. Washington, D.C., 1970. pp. 89-103.
1950   _____. The 1968 Campaign: Anatomy of a Critical Election. Washington, D.C., 1970.
1951   Chester, Lewis, Godfrey Hodgson, and Bruce Page. An American Melodrama: The Presidential Campaign of 1968. New York: 814p. A massive study originally penned for a British audience, which takes the story from the New Hampshire primaries through the conventions to election night; includes comments on the perceived influence of network news.
1952   Cott, Suzanne. "The Function of Television in the Presidential Election Campaign of 1968." Unpublished PhD Dissertation, Columbia University, 1972.
1953   English, David. Divided They Stand. Englewood Cliffs, N.J.: Prentice-Hall, 1969. 428p. Another chronicle of the crisis-laden 1968 election; this work looks at the differences between the major candidates on such issues as Vietnam and Civil Rights.
1954   Graber, Doris. "The Press as Opinion Resource on the 1968 Presidential Campaign." Public Opinion Quarterly, XXXV (Summer 1971), 168-172.
1955   _____. "Press Coverage Patterns of Campaign News: The 1968 Presidential Race." Journalism Quarterly, XLVIII (Autumn 1971), 501-512.
1956   Hickey, Neil and Richard K. Doan. "It Began in New Hampshire." TV Guide, XVI (December 7, 1968), 7-9.
1957   Just, Ward S. "Great Moments in American Journalism: Television's Ascendency Over the Press." Atlantic, CCXLV (January 1980), 37-39.

1958   McGinniss, Joe.   The Selling of the President, 1968.   New
        York: Trident Press, 1969.   253p.   From the viewpoint of
this guide, the most telling work to emerge from the 1968
elections; McGinniss chronicles the manner in which Richard
Nixon and his associates "packaged" the Republican national
ticket in such a fashion as to make it appear, via commercials
and "media events," much more palatable than the crisis-ridden
Democrats.

1959   NBC News.   The Huntley-Brinkley Chronicle and NBC
        News Supplement to Election Year Viewing.   New   York:
        National Broadcasting Company, 1968.   15p.

1960   Robinson, John F.   "Perceived Media Bias and the 1968
        Vote: Can the Media Affect Behavior After All?"   Journa-
        lism Quarterly, XLIX (Summer 1972), 239-246.

1961   Whale, John.   The Half-Shut Eye: Television and Politics
        in Britain and America.   New York: St. Martin's Press,
1970.   219p.   Studies the impact of network television on politics
in both Great Britain and the United states, with the American
example being the 1968 presidential campaign.

1962   White, Theodore H.   The Making of the President,1968.
        New York: Atheneum, 1969.   459p.   The third in White's
award-winning series, this title includes ample coverage of the
role of the media in the campaign.

THE 1972 CAMPAIGN

1963   Alternative Educational Foundation.   Report on Network
        News Treatment of the 1972 Democratic Presidential Candi-
        dates.   Bloomington, Ind., 1972.   245p.

1964   Bagdikian, Ben H.   "Election Coverage '72:   The Fruits
        of Agnewism."   Columbia Journalism Review, XI (January-
        February 1973), 9-23.

1965   Black, Edwin.   "Electing Time."   Quarterly Journal of
        Speech, LIX (Spring 1973), 125-129.

1966   CBS News.   CBS News, Campaign '72:   Special Research
        Bulletin.   New York: Holt Information Systems, 1972.
        Unpaged.

1967   Crouse, Timothy.   The Boys on the Bus: Riding with
        the Campaign Press Corps.   New York: Random House,
1973.   383p.   "The" 1972 election history in journalism circles;
Crouse explains what it was like for print and broadcast reporters to follow the 1972 candidates, deal with their media staffs,
and participate in a number of "media events."

1968   Doan, Richard K.   "TV Watches Election '72."   TV Guide,
        XX (March 4, 1972), 8-12.

1969   Doll, Howard and Bert Bradley.   "A Study of the Objec-
        tivity of Television News Reporting of the 1972 Presidential
Campaign."   Central States Speech Journal,   XXV   (Summer
1974), 254-263.

1970   Einsiedel, Edna F.   "Television Network News Coverage of
        the Eagleton Affair: A Case Study."   Journalism Quarterly,
        LII (Spring 1975), 56-60.

1971   Evarts, Dru and Guido H. Stempel.   "Coverage of the
       1972 Campaign by TV, News Magazine, and Major News-
papers."   Journalism Quarterly, II   (Winter   1974),   645-648.
1972   Frank, Robert S.   Message Dimensions of Television News
       Lexington, Mass.:   D.C. Heath, 1973.   120p.   In an effort
to more accurately portray the various characteristics of network news, the author studies the message content of 1972
campaign broadcasts.
1973   Greene, Bob.   Running: Nixon-McGovern.   Chicago,
       Ill.:   Henry Regnery,   1975.   267p.   One journalist's
recollections of covering the candidates in the 1972 election
campaign; a print reporter, Greene now works for ABC News.
1974   Hofstetter, C. Richard.   Bias in the News: Network
       Television Coverage of the 1972 Election Campaign.   Colum-
bus, Ohio: Ohio State University Press, 1976.   213p.   An
extraordinary attempt to monitor the more than 4,000 campaign
stories broadcast on the evening news shows of the three
commercial networks between July 10 and November 6, 1972
using advanced techniques of social-scientific analysis in an
effort to uncover bias for or against various candidates; the
results provide food for thought by both critics and proponents
of the role of network news in presidential coverage.
1975   _____, and Cliff Zukin. "TV Network News and Adver-
       tising in the Nixon and McGovern Campaign." Journalism
       Quarterly, LVI (Spring 1979), 106-115, 152.
1976   Isaacs, Stephen.   "Election Coverage '72:   Were Polls
       Overemphasized?"   Columbia Journalism Review, XI (Janu-
       ary-February 1973), 29-30.
1977   Kiebs, Albin.   "Walter Cronkite: Do Politicians Fool the
       TV Camera and You?"   Good Housekeeping, CLXXV (July
       1972), 32+.
1978   Lowry, Dennis T.   "Measures of Network News Bias in
       the 1972 Presidential Campaign?" Journal of Broadcasting,
       CLXXV (Fall 1974), 387-402.
1979   McClure, Robert D. and Thomas E. Patterson.   "Television
       News and Political Advertising: The Impact of Exposure
and Voter Beliefs."   Communication Research, I (January 1974),
3-31.
1980   Malaney, Carl D. and Terry F. Buss.   "AP Wire Reports
       vs.   CBS News Coverage of a Presidential Campaign."
       Journalism Quarterly, LVI (Autumn 1979), 602-610.
1981   Meadow, Robert G.   "Cross-Media Comparison of Coverage
       of the 1972 Presidential Campaign." Journalism Quarterly,
       L (Autumn 1973), 482-488.
1982   Myers, Davis S.   "Editorials and Foreign Affairs in the
       1972 Presidential Campaign."   Journalism Quarterly, LI
       (Summer 1974), 251-257.
1983   NBC News.   "Chronicles of One Television Network's
       Campaign Coverage During the Last Month of the 1972
Election."   In: Thomas E. Patterson and Robert D. McClure.
The Unseeing Eye: The Myth of Television Power in National
Elections.   New York: G. P. Putnam, 1976.   pp.   42-46,
208-218.

1984   Patterson, Thomas E. and Robert D. McClure. "Political
       Campaigns: TV Power is a Myth." Psychology Today, X
       (July 1976), 61-62+.
1985   . The Unseeing Eye: The Myth of Television
       Power in National Politics. New York: G. P. Putnam,
1976. 218p. Based on extensive campaign research (though
perhaps not quite so extensive as Hofstetter's), the conclusion
here is that network news had no effect on voter decisions in
1972.
1986   Perry, James M. Us and Them: How the Press Covered
       the 1972 Election. New York: Clarkson N. Potter, 1973.
292p. After four years of government attack headed by Spiro
T. Agnew, the press still found itself able to search out the
hard news stories and report them to the American electorate.
1987   Sevenson, David L. "Political Information, Influence, and
       Judgment in the 1972 Presidenial Campaign." Quarterly
       Journal of Speech, LIX (Spring 1973), 130-142.
1988   "TV Campaign Coverage." Senior Scholastic, CIX (Sep-
       tember 9 and 23, 1976), 12-13, 18-19.
1989   Thompson, Hunter S. Fear and Loathing: On the Cam-
       paign Trail, '72. New York: Popular Library, 1974.
512p. Another look at the trials and difficulties faced by
reporters trying to cover the 1972 campaign, especially that of
Richard Nixon.
1990   White, Theodore H. The Making of the President, 1972.
       New York: Atheneum, 1973. 391p. The last in White's
popular series, this title gives some thought to the role of the
media in covering the campaign.
1991   Witcover, Jules. "Election Coverage '72: The Trials of a
       One-Candidate Campaign." Columbia Journalism Review,
       XI (January-February 1973), 24-28.
1992   . "How We Missed the McGovern Phenomenon."
       Columbia Journalism Review, XI (September-October 1972),
       38-41.

THE 1976 CAMPAIGN

1993   Aulette, Ken. "Covering Carter is Like Playing Chess
       with Bobby Fischer." More, VI (October 1976), 12+.
1994   "The Broadcasting Media and the Political Process, 1976.
       Broadcasting, XCII (January 3, 1977), 33-76.
1995   Friedman, Howard S., M. Robin DiMatteo, and Timothy I.
       Mertz. "Non-verbal Communication on Television News:
The Facial Expressions of [Five Network] Broadcasters During
Coverage of a Presidential Election Campaign." Personality and
Social Psychology, VI (September 1980), 427-435.
1996   Gold, Vic. "The Making of the President, 1976." Wash-
       ington Monthly, XI (March 1976), 100+.
1997   . PR as in President: A Pro Looks at Press
       Agents, Media and the 1976 Candidates. Garden City,
N.Y.: Doubleday, 1977. 251p. Examines the co-ordination of
media use by the paid press and tv commercial pros in both the
Carter and Ford camps.

1998   Hickey, Neil. "How TV Will Cover the 1976 Election."
       TV Guide, XXIV (January 31, 1976), 3-5.
1999   Kline, F. Gerald. "Media Vital to Current Political Cam-
       paign." Rackham Reports, III (1976), 2+.
2000   Mowlana, Hamid. "The Mass Media and the 1976 Presiden-
       tial Campaign." Intellect, CV (February 1977), 244-245.
2001   Patterson, Thomas E. The Mass Media Election: How
       Americans Choose Their President. New York: Praeger,
1980. 220p. One of the most comprehensive studies ever done
on news coverage of presidential candidates, Patterson's study
is based on interviews with 1,250 people and demonstrates the
complex relationship between the media and the public.
2002   Reeves, Richard. "Mea Culpa: The Candidates Were Not
       the Only Clowns." New York, IX (November 15, 1976),
       142.
2003   Roberts, Churchill L. "Media Use and Difficulty of
       Decision in the 1976 Presidential Campaign." Journalism
       Quarterly, LVI (Winter 1979), 794-802.
2004   Ryan, Michael. "As America Decides." TV Guide, XXIV
       (October 30, 1976), 4-6.
2005   Schram, Martin. Running for President 1976: The Carter
       Campaign. New York: Stein & Day, 1977. 406p. Follows
the Georgian's efforts from June 9, 1975 to November 1976
making a variety of comments on media coverage and devoting
three chapters to the television debates with President Ford.
2006   Swanson, David L. "And That's the Way It Is: Was?:
       Television Coverage of the 1976 Presidential Campaign."
       Quarterly Journal of Speech, LXIII (Fall 1977), 239-248.
2007   Swertlow, Frank S. "Election '76: How TV Will Cover
       the Issues." TV Guide, XXIV (April 24, 1976), 4-6.
2008   United States. Congress. House. Committee on House
       Administration. The Presidential Campaign 1976. 3 vols.
in 5. 94th Cong., 2nd sess. Washington, D.C.: U.S. Government Printing Office, 1979.
2009   Weaver, David H., et al., eds. Media-Agenda-Setting
       in a Presidential Election: Issues, Images, and Interest.
New York: Praeger, 1981. 238p. Agenda-setting, defined as
including those candidates, issues, and impressions to be covered during the entire campaign, is studied in terms of interviews with 1,000 people in three different kinds of communities
and content analysis of the thousands of newspaper and network news stories which appeared; for our purposes, the
conclusions are that television coverage of a campaign plays its
major role as a stimulant of voter interest thereby causing
greater attention to and learning from campaign coverage.
2010   Weaver, Paul H. "Captives of Melodrama." New York
       Times Magazine, (August 29, 1976), 6, 48-56.

THE 1980 CAMPAIGN

2011   Arlen, Michael J. "Modulating of the Presidency." New
       Yorker, LVI (Octobe 1980), 172-174.
2012   Bonafede, Dom. "The Boys on the Run, 1980." Washing-
       ton Journalism Review, I (November-December 1979),
       22-25.

2013   Brokaw, Tom.   "TV and the Election."   USA Today, CVIII (June 1980), 15.

2014   "Candidates--Getting Their Acts Together: A Special Report."   Broadcasting, XCVII (November 5, 1979), 30+.

2015   "Covering the Campaign: Top Newspaper and Network Chiefs Reveal Strategy on Horse-Race Issues, Rotating Reporters, and Playing The Polls."   Washington Journalism Review, II (October 1980), 38-41.

2016   Diamond, Edwin.   "Beyond Narcissus and Media Events." Washington Journalism Review, II (October 198), 23.

2017   _____.   "The Search for the Smoking Gun."   Washington Journalism Review, IV (April 1982), 19.

2018   Drew, Elizabeth. Portrait of an Election: The 1980 Presidential Campaign.   New York: Simon and Schuster, 1981. 459p.   A collection of New Yorker pieces written during the campaign '80 season which reflect not only the issues and personalities, but the changing political climate as well.

2019   "Early Retrospect on Campaign '80."   Broadcasting, XCIX (October 27, 1980), 29-31.

2020   Evans, Katherine W.   "Candidates and Their Gurus Criticize Coverage." Washington Journalism Review, II (September 1980), 28-31.

2021   Germond, Jack W. and Jules Witcover.   Blue Smoke and Mirrors: How Reagan Won and Why Carter Lost the Election of 1980.   New York: Viking Press, 1981.   337p.   Explains how Jimmy Carter came to be perceived as a weak chief executive in a time of crisis (Iran) and how Reagan, professing and portraying traditional leadership virtues was able to capitalize on his excellent media perception.

2022   Glass, Andrew J. "Carter's Press Operation." Washington Journalism Review, II (October 1980), 36.

2023   Greenfield, Jeff.   "How You Can Get Elected by Using Television."   Panorama, I (June 1980), 60-65.

2024   _____.   Playing to Win: An Insider's Guide to Politics. New York: Simon and Schuster, 1980.   259p.   The well-known CBS critic contends that "television has changed our political life less radically than you have been told," suggesting that the influence of network news coverage on the outcome of elections is more myth than reality.

2025   _____.   The Real Campaign: The Media and the Battle for the White House.   New York: Simon and Schuster, 1982.   288p.   The CBS commentator on the 1980 presidential campaign demonstrates that the media covered that event with very little reference to the issues and a deep day-to day concern not with the political process but with the battle for votes, leading to such false starts as saturation coverage of the Florida straw vote, how Anderson's campaign affected media coverage of Ronald Reagan, usage of the polls by the media, and the untrue picture of an election "too close to call"; the electorate, the author contends, knew of these weaknesses and made up its mind the best it could.

2026   Larson, C. U.   "The Influence of Mass Media Coverage on Campaign '80."   USA Today, CIX (March 1981), 61-63.

2027   Leubsdorf, Carl P. "Reagan's Press Operation." Washington Journalism Review, II (October 1980), 37.

2028   MacNeil, Robert. "The Edge of Apathy." Dial, I (Septem-
       ber 1980), 33-37.
2029   Moore, Jonathan, ed. The Campaign for President: 1980
       in Retrospect.   New   York: Ballanger, 1981.   304p.
Proceedings of a conference held in December 1980 at the John
F. Kennedy School of Government, Harvard University; contains
some comments on the role of the media.
2030   Nessen, Ron.   "Now Television's the Kingmaker."   TV
       Guide, XXVIII (May 10, 1980), 4-8.
2031   Phillips, Dean and Erica Max.   "Covering Campaign Eco-
       nomic Issues, Trying to Make Love to a Porcupine...."
Washington Journalism Review, II (July-August 1980), 43-47+.
2032   "Reflections on the Media and the Campaigns."   Broad-
       casting, XCIX (November 24, 1980), 54-55+.
2033   Robinson, Michael J. and Margaret Sheehan. "The Elev-
       enth-Hour Conversion of CBS: How the Networks Learned
to Love the Issues in the 1980 Presidential Campaign."
Washington Journalism Review, II (December 1980), 15-19.
2034   Salant, Richard S.   "Report the Issues!"   Washington
       Journalism Review. I (November-December 1979), 46-47.
2035   Scheer, Robert. What Happened?: The Story of Election
       1980.   New York: Random House, 1981.   Attempts to
assess the variety of factors, economic, foreign, political,
personality, expectations, and others which changed the electorate's opinion of Carter in favor of Reagan; includes thoughts
on the role of the media.
2036   Schorr, Daniel. "The Television Factor." Geo, II (Novem-
       ber 1980), 152-153.
2037   Simon, Roger. "Campaign Reporting Hazards of the Trade:
       Beer Bombs, Tedium, and Defiant Crews." Panorama, I
       (November 1980), 6-7.
2038   .   "Message to Losing Candidates: Don't Blame
       TV." Panorama, I (September 1980), 9+.
2039   Stacks, John F. Watershed: The Campaign for the Presi-
       dency, 1980.   New York: Times Books, 1982.   288p.   In
a somewhat shorter book, Stacks attempts to do what White does
in entry 2044:   assess the mood of America and show how
politics went from liberal to conservative, sufficient enough to
see Reagan elected with a Republican majority in the U.S.
Senate.
2040   Swerdlow, Joel. "The Decline of the Boys on the Bus."
       Washington Journalism Review, III (January-February 1981),
       14-20.
2041   Townley, Rod.   "Waiting for Election Night."   TV Guide,
       XXVIII (October 25, 1980), 2-5.
2042   Weisman, John and Sally Bedell.   "Something is Missing in
       TV's Political Coverage."   TV Guide, XXVIII (July 5,
       1980), 24-30.
2043   White, Ray, ed. "Press on Press: The 1980 Campaign."
       Washington Journalism Review, II (January-February 1980),
       55-63.
2044   White, Theodore H.   American in Search of Itself: The
       Making of the President, 1956-1980.   New York: Harper &
Row, 1982.   480p.   White's tale is more than just that of the
election campaign of 1980 or of those since 1956 prior to it, but

of the flows and stresses in American society since the time of Dwight D. Eisenhower; the role of the media and the growth of electronic journalism is covered.

VII-F. ELECTION NIGHT COVERAGE

2045 Bohn, Thomas W. "Broadcasting National Election Returns, 1952-1980." Journal of Communications, XXX (Autumn 1978), 140-153.

2046 Brown, James and Paul I. Hain. "Reporting the Vote on Election Night." Journal of Communications, XXVIII (Autumn 1978), 132-139.

2047 "CBS News Returns fo Election Night Coverage." Broadcasting, LXVIII (September 21, 1964), 90-91.

2048 Cronkite, Walter. "Victorygraph--The CBS Election Night Program: An Interview." New Yorker, XLII (November 5, 1966), 51-53.

2049 Edwin, Ed. "How to Pick the Winner on Election Night." TV Guide, VIII (November 5, 1960), 5-9.

2050 "Election Night Razzle-Dazzle." Time, CXVI (November 3, 1980), 74.

2051 "Election Night Sponsors Get Their Money's Worth." Broadcasting, LIX (November 14, 1960), 36+.

2052 "Electronic Vote Analysis and Digital-to-Video Converter Aid NBC's Election Team." Broadcasting, LXVII (October 26, 1964), 60+.

2053 Hickey, Neil. "How TV Will Count the Votes." TV Guide, XVI (November 2, 1968), 6-9.

2054 _____. "November 3: The Night of the Computer." TV Guide, XII (October 31,1964), 6-9.

2055 _____. "TV Covers Election Night." TV Guide, XX (November 4, 1972), 8-12.

2056 "How Networks Plan to Cover the Election." Broadcasting, LXVII (November 2, 1964), 30-32.

2057 James, Edwin. "The Trouble $2,475,000 Can Buy." Television, XXI (December 1964), 72-86. NBC computer problems.

2058 Kerrigan, Marybeth. "We Interrupt This Election." Washington Journalism Review, III (September 1981), 15-16.

2059 "Long Night at the Races." Time, CVIII (November 15, 1976), 84-85.

2060 Lubell, Samuel. "The New Technology of Election Reporting." Columbia Journalism Review, III (Summer 1964), 4-8.

2061 "One Hundred Million Box Seats for the Show." TV Guide, IV (August 11, 1956) 4-7.

2062 Pepper, Robert. "Election Night, 1972: Television Network Coverage." Journal of Broadcasting, XVIII (Winter 1973-1974), 27-38.

2063 Ryan, Michael. "Election '76: How TV Will Cover the Big Night." TV Guide, XXIV (October 30, 1976), 4-6.

2064 Skedgell, Robert A. "How Computers Pick an Election Winner." Trans-action, IV (November 1966), 42-46.

2065 Waters, Harry F. "The Peacock's [NBC] Night to Crow."
Newsweek, XCVI (November 17, 1980), 82.
2066 "The Winner is . . . ." Newsweek, LXXII (November 4,
1968), 72-73.

VII-G. INAUGURATION COVERAGE

2067 Edwin, Ed. "TV Covers the Inauguration." TV Guide,
IX (January 14, 1961), 17-19.
2068 "Hail to the Chief: Reporting the Inaugural." Time, LIII
(January 31, 1949), 55.
2069 "Inauguration by Video." Newsweek, XXXIII (January
31, 1949), 49.
2070 "Johnson's Inauguration a Broadcaster's Field Day." Broadcasting, LXVIII (January 25, 1965), 72-73.
2071 "TV Covers the Inauguration." TV Guide, V (January
19, 1957), 6-7.
2072 Weisman, John. "The Inauguration of Jimmy Carter."
TVGuide, XXV (January 15, 1977), 4-6.
2073 _____. "It's a Great American Tradition." TV Guide,
XXIX (January 17, 1981), 6-8. A general review of television coverage of past inaugurals, with a look ahead to Reagan's.

VIII. TELEVISION NETWORK NEWS AND THE
FOREIGN AFFAIRS/DEFENSE COMMUNITIES

The foreign correspondent, sometimes doubling as war reporter, has been a feature of broadcast journalism almost from its inception. Some of the great names in network television news history received their training or early distinction as overseas commentators, men such as Walter Cronkite, Charles Collingwood, Eric Sevareid, Howard K. Smith, and the legendary Edward R. Murrow, in radio first and then in the new medium of television. Indeed it has sometimes been said that for a network correspondent to become a well-rounded reporter, he must demonstrate effectiveness in the overseas tour. For some the tour is rather short and undistinguished, but for others, such as ABC's Peter Jennings or CBS's Morley Safer, foreign duty marks the beginning of long foreign service and great distinction.

Is there an ebb-and-flow to foreign news on American television? Watching it night after night, "news buffs" might be inclined to suggest that there is. As this guide was completed, a recent crisis had been the lead on each evening news broadcast--that involving the war between Britain and Argentina over the Falkland Islands, or Malvinas. Every night for a couple of months, America saw either first or second on each network's (including CNN) evening news shows reports concerning the key events, ships, planes, personalities, and issues. The South Atlantic shooting war replaced a series of other crises, such as El Salvador, Poland, Iran, and Afghanistan, which competed for dominancy in the news as had Vietnam, the Cuban crises, Suez, and the Korean War. The thirty-year un-peace in the Middle East may hold the record for providing evening news stories, but in the spring of 1982, unless a terrorist bomb exploded, the Middle East receded to the "back page" of network coverage in favor of the Falklands.

One of the more interesting, and little noticed, facets of foreign news coverage in the 1980's was recently brought home in a summation of an ABC Viewpoint broadcast by Ted Koppel. The technology of television today is such that viewers sitting in their living room have the world literally at their fingertips in a manner unknown a few decades ago. Satellites make it possible for one to almost believe that everything reported from around the globe is occurring simultaneously and is instantly covered--even though half the world is asleep when the network news evening shows air. ABC's World News Tonight is predicated on the fact that one of its three anchors reports nightly by satellite from London and while it is dinner time here, it is after midnight in Great Britain. Technoloy and time are almost merged; indeed, one might have marveled as he watched simultaneous reports from London and Buenos Aires on the Falklands/Malvinas crisis that it was nighttime on the Thames as the sun shone over the Pampas.

Central to foreign news coverage is war reporting. Many of the subsections below deal with wars. Directly connected is the provision of information concerning national defense. Here government secrets are sometimes a stumbling block, but information often emerges, for example, My Lai, the "stealth bomber," etc. In only a few cases, such as during the Cuban missile crisis, have government pleas for secrecy been upheld. It was also revealed in the mid-1970's that certain newsmen and networks had connections with the CIA, while to this day controversy surrounds the manner in which news of international terrorism is reported.

The citations in this section address the questions of foreign news coverage by American network television news since the days of the Korean War, the relationship of the electronic press to the defense and intelligence communities, and the role of electronic journalism in covering stories in various regions and nations around the globe, including those dealing with terrorism.

VIII-A.   NATIONAL DEFENSE

2074   Baker, Brent. "Leakology: The War of Words." U.S. Naval Institute Proceedings, CIII (July 1977), 43-49.

2075   Bant, Bruce N. "The Pentagon Said Today . . . ." Soldiers, XXXIII (May 1978), 45-49.

2076   Brozska, Michael. "The Reporting of Military Expenditures." Journal of Peace Research, XVIII (Summer 1981), 261-275.

2077   Buchanan, Patrick. "Military Spending: Are We Hearing All the Facts?" TV Guide, XXII (May 25, 1974), A3-A4.

2078   "CBS Charged with Undercovering Advocates of Military Power." Broadcasting, XCI (September 13, 1976), 28+.

2079   Clotfelter, James and B. G. Peters. "The Mass Media and the Military: Selected Ratings of Fairness." Journalism Quarterly, LI (Summer 1974), 332-333.

2080   Curry, Jerry R. ". . .And That's the Way It Is?: The Military and the Media." Defense 80, no. 6 (June 1980), 19-24.

2081   Edwards, Douglas. "The Role of the News Media: An Address to the American Logistics Association 1972 Convention." Review, LII (November-December 1972), 25+.

2082   Gervazi, Thomas. "The Doomsday Beat." Columbia Journalism Review, XVIII (May 1979), 34-40.

2083   Heise, Juergen A. "Defense Department Handling of Negative, Unrestricted Information of Interest to the Media." Unpublished PhD Dissertation, Syracuse University, 1975.

2084   _____. Minimum Disclosure: How the Pentagon Manipulates the News. New York: W. W. Norton, 1979. 221p.

Revised from the author's PhD dissertation cited below; examines the secrecy and censorship procedures of the U.S. military, specifically as they relate to giving information to representatives of the media for dissemination to the public.

2085 Hersh, Seymour N. "But Don't Tell Anyone I Told You: Private Briefings of the Pentagon Press Corps by Top Officials." New Republic, CLVII (December 9, 1967), 13-14.

2086 Hofstetter, C. Richard and David W. Moore. "Watching TV News and Supporting the Military--A Suprising Impact of the News Media." Armed Forces and Society, V (Winter 1979), 261-269.

2087 Kondracks, Norton. "Eye on the Pentagon: Is TV Telling Us Enough?" TV Guide, XXVII (August 25, 1979), 2-10.

2088 Lefever, Ernest W. TV and National Defense: An Analysis of CBS News, 1972-1973. Boston, Va.: Institute for American Strategy Press, 1975. 209p. An often noted study by pro-military scholars, based on a content examination of the CBS Evening News and 60 Minutes programs recorded by the Vanderbilt News Archive for the period; emphasis is on the "bias" demonstrated by those programs in their handling of military and national defense issues.

2089 Massing, Michael. "The 'Invisible' Story." Columbia Journalism Review, XIX (November-December 1980), 51-52+.

2090 Migdail, Carl J. "A Perspective of the Military and the Media." Naval War College Review, XXVIII (Winter 1976), 2-9.

2091 "Military-Media Symposium at the Naval War College." Naval War College Review, XXV (January-February 1973), 48-51.

2092 Norman, Lloyd. "The Love-Hate Affair Between the Pentagon and the Press." Army, XXX (Febuary 1980), 14-20.

2093 Schemmer, Benjamin F. and Robin J. Stein. "The Reporters Who Bring You the Defense News--and How They Rate the Men Who Make It." Armed Forces Journal International, CXVI (August 1979), 20-22+.

2094 Singletary, W. "Attitudes of Military Censors and Other Officers on Mass Media Issues." Journalism Quarterly, LIV (Winter 1977), 727-732.

2095 United States. Department of the Army. Field Press Censorship. Field Manual 45-25. Washington, D.C., 1967. 82p.

2096 White, Jack M. "The Military and the Media." U.S. Naval Institute Proceedings, C (July 1974), 47-51.

2097 Williams, John D. "Interaction: The Military and the Media." Air University Review, XXVI (November-December 1974), 54-58.

2098 Wise, Kenneth L. "The War News System." Unpublished PhD Dissertion, American University, 1967.

2099 Witcover, Jules. "The Surliest Crew in Washington: The Two Dozen Correspondents Who Spend Their Working Lives in the Pentagon." Columbia Journalism Review, IV (Spring 1965), 11-15.

2100 Zubkoff, Harry M. "News--of Views?" Strategic Review, I (Summer 1976), 104-110.

VIII-B. THE C.I.A.

2101 Bagdikian, Ben H. "An Unsecretive Report on the CIA."
New York Times Magazine, (October 27, 1963), 184.
2102 Barbosa, Roberto. "The CIA and the Press: Foreign
Reactions to Disclosures of Media Manipulation." Atlas,
XXV (March 1978), 22-25.
2103 Bernstein, Carl. "The CIA and the Media: How America's
Most Powerful News Media [CBS] Worked Hand in Glove
with the CIA and Why the Church Committee Covered It Up."
Rolling Stone, (October 20, 1977), 55-67.
2104 Bray, Howard. "Journalists as Spooks: The CIA Use of
Newsmen on Intelligence Operations." Progressive, XLI
(February 1977), 9-10.
2105 Buchanan, Patrick. "Are Newsmen Who Asisisted the CIA
Scoundrels or Patriots?"   TV Guide, XXIV (March 13,
1976), A3-A4.
2106 "CIA   Admits Help from Twenty-Five in U.S. Media,
But Won't Give Any Names." Broadcasting, XC (May 3,
1976), 32-33.
2107 "CIA, FBI, and the Media: Excerpts from the Senate
Report on Intelligence Activities."   Columbia Journalism
Review, XV (July 1976), 37-42.
2108 "CIAntics: U.S. Journalists Abroad as Undercover A-
gents." New Republic, CLXIX (December 15, 1973), 7-8.
2109 "The CIA in Wonderland: The Controversy as Reflected
in the Media." National Review, XXVII (January 31,
1975), 88+.
2110 Colby, William E. "When TV Probes, Can the Government
Keep a Secret? TV Guide, XXV (February 12, 1977), 2-6.
2111 Crile, George, 3rd. "The Fourth Estate: A Good Word
for the CIA."   Harper's, CCLII (January 1976), 28-30.
2112 Crock, Stan. "Schlesinger Says Leaks Curb CIA: Reprinted from the Washington Post, August 3, 1975." Congressional Record, CXXI (October 28, 1975), 33896.
2113 Cuneo, Ernest. "What's the Story Behind the CIA and
Newsmen Abroad?" Human Events, XXXIII (December 22,
1973), 84.
2114 Efron, Edith. "'Amnesia' Epidemic Sweeps Press and
Politics." TV Guide, XXIII (July 19, 1975), A5-A6.
2115 Gelb, L.H. "The CIA and the Press: Bearing Out Seymour Hersh." New Republic, CLXXII (March 22, 1975),
13-16.
2116 Halperin, Morton H. "'CIA News Management' and 'How
the CIA Managed the News After Agent's Murder in '75':
Reprinted from the Washington Post and the Washington Sunday
Times, January 23, 1977." In: United States, Congress, House,
Permanent Select Committee on Intelligence, Subcommittee on
Oversight. The CIA and the Media: Hearings. 95th Cong.,
1st and 2nd sess. Washington, D.C.: U.S. Government Printing Office, 1978. pp. 441-442.
2117 Johnson, Oswald. "Journalists Doubling as CIA Contacts: Reprinted from the Washington Star-News, November
30, 1973." In: United States, Congress, House, Select Committee on Intelligence. U.S. Intelligence Agencies and Activ-

ities--Risks and Control of Foreign Intelligence: Hearings. 95th
Cong., 1st and 2nd sess. Washington, D.C. : U.S. Government Printing Office, 1978. pp. 441-442.
2118   Karnow, Stanley. "Associating With the Agency." News-
       week, XCI (October 10, 1977),11.
2119   Kirwin, Charles. "Thirty Year Survey: The Impact
       of Media Coverage on the CIA." In: Failures in Covert
Operations. Providence, R.I.: Brown University,1979. Chapt. 2.
2120   Ledeen, Michael A. "Scoop and Dagger." Harper's,
       CCLVIII (January 1979), 91-94.
2121   Loory, Stuart H. "The CIA's Use of the Press." Colum-
       bia Journalism Review, XIII (September-October 1974),
       9-18.
2122   Marchetti, Victor and John D. Marks. The CIA and the
       Cult of Intelligence. New York: Alfred A. Knopf, 1974.
398p.   A noted title which saw legal contests between the
authors and the Agency resulting in the publisher printing the
book with large gaps where material was censored in review;
contains some information on the relationship between Langley
and the press.
2123   "Networks Deny Assertions That Their Newsmen Aided
       CIA, FBI." Broadcasting, XC (February 16, 1976),
       21-22.
2124   "No Newsmen in the CIA's Future, but the Past Still
       Haunts Some." Broadcasting, XC (February 16, 1976),
       22-24.
2125   Roche, John P. "CIA 'Exposure' Put Network Newsmen in
       Mood to Save Souls." TV Guide, XXIV (February 14,
       1976), A3-A4.
2126   Salant, Richard S. "CBS-CIA Connection Confirmed by
       Salant." Broadcasting, XCII (May 30, 1977), 22-23.
2127   Schorr, Daniel. "Are CIA Assets a Press Liability?"
       More, VIII (February 1978), 18-23.
2128   _____. "The CIA at CBS: Cloak-and-Camera at Black
       Rock." New York, X (September 26, 1977), 40+.
2129   Seib, Charles B. "The Press/Spy Affair-- Cozy and Still
       Murkey. Reprinted from the Washington Post, October
11, 1977." In: United States, Congress, House, Permanent
Select Committee on Intelligence, Subcommittee on Oversight.
The CIA and the Media: Hearings. 95th Cong., 1st and 2nd
sess. Washington, D.C.: U.S. Government Printing Office,
1978. p. 338.
2130   "Tinker, Tailor, Newsman, Spy?" Broadcasting, XC (Feb-
       ruary 2, 1976), 33+.
2131   Trenton, Joe, and Dave Roman. "The Spies Who Came in
       from the Newsroom." Penthouse, VIII (August 1977), 44+.
2132   United States. Congress. House. Committee on Stand-
       ards of Official Conduct. Investigation of the Publication
of Select Committee on Intelligence Report: Hearings. 84th Cong.,
2nd sess. Washington, D.C.: U.S. Government Printing Office,
1976. 748p.
2133   _____.   _____.   _____. Permanent Select Com-
       mittee on Oversight. The CIA and the Media: Hearings.
95th Cong., 1st and 2nd sess. Washington, D.C.: U.S.
Government Printing Office, 1978. 627p.

2134   Weisman, John. "Why American TV Is So Vulnerable to
Propaganda Disinformation." TV Guide, XXX (June 12,
1982), 4-10.

VIII-C. FOREIGN AFFAIRS

GENERAL WORKS--Books

2135   Batscha, Robert M. Foreign Affairs News and the Broadcast Journalist. New York: Praeger, 1975. 254p. An
examination of the behavior of those individuals who control the
composition of foreign news on network news broadcasts.
2136   Chittick, William O. State Department Press and Pressure
Groups: A Role Analysis. New York: Wiley-Interscience,
1970. 373p. Looks at the press, including network newsmen,
as one of the press groups which have to be "handled" carefully; demonstrates the relationship between briefer and briefee,
and the methods and materials by which the former communicate
with the latter.
2137   Freidin, Seymour and George Bailey. The Experts. New
York: Macmillan, 1968. 398p. Contends that commentary
offered by the likes of Eric Severeid and Howard K. Smith on
the evening news shows of the late 1960's were biased with
regards to foreign news.
2138   Kissinger, Henry A. Memoirs. 2 vols. Boston, Mass.:
Little, Brown, 1979-1982. Vol. I The White House Years
and Vol. II Years of Upheaval cover the former Secretary of
State's service under Presidents Nixon and Ford; although the
bulk of the titles naturally relate to foreign affairs, the one-
time Harvard teacher's comments on the media are of interest to
students of network news reporting of non-domestic events.
2139   Morris, Roger. Uncertain Greatness: Henry Kissinger
and American Foreign Policy. New York: Harper & Row,
1977. An assessment of the former Secretary of State's contribution to the formulation and execution of America's foreign
relations with some thoughts on the role of the media.
2140   Pollock, John C. The Politics of Crisis Reporting: American Journalism and Foreign Affairs. New York: Praeger,
1978. 200p. A study of the factors which shape foreign correspondents' perspectives toward crisis reporting which concludes
that experience and decisions in a young reporter's career will
exert a decisive impact on his later professional judgments.
2141   Valeriani, Richard. Travels With Henry. Boston, Mass.:
Houghton-Mifflin, 1979. 448p. Currently working for NBC,
Valeriani traces his experience (and indirectly that of others)
in following Henry Kissinger's "shuttle-diplomacy" trips and
other foreign policy adventures during the Nixon-Ford years.

GENERAL WORKS--Articles

2142   Anderson, James. "The Follies of Grandeur." Washington
Journalist Review, II (March 1980), 57-59. State Department
spokesman Hodding Carter, 3rd.

2143   Angle, J. L.   "News Coverage of Foreign Affairs."   USA Today, CIX (October 1980), 7-8.

2144   Arlen, Michael J.   "Eyes and Ears of the World: Reporting Overseas News."   New Yorker, L (January 6, 1975), 52-56.

2145   Boafo, Samuel T. K.   "International News Coverage on U.S. Television Network Newscasts: A Gratification Study." Unpublished PhD Dissertation, Michigan State University, 1980.

2146   Chittick, William C.   "American Foreign Policy Elites: Attitudes Toward Secrecy and Publicity."   Journalism Quarterly, XLVII (Winter 1970), 689-696.

2147   _____.   "State Department-Press Antagonism: Opinion Versus Policy-Making Needs?"   Journal of Politics, XXXI (August 1969), 756-771.

2148   Collingwood, Charles.   "Good-bye to All That."   TV Guide, XXVIII (April 19, 1980), 6-12.

2149   _____.   "Touring Europe with a TV Camera."   TV Guide, VIII (August 6, 1960), 24-27.

2150   Collins, Catherine A.   "Kissinger's Press Conference, 1972-1974:   An Exploration of Form and Role Relationships on News Management."   Central States Speech Journal, XXVIII (Spring 1977), 185-193.

2151   Cronkite, Walter.   "Kissinger, Congress, and U.S. Foreign Policy: Transcript of a CBS Radio Commentary, February 11, 1976."   Congressional Record, CXXII (March 29, 1976), 8467.

2152   Davison, Phillips.   "The News Media and International Negotiations."   Public Opinion Quarterly, XXXVIII (Summer 1874), 174-191.

2153   Fulbright, J. William.   "Fulbright on the Press."   Foreign Service Journal, LIII (February 1976), 4-6, 15-18.

2154   Haisman, Stephen F.   "Television's World Views: One Month of Network International News."   Unpublished PhD Dissertation, University of Iowa, 1970.

2155   Hohenburg, John.   "Tomorrows for Correspondents."   In: Gerald Cross, ed.   The Responsibility of the Press.   New York: Fleet Publishing Co., 1966.   pp. 207-224.

2156   Kroeger, Albert R.   "Television's Men-at-War: in South Vietnam and in Santo Domingo, TV Crews are on the Scene." Television, XXII (July 1965), 35-39+.

2157   Larson, James F.   "America'a Window on the World: U.S. Network Television Coverage of International Affairs, 1972-1976."   Unpublished PhD Dissertation, Stanford University, 1978.

2158   _____.   "International Affairs Coverage on U.S. Network Television."   Journal of Communications, XXIX (Spring 1979), 136-147.

2159   _____.   and Andy Hardy.   "International Affairs Coverage on Network Television News: A Study of News Flows." Gazette, XXIII (Fall 1977), 241-256.

2160   Lefever, Ernest W.   "Prestige Press, Foreign Policy, and American Survival."   Orbis, XX (Spring 1976), 207-225.

2161   Levin, Eric.   "It Takes More Than a Trenchcoat."   TV Guide, XXIII (October 11, 1975), 6-10.

2162   Mayer, Martin.   "How Television News Covers the World, in 4,000 Words or Less."   Esquire, LXXVII (January 1972), 86-91.

2163 Morris, Roger. "Kissinger and the Media." In: Michael
      C. Emery and Ted C. Smythe, eds. Readings in Mass
Communications: Concepts and Issues in the Mass Media. 2nd
ed. Dubuque, Ia.: William C. Brown, 1974. pp. 154-181.
2164 "NBC Nets Expertise of Henry Kissinger." Broadcasting,
      XCII (Februay 21, 1977), 23-24.
2165 Oberdorfer, Don. "News and the Perception of Reality."
      Proceedings of the American Philosophical Society, CXIII
      (Summer 1979), 129+.
2166 Palumbo, Dennis. "Apocalypse on the Nightly News."
      Emmy, II (Winter 1980), 16+.
2167 Reischaur, Edwin O. "The Global View: Television and
      Foreign Affairs." TV Guide, XXIV (January 3, 1976),
      4-7.
2168 Reston, James. "The Press, the President, and Foreign
      Policy." In: Charles S. Steinberg, ed. Mass Media and
Communications. New York: Hastings House, 1972. pp. 413-
414.
2169 Robinson, John P. "World Affairs Informations and Mass
      Media Exposure." Journalism Quarterly, XLIV (Spring
      1967), 23-31.
2170 Roche, John P. "TV News Missing New Public Attitudes
      on Foreign Affairs." TV Guide, XXV (July 23, 1977),
      A3-A4.
2171 Rubin, Barry. International News and the American Media.
      Washington Papers, vol. 5, no. 49. Beverly Hills, Calif.:
      Sage Publications, 1977. 71p.
2172 Stone, Jan. "The Picture from Abroad." In: Marvin
      Barrett and Zachary Sklar, eds. The Eye of the Storm:
The Alfred I. DuPont-Columbia University Survey of Broadcast
Journalism. New York: Lippincott-Crowell, 1980. pp. 215-226.
2173 Trewhitt, Henry L. "Hodding Carter, 3rd: Candor and
      Style at the State Department." Washington Journalism
      Review, I (January-February 1978), 7-8.
2174 "TV's Biggest Show: Foreign News." TV Guide, VI
      (March 1, 1958), 5-7.
2175 United States. Congress. House. Committee on Inter-
      national Relations, Subcommittee on Future Foreign Policy
Research and Development. The Press and Foreign Policy:
Hearings. 94th Cong., 1st sess. Washington, D.C.: U.S.
Government Printing Office, 1975. 34p.
2176 Warrier, Malcolm. "TV Coverage of International Affairs."
      Television Quarterly, VII (Spring 1968), 60-75.
2177 White, Ray, ed. "Press on Press: The New Foreign
      Correspondent." Washington Journalism Review, II (March
      1980), 39-47.
2178 Wilhelm, John. "The Reappearing Foreign Correspondent."
      Journalism Quarterly, XL (Spring 1963), 147-168.
2179 Wolzien, Tom. "Watch Your Loved One Brave Bombs and
      Bullets." TV Guide, XXVIII (January 26, 1980), 6-10.
An NBC producer's thoughts on the ethics of war reporting.
2180 Yoder, Amos. "The News Media and One World." Politi-
      cal Communication and Persuasion, I (Fall 1981), 17-29.
Asks if U.S. citizens receive enough information from foreign
reporting to make intelligent decisions.

INTERNATIONAL TERRORISM

2181 "ABC's Grim TV First: Coverage of Terrorist Raid on
Munich Olympics." Newsweek, LXXX (September 18,
1973), 67-68.
2182 Alexander, Yonah. "Communications Aspects of International Terrorism." International Problems, XVI (Spring
1877), 55-60.
2183 _____. "Terrorism, the Media, and the Police." Journal of International Affairs, VII (Spring-Summer 1978),
101-114. Reprinted in Police Studies, I (June 1978), 45-52.
2184 Bell, J. Bowyer. "Chroniclers of Violence in Northern
Ireland: The First Wave Interpreted." Review of Politics,
XXXIV (April 1972), 147-157.
2185 _____. "Chroniclers of Violence in Northern Ireland
A Tragedy in Endless Acts." Review of Politics, XXXVIII
(October 1976), 10-33.
2186 _____. "Chroniclers of Violence in Northern Ireland
Revisited: The Analysis of Tragedy." Review of Politics,
XXXVI (October 1974), 521-543.
2187 _____. "Terrorist Scripts and Live-Action Spectaculars."
Columbia Journalism Review, XVII (May 1978), 47-50.
2188 Buchanan, Patrick. "Television: Patsy and Promoter for
Terrorists." TV Guide, XXV (March 26, 1977), A5-A6.
2189 CBS News. "CBS Rules on Terrorist Coverage." In:
Marvin Barrett, ed. Rich News, Poor News: The Alfred
I. DuPont-Columbia University Survey of Broadcast Journalism.
New York: T. Y. Crowell, 1978. pp. 224-226.
2190 "CBS News' Ground Rules for Terrorist Coverage Backed
by Peers, Law Enforcers." Broadcasting, XCIII (November 7, 1977), 42-43.
2191 Clutterbuck, Richard. The Media and Political Violence.
New York: Humanities Press, 1981. 191p. A noted British
expert on terrorism, using events from British/Northern Ireland
or coverage of same, assesses the role of print and electronic
journalism in both the philosophies of terrorists and the pro-
long ing of terrorist misdeeds; suggests strongly the need for
internal or government control of media access to the scenes of
terrorism.
2192 Cooper, H. H. A. "Terrorism and the Media." Chitty's
Law Journal, XXXIV (September 1976), 226-232.
2193 Drummond, William J., and Augustine Zycher. "Arafat's
Press Agents." Harper's, CCLII (March 1976), 24-30.
2194 Gladis, Stephen D. "Hostage/Terrorist Situations and the
Media." FBI Law Enforcement Bulletin, XLVIII (September
1979), 11-15.
2195 Halloran, J. B. "Mass Communications: Symptom or
Cause of Violence?" International Social Science Journal,
XXX (Fall 1978), 816-833.
2196 Heron, Paddy. "Television's Role in Reporting Ulster
Violence." Harrangue, a Political and Social Review (Belfast), I (Summer 1974), 2+.
2197 Hickey, Neil. "How Television Affects the Battle for
Northern Ireland." TV Guide, XXIX (September 26, 1981),
8-12.

2198 _____. "Terrorism and Television." TV Guide, XXIV
(July 31-August 7, 1976), 2-6, 10-13.
2199 Hoge, James, ed. The Media and Terrorism: A Seminar
Sponsored by the Chicago Sun-Times and Chicago Daily
News. Chicago, Ill.: Field Enterprises, 1977. 38p.
2200 McKay, Jim. My Wide World. New York: Macmillan,
1973. 272p. In Munich in 1972, this noted ABC sports-
caster found himself and his colleagues immersed into the role of
foreign correspondents in reporting the Black September attack
on the Israeli atheletes at the Olympic Games.
2201 Magagnini, Stephen. "Media Coverage and the Spread of
Terrorism." IPI Report, (September 1975), 8-10.
2202 Methvin, Eugene H. "Objectivity and the Tactics of
Terrorists." Seminar, (September 1974), 22-25.
2203 Mickolus, Richard F. Assessing the Degrees of Error in
Public Reporting of Transnational Terrorism. Langley, Va.:
Office of Political Research, Central Intelligence Agency, 1976.
Unpaged.
2204 Mosse, Hilde L. "The Media and Terrorism." In: Marius
H. Livingston, ed. International Terrorism in the Contemporary World. Westport, Conn.: Greenwood Press, 1978. pp.
282-286.
2205 Redlick, Amy S. "The Transnational Flow of Information
as a Cause of Terrorism." In: Yonah Alexander, David
Carlton, and Paul Wilkinson, eds. Terrorism: Theory and
Practice. Boulder, Col.: Westview Press, 1979. Chpt. 3.
2206 Snider, Marie, ed. Media and Terrorism: The Psychological Impact. Newton, Ka.: Prairie View, 1978. 51p.
2207 Weisman, John. "When Hostages' Lives are at Stake."
TV Guide, XXVI (August 26, 1978), 4-9.
2208 Winchester, Simon. Northern Ireland in Crisis: Reporting the Ulster Troubles. New York: Holmes and Meier,
1975. 256p. Looks at the role of print and electronic reporters
in covering the "troubles" in Northern Ireland, especially
around Belfast, since 1969 and suggests that the press may
have been employed by the IRA as a vehicle for getting its
revolutionary message across to various constituencies, including the British government, Irishmen, and funding sources in
America.

EUROPE

2209 "Across the Atlantic Racing the Sun: How NBC Utilized
In-air Time for On-air Coverage of Winston Churchill's
Funeral." Sponsor, XIX (February 8, 1965), 21-23.
2210 Burgess, Anthony. "The Royal Wedding: Prince Charles
and Lady Diana, Comes to TV." TV Guide, XXIX (July
25, 1981), 2-8.
2211 Castro, Janice. "The Vows Heard Round the World."
Time, CXVIII (August 10, 1981), 66-67.
2212 Csida, John. "TV Had It All Over Print on the 'Summit
Story.'" Sponsor, XIV (May 28, 1960), 14+.
2213 Fromson, Murray. "Dateline Moscow: Censorship of Our
TV News." Columbia Journalism Review, XIV (September
1975), 32-34.

2214   Harding, Henry. "TV Coverage of Winston Churchill's Funeral Ceremonies." TV Guide, XIII (February 6, 1965), 32-34.
2215   Jobin, Judith. "Filming the Soviet Invasion of Czechoslovakia." TV Guide, XVII (January 25, 1969), 24-27.
2216   LeDuc, Don R. "Television Coverage of NATO Affairs." Journal of Broadcasting, XXIV (Fall 1980), 449-466.
2217   Levine, Irving R. "The Days and Nights of a Correspondent in Rome." TV Guide, XIII (February 27, 1965), 10-14.
2218   Quint, Bert. "Television and the Pope: A Perfect Match." TV Guide, XXVII (September 29, 1979), 4-9.
2219   Salisbury, Harrison E. "Is TV's Coverage of the Soviet Union Adequate?" TV Guide, XXX (July 10, 19820, 2-6.
2220   Schorr, Daniel. "Correspondents Need a Touch of Larceny." TV Guide, IX (March 25, 1961), 28-29.
2221   "TV's Splurge on the Eisenhower Trip." Business Week, (December 12, 1959), 29-31.
2222   Wren, Christopher. "From Russia with Difficulty." TV Guide, XXVI (April 22, 1978), 28-32.

LATIN AMERICA

2223   "ABC Newsman's Role in the Cuban Missile Crisis." Broadcasting, LXVIII (August 10, 1964), 52.
2224   Abel, Elie. The Missile Crisis. New York: Macmillan, 1966. 220p. Written from the viewpoint of the former NBC correspondent, this account of the October 1962 event includes comments on the role of the press, especially ABC Newsman John Scali.
2225   Christian, Shirley. "How the Press Covered the Sandinistas." Washington Journalism Review, IV (March 1982), 32-39.
2226   Clark, Gerald. "Covering the Uncoverable War." Time, CIX (May 17, 1982), 53.
2227   Cline, Carolyn G. "Our Neglected Neighbors: How the U.S. Elite Media Covered Latin America in 1977." Unpublished PhD Dissertation, Indiana University, 1981.
2228   Cooke, Gerald E. "News Media Perception and Projection of the Castro Rebellion, 1957-1958: Some Image Theme Affects in the Foreign Policy System." Unpublished PhD Dissertation, University of Maryland, 1969.
2229   Diederich, Bernard. "Searching for Bang-Bang: Competition Heats Up for Vietnam-Style Coverage in El Salvador." Time, CXIX (March 8, 1982), 97.
2230   "Difficulties and Dangers in Reporting a Revolution." Center Magazine, XV (January-February 1982), 48-54.
2231   Halberstam, David. "A Look at the Cuban Missile Crisis." TV Guide, XXII (December 14, 1974), 3-5.
2232   Harding, Henry. "ABC Newsman John Scali's Key Role in the Cuban Crisis." TV Guide, XII (August 15, 1964), A-1.
2233   _____. "TV's Role During the Cuban Missile Crisis." TV Guide, X (November 3, 1962), A-1.

2234 Henry, William A., 3rd. "Missing a Story in El Salvador: The High [Voter] Turnout Startled Everyone--Including Journalists." Time, CXIX (April 12, 1982), 44.

2235 Houghton, Neal D. "The Cuban Invasion of 1961 and the U.S. Press in Retrospect: A Study of the 'Bay of Pigs' Disaster and of U.S. Press Reaction to American Involvement in Cuban Affairs." Journalism Quarterly, XLII (Summer 1965), 422-432. Originally penned in late 1962.

2236 Kaiser, Charles. "Behind 'Enemy' Lines." Newsweek, XCIX (April 26, 1982), 57.

2237 Leo, J. "A War Even Tougher to Cover." Time, CXIX (May 24, 1982), 70.

2238 Lord, Arthur A. "Q: When Does the Revolution Start?, A: When Can You Get There?" TV Guide, XXVII (June 30, 1979), 14-20.

2239 McColm, R. Bruce. "El Salvador: The Media Image." Freedom at Issue, (November-December 1981), 12-16.

2240 "Man in the Middle." Newsweek, LXIV (August 17, 1964), 80-81. John Scali.

2241 "The Media's War: Reprinted from the Wall Street Journal, February 10, 1982." Congressional Record, CXXVIII (February 10, 1982), S725-S726.

2242 "Mr. [Howard K.] Smith Goes to Cuba: A Picture Feature." TV Guide, XXV (February 26, 1977), 12-14.

2243 "News Ranks Escalate for Election Coverage." Broadcasting, CII (April 5, 1982), 38-39.

2244 Szulc, Tad. "Isn't Latin America Important Too?" TV Guide, XXVII (September 29, 1979), 37-38.

2245 Townley, Rod. "Covering the War in El Salvador." TV Guide, XXIX (May 9-16, 1981), 6-13, 36-42.

2246 Wiley, C. W. "Two Faces of Fidel Castro: Contrasting Views Presented by News Reporters and Documentaries." National Review, XXVIII (April 30, 1976), 442-444.

MIDDLE EAST

2247 Adams, William C., ed. Television Coverage of the Middle East. Norwood, N.J.: Ablex Publishing Corp., 1981. 167p. An examination of how the three big commercial American networks portray the various crises of the Middle East; looks at that portrayal in terms of bias and questions concerning specific issues such as the PLO.

2248 Alpern, David M. "Cronkite Summit." Newsweek, XC (November 28, 1977), 29.

2249 Altheide, David. "The Failure of Network News." Washington Journalism Review, III (May 1981), 28-29.

2250 Anderson, Jim. "The Son of Deep Throat Tips Off NBC on the Rescue Mission Story." Washington Journalism Review, II (June 1980), 10.

2251 Arlen, Michael J. "Tourists in Teheran: or, Cameras in Command." New Yorker, LV (January 21, 1980), 98-101.

2252 Asi, Morad O. "Arabs, Israelis, and U.S. Television Networks: A Content Analysis of How ABC, CBS, and

NBC Reported the News Beween 1970-1979." Unpublished PhD Dissertation, Ohio University, 1981.
2253 "Behind Cronkite's Coup." Time, CX (November 28, 1977), 47.
2254 Castro, Janice. "Groping for News from Cairo." Time, CXVIII (October 19, 1981), 62.
2255 Dimitman, E. E. "How Television is Watching the Eichman Trail." TV Guide, IX (May 6, 1961), A2-A3.
2256 Emerson, Gloria. "'Heard the News Today--Oh, Boy!.'" Channels, I (April-May 1981), 17+. I heard.
2257 Ephron, Nora. "The War [of Yom Kippur] Follows." New York, (November 12, 1973), 49-53.
2258 Frye, Robert E. "The Diary of 'Tango Delta': An Insider's Account of ABC's 'Secret Negotiations.'" Washington Journalism Review, III (May 1981), 30-36.
2259 Goren, Dina N., et al. "Reporting of the Yom-Kippur War from Israel." Journalism Quarterly, LII (Summer 1975), 199-206.
2260 Hickey, Neil. "For Walter Cronkite They Raised Lake Nasser Three Feet." TV Guide, XXVIII (June 28, 1980), 28-30.
2261 "The High Cost of [6-Day War] Mideast News." Broadcasting, LXXII (June 19, 1967), 51-52.
2262 Hill, Frederic B. "Media Diplomacy." Washington Journalism Review, III (May 1981), 23-27.
2263 Lane, Raymond M. "[Frank] Reynolds Held Hostage by ABC Specials." Washington Journalism Review, II (March 1980), 11.
2264 "The Media and the Islamic World: A Roundtable." Middle East Journal, XXXV (Autumn 1981), 465-505.
2265 "Media Diplomacy: Television Reporting and the Israeli-Egypt Peace Talks." New Republic, CLXXVIII (January 14, 1978), 5-6.
2266 Mortimer, Edward. "Islam and the Western Journalist." Middle East Journal, XXXV (Autumn 1981), 492-505.
2267 Mosettig, Michael D. "The Revolution in Communications and Diplomacy." Academy of Political Science Proceedings, XXXIV (Summer 1981), 190-201.
2268 "The NBC Hostage Interviews: Getting the Story." Inquiry, III (February 4, 1980), 3-4.
2269 Networks Mount Offensive for [6-Day] War News." Broad casting, LXXII (June 12, 1967), 72-73.
2270 "News Gathering Under the Gun: Israel Accuses U.S. Journalists of Suppressing Stories, Out of Fear." Time, CXIX (March 1, 1982), 87.
2271 Oberdorfer, Don. "Now That It's Over the Press Needs to Reflect on Its Role." Washington Journalism Review, III (May 1981), 37-38.
2272 Powers, Ron. "You Didn't Know Where the Next Bullet was Coming From." TV Guide, XVII (May 26, 1979), 4-10.
2273 Quint, Bert. " Dateline Teheran: There was a Touch of Fear." TV Guide, XXVIII (April 5, 1980), 6-12.
2274 Rosen, Barbara and Barry. The Destined Hour: The Rosen's Revealing Personal Account of Iran and the Hostage Crisis. Garden City, N.Y.: Doubleday, 1982. Includes

many comments on the role of the media in covering the long
crisis.

2275   Rubin, Barry. "Iran." Washington Journalism Review,
       II (April 1980), 35-39.
2276   Said, E. W. "Iran." Columbia Journalism Review, XVIII
       (March-April 1980), 23-33.
2277   _____. "Inside Islam." Harper's, CCLXII (January-
       February 1981), 25-32.
2278   Salinger, Pierre. America Held Hostage: The Secret
       Negotiations. Garden City, N.Y.: Doubleday, 1981.
349p. ABC's Paris bureau chief provides a very enlightening
description of the role of the media throughout the long crisis
and delicate negotiations.
2279   Simmons, Peter. "Running the Green Line in Lebanon."
       TV Guide, XXVII (February 3, 1979), 4-10.
2280   Sreebny, Daniel. "American Correspondents in the Middle
       East: Perceptions and Problems." Journalism Quarterly,
       LVI (Summer 1978), 386-388.
2281   "TV: Middleman in the Middle East." Broadcasting,
       XCIII (November 28, 1977), 25.
2282   "Television's Intercontinental Triumph." Broadcasting, C
       (January 26, 1981), 20-22.
2283   Townley,Rod. "The War TV News Can't Cover." TV
       Guide, XXIX (January 3, 1981), 4-8. Iran-Iraq.
2284   Trotta, Liz. "A News Correspondent's Recollections of
       the Arab-Israeli War." TV Guide, XXI (December 22,
       1973), 5-7.
2285   United States. Congress. House. Committee on Foreign
       Affairs.   The Iran Hostage Crisis--A Chronology of Daily
Developments: A Report Prepared by the Foreign Affairs and
National Defense Division, Congressional Research Service, Library of Congress. 97th Cong., 1st sess. Washington, D.C.:
U.S. Government Printing Office, 1981. 421p.
2286   _____. _____. _____. _____. The Iran
       Hostage Crisis--A Chronology of Daily Developments, Janu-
ary 1-25, 1981: A Report Prepared by the Foreign Affairs and
National Defense Division, Congressional Research Service, Library of Congress. 97th Cong., 1st sess. Washington, D.C.:
U.S. Government Printing Office, 1981. 36p.
2287   _____. _____. _____. _____. Iran's Seizure
       of the United States Embassy: Hearings. 97th Cong., 1st
sess. Washington, D.C.: U.S. Government Printing Office,
1981. 285p.
2288   Von Hoffman, Nicholas. "ABC Held Hostage." New Re-
       public, CLXXXIX (May 10, 1980), 15-17.
2289   Weisman, John. "How a Weary Barbara Walters Scooped
       Her Rivals on the Carter Peace Victory." TV Guide,
       XXVII (May 12, 1979), 16-20.
2290   _____. "TV's Blind Spot in the Middle East: [The
       Palestinians]." TV Guide, XXIX (October 24-31, 1981),
       6-10, 10-15.
2291   "Without Portfolio: Delicate Dilemma of TV Journalism."
       Broadcasting, XCVII (December 24, 1979), 23+.

CHINA, KOREA, NIGERIA

2292 Doan, Richard K., and Andrew Mills. "How TV Will Take
      You Along on the President's [Nixon] Eight-Day Trip to
      China." TV Guide, IX (February 19, 1972), A1-A3.
2293 Hamburger, Philip. "This is Korea, Christmas, 1951."
      New Yorker, XXVIII (January 10, 1953), 58+.
2294 "Korean Coverage." Newsweek, XXXVI (September 4,
      1950), 48.
2295 "Living Room Front." Time, LVI (July 31, 1950), 40.
2296 "Made for Television: Covering Richard Nixon's China
      Visit." Newsweek, LXXIX (February 21, 1972), 100.
2297 Oberdorfer, Don. "Media Manipulation: The Press Dele-
      gation on Nixon's Visit to China." Nation, CCXIV (March
      27, 1972),394-397.
2298 "The Perils of Peking." Time, CXIII (March 4, 1974),
      42-47.
2299 Sambe, John A. "Network Coverage of the Civil War in
      Nigeria." Journal of Broadcasting, XXIV (Winter 1980),
      61-68.
2300 Simon, Edelgard. "Correspondents in China." Matrix,
      LXI (Winter 1975-1976), 23-25.
2301 Upshaw, Jim. "Covering Asia for a TV Network [NBC]."
      TV Guide, XXIX (July 4, 1981), 12-17.
2302 Weisman, John. "TV News and President Ford's China
      Trip." TV Guide, XXIV (January 26, 1976), 4-9.

THE VIETNAM WAR--Books

2303 Braestrup, Peter. Big Story: How the American Press
      and Television Reported and Interpreted the Crisis of Tet
1968 in Vietnam and Washington. Garden City, N.Y.: Double-
day-Anchor Books, 1978. 606p. Possibly the most important
book to emerge on the role of network news in the Vietnam
War; contends that the media, especially television, was largely
responsible for giving the impression that the massive Communist attack demonstrated that the war could not be "won" in a
military sense; examples of faulty reporting include the sapper
attack on the American embassy complex in Saigon.
2304 CBS News. Vietnam Perspectve: CBS Special Report--
      Analysis by Walter Cronkite. New York: Pocket Books,
1965. 112p. A favorable review of the American effort in
Indochina, especially the military push.
2305 Goulden, Joseph C. Truth is the First Casualty: The
      Gulf of Tonkin Affair--Illusion and Reality. Chicago, Ill.:
Rand-McNally, 1969. 285p. A study of the 1964 naval events
in the Gulf of Tonkin area which questions whether some of the
attacks on U.S. warships actually took place and the manner in
which those reports were communicated to the Congress and
American people.
2306 Halberstam, David. The Best and the Brightest. New
      York: Random House, 1972. 688p. A well-known account
of how Kennedy, Johnson, and their advisors escalated the
Vietnamese conflict; includes several comments concerning the

role of the press in attempting to uncover what was going on both "in country" and in Washington.
2307   Kalb, Marvin and Elie Abel. Roots of Involvement: The
       U.S. in Asia, 1784-1971. New York: W. W. Norton, 1972.
336p. A pair of broadcast journalists known for their expertise on foreign affairs examine American far eastern policy; neither are sympathetic toward U.S. involvement in Indochina.
2308   Kinnard, Douglas. The War Managers. Hanover, N.H.:
       University Press of New England, 1977. 216p. Interviews with a variety of U.S. field officers who served in Vietnam; interestingly enough, about the only thing they all agree on is that network television news coverage of the conflict was all bad.
2309   Minow, Dale. The Information War. New York: Haw-
       thorn Books, 1970. 212p. A contemporary study of the bitter conflict between reporters, both print and electronic, and government officials in Saigon.
2310   Oberdorfer, Don. Tet! Garden City, N.Y.: Doubleday,
       1971. 385p. An account of the massive enemy attacks of early 1968 and the reaction to them in the United States; should be compared with Peter Braestrup's book cited above.
2311   Schandler, Herbert Y.   The Unmaking of a President:
       Lyndon B. Johnson and Vietnam.   Princeton,   N.J.:
Princeton University Press, 1977. 419p. Carefully weighs the impact of media coverage against those other factors that influenced LBJ's post-Tet decisions in an effort to avoid the "stab-in-the-back" theory of more hawkish Vietnam historians.
2312   Sharp, U.S. Grant. U.S. Strategy for Defeat: Vietnam
       in Retrospect. San Rafael, Calif.: Presidio Press, 1978.
324p. The C-in-C of the U.S. Pacific Fleet reflects upon why the U.S. military did so poorly in Vietnam and has few tender words for the press, especially television.
2313   Snepp, Frank W., 3rd. Decent Interval: An Insider's
       Account of Saigon's Indecent End.   New York: Random
House, 1977. 590p. A controversial book by a former CIA agent who was on the scene before and during the American evacuation of South Vietnam in April 1975: contains some revealing thoughts on the work of television crews in covering both the government's collapse and the final U.S. pull-out.
2314   Stein, Meyer L. Under Fire: The Story of American War
       Correspondents. New York: Julian Messner, 1968. 256p.
Includes a final chapter on the work of network television news reporters in South Vietnam.
2315   United States. Congress. Senate. Committee on Foreign
       Relations. News Policies in Vietnam: Hearings. 87th Cong.,
2nd sess. Washington, D.C.: U.S. Government Printing Office, 1966. 161p.
2316   Westmoreland, William C. A Soldier Reports. Garden
       City, N.Y.: Doubleday, 1976. 446p. The commanding officer of U.S. military forces in South Vietnam for much of the period after 1964, Westmoreland is a vocal critic of television reporting on the conflict; see also the controversy surrounding the CBS Reports piece, "Uncounted Enemy," cited as Section III:D:2:h above.

THE VIETNAM WAR--Articles

2317 Adams, A. A. "A Study of Veteran Viewpoints on Television Coverage of the Vietnam War." Journalism Quarterly,
LIV (Summer 1977), 248-253.
2318 Arlen, Michael J. "CBS Documentary Vietnam Perspective:
Air War in the North." New Yorker, XLIII (March 4,
1967), 148+.
2319 _____. "CBS News Show About Con Thien, by Correspondent John Laurence." New Yorker, XLIII (September
30, 1967), 161-164.
2320 _____. "Morley Safer's Vietnam." New Yorker, XLIII
(April 15, 1967), 184+.
2321 _____. "News About the Vietnam War from Television."
New Yorker, XLII (October 15, 1966), 200-202.
2322 _____. "The Road from Highway One." Columbia
Journalism Review, XIV (July 1975), 22-26.
2323 _____. "Snapshots from Operation Attleboro: Vietnam
War." New Yorker, L (December 9, 1974), 163-164+.
2324 _____. "Television and the Press in Vietnam." New
Yorker, XLIII (October 21, 197), 173-180.
2325 _____. "They [Network Cameramen] Bear Witness."
In: Marvin Barrett, ed. Year of Challenge, Year of
Crisis: The Alfred I. DuPont-Columbia University Survey
of Broadcast Journalism, 1969-1970. New York: Grosset and
Dunlap, 1970. pp. 98-102.
2326 _____. "Viet Cong [Tet] Attacks." New Yorker, XLIII
(February 17, 1968), 102+.
2327 Arnett, Peter. "Tet Coverage: A Debate Renewed."
Columbia Journalism Review, XVI (January 1978), 44-47.
2328 Arnot, C. "The Tough Job of Getting News Out of Vietnam." Broadcasting, LVIII (May 31, 1965), 52-53.
2329 "As Newsmen See the Vietnam War." War/Peace Report,
VIII (March 1968), 6-11.
2330 Bailey, George A. "Interpretive Reporting of the Vietnam
War by Anchormen." Journalism Quarterly, LIII (Summer
1976), 319-324.
2331 _____. "Television War: Trends in Network Coverage
of Vietnam, 1965-1970." Journal of Broadcasting, XX
(Spring 1976), 147-158.
2332 _____, and Lawrence W. Lichty. "Rough Justice on a
Saigon Street: A Gatekeeper Study of NBC's Tet Execution
Film." Journalism Quarterly, XLIX (Summer 1972), 221-229.
2333 _____. "The Vietnam War According to Chet, David,
Walter, Harry, Peter, Bob, Howard, and Frank: A Content Analysis of Journalistic Performance by the Network Television Evening News Anchormen, 1965-1970." Unpublished PhD
Dissertation, University of Wisconsin, 1973.
2334 _____. "The War According to Walter: Network Anchormen and Vietnam. Milwaukee, Wisc.: Department of
Mass Communications, University of Wisconsin, 1975.
2335 Bain, Chester A. "Viet Cong Propaganda Abroad." Foreign Service Journal, XLV (October 1968), 18-21.
2336 Baldwin, Hanson W. "The Information War in Saigon."
Reporter, XXXIV (February 24, 1966), 29-31.

2337   Bishop, Donald M.   "The Press and the Tet Offensive:
A Flawed Institution Under Stress." Air University Review,
XXX (November-December 1978), 84-88.
2338   Blanchard, Ralph.   "The Newsmen in Vietnam."   U.S.
Naval Institute Proceedings, XCV (February 1969), 50-7.
2339   _____.   "The Newsman in Vietnam: Responsible or
Irresponsible?"   Naval War College Review, XX (June 1968),
14-42.
2340   Boylan, James.   "TV's Month [February 1966] of Tumult."
Columbia Journalism Review, V (Spring 1966), 15-21.
2341   Braestrup, Peter.   "Covering the Vietnam War."   Nieman
Report, XXIII (December 1969), 8-13.
2342   _____.   "The Press Corps in Vietnam."   Freedom at
Issue, (May-June 1977), 9-11.
2343   Browne, Malcolm W.   "A Reporter [for ABC News] Looks
Back: The CIA and the Fall of Vietnam."   Washington
Journalism Review, I (January-February 1978), 18-21.
2344   _____.   "Vietnam Reporting: Three Years of Crisis."
Columbia Journalism Review. III (Fall 1964), 4-10.
2345   Buckley, William F., Jr. "Elegant, Encounter, and Safer."
National Review, XXXIII (December 11, 1981), 1508-1509.
Morley   Safer's   "attack"   on   the   Vietnam   views   of   Robert   S.
Elegant.
2346   Bunge, Walter, Robert V. Hudson, and Chung Woo Suh.
"Johnson's Information Strategy for Vietnam: An Evaluation."   Journalism Quarterly, XLV (Autumn 1968), 419-425.
2347   Carroll, Raymond L., and Lawrence W. Lichty. "Network
News-Interview Programs and the "Television War": A Paper
Presented Before the Annual Meeting of the Association for Education in Journalism.   University, Ala.: Department of Communications, University of Alabama, 1981.   28p.   Available as ERIC
document ED 205 971.
2348   Chomsky, Noam.   "Reporting Indochina: The News Media
and the Legitimation of Lies." Social Policy, IV (September-
October 1973), 4-9.
2349   "Chopper Warfare: ABC's 'Letters from Vietnam.'" Newsweek, LXIV (September 14, 1964), 84.
2350   "Chroniclers of Chaos."   Time, XV (April 14, 1975),
55-56.
2351   "Cronkite Takes a Stand."   Newsweek, LXX (March 11,
1968), 108.
2352   Davison, W. Phillips.   "Making Sense of Vietnam News."
Columbia Journalism Review, V (Winter 1966-1967), 5-9.
2353   Dimmick, John.   "The Belief System of War Correspondents: A   Bayesian   Analysis."   Journalism Quarterly, L
(Autumn 1973), 560-562.
2354   Doan, Richard K.   "How Top Newsman View Vietnam."
TV Guide, XVI (March 16, 1968), A-1.
2355   Dunne, J. G.   "The Networks on Vietnam."   New Republic, CLIV (January 8, 1966), 36-37.
2356   Efron, Edith.   "Massive Study [Braestrup's] Indicts Media
Coverage of Vietnam."   TV Guide, XXV (July 9, 1977),
A5-A6.
2357   _____.   "Why Were the Vietnam Facts Misrepresented?"
TV Guide, XXV (July 16, 1977, A5-A6.

2358   Elegant, Robert. "Looking Back at Vietnam: How to Lose a War--Reflections of a Foreign Correspondent." En-counter, LVII (August 1981), 73-90.

2359   Emergy, Edwin. "The Press in the Vietnam Quagmire." Journalism Quarterly, XLVIII (Winter 1971), 619-626.

2360   Emerson, Gloria. "The War That Murdered Honor." Dial, I (December 1980), 46+.

2361   "Epilogue in Vietnam Proves Hard." Broadcasting, LXXXVIII (May 5, 1975), 36-37.

2362   Epstein, Edward J. "The Pentagon Papers: Reviewing History." In: his Between Fact and Fiction: The Problem of Journalism. New York: Random House, 1975. pp. 78-100.

2363   _____ . "TV and the Vietnam War." TV Guide, III (September 29-October 13, 1973), 6-10, 20-23, 49-54.

2364   Erwin, Robert. "Authorities Assay TV's War Coverage." Editor and Publisher, XCIX (April 2, 1966), 14+.

2365   "Eric Severeid vs. Alexander Solzhenitsyn on News Media Coverage of the Hue Massacres of 1968: Reprinted from a Report by Accuracy in Media, November 1973." Congressional Record, CXIX (December 4, 1973), 39457-39460.

2366   Faulkner, Francis D. "Bao Chi: The American News Media in Vietnam, 1960-1975." Unpublished PhD Disserta-tion, University of Massachusetts, 1981.

2367   Fitzgerald, Frances. "Covering the Happy Ending." More, VI (July 1976), 6+.

2368   Gitlin, Todd. "Spotlight and Shadows: Television and the Culture of Politics." College English, XXXVIII (Spring 1977), 789-801.

2369   Glass, Andrew J. "Nixon, the Press, and Vietnam." New Leader, LV (January 24, 1972), 5-6.

2370   Greenwald, J. "TV Newsmen Caught in Asian Hurricane." Editor and Publisher, XCVIII (July 24, 1965), 16+.

2371   Halberstam, David. "Getting the Story in Vietnam." Commentary, XXXIX (January 1965), 30-34.

2372   Hallin, Daniel C. "The Mass Media and the Crisis in American Politics: The Case of Vietnam." Unpublished PhD Dissertation, University of California at Berkeley, 1980.

2373   Hart, John. "Set the Watchdogs Loose." Quill, LX (July 1972), 4+.

2374   Herr, Michael. "Hearts and Minds." Columbia Journalism Review, XVI (January 1978), 47-48.

2375   Herz, Martin F. The Prestige Press and the Christmas Bombing, 1972: Images and Reality in Vietnam. Washington, D.C.: Ethics and Public Policy Center, 1980. 103p.

2376   _____ . "Tet vs. Electronic Journalism." Officer, LIII (August 1977), 8-9+.

2377   Hickey, Neil. "The Vietnam War: Is Television Giving Us the Picture?" TV Guide, XIV (October 1-22, 1966), 6-13, 26-32, 13-18, 36-40.

2378   Jacobsen, K. C. "Television and the War: The Small Picture." U.S. Naval Institute Proceedings, CI (March 1975), 54-60.

2379   Jakes, John W. "Walter Cronkite on the Air: A Strange War, a New Breed." In: his Great War Correspondents. New York: G.P. Putnam, 1968. Chpt. 10.

2380 Johnson, DeWayne B. "Vietnam: A Report Card on the Press Corps at War." Journalism Quarterly, XLVI (Spring 1969), 9-19.

2381 Joyce, Dick. "TV Coverage in Vietnam." Army Digest, XXII (January 1967), 37-39.

2382 Karnow, Stanley. "The Newsmens' War in Vietnam." Nieman Reports, XVI (December 1963), 3-8.

2383 Kirk, Gerry. "Heads They Win, Tails We Lose: TV and the War." New Guard, XII (December 1972), 8-10.

2384 Knightly, Phillip. "'Vietnam' [and] 'War is Fun, 1954-1975.'" In: his The First Casualty: From the Crimea to Vietnam--The War Correspondent as Hero, Propagandist, and Myth Maker. New York: Harcourt Brace Jovanovich, 1975. pp. 373-426.

2385 Kroeger, Albert R. "Vietnam: Television's Cruelist Test." Television, XXIII (May 196), 24-27.

2386 LaFeber, Walter. "Vietnam and the Next War." Democracy, I (January 1981), 93-103. Challenges the idea of a media "stab-in-the-back" on Vietnam.

2387 Lefever, Ernest R. "The Cambodian Blood Bath and the Great [TV] Silence." TV Guide, XXV (April 30, 1977), A5-A6.

2388 Lichty, Lawrence W. "The Night at the End of the Tunnel: How Television Reported the End of the Indochina War." Film Comment, XI (July-August 1975), 32+.

2389 _____. "The War We Watched on Television: A Study in Progress." American Film Institute Report, IV (Winter 1973), 29-37.

2390 _____, and Murray Fromson. "Comparing Notes on Television's Coverage of the War." Center Magazine, XII September 1979), 42-46.

2391 "Lid in Vietnam: Restrictions on Newsmen." Newsweek, LXV (March 29, 1965), 58-59.

2392 "Living-Room War: The Impact of TV." U.S. News and World Report, LXIV (March 4, 1968), 28-29.

2393 Lofton, John D., Jr. "Networks were Busy--There was No Time for Saigon's Side: Reprinted from the Philadelphia Inquirer, February 28, 1975." Congressional Record, CXXI (March 5, 1975), 5337.

2394 Lord, Arthur A. "Missing in Action: Journalists in Indochina." TV Guide, XXI (June 2, 1973), 14-16.

2395 Lower, Elmer W. "Are Newsmen Hampered?: Blasts Restrictions in Vietnam." Broadcasting, LXX (April 18, 1966), 56.

2396 Lunch, William M. and Peter W. Sperlich. "American Public Opinion and the War in Vietnam." Western Political Quarterly, XXXII (March 1979), 21-44.

2397 McLaughlin, John. "Siagon Newsgathering." America, CXIX (November 2, 196), 418-420.

2398 McNulty, Thomas H. "Vietnam Specials: Policy and Content." Journal of Communications, xiv (Autumn 1975), 173-180.

2399 Mahoney, John. "How the Vietnam War Changed Television News Operations." EBU Review, (July 1975), 16-17.

2400   Maloney, Martin. "Does TV Confuse Americans About Vietnam?" TV Guide, XV (December 2, 1967), 7-10.

2401   Marshall, Samuel L. A. "Press Failure in Vietnam: America's Sedentary War Correspondents." New Leader, XLIX (October 10, 1966), 3-5.

2402   "The Media and Vietnam: An Appraisal." Columbia Journalism Review, IX (Winter 1970-1971), 26-27.

2403   "The Media and Vietnam: Comment and Appraisal." In: Michael C. Emery and Ted C. Smythe, eds. Readings in Mass Communications: Concepts and Issues in the Mass Media. 2nd ed. Dubuque, Ia.: William C. Brown, 1974. pp. 435-440.

2404   Middleton, Drew. "Vietnam and the Military Mind." New York Times Magazine, (January 10, 1982), 34-37+.

2405   "Moral Issues are Involved in the TV Coverage of the Vietnam War: Reprinted from the Rolla [No.] Daily News, July 24, 1967." Congressional Record, CXIII (July 25, 1967), 20013.

2406   "Mortars at Martini Time." Time, XC (December 1, 1967), 86-87.

2407   Mortensen, C. David. "The Influence of Television on Policy Decision." Quarterly Journal of Speech, LIV (October 1968), 277-281.

2408   Moyers, Bill D. "One Thing We Learned." Foreign Affairs, XLVI (1968), 657-664.

2409   "Networks Escalate Vietnam Coverage." Broadcasting, LIX (February 7, 1966), 58-59.

2410   Nobile, Philip. "Placing the Blame for Vietnam." Insight: Sunday Magazine of the Milwaukee Journal, (December 3, 1972), 30-35.

2411   Oberdorfer, Don. "Tet: The Turning Point." Washington Post Magazine, (January 28, 1978), 10-11, 17-19.

2412   O'Meara, Andrew P. "Vietnam in Perspective." Armor, LXXXIV (November-December 1975), 8-14.

2413   Padgett, Harry E. "A Close Look at the Controversial U.S. Press Corps in Vietnam." Navy, XI (May 1968), 8-14.

2414   Pride, Richard A. and Gary L. Wormsley. "Symbol Analysis of Network Coverage of the Laos Incursion." Journalism Quarterly, XLIX (Winter 1972), 635-647.

2415   "The Problems of Vietnam." Broadcasting, LXXIII (September 18, 1967), 67-68.

2416   Reeves, Richard. "Fallibility and the Fourth Estate." Esquire, LXXXIX (February 1978), 8+.

2417   Rigg, Robert B. "How Not to Report a War." Military Review, XLIX (June 1969), 14-24.

2418   Roche, John P. "The Media's Influence on the Course of the War Has Been Misjudged." TV Guide, XXIII (July 5, 1975), A3-A4.

2419   _____. "New Book [Braestrup] on Tet Offensive Shows Shameful Behavior of the Press: Reprinted from the Washington Star, July 27, 1977." Congressional Record, CXXIII (August 2, 1977), 26228.

2420   Roundy, Peter E. "Images of Vietnam: 'Catch-22,' New Journalism, and the Post-Modern Imagination." Unpublished PhD Dissertation, Florida State University, 1981.

2421   Russo, Frank D.   "A Study of Bias in TV Coverage of
       the Vietnam War: 1969 and 1970." Public Opinion Quarterly,
       XXXV (Winter 1971-1972), 539-543.
2422   Saarinen, Aline.   "Newswomen in Vietnam."   TV Guide,
       XIV (January 29, 1966), 8-11.
2423   Safer, Morley.   "Television Covers the War: Reprinted
       from Overseas Press Club of America's Dateline 1966
Covering War."   Congressional Record, CXII (May 12, 1966),
10467-10468.
2424   "'Saigon Follies?':   Newsmen Accuse USIS of Withholding
       News."   Newsweek.   LXVIII (August 15, 1966), 54-55.
2425   Semple, Robert.   "The Media and Vietnam."   In: R.
       Gordon Harris, ed.   The White House--Organization and
Operations: Proceedings of the 1970 Montauk Symposium on the
Office of the President of the United States.   New   York:
Center for the Study of the Presidency, 1971.   pp. 43-45.
2426   Shelton, John S.   "A Comparison of Network Television
       News Coverage and Audiences: The War in Vietnam,
February-May '70."   Unpublished PhD Dissertation, American
University, 1973.
2427   Stanton, Frank.   "The Face of War."   Quill, LIV (March
       1966), 27. Reprinted in Congressional Record, CXII (March
       10, 1966), A1393-A1394.
2428   _____.   "Why War News Must Be Honest."   Broadcasting,
       LXX (January 31, 1966), 56-57.
2429   Stillman, Don.   "Tonkin Gulf: What Should Have Been
       Asked?"   Columbia Journalism Review, IX   (Winter 1970-
       1971), 21-25.
2430   Sylvester, Arthur.   "Vietnam and the News."   Broad-
       casting, LXXI (September 5, 1966), 59-60.
2431   Thompson, K. S.   " Photographic Imagery and the Viet-
       nam War: An Unexamined Perspective."   Journal of Psy-
       chology, LXXXVII (July 1974), 279-292.
2432   Trotta, Liz.   "A Female War Correspondent in Vietnam."
       TV Guide, XVII (April 19, 1969), 6-10.
2433   "Tough Job Getting News Out of Vietnam."   Broadcasting,
       LXVIII (May 31, 1965), 52-53.
2434   "TV Newsmen Take Strong Stands on Vietnam."   Broad-
       casting, LXXIV (March 18, 1968), 66-67.
2435   "The Ultimate Weeper: Coverage of POW's Homecoming."
       Newsweek, LXXXI (February 26, 1973), 55.
2436   "U.S. National Interest Not Considered Before Spreading
       Enemy Propaganda Say Network News, Wire Service Execu-
tives: Reprinted from Monday, May 16, 1972."   Congressional
Record, CXVIII (May 16, 1972.) 17493-17494.   Showing North
Vietnamese film by network news.
2437   Voudouris, Arthur C.   "Language as a Factor in Airpower."
       Aerospace Historian, XII (April 1965), 56-59.
2438   Welch, Susan.   "Vietnam: How the Press Went Along."
       Nation, CCXIII (October 11, 1971), 327-330.
2439   Witze, Claude.   "Hanoi Manages Our News."   Air Force
       and Space Digest, L (February 1967), 12+.
2440   Zeidenberg, Leonard.   "The 21-Inch View of Vietnam."
       Television, XXV (January 1968), 28-33+.

2441 _____ . "Vietnam and Electronic Journalism: Lessons of the Living-Room War." Broadcasting, LXXXVIII (May 19, 1975), 23+.

2442 Zorthian, Barry. "The Cluttered View from SEA." Air Force and Space Digest, LI (November 1968), 52-54+.

IX. BIOGRAPHY

The materials immediately below are devoted in a general way to persons involved in network news. In addition, some examine the "star" system of reporters and anchormen or women, and some cover blacks, salaries and the talents necessary for certain positions. Following the Collective Biography articles come individual persons, in alphabetical order. They are also all in the Index.

COLLECTIVE BIOGRAPHY--Books

2443   Abrams, Alan E., ed.   Journalists Biographical Master Index: A Guide to More Than 82,000 Sketches of and References to Historical and Modern Journalists in Over 200 Biographical Directories and Other Sources.   Gale Biographical Index Series, v. 4. Detroit, Mich.: Gale Research Company, 1979. As is the case with our next entry, this is not a directory but an index to sources where one can find information about a variety of journalists, both print and broadcast.

2444   Biography Index. New York: H. W. Wilson Co., 1947--, v. 1--. A noted reference tool which provides listings to books, articles, and other materials about a variety of personnel in many walks of life; for our purposes, this is an important source on reporters and broadcast personnel which is usually available in public or college libraries.

2445   Current Biography. New York: H.W. Wilson Co., 1947--. v. 7--. A useful source for direct biographical information on the more important network personnel; data presented is often lengthy and complete, unfortunately, however, less than 50 biographies relative to this guide have been entered in Current Biography since 1947.

2446   Downie, Leonard.   The New Muckrakers.   Washington, D.C.: New Republic Book Company, 1976. 296p. A look at print and broadcast journalists who have come to specialize in investigative reporting since the 1960's.

2447   Dygert, James H.   The Investigative Journalist: Folk Heroes of a New Era.   Englewood Cliffs, N.J.: Prentice-Hall, 1976. 282p. Examines the work of print and broadcast journalists who have made a specialty of learning and reporting such cases as Watergate, problems in Vietnam, etc.

2448   Facts on File, Editors of.   Obituaries on File [1940-1978]. 2 vols. New York: Facts on File, Inc., 1979. A useful

source for biographical information on broadcast journalists who
died before 1978, e.g., Chet Huntley, Edward R. Murrow, and
Frank McGee.
2449   New York Times Obituary Index, 1858-1968.   New York:
       New York Times Company, 1970. 1,136p. Provides obitu-
aries on broadcast personnel who died before 1968 as reported
in the pages of the New York Times.
2450   Powers, Ron.   The Newscasters: The News Business as
       Show Business. New York: St. Martin's Press, 1977.
243p. In addition to looking at the rotation of local news
personnel, Powers, a frequent contributor to TV Guide, tells us
the stories of many noted network news reporters and anchormen.
2451   Steinberg, Barbara.   Who Puts the News on Television?
       New York: Random House, 1976.   75p. A juvenile title
which studies the work of all involved including writers, producers, anchormen, etc.
2452   Who's Who in America. Chicago, Ill.:   Marquis, 1947--,
       v. 9--. A unique source and one of the best for concise
biographies of network news personnel; the latest edition contains data on all but a handful of network reporters and producers and varies in length according to what the candidate
submits.

COLLECTIVE BIOGRAPHY--Articles

2453   Brinkley, David. "TV News and the Star System." Tele-
       vision Quarterly, V (Spring 1966), 13-18.
2454   . "What are Sponsors Buying?:   News or a TV
       News Star?" Sponsor, XXI (January 23, 1967), 38-39.
2455   Burgoon, J. K. "Attributes of the Newscasters Voice as
       Predictors of His Credibility." Journalism Quarterly, LV
       (Summer 1978), 276-281.
2456   Corliss, Richard. "Sex Stars of the '70's: Newscasters."
       Film Comment, XV (July 1979), 27-29.
2457   Cronkite, Walter. "On Choosing--and Paying--Anchor-
       people." Columbia Journalism Review, XV (July 1976),
       24-25.
2458   Doan, Richard K. "Newscasting: No Longer a White
       Man's Club." TV Guide, IX (December 4, 1971), 7-10.
2459   "Faces of Faceless Men: Producers Wallace Westfield, Av
       Westin, Les Midgley." Newsweek, LXXIV (November 24,
       1969), 92.
2460   "Fates and Fortunes: News and Public Affairs." In:
       each weekly issue of Broadcasting: Magazine of the Fifth
Estate (Washington, D.C.:   Broadcasting Publications, Inc.,
1935--). A good way to keep up with the movements of network
news personnel; for example, on p. 93 of the April 19, 1982
issue, one finds that NBC correspondent Bill Sternoff has
joined Los Angeles station KNXT-TV as an anchor-reporter.
2461   Gates, Gary P. "If You Can't Beat 'Em, Raid 'Em."
       TV Guide, XXVIII (February 9, 1980), 5-9.
2462   Goldhabar, Gerald M. "Network Newsmen: Who's Got the
       Most Charisma?" TV Guide, XXIX (May 2, 1981), 4-10.

In order, Walter Cronkite, Roger Mudd, John Chancellor, Frank
Reynolds, Peter Jennings, Max Robinson, Dan Rather.
2463 Halberstam, David. "They Ought to Play Up the News--
      Not the Newscasters." TV Guide, XXVII (January 20,
      1979), 31-34.
2464 Levine, Richard M. "The Plight of Black Reporters."
      TV Guide, XXIX (July 18-25, 1981), 2-7, 26-38.
2465 "News Talent Commanding Ever-Higher Pay Scales." Broad-
      casting, XCVIII (April 7, 1980), 100+.
2466 "Out-of-Office Politicians Join Ranks of Broadcast Person-
      alities." Broadcasting, XCII (March 7, 1977), 57.
2467 Pierce, John C. "Party, Ideology, and Public Evaluations
      of the Power of Television Newspeople." Journalism Quar-
      terly, LIV (Summer 1977), 307-312.
2468 Pincus, Ann. "The Best Television Reporters." Washing-
      ton Monthly, XI (December 1975), 134-139.
2469 Ryan, Michael. "TV Newsmen: Well Paid for Lecturing."
      TV Guide, XXV (March 19, 1977), 24-25.
2470 Thrush, Robin. "Behind TV News: The Top Newscasters
      Talk About How They See Their Jobs." Family Weekly,
      (February 1, 1976), 4-7.
2471 Townley, Richard. "The Best Charisma Money Can Buy."
      TV Guide, XXIV (October 16, 1976), 42-45.
2472 Valeriana, Richard. "The Uncertain Celebrity of TV
      Newsmen." TV Guide, XXV (November 22, 1975), 6-8.
2473 Vallejo, Fred. "The Best in the Business: Reporters
      Rate Their Prime Time Peers." Washington Journalism
      Review, II (December 1980), 32-33.
2474 Wadler, Joyce. "Super Media Men." Viva, III (February
      1976), 50-54.
2475 Weisman, John. "How Politicians Rate TV's Reporters."
      TV Guide, XXIX (September 5, 1981), 6-10.
2476 "Whom Can You Trust in Network News?" Broadcasting,
      LXXXVI (June 17, 1974), 33.
2477 Wood, William A. "TV News Stars." In: Judy Fireman,
      ed. TB Books, the Ultimate TV Book. New York: Work-
      man Publishing Co., 1977. p 258.

AGRONSKY, MARTIN

2478 "Martin Agronsky: A Broadcast Journalist Who's Covered
      the World." Broadcasting, CI (November 2, 1981), 103.
2479 "A Skillful Reporter." Newsweek, XLI (May 4, 1953), 84.
2480 Turck, Nancy. "Martin and Hugh and Carl and Peter
      and Klipo." Washington Monthly, X (February 1975),
      175-181.

ARLEDGE, ROONE

2481 "ABC Hopes for News Rest Now with Sports Wizard Ar-
      ledge." Broadcasting, XCII (May 9, 1977), 44+.
2482 "ABC's Wider World of News: The Appointment of Roone
      Arledge." Time, CIX (May 16, 1977), 79-80.

2483   Arledge, Roone. "Roone at the Top: Excerpts from an Interview." Newsweek, LXXXIX (May 16, 1977), 103-104.
2484   _____. "Going In: A Selection of Arledgisms on TV News." Broadcasting, XCII (May 9, 1977), 30.
2485   Buckley, Tom. "Wide World of News: The Work of Roone Arledge." Horizon, XXI (September 1978), 66-70.
2486   Diamond, Edwin. "ABC's Captain Success." Washington Journalism Review, I (October 1977), 14-19.
2487   Swertlow, Frank. "ABC's Prince: The Most Powerful Man in Television." New York, X (October 10, 1977), 39-43.

BERGMAN, JULES

2488   "Jules Bergman, TV's Science Editor." TV Guide, XI (August 24, 1963), 15-17.

BITTERMAN, JIM

2489   Dupont, Joan. "Part Clark Kent, Part James Bond." TV Guide, XXIX (June 6, 1981), 613.

BLAIR, FRANK

2490   Blair, Frank with Jack Smith. "Let's Be Frank About It. Garden City, N.Y.: Doubleday, 1979. 377p. Autobiography.
2491   Hickey, Neil. "Newscaster Frank Blair." TV Guide, XX (February 26, 1972), 44-46.
2492   _____. "Today's Producer Starts His Day with Homework." TV Guide, XII (August 1, 1964), 4-7.

BRADLEY, ED

2493   Reise, Bob. "Profile: Ed Bradley." Washington Journalism Review, III (May 1981), 40-44.
2494   Tait, E. V. "Ed Bradley: Life in the Fast Lane." Encore, VI (August 1, 1977), 26-31.
2495   Townley, Rod. "Ed Bradley of 60 Minutes." TV Guide, XXX (February 20, 1982), 28-33.
2496   Weisman, John. "For Ed Bradley, the White House is Not a Home." TV Guide, XXV (August 10, 1977), 10-12.

BRINKLEY, DAVID

2497   Ball, A. L. "People on the Cover: David Brinkley." Redbook, CXLVI (May 1976), 4+.
2498   Braun, Saul. "Brinkley on Brinkley." TV Guide, XX (April 15, 1972), 36-40.
2499   Brinkley, Ann F. "Ex Marks the Spot." Ladies Home Journal, XCV (February 1978), 147-149.
2500   Brinkley, David. "The Washington Establishment and Education: Excerpts from an Address." Education Digest, XLII (September 1976), 6-8.

2501 "Brinkley to ABC." Broadcasting, CI (September 28, 1981), 45.
2502 "Brinkleymanship." Newsweek, LIX (May 14, 1962), 98.
2503 Clurman, S. "Host." People, IX (February 6, 1978), 78-80.
2504 Crawford-Mason, C. "Can A Dubious Eyebrow Slant the News?" People, XII (November 12, 1979), 44-46.
2505 "David Brinkley." In: Current Biography Yearbook, 1960. New York: H. W. Wilson Co., 1961. pp. 51-53.
2506 _____. In: Eleanora W. Schoenebaum, ed. Political Profiles: The Kennedy Years. New York: Facts on File, Inc., 1976. pp. 49-50.
2507 "David Brinkley Adds Punchlines to Headlines." TV Guide, VII (May 16, 1959), 12-14.
2508 "David Takes on a Goliath." Time, CXVI (September 8, 1980), 61.
2509 "David's New Dateline." Newsweek, LXXII (December 30, 1968), 46.
2510 Efron, Edith. "David Brinkley." TV Guide, X (July 7-14, 1962), 6-9, 22-25.
2511 Evans, Katherine W. "A Conversation with David Brinkley." Washington Journalism Review, III (November 1981), 15-20.
2512 "Good Night, David, from NBC." Newsweek, XCIV (October 15, 1979), 96.
2513 Kaye, Dena. "Where I Go When I Want to Escape: An Interview with David Brinkley." Travel and Leisure, VI (January 1976), 36+.
2514 Liston, J. "At Home with Brinkley." American Home, LIV (September 1961), 13-14+.
2515 "Mr. Brinkley Goes to New York." Time, XCIII (March 14, 1969), 82+.
2516 "This is David Brinkley." Newsweek, LV (January 4, 1960), 40.
2517 Wren, C. S. "David Brinkley and His Golden Key." Look, XXVIII (February 25, 1964), 44+.
2518 "The Wry World of David Brinkley." Look, XXIV (April 26, 1960), 73-74+.

BROKAW, TOM

2519 Bedell, Sally. "Tom Brokaw: Anchorman on the Go." TV Guide, XXX (April 10, 1982), 26-32.
2520 Brokaw, Tom. "A Day in the Life of a White House Correspondent." Washington Monthly, XI (December 1975), 138-139.
2521 "But Tom Decides to Stay [at NBC]." Time, CXVIII (July 13, 1981), 62.
2522 McNurran, K. "NBC Played Hardball to Sign Tom Brokaw for Nightly News." People, XVI (July 13, 1981), 30-31.
2523 Ryan, Michael and Sally Bedell. "Tom Brokaw of Today." TV Guide, XXV (May 14, 1977), 14-18.
2524 Thompson, Toby. "The Prince of News: Tom Brokaw." Rolling Stone, (May 13, 1982), 26-29.
2525 "Tom Brokaw." In: Current Biography Yearbook 1981. New York: H. W. Wilson Co., 1982. pp. 36-39.

2526   White, B.   "Tom Brokaw: By Dawn's Early Light." Saturday Evening Post, CCL (May 1976), 78-80.

BROUN, HEYWOOD HALE

2527   Broun, Heywood Hale. A Studied Madness.   Garden
City, N.Y.: Doubleday, 1965. 298p.
2528   _____ . Tumultuous Merriment. New York: Richard
Marek, 1979. 278p.
2529   Higgins, Robert.   "Heywood Hale Broun Isn't Sure About
His Career."   TV Guide, XVI (January 6, 1968), 25-27.

CHANCELLOR, JOHN

2530   Bennette, L.   "John Chancellor." Biographical News, II
(May 1975), 503-504.
2531   Burke, Tom.   "John Chancellor of NBC News." TV Guide,
XXII (June 22, 1974), 20-24.
2532   Chancellor, John.   "Don't Beat the Messenger." TV Guide,
XXIII (March 8, 1975), A5-A6.
2533   _____ .   "Things Quite Often Go Wrong."   TV Guide,
XXVII (November 3, 1979), 6-12.
2534   "Chancellor on His Own."   Newsweek, LXXVIII (August
2, 1971), 71.
2535   Diamond, Edwin.   "Politics and Pizza a Threat to TV
News: An Interview with John Chancellor."   Politicks,
I (January 31, 1978), 7-9.
2536   Drew, H. H. "Ambulatory Anchor Man."   Biographical
News, I (June 1974), 625.
2537   Gans, Herbert J.   "Letters to an Anchorman."   Journal
of Communications, XXVII (Summer 1977), 86-91.
2538   "Iron Chancellor."   Time, XCVIII (August 2, 1971), 55.
2539   "John   Chancellor."   In: Current Biography Yearbook
1962.   New York: H. W. Wilson Co., 1963. pp. 81-83.
2540   _____ . In: Eleanora W. Schoenebaum, ed. Political
Profiles: The Johnson Years.   New York: Facts on File,
Inc., 1976. p. 101.
2541   Millstein, Gilbert.   "John Chancellor: The Man Who Suc-
ceeded Garroway." TV Guide, X (January 20, 1962), 10-13.
2542   Nobile, Philip. "John Chancellor on the Record: An
Interview."   More, VI (May 1976), 7-11.
2543   Waters, Harry F.   "Hoisting Anchor."   Newsweek, XC
(December 12, 1977), 98.
2544   Whittemore, Reed.   "John Chancellor."   New Republic,
CLXXIV (January 3, 1976), 25-26.

CHASE, SYLVIA

2545   Hall, Jane. "Sylvia Chase of CBS's Magazine." TV Guide,
XXIV (June 19, 1976), 8-9.

CHUNG, CONNIE

2546   Cimons, Marlene.   "Why Network Newsmen Decide to Go
Local." TV Guide, XXIV (August 28, 1976), 12-16.

2547   Saunders, Mary J. and Yusef Mageni. "The Straight and Narrow." Twin Cities Journalism Review, (June 1975), 8-9.
2548   Waters, Craig. "Come Back in About Ten Years." TV Guide, XXIII (April 19, 1975), 24-25.

COCHRAN, RON

2549   "ABC's Ron Cochran." TV Guide, XII (March 26, 1964), 12-14.

COMPTON, ANN

2550   Weisman, John. "Little Girl, How Would You Like to be a White House Correspondent?" TV Guide, XXIII (September 13, 1975), 26-27.

CRONKITE, WALTER

2551   "A.S.J.S.A. Honors Walter Cronkite as the Outstanding Broadcast Journalist of the 1970's." Journalism Education, XXXV (October 1980), 11-14.
2552   Bayless, Pamela. "Favorite Father Figure Finds Show-Me Healthy." City, I (April 1978), 30-31.
2553   Bennetts, L. "And That's the Way It Is." Biographical News, II (March 1975), 299-300.
2554   Buckley, William F., Jr. "The Unhappy Dilemma of Walter Cronkite." National Review, XXIV (December 8, 1972), 1370-1371.
2555   Carter, Betsey. "Walter Cronkite: A Dossier." Esquire, XCIV (December 1980), 88-89.
2556   Coates, C. "Cronkite Move Seen as Boon to ABC." Advertising Age, LI (March 3, 1980), 4+.
2557   Considine, Bob. "Walter Cronkite: A Personal Perspective." In: Barbara Nykoruk, ed. Authors in the News. 2 vols. Detroit, Mich.: Gale Research Co., 1976. II, 70-73.
2558   Cronkite, Betsey. "Mrs. Cronkite Shares Her Family Pictures and Memories: An Interview." McCall's, CVIII (February 1981), 100-101+.
2559   Cronkite, Kathy. "Life with Father." McCall's, CVIII (February 1981), 98-101.
2560   _____. "My Father, Walter Cronkite." McCall's, CV (November 1977), 222-223+.
2561   _____. On the Edge of the Spotlight. New York: William Morrow, 1981. 318p.
2562   Cronkite, Walter. "And That's the Way It Is: An Interview." Columbia Journalism Review, XIX (May-June 1980), 50-51.
2563   _____. "And That's the Way It Was: An Interview." Broadcasting, XCIX (December 1, 1980), 53-54.
2564   _____. An Evening with Walter Cronkite: Transcript of an Interview at the Speech Communications Association Summer Conference on Mass Communications in Education and Society. Ausin, Tx.:, 1975. 16p. ERIC document ED 157 128.
2565   _____. Eye on the World. New York: Cowles Communications, 1971. 310p.

2566 _____ . "An Interview with John Love." Quest 81, V (March 1981), 96.

2567 _____ . "An Interview with Lally Weymouth." Washington Journalism Review, III (January-February 1981), 21-25.

2568 _____ . "Why I Believe: An Interview." Today's Health, L (February 1972), 20-24.

2569 Daly, George. "After 19 Years as TV's Most Unimpeachable Source, Walter Cronkite Weighs Anchor." People, XV (March 9, 1981), 26-31.

2570 Fallaci, Oriana. "What Does Walter Cronkite Really Think?" Look, XXXIV (November 17, 1970), 57-62.

2571 Gehman, Richard. "Walter Cronkite: The Deliberate Dutchman." TV Guide, XI (June 29, 1963), 24-27.

2572 Genn, Lillian C. "An Interview with Walter Cronkite." Modern Maturity, XVIII (September-October 1975), 9-10.

2573 Gorkin, M. "Walter Cronkite: Why He's the Most Trusted Man in America." 50 Plus, XIX (November 1979), 14-19.

2574 Greene, Bob. "Anchor's Aweigh." Esquire, XCIV (December 1980), 19-20.

2575 Griffith, Tom. "The Age of Cronkite Passes." Time, CXVII (March 9, 1981), 42-43.

2576 Harding, Henry. "Cronkite Relieved of Anchorman Duties for 1964 Democratic Convention." TV Guide, XII (August 8, 1964), A-1.

2577 Hoffman, A. "Eyes on Cronkite." Esquire, LXXIX (April 1973), 85.

2578 Howell, Chauncey. "That's the Way It Is: An Interview with Walter Cronkite." Women's Wear Daily, CXXII (February 9, 1971), 4-5.

2579 Krementz, Jill. "The Great Anchorman Off Camera." Life, III (November 1980), 133+.

2580 Lapham, L. H. "The Secret Life of Walter (Mitty) Cronkite." Saturday Evening Post, CCXXXVI (March 16, 1963), 65-67.

2581 Martorelli, D. "Walter Cronkite Speaks to Teachers." Instructor, XC (November 190), 38-40.

2582 Miller, M. C. "And That's the Way It Seems." New Republic, CLXXXIV (February 14, 1981), 19-23.

2583 _____ . "Walter Cronkite: And That's the Way It Seems." Current, CCXXXII (May 1981), 20-28.

2584 Morgan, Al. "A Conversation with Walter Cronkite." TV Guide, XX (March 4, 1972), 18-20.

2585 Morgan, Neil. "Walter Cronkite's Plans." Dial, I (September 1980), 77-78.

2586 "A Most Intimate Medium." Time, LXXXVIII (October 14, 1966), 56-58.

2587 O'Neil, Peter. "The Prime Time of Walter Cronkite." Life, LXX (March 26, 1971), 50A-50B.

2589 Orr, Rita. "Walter Cronkite: Playboy Interview." Playboy, XX (June 1973), passim.

2590 Reddy, J. "The Unflappable Walter Cronkite." Reader's Digest, XCV (December 1969), 193-194.

2591 Reeves, Richard. "Which Is More Real?: Walter Cronkite or Alan Alda?" Panorama, I (May 1980), 10-11.

2592 Rein, Rich. "Walter Cronkite Is Back on the Space Beat,"
      People, IV (July 21, 1975), 54-59.
2593 Reinert, Al. "The Secret World of Walter Cronkite."
      Texas Monthly, IV (January 1976), 62+.
2594 Ronge, Peter R. "You Can Hardly Beat It for a Long-
      Running Story: An Interview with Walter Cronkite." Pano-
      rama, I (June 1980), 16-21.
2595 Schickel, Richard. "Walter Cronkite Must be Doing Some-
      thing Right." TV Guide, XIV (July 2, 1966), 15-18.
2596 Shaw, David. "And That's the Way He Is." TV Guide,
      XXVII (April 21, 1979), 32-40.
2597 Taves, I. "Walter Cronkite: Why Won't He Be Himself
      on TV?" Look, XXVIII (August 25, 1964), 74+.
2598 Taylor, Paula and Norita Larson. Walter Cronkite. Cre-
      ative Education Close-ups. Mankato, Mn.: Creative Educa-
      tion, 1975. 29p.
2599 "A Television Institution: Newsman Walter Cronkite."
      Broadcasting, LXXXV (October 15, 1973), 57.
2600 "That's the Way It Is." Newsweek, LXXXII (November
      12, 1973), 87-88.
2601 Tivnam, Edward. "The Cronkite Syndrome." Dial, I
      (November 1980), 44+.
2602 Tornabene, Lynn. "Walter Cronkite Cannot Tell a Lie."
      Cosmopolitan, CLXXXV (October 1978), 251+.
2603 Unger, A. "Cronkite in Retirement." Current, CCXXXII
      (May 1981), 32-36.
2604 Vallejo, Fred. "The Best in the Business." Washington
      Journalism Review, II (December 1980), 32-33.
2605 Vonnegut, Kurt. "The Reluctant Big Shot." Current,
      CCXXXII (May 1981), 36-37.
2606 "Walter Cronkite." In: Current Biography Yearbook 1956.
      New York: H. W. Wilson Co., 1957. pp. 130-132.
2607 _____. In: Current Biography Yearbook 1975). New
      York: H. W. Wilson Co., 1976). pp 95-98.
2608 _____. In: Eleanora W. Schoenbaum, ed. Political
      Profiles: The Johnson Years. New York: Facts on File,
      Inc., 1976. pp. 136-137.
2609 _____. In: Eleanora W. Schoenbaum, ed. Political
      Profiles: The Kennedy Years. New York: Facts on File,
      Inc., 1976. pp. 103-104.
2610 _____. In: Eleanora W. Schoenbaum, ed. Political
      Profiles: The Nixon/Ford Years. New York: Facts on
      File, Inc., 1979. p. 155.
2611 _____. U.S., 1 (January 10, 1978), 18-21.
2612 Waters, Harry F. "A Man Who Cares." Newsweek, LCVII
      (March 9, 1981), 57-58.
2613 Westman, Paul. Walter Cronkite: The Most Trusted Man
      in America. Minneapolis, MN.: Dillon Press, 1980. 47p.
2614 Weymouth, Lally. "Cronkite Remembers: An Interview."
      Washington Journalism Review, III (January-February 1981),
      21-25.
2615 White, Theodore H. "A Hard Act to Follow." Rolling
      Stone, (April 2, 1981), 10-15.
2616 _____. "Is Walter Cronkite as Good as His Ratings?"
      Panorama, II (January 1981), 54+.

2617 _____. "Walter, We Hardly Knew You." Rolling Stone, (February 5, 1981), 17-19.
2618 "Who Runs America? U.S. News and World Report, LXXXII (April 18, 1977), 36; LXXXIV (April 17, 1978), 36.
2619 "You Want Uncle Walter." Esquire, XCVII (April 1973), 83-85.

DALY, JOHN

2620 "John Daly." TV Guide, 1 (November 20, 1953), 15-17.
2621 "John Daly's Line: News Expert." TV Guide, VIII (July 23, 1960), 8-11.
2622 "Vanishing Newsman." Time, LVIII (September 17, 1951), 79-80.

DANCY, JOHN

2623 Dancy, John. "White House Shadow." TV Guide, XXVII (August 11, 1979), 23-28.

DICKERSON, NANCY

2624 Dickerson, Nancy. Among Those Present: A Reporter's View of 25 Years in Washington. New York: Random House, 1976. 238p.
2625 Gottehrer, Barry. "Television's Princess of the Press Corps." Saturday Evening Post, CCXXXVII (October 31, 1964), 36-37.
2626 Rollin, Betty. "Nancy Dickerson: Washington's Most Serious Butterfly." Look, XXXI (September 5, 1967), 28-30.
2627 "TV's Newswoman." TV Guide, X (June 16, 1962), 6-9.

DOBYNS, LLOYD

2628 "How to Kiss an Elephant." TV Guide, XXVIII (February 23, 1980), 34-35.

DONALDSON, SAM

2629 Piantadosi, Roger. "Profile: Sam Donaldson." Washington Journalism Review, IV (March 1982), 45-49.
2630 Thompson, Toby. "Forgive Them Jody [Powell]." Washington Monthly, XIII (May 1978), 141+.
2631 Weisman, John. "'I'm Not Too Proud to Leap and Yell." TV Guide, XXVI (July 29, 1978), 8-10.

DOWNS, HUGH

2632 Bernard, Bina. "Hugh Downs is an Uneasy Rider in Retirement." People, III (March 3, 1975), 29-30.
2633 Downs, Hugh. "People Who Fly--Hugh Downs: An Interview." Flying, CVIII (December 1981), 84-86.
2634 Efron, Edith. "Hugh Downs, Egghead." TV Guide, IX (August 26, 1961), 4-7.

2635 "Hugh Downs." In: Current Biography Yearbook 1965.
New York: H. W. Wilson Co., 1966. pp. 127-130.

EDWARDS, DOUGLAS

2636 "Doug Edwards and the News." TV Guide, 1 (December
11, 1953), 22-23.
2637 Edwards, Douglas. "The One World of Television." Parent's Magazine, XXVI (March 1951), 160.
2638 "The News About Douglas Edwards." TV Guide, VI (May
17, 1958), 17-19.
2639 "A Very Happy Family on Kettle Creek Road . . . and a
Budget." Newsweek, XLIX (June 3, 1957), 88-89.

ELLERBEE, LINDA

2640 Cimons, Marlene. "No Jeans and Sneakers Around That
House." TV Guide, XXV (January 1, 1977), 14-15.

FENTON, TOM

2641 Fenton, Tom. "Bringing You Today's War--Today." TV
Guide, XXVIII (November 15, 1980), 36-38.

FETTER, DIANA

2642 Efron, Edith. "Diana Fetter of ABC News." TV Guide,
XVIII (May 16, 1970), 45-48.

FRANK, REUVEN

2643 "Reuven Frank is Back." Broadcasting, CII (March 8,
1982), 44.
2644 "Reuven Frank: Innovator at NBC News." Broadcasting,
LXXV (September 1968), 85.

FREDERICK, PAULINE

2645 "Busy Redhead Reporting." Newsweek, LII (August 11,
1958), 54.
2646 Clymer, Eleanor and Lillian Ehrlich. "Pauline Frederick."
In: their Modern American Career Woman. New York:
Dodd, Mead, 1959. pp. 141-149.
2647 "Newscaster Pauline Frederick." TV Guide, V (May 4,
1957), 22-23.
2648 Parshalle, Eve. "Pauline Frederick." In: her Kashmir
Bridge-Woman. New York: Oxford University Press,
1965. pp. 183-185.
2649 Talese, G. "The Perils of Pauline." Saturday Evening
Post, CCXXXVI (January 26, 1963), 20-22.

FRIENDLY, FRED

2650 "Bloody Test of Wills at CBS." Broadcasting, LXX (February 21, 1966), 72-75.

2651   Doan, Richard K.   "Public TV's Fred Friendly."   TV
Guide, XXI (April 15, 1973), 6-10.
2652   Efron, Edith.   "TV: America's Timid Giant."   TV Guide,
XI (May 18, 1963), 4-11.
2653   "Fred W. Friendly."   In: Current Biography Yearbook
1957.   New York: H. W. Wilson Co., 1958, pp. 196-198.
2654   Friendly, Fred W.   Due to Circumstances Beyond Our
Control . . .   New York: Random House, 1968, 339p.
2655   _____ .   "Fred Friendly Talks About TV News."   TV
Guide, XXIX (August 1, 1981), 24-29.
2656   _____ .   Television Can Open America's Eyes."   TV
Guide, VIII (December 10, 1960), 5-7.
2657   _____ .   Harding, Henry.   "Fred Friendly Resigns as
Head of CBS News."   TV Guide, XIV (February 26, 1966),
A-1.
2658   _____ .   "Fred W. Friendly New Head of CBS News."
TV Guide, XII (March 14, 1964), A-1.
2659   "Showdown at CBS."   Television, XXIII (March 1966),
7-9.
2660   Stanton, Frank.   "Comments on Friendly's Resignation."
Broadcasting, LXX (March 7, 1966), 58.

GARROWAY, DAVE

2661   "Dave Garroway."   In: Current Biography Yearbook 1952.
New York: H. W. Wilson Co., 1953.   pp. 207-209

GRAHAM, FRED

2662   Lofton, John D., Jr.   "Tape, Cocktails, TV Journalism,
and Legal Ethics."   TV Guide, XXII (March 2, 1974),
A3-A4.

GREENE, BOB

2663   Greene, Bob.   "A Print Reporter Ventures Into TV."
TV Guide, XXX (January 30, 1982), 6-10.

GUMBEL, BRYANT

2664   Henry, M.   "Today's New Mr. Natural."   Newsweek,
XCVIII (December 14, 1981), 101.
2665   Piantodosi, Roger.   "Profile: Bryant Gumbel."   Washington Journalism Review, IV (January-February 1982), 25-28.

HART, JOHN

2666   Hickey, Neil.   "Newsman John Hart."   TV Guide, XX
(March 25, 1972), 13-15.

HARTMAN, DAVID

2667   "David Hartman."   In: Current Biography Yearbook 1981.
New York: H. W. Wilson Co., 1982.   pp. 195-198.
2668   _____ .   U.S., 1 (September 6, 1977), 60-65.

HARTZ, JIM

2669 Hickey, Neil. "Jim Hartz of Today." TV Guide, XXIII
      (January 25, 1975), 8-12.
2670 "Jim Hartz Picked as McGee Successor." Broadcasting,
      LXXXVII (July 29, 1974), 36-37.

HEWITT, DON

2671 "The Man Who Makes 60 Minutes Tick." Broadcasting,
      XCVIII (February 11, 1980), 76-77.

HILL, SANDY

2672 Levin, Eric. "'I Love Playing Sponge.'" TV Guide,
      XXVI (January 28, 1978), 20-22.
2673 Hottelet, Richard C. "Words Take the Place of Blood."
      TV Guide, XXVII (October 6, 1979), 2-8.

HUNTLEY, CHET

2674 Barrett, B. "Chet Huntley: The Fatherly Rebel." Bio-
      graphical News, 1 (April 1974), 416.
2675 "The Calm Controversialist." Newsweek, XLIII (April
      19, 1954), 54.
2676 "Chet Huntley." In: Current Biography Yearbook 1956.
      New York: H. W. Wilson Co., 1957. pp. 290-291.
2677 _____. In: Eleanore W. Schoenebaum, ed. Political
      Profiles: The Kennedy Years. New York: Facts on File,
      Inc., 1976. pp. 242-243.
2678 "Chet Huntley Obituary: Transcript from NBC Nightly
      News, March 20, 1974." Congressional Record, CXX (March
      29, 1974), 8921-8922.
2679 Efron, Edith. "The Travels of Chester Huntley." TV
      Guide, XIII (June 19, 1965), 6-8.
2680 Frost, David. "Chet Huntley." In: his The Americans.
      New York: Stein & Day, 1970. pp. 185-188.
2681 "Good-bye Chet." Newsweek, LXXIX (April 10, 1972),
      57.
2682 Huntley, Chet. "Chet Huntley Speaks His Mind: An
      Interview." National Wildlife, X (June 1972), 34-35.
2683 _____. "Educationists: An Address, April 7, 1973."
      Vital Speeches, XXXIX (July 15, 1973), 601-603.
2684 _____. Generous Years: Remembrances of a Frontier
      Boyhood. New York: Random House, 1968. 215p.
2685 _____. "Good Night All." TV Guide, XVIII (August
      1, 1970), 8-11.
2686 Kaufman, Michael T. "Chet Huntley, 62, Is Dead: Re-
      printed from the New York Times, March 21, 1974." Con-
      gressional Record, CXX (March 21, 1974), 7654.
2687 Liston, J. "At Home with Huntley." American Home,
      LXIV (September 1961), 12+.
2688 Matloff, S. "The Saco Kid." Newsweek, LXXII (October
      7, 1968), 112-113.

2689   Polier, R. "His Co-Workers Respected Huntley." Bio-graphical News, 1 (April 1974), 416.
2690   "The Rugged Anchor Man." Time, CIII (April 1, 1974), 44.
2691   Schanche, Don A. "Good Night, NBC--Hello, Montana." Today's Health, L (May 1972), 54-58.
2692   Seventeen, Editors of. "Chet Huntley." In: their In My Opinion. New York: Macmillan, 1966. pp. 121-124.
2693   Thompson, T. "Chet Heads for the Hills." Life, LXIX (July 16, 1970), 33+.
2694   Weintraub, B. "Chet Huntley: He Changed TV News." Biographical News, 1 (April 1974), 415.
2695   "The World is Chet Huntley's Beat." TV Guide, VI (August 23, 1958), 17-19.

JENNINGS, PETER

2696   Hickey, Neil. "In ABC's Corner: Peter Jennings." TV Guide, XIII (August 14, 1965), 6-9.

JONES, PHIL

2697   Weisman, John. "He's the Gadfly of Capitol Hill." TV Guide, XXVIII (April 12 1980), 10-11.

KALB, BERNARD

2698   "Kalb Is Latest CBS Veteran to Switch to NBC." Broadcasting, XCVIII (June 23, 1980), 23-24.
2699   Weisman, John. "Bernard Kalb's China Syndrome Keeps Him Going." TV Guide, XXIX (July 11, 1981), 8-10.

KALB, MARVIN

2700   Hickey, Neil and Susan Ludel. "Is TV Looking at Russia Through Red-Colored Glasses?" TV Guide, XV (August 5-12, 1967), 6-11, 19-23.

KOPPEL, TED

2701   Albin, Len. "H-e-e-e-re's Ted." Family Weekly, (February 21, 1982), 18.
2702   Koppel, Ted. "Making the Great Leap Forward Into China." TV Guide, XXVII (July 14, 1979), 4-8.
2703   Piantadosi, Roger. "Profile: Ted Koppel." Washington Journalism Review, III (March 1981), 22-25.
2704   Waters, Harry F. "The Unflappable Koppel." Newsweek, XCVII (February 16, 1981), 75.
2705   Weisman, John. "ABC Correspondent Ted Koppel." TV Guide, XXIX (April 18, 1981), 22-25.

KURALT, CHARLES

2706   "CBS's Charles Kuralt." Broadcasting, CI (September 7, 1981), 119.

2707   Doan, Richard K. "Travels with Charlie Kuralt." TV
Guide, XVI (May 18, 1968), 20-21.
2708 "Charles Kuralt." In: Current Biography
Yearbook 1981. New York: H. W. Wilson Co., 1982.
pp 259-262.
2709 Hill, Doug. "The Importance of Being Irrelevant." TV
Guide, XXIV (November 20, 1976), 18-21.
2710 "Into the Heartland: Charles Kuralt's Essays."
Newsweek, LXXI (January 1, 1968), 54.
2711 Kuralt, Charles. "A Conversation with Charles Kuralt."
In: Frederick Shook and Dan Lattimore, eds. The Broadcast News Process. Denver, Colo.: Morton Publishing Co.,
1979. pp. 115-119.
2712 _____. "Dateline America: An Interview." Current,
CCXVII (November 1979), 8_13.
2713 _____. "Good Evening, Ain't It Pretty." Oklahoma
Observer, VII (November 25, 1975), 10.
2714 _____. "What Are We Afraid Of?" Reader's Digest,
CXVI (February 1980), 175-178.
2715 Phillips, Kevin. "What Television Needs Is More Kuralts."
TV Guide, XXIV (August 28, 1976), A3-A4.
2716 Segal, S. A. "On the Road with Charles Kuralt." Reader's Digest, CXIII (December 1978), 132-135.
2717 "Travels with Charlie: Charles Kuralt's Reports from
Small Towns." Time, XCI (January 19, 1968), 44-45.
2718 West, Richard. "Super Sundays with Charles Kuralt."
New York, XIV (June 1, 1981), 24-29.

LAWRENCE, BILL

2719   Lawrence, Bill. Six Presidents, Too Many Wars. New
York: Saturday Review Press, 1972. 307p.

LEHRER, JIM

2720 Droesch, Paul. "PBS Newsman Jim Lehrer" TV Guide,
XXX (January 23, 1982), 11-14.

LEONARD, BILL

2721 "Bill Leonard." In: Current Biography Yearbook 1960.
New York: H. W. Wilson Co., 1961. pp. 234-235.
2722 "Bill Leonard: Going Out on a High with CBS News."
Broadcasting, XCV (July 24, 1978), 34.
2723 Leonard, Bill. "Diary of a CBS News President." Broadcasting, CII (March 1, 1982), 78-92.
2724 _____. "An Interview." Washington Journalism Review,
1 (September-October 1978), 29-33, 86-87.
2725 Trachtenberg, J. A. "Bill Leonard: Behind the Faces
of CBS News." W, IX (August 15, 1980), 10.

LEVINE, IRVING R.

2726 "Irving R. Levine." In: Current Biography Yearbook
1959. New York: H. W. Wilson Co., 1960. pp. 258-260.

2727   Levine, Irving R.   "Adventures on the Lecture Circuit."
       TV Guide, XVIII (June 6, 1970), 8-12.

LOWER, ELMER W.

2728   Lower, Elmer W.   "My Twenty Years of TV Journalism."
       TV Guide, XXII (June 1, 1974), 6-11.

McGEE, FRANK

2729   Benchley, Peter.   "Frank McGee, Newsman."   TV Guide,
       XIV (June 25, 1966), 14-16.
2730   "Biographical Sketch of Frank McGee."   Congressional
       Record, CXX (April 24, 1974), 11765-11766.
2731   Farinet, Gene.   "Frank McGee, 1921-1974."   TV Guide,
       XXII (April 27, 1974), A3-A4.
2732   "Frank McGee." In: Current Biography Yearbook 1964.
       New York: H. W. Wilson Co., 1965. pp. 265-266.
2733   Miller, Merle.   "Buttoned-Up Frank McGee."   TV Guide,
       XIX (December 25, 1971), 10-12.

MACKIN, CATHERINE

2734   Drake, Ross.   "Newswoman Catherine Mackin." TV Guide,
       XX (August 12, 1972), 23-24.

MacNEIL, ROBERT

2735   MacNeil, Robert.   The Right Place at the Right Time: A
       Memoir.   Boston, Mass.: Little, Brown, 1982. 320p.
2736   Piantadosi, Roger.   "Profile: Robert MacNeil and Jim
       Lehrer."   Washington Journalism Review, III (December
       1981), 23-27.
2737   "Robert MacNeil." In: Current Biography Yearbook 1980.
       New York: H. W. Wilson Co., 1981. pp. 236-239.

MORGAN, EDWARD P.

2738   "Edward P. Morgan." In: Current Biography Yearbook
       1964. New York: H. W. Wilson Co., 1965. pp. 296-298.
2739   Morgan, Edward P. Clearing the Air. Washington, D.C.:
       Robert B. Lucas, 1963. 267p.

MOYERS, BILL

2740   "Bill Moyers." In: Current Biography Yearbook 1976.
       New York: H. W. Wilson Co., 1977. pp 274-277.
2741   _____. In: Eleanora W. Schoenebaum, ed. Political
       Profiles: The Johnson Years. New York: Facts on File,
       Inc., 1976. pp. 441-443.
2742   Crittenden, Ann.   "The Perplexing Mr. Moyers." Chan-
       nels, 1 (October-November 1981), passim.
2743   Fallows, J.   "Bill Moyers: His Heart Belongs to Daddy."
       Washington Monthly, X (July 1974), 37-50.

2744   "Moyers Returns to CBS as Senior News Analyst." Broadcasting, C (May 25, 1981), 46.
2745   Roberts, Charles. LBJ's Inner Circle. New York: Dial
Press, 1966. 223p. Includes a section on Moyers.
2746   Smith, L. E. "Bill Moyers." People, XVII (February 22,
1982), 47-48+.

MUDD, ROGER

2747   "Roger Mudd." In: Current Biography Yearbook 1981.
New York: H. W. Wilson Co., 1982. pp. 311-314.
2748   Schardt, Allen. "CBS's Mudd Drops Anchor at NBC."
Newsweek, XCVI (July 14, 1980), 64.
2749   "The Unmuddling of Mudd." Time, CXVI (July 14, 1980),
75.

MURROW, EDWARD R.

2750   Altman, W. "Edward R. Murrow." Contemporary Review,
CXCIX (June 1961), 279-283.
2751   Bilski, Theodore J., Jr. "A Descriptive Study: Edward
R.   Murrow's   Contribution   to   Electronic   Journalism."
Unpublished PhD Dissertation, Case-Western Reserve University,
1971.
2752   Bliss, Edward, Jr. "Remembering Edward R. Murrow."
Saturday Review, II (May 31, 1975), 17-20.
2753   "Busy Murrow: He Begins with Lunch." Newsweek, XLII
(December 7, 1953), 66.
2754   Crist, Judith. "Mike Man." Scholastic, LXIII (November
11, 1953), 6.
2755   "Deep Marks That Ed Murrow Left: The Profession That
He Did Much to Mold, Mourns Famed Newsman." Broadcasting, LXVIII (May 3, 1965), 44-46.
2756   Doyle, J. "Murrow: The Man, the Myth, and the McCarthy
Fighter." Look, XVIII (August 24, 1954), 23-27.
2757   "Edward R. Murrow." In: Current Biography Yearbook
1953. New York: H. W. Wilson Co., 1954. pp. 448-451.
2758   _____ .   In: Eleanora W. Schoenebaum, ed.   Political
Profiles: The Eisenhower Years. New York: Facts on
File, Inc., 1977. pp. 447-449.
2759   _____ .   _____ .   :   The Kennedy Years.
New York: Facts on File, Inc., 1976. pp. 379-380.
2760   "Edward R. Murrow of CBS: Diplomat, Poet, Preacher."
Newsweek, XLI (March 0, 1953), 40-41.
2761   Faber, Harold and Doris.   "Edward R. Murrow." In:
their American Heroes of the Twentieth Century. New York:
Random House, 1967. pp. 109-115.
2762   Fedo, Michael. "Ethical Proof in the Life and Speaking
of Edward R. Murrow." Unpublished MA thesis, Kent
State University, 1965.
2763   Forsee, Ayless.   "Edward R.   Murrow." In: his Head-
liners.   New York: Macrae Smith, 1967.   pp. 153-185.
2764   Kendrick, Alexander.   Prime Time: The Life of Edward
R. Murrow. Boston, Mass.: Little, Brown, 1969, 548p.

2765 Kuralt, Charles. "Edward R. Murrow." North Carolina
Historical Review, XLVIII (April 1971), 162-170.

2766 Lesueur, L. "The Most Unforgettable Character I've Ever
Met." Reader's Digest, LCIV (May 1969), 92-96.

2767 Levy, Elizabeth. "Edward R. Murrow." In: her By-
Lines: Profiles in Investigative Journalism. New York:
Four Winds Press, 1975. Chpt 2.

2768 Lichello, Robert. Edward R. Murrow, Broadcaster of
Courage. Outstanding Personalities, no 4. Charlotteville,
N.Y.: Sam Har Press, 1971. 31p.

2769 Lorenz, Lawrence. "Truman and the Broadcaster." Journal of Broadcasting, XIII (Winter 1968-1969), 17-22.

2770 McGrory, Mary. "Edward R. Murrow--A Startlingly De-
cent Man, He Symbolized Integrity: Reprinted from the
Washington Evening Star, April 28, 1965." Congressional Record,
CXI (April 29, 1965), 8956.

2771 Martin, Peter. "I Call on Edward R. Murrow." Saturday
Evening Post, CCXXX (January 18, 1958), 32-33.

2772 Murrow, Edward R. "Address to the Radio and Television
News Directors' Association Convention." In: Harry J.
Skornia. Television and Society. New York: McGraw-Hill,
1965. pp. 227-238

2773 _____. "A Broadcaster Talks to His Colleagues." Reporter, XIX (November 13, 1958), 32-32.

2774 _____. In Search of Light: The Broadcasts of Edward
R. Murrow (1938-1961). Edited by Ed Bliss. New York:
Alfred A. Knopf, 1967. 364p.

2775 _____. "Murrow's Indictment of Broadcasting." Columbia Journalism Review, IV (Summer 1965), 27-32.

2776 "The Other Voice of America." New Statesman and Nation,
XLIX (June 4, 1955), 780-781.

2777 Pedell, Katherine. "This is Murrow . . ." TV Guide,
III (February 5, 1955), 4-7.

2778 Price, W. "Murrow Sticks to the News." Saturday Evening Post, CCXXII (December 10, 1949), 25+. Abridged
in Reader's Digest, LVI (March 1950, 115-118, as "He Has America by the Ears."

2779 Reston, James. "Farewell to Brother Ed: Reprinted from
the New York Times, April 28, 1965." Congressional Record, CXI (April 28, 1965), 8692.

2780 Reynolds, O. T "Reporter as Orator: Edward R. Murrow." In: Loren Reid, ed. American Public Address.
Columbia, Mo.: University of Missouri Press, 1961. pp. 311-
331.

2781 Seldes, Gilbert V. "At Home with Edward R. Murrow
Person-to-Person." McCall's, LXXXI (February-March
1954), 24-25+, 53+.

2782 Smith, H. A. "An Intimate Chat with Ed Murrow." Good
Housekeeping, CXLV (November 1957), 84-85.

2783 Sorensen, Thomas C. "The Murrow Years: Tragedy and
Triumph." Foreign Service Journal, XLV (May 1968),
16-21, 28-30.

2784 Talmey, A. "See Them Now: Ed Murrow and the Man
Behind Him, Fred Friendly." Vogue, CXXIII (February
1, 1954), 144-145.

2785 Taves, I. "Edward R. Murrow." McCall's, LXXXI (February-March 1954), 24-25+, 53.
2786 _____. "A Visit with Edward R. Murrow." Look, XXIII (August 18, 1959), 19-23.
2787 Taylor, Telford. "This is Edward R. Murrow." Coronet, XXXV (December 1953), 114-118.
2788 "They Call Him Ed." TV Guide, 1 (November 6, 1853), 10-11.
2789 "This Is Murrow." Time, LXX (September 30, 1957), 48-51.
2790 "This--Is the News." Newsweek, LV (May 9, 1960), 106-107.
2791 "The Voice of a Generation." Newsweek, LXV (May 10, 1965), 77-78.
2792 "The Voice of Crisis." Time, LXXXV (May 7, 1965), 63.
2793 Wertenbacker, C. "The World on His Back." New Yorker, XXIX (December 26, 1953), 28-30+.
2794 Whitcomb, Jules. "Whitcomb to Murrow Person-to-Person." Cosmopolitan, CXL (April 1956), 20-25.
2795 White, S. "Interesting People: Edward R. Murrow." Good Housekeeping, CXXXVIII (February 1954), 18.
2796 Zito, Stephen. "The Lost Legacy of Edward R. Murrow." American Film, II (March 1977), 30+.

NESSEN, RON

2797 "Man in the News." Broadcasting, LXXXVII (October 7, 1974), 26-27.
2798 Nessen, Ron. It Sure Looks Different from the Inside. New York: Simon and Schuster, 1978. 367p.
2799 "Predecessors Haunt Nessen After Six Months." Broadcasting, LXXXVIII (March 24, 1975), 43-44.
2800 "Ron Nessen." In: Current Biography Yearbook 1976. New York: H. W. Wilson Co., 1977. pp. 284-286.

NEWMAN, EDWIN

2801 "Can We Get Ed Newman?" Life, LXV (November 15, 1968), 53-54+.
2802 "Edwin Newman." In: Current Biography Yearbook 1967. New York: H. W. Wilson Co., 1968. pp. 317-319.
2803 Gross, Martin L. "Conversation with an Author: Edwin Newman." Book Digest, III (February 1976), 168-176.
2804 "A Healthy Jaundice." Time, XCI (November 15, 1968), 53-54+.
2805 Newman, Edwin. A Civil Tongue. Indianapolis, Ind.: Bobbs-Merrill, 1976. 207p.
2806 _____. Strictly Speaking. Indianapolis, Ind.: Bobbs-Merrill, 1974. 205p.
2807 "Newman-at-Large." Newsweek, LXIX (June 26, 1967), 79.
2808 Pomeroy, Malcolm G. "The Bodacious American Language: Edwin Newman." American Legion Magazine, XCVIII (January 1975), 10+.

2809   Probst, Leonard. "Edwin Newman: An Interview." TV
       Guide, XXIII (November 29, 1975), 4-8.
2810   "The Sung Hero." Newsweek, LVIII (August 14, 1961),
       67.

OSGOOD, CHARLES

2811   Osgood, Charles. Nothing Could Be Better Than a Crisis
       That is Minor in the Morning. New York: Holt, Rinehart
       and Winston, 1979.

PALEY, WILLIAM S.

2812   Davidson, Bill. "William S. Paley of CBS." TV Guide,
       XI (January 5, 1963), 10-13.
2813   Paley, William S. As It Happened: A Memoir. Garden
       City, N.Y.: Doubleday, 1979. 418p.
2814   Thomas, Dana L. Media Moguls: From Joseph Pulitzer to
       William S. Paley, Their Lives and Boisterous Times. New
       York: G. P. Putnam, 1981.
2815   "William S. Paley." In: Current Biography Yearbook
       1951. New York: H. W. Wilson Co., 1952. pp. 469-471.

PAULEY, JANE

2816   Ball, A. "Jane Pauley and Sandy Hill: This is Your
       Life." Redbook, CL (November 1977), 94+.
2817   "Barbara's Heir." Forbes, CXX (October 1, 1977), 102.
2818   Birmingham, F. A. "Jane Pauley: The Girl Next Door
       Makes Good." Saturday Evening Post, CCXLIX (February
       1977), 48-50+.
2819   Harayda, Janice. "Talking with Today's Jane Pauley."
       Glamour, LXXV (March 1977), 120+.
2820   Hickey, Neil. "Too Big, Too Soon?" TV Guide, XXV
       (August 27, 1977), 22-28.
2821   Jacobs, Linda. Jane Pauley: A Heartland Style. St.
       Paul, Minn.: EMC Corp., 1978. 39p.
2822   "Jane Pauley." U.S., 1 (November 15, 1977), 26-29.
2823   Levy, Stephen. "Princess Jane--Approximately." Craw-
       daddy, (April 1977), 42-47.
2824   "Pauley Signs On." Time, CVIII (October 11, 1976), 76.

PETTIT, TOM

2825   Drake, Ross. "The Persistent Tom Pettit." TV Guide,
       XIX (July 3, 1971), 14-17.

PIERPOINT, ROBERT

2826   Pierpoint, Robert. At the White House: Assignment to
       Six Presidents. New York: G. P. Putnam, 1981. 240p.
2827   Yoffe, Sally. "Profile: Robert Pierpoint." Washington
       Journalism Review, II (December 1980), 46-50.

QUINN, SALLY

2828 "Apologia pro Sally Quinn." Broadcasting, LXXXIX (July 28, 1975), 34.
2829 Burke, Ted. "Focus on Sally Quinn, with an Interview." Harper's Bazaar, CVI (October 1973), 121+.
2830 "The CBS Morning Blues." Newsweek, LXXXII (August 20, 1973), 65.
2831 Francke, L. B. "Avenging Angel: Sally Quinn and the CBS Morning News." Newsweek, LXXXVI (July 7, 1975), 43-44.
2832 "Pretty Poison." Newsweek, LXXXII (July 2, 1973), 50.
2833 Quinn, Sally. "Live a New Way." Vogue, CLXVI (June 1976), 114+.
2834 _____. "'So There I was on TV!--Me, Sally Quinn!--Oh, My God!'" Esquire, LXXXIV (August 1975), 104-107+.
2835 _____. We're Gona Make You a Star. New York: Dell Books, 1976. 286p.
2836 "Sallying Forth." Time, CII (August 20, 1973), 63-64.

RABEL, ED

2837 Buchanan, Patrick. "What's Needed to Wipe Away Ed Rabel's Tears." TV Guide, XXIII (February 22, 1975), A3-A4.

RATHER, DAN

2838 "And This is the Way It Will Be: Rather to Get Cronkite Job." Broadcasting, XCVIII (February 18, 1980), 44-45.
2839 Arlen, Michael J. "The Prosecutor." New Yorker, LIII (November 28, 1977), 166-173.
2840 Baker, J. F. "Publisher's Weekly Interviews Dan Rather." Publisher's Weekly, CCXI (May 9, 1977), 8-9.
2841 Bedell, Sally. "Dan Rather's Dilemma." TV Guide, XXIX (May 30, 1981), 15-25.
2842 Bennetts, L. "He'd Rather Get the News." Biographical News, 1 (April 1974), 449-450.
2843 Collins, Nancy. "Twenty Questions [for] Dan Rather: An Interview." Playboy, XXVI (May 1979), 189+.
2844 "Dan Rather." In: Current Bigraphy Yearbook 1975. New York: H. W. Wilson Co., 1975. pp. 337-340.
2845 _____. In: Eleanora W. Schoenebaum, ed. Political Profiles: The Nixon/Ford Years. New York: Facts on File, Inc., 1979. pp. 507-508.
2846 "Dan Rather: Lightning Rod in White House Hostility." Broadcasting, LXXXV (December 10, 1973), 67.
2847 Emerson, Gloria. "Newsman Tuned in to the Temper of Our Times." Vogue, CLXXI (September 1981), 199+.
2848 "The Houston Hurricane." Time, CXV (February 25, 1980), 72-74.
2849 Jahr, C. "Dan Rather: Soft Side of a Tough Anchorman." Ladies Home Journal, XCVII (July 1980), 76+.

2850 Janssen, P. A. "Dan Rather: Did His Family Pay for
His Success?" Parent's Magazine, LIII (August 1978),
50-51+.

2851 Latham, Aaron. "The Reporter the President Hates."
New York, VII (January 21, 1974), 34-43.

2852 "The New Face of TV News." Time, CXV (February 25,
1980), 64-66.

2853 Nobile, Philip. "Dan Rather is Going Fishing: CBS News
White House Correspondent." Esquire, LXXXI (April 1978),
106-108+.

2854 Rather, Dan. "Barbara, Eric, Walter, and Me." Family
Circle, XC (June 28, 1977), 4+.

2855 _____ . The Camera Never Blinks: Adventures of a
TV Journalist. New York: William Morrow, 1977. 320p.

2856 _____ . _____ . Book Digest, IV (August 1977),
35+.

2857 _____ . "A Hard Act [Walter Cronkite] to Follow: An
Interview." Rolling Stone, (April 2, 1981), 10-15.

2858 "Rather Lather." Newsweek, LXXXIV (September 2,
1974), 49.

2859 "Rather Rattled: CBS White House Correspondent." Time,
LXXXV (February 5, 1965), 94+.

2860 Smilgis, Martha. "His Name Is Mud to CBS Rivals, But
Dan Rather Says That's the Way It Is." People, XIII
(March 3, 1980), 32-33.

2861 "The 25 Most Intriguing People of 1980: Dan Rather."
People, XIV (December 29, 1980-January 5, 1981), 80.

2862 Waters, Harry F. "Dan Rather, Anchorman." Newsweek,
XCV (February 25, 1980), 71-72.

2863 "What Rather is Running For." Broadcasting, LXXXVIII
(January 27, 1975), 64.

REASONER, HARRY

2864 "ABC Tells CBS to Keep Its Hands Off Harry Reasoner."
Broadcasting, XCIV (January 30, 1978), 85.

2865 Bedell, Sally. "What Made Harry Reasoner Switch Back
to CBS?" TV Guide, XXVII (January 27, 1979), 24-30.

2866 "Cloaking Pitfalls in Smiles." Time, XCIII (January 10,
1969), 30.

2867 Efron, Edith. "The Reasoner Touch." TV Guide, XII
(July 25, 1964), 15-17.

2868 "Harry Reasoner." In: Current Biography Yearbook
1966 New York: H. W. Wilson Co., 1967. pp. 322-324.

2869 Hickey, Neil. "Harry Reasoner Answers Some Questions."
TV Guide, XIX (March 20, 1971), 6-12.

2870 Reasoner, Harry. Before the Colors Fade. New York:
Alfred A. Knopf, 1981. 224p.

2871 _____ . The Reasoner Report. Garden City, N.Y.:
Doubleday, 1966. 168p.

2872 Scavrillo, Francesco. "Harry Reasoner: An Interview."
Qui, VI (November 1977), 72+.

REYNOLDS, FRANK

2873   Doan, Richard K. "Frank Reynolds Will Become ABC Nightly News Anchor." TV Guide, XVI (May 18, 1968), A-3.
2874   "Reynolds Is Replaced by Reasoner on ABC-TV." Broadcasting, LXXIX (November 9, 1970), 54.
2875   Weisman, John. "Drop in at Frank's Place--or Else." TV Guide, XXVII (September 1, 1979), 18-21.

RIVERA, GERALDO

2876   Bedell, Sally. "ABC Divisions Fight for Services of 'Soulful' Newsman." TV Guide, XXV (August 20, 1977), A-3.
2877   "Geraldo Rivera." In: Current Biography Yearbook 1975. New YorK: H. W. Wilson Co., 1976. pp. 358-361.
2878   _____. New York Sunday News Magazine, (September 10, 1972), passim.
2879   Weisman, John. "The Stange Case of Geraldo Rivera." TV Guide, XXVIII (December 6, 1980), 21-27.

ROBINSON, MAX

2880   "Seafood Is His Specialty." Ebony, XXXVI (March 1981), 104-105.
2881   Simon, Roger. "No Longer Invisible." TV Guide, XXVI (December 2, 1978), 18-20.

ROONEY, ANDY

2882   Koper, Peter. "Boldface: A Profile of Andy Rooney." Washington Journalism Review, II (Jauary-February 1980), 70-75.
2883   Levine, Martin. "A Few More Minutes with Andy Rooney: An Interview." Book Digest, IX (April 1982), 52-58.
2884   Rooney, Andrew A. A Few Minutes with Andy Rooney. New York: Atheneum, 1981. 245p.
2885   _____. _____. Book Digest, IX (April 1982), 52-58.
2886   _____. "A TV Writer Copes with American History." TV Guide, XXIII (June 28, 1975), 32-34.
2887   _____. "A Writer's Complaint." TV Guide, XIX (October 2, 1971), 45-48.

RUDD, HUGHES

2888   Hickey, Neil. "His Attitude Is Casual." TV Guide, XXIII (December 27, 1975), 20-22.
2889   Polier, R. "The Seven O'Clock Sage Is a Texan Named Rudd." Biographical News, 1 (July 1974), 827-828.
2890   "Roone Gets Rudd." Broadcasting, XCVI (June 25, 1979), 62-63.
2891   Rudd, Hughes. "Hughes Rudd's West Side Story." TV Guide, XXVI (July 8, 1978), 20-22.
2892   "A Sardonic Man in Moscow." Time, LXXXVII (May 27, 1966), 69-79.

SAARINEN, ALINE

2893 Efron, Edith. "A Portrait of Aline Saarinen." TV Guide,
      XVIII (April 25, 1970), 28-32.

SAFER, MORLEY

2894 "Morley Safer." In: Current Biography Yearbook 1980.
      New York: H. W. Wilson Co., 1981. pp. 355-359.
2895 Vespa, Mary. "If Anthropologist Jane Safer Finds Hus-
      band Morley Home, It's Rarely for More than 60 Minutes."
      People, XI (January 15, 1979), 62-67.

SALANT, RICHARD S.

2896 "Dick Salant and the Purity of the News." Broadcasting,
      XCIII (September 19, 1977), 105.
2897 "Never a Newsman, Always a Journalist." Broadcasting,
      XCVI (February 26, 1979), 90-94.
2898 "Richard S. Salant." In: Current Biography Yearbook
      1961. New York: H. W. Wilson Co., 1962. pp. 404-406.
2899 "Salant's Jump [from CBS to NBC]." Time, CIII (April
      9, 1979), 69-70.
2900 "Up, Out, and Over to NBC." Newsweek, XCIII (April
      9, 1979), 101-102.

SALINGER, PIERRE

2901 DeRoos, Robert. "Pierre Salinger in the Early Days of
      TV." TV Guide, XVII (April 26, 1969), 6-8.
2902 "Pierre Salinger." In: Current Biography Yearbook 1961.
      New York: H. W. Wilson Co., 1962. pp. 406-408.

SAUTER, VAN GORDON

2903 "Heaving Up the Hierarchy at CBS." Broadcasting, CI
      (November 16, 1981), 32-33.
2904 Levin, Eric. "Censors in Action." TV Guide, XXV (De-
      cember 10-17, 1977), 4-10, 18-22.
2905 "A New Helmsman for CBS News." Broadcasting, CII
      (February 15, 1982), 72-73.
2906 Waters, Harry F. "CBS News Gets a New Boss." News-
      week, XCVIII (December 7, 1981), 123.

SAVITCH, JESSICA

2907 Carter, Bill. "NBC's Golden Girl." Newsweek, XCIII
      (January 15, 1979), 86.
2908 Cohen, Rich. "The First Time I Saw Houston: An Inter-
      view with Jessica Savitch." Houston, IV (March 1980), 60-
      61.
2909 Hennessee, Judith A. "What It Takes to Anchor the
      News." Ms., VIII (August 1979), 84-94.

2910   Range, Peter R.   "'I'm Not Going to Apologize for My
       Looks Any More.'"   TV Guide, XXVII (March 3, 1979),
       13-18.
2911   Rein, Richard K.   "Yes, Jessica Savitch, the Fresh Claim-
       ant to NBC News' Peacock Throne Is Pretty--Pretty Tough."
       People, XIV (November 10, 1980), 88-90, 95.

SAWYER, DIANE

2912   Bent, T.   "Risen from the Ashes of the Nixon White
       House, Diane Sawyer Becomes CBS' Morning Star."   People,
       XVI (November 9, 1981), 50-52.
2913   Gildea, William.   "CBS Correspondent Diane Sawyer."
       TV Guide, XXIX (February 28, 1981), 24-26.
2914   Gross, Edith L.   "TV's Newest . . . Diane Sawyer."
       Vogue, CLXXII (January 1982), 166-169, 228.

SCALI, JOHN

2915   Hickey, Neil.   "How Ex-Diplomat Views His Return to
       Network News."   TV Guide, XXIII (August 16, 1975),
       A-1.
2916   "John Scali."   In: Current Biography Yearbook 1973.
       New York: H. W. Wilson Co., 1974. pp. 376-378.
2917   _____.   In: Eleanora W. Schoenebaum, ed. Political
       Profiles: The Kennedy Years.   New York: Facts on
       File, Inc., 1976. p. 463.

SCHIEFFER, BOB

2918   Hickey, Neil.   "If His Accent Gets Thicker, Watch Out."
       TV Guide, XXVIII (October 11, 1980), 26-28.
2919   Schieffer, Bob.   "The President's Road Show."   New
       Leader, LVIII (March 31, 1975), 6-8.

SCHOENBRUN, DAVID

2920   "David Schoenbrun."   In: Current Biography Yearbook
       1960.   New York: H. W. Wilson Co., 1961. pp. 360-362.
2921   Harding, Henry.   "David Schoenbrun Leaves CBS."   TV
       Guide, XI (July 6, 1963), A-1.

SCHORR, DANIEL

2922   Alpern, David .   "The Question of Leakage: Publication
       of CIA Report in the Village Voice."   Newsweek, LXXXVII
       (February 23, 1976), 12-13.
2923   Anderson, Jack.   "News Leaks and Hypocrisy: Reprinted
       from The Washington Post, March 28, 1976."   In: Francis
       H. and Ludmila A. Voelker, eds.   Mass Media: Forces in Our
       Society.   New York: Harcourt Brace Jovanovich, 1978. pp.
       86-88.
2924   Buchanan, Patrick.   "Regarding the Ethics and Veracity
       of Daniel Schorr."   TV Guide, XXIV (March 13, 1976),
       A3-A4.

2925 "CBS Offers Its Perspective on Bernstein, Schorr Replays of CIA Link." Broadcasting, XCIII (September 26, 1977), 52.

2926 "CBS Suspends Schorr: Reporter's Group Declines Payment for Pike Report." Editor and Publisher, CIX (February 28, 1976), 11+.

2927 Claiborne, William and Laurence Stern. "Voice Melodrama: Reprinted from the Washington Post, February 12, 1976." In: Francis H. and Ludmila A. Voelker, eds. Mass Media: Forces in Our Society. New York: Harcourt Brace Jovanovich, 1978. pp. 79-81.

2928 "Daniel Schorr." In: Current Biography Yearbook 1959. New York: H. W. Wilson Co., 1959. pp. 407-408.

2929 _____. In: Current Biography Yearbook 1978. New York: H. W. Wilson Co., 1979. pp. 363-367.

2930 _____. In: Eleanora W. Schoenebaum, ed. Political Profiles: The Nixon/Ford Years. New York: Facts on File, Inc., 1979. pp. 576-578.

2931 Furlong, William B. "Dan ('Killer') Schorr, the Great Abrasive." New York, VIII (June 16, 1975), 41-44.

2932 Gelman, D. "Defender of the Faith." Newsweek, LXXXVIII (September 27, 1976), 85.

2933 Getlein, F. "Daniel Schorr: At the Eye of Several Storms." In: Barbara Mykoruk, ed. Authors in the News. 2 vols. Detroit, Mich.: Gale Research Company, 1976. II, 239-240.

2934 Ignatius, David. "Dan Schorr: The Secret Sharer." Washington Monthly, VIII (April 1976), 6-20.

2935 Keerdoja, E. "Broadcaster Bounces Back." Newsweek, XCIII (May 14, 1979), 22-23.

2936 Panitt, Merrill. "First Amendment: No License to Steal." TV Guide, XXIV (October 16, 1976), A5-A6.

2937 Roche, John P. "Confessions of an Unrepentant Leaker of Secrets." TV Guide, XXIV (April 3, 1976), A3-A4.

2938 "Salant Defends Schorr--Up to a Point." Broadcasting, XC (May 10, 1976), 53-54.

2939 "Schoenbrun, Defends CBS's Dan Schorr; Rather Adds Ominous Note." Broadcasting, XC (March 8, 1976), 26.

2940 Schorr, Daniel. "Behind the Lines with Daniel Schorr: An Interview." Christianity and Crisis, XXXVI (April 26, 1976), 93-98.

2941 _____. Clearing the Air. Boston, Mass.: Houghton-Mifflin, 1977. 333p.

2942 _____. "Covering My Own Story." Newsweek, LXXXVIII (October 11, 1976), 17.

2943 _____. "The FBI and Me." Columbia Journalism Review, XIII (November 1974), 8-14.

2944 _____. "My Eighteen Months on the CIA Watch: A Backstage Journal." Rolling Stone, (April 8, 1976), 32+.

2945 _____. "Of Secret Documents: Reprinted from the New York Times, February 22, 1976." In: Francis H. and Ludmila A. Voelker, eds. Mass Media: Forces in Our Society. New York: Harcourt Brace Jovanovich, 1978. pp. 83-84.

2946 _____ . "Schorr Revisits His Own Problems and Those of CBS." Broadcasting, XCIII (October 31, 1977), 42-44.

2947 _____ . "Schorr Statement on House CIA Report." In: Robert A. Diamond, ed. Historic Documents of 1976. Washington, D.C.: Congressional Quarterly, Inc., 1977. pp. 683-687.

2948 _____ . "Schorr Strikes Back." More, VII (September 1977), 48+.

2949 _____ . "Schorr's Thoughts on Leak Inquiry." Broadcasting, XCI (July 26, 1976), 35-36.

2950 _____ . "Shadowing the Press." New Leader, LV (February 21, 1972), 8-10.

2951 "Schorr Signs Off." Time, CVIII (October 11, 1976), 76.

2952 "Schorr Suspended from Reporting: CBS Will Go Only Part of the Way in Defending Him." Broadcasting, XC (March 1, 1976), 55-56.

2953 Seib, Charles B. "The Secret Report Caper: Reprinted from the Washington Post, February 20, 1976." In: Francis H. and Ludmila A. Voelker, eds. Mass Media: Forces in Our Society. New York: Harcourt Brace Jovanovich, 1978. pp. 84-86.

2954 Stern, Laurence. "The Daniel Schorr Affair: With Reply by Daniel Schorr." Columbia Journalism Review, XV (May and July 1976), 20-25, 48-49.

2955 Stone, Isidor F. "The Schorr Case: The Real Dangers." New York Review of Books, XXIII (April 1, 1976), 6-11.

2956 Waters, Harry F. and Tom Joyce. "What Makes Danny Run?" Newsweek, (February 23, 1976), 49.

2957 "White Hat or Black or CBS's Dan Schorr?" Broadcasting, XC (March 15, 1976), 22-23.

SCOTT, WILLARD

2958 Langdon, Dolly. "Fearing Today was Too Dry, NBC Threw in Willard Scott, the Clown Wince of Weathermen." People, XIV (September 1, 1980), 89-91.

2959 Reiss, Bob. "Boldface; Willard Scott." Washington Journalism Review, II (July-August 1980), 49-51.

SEVAREID, ERIC

2960 Alpern, David M., et al. "He Looked Like God." Newsweek, XC (November 28, 1977), 130.

2961 Buchanan, Patrick. "The Sacking Out of a Big Cat Named Sevareid." TV Guide, XXIV (September 4, 1976), A3-A4.

2962 "Eric: Conversations." New Republic, CLXXIII (September 20, 1975), 26-28.

2963 "Eric Sevareid." Current Biography Yearbook 1966. New York: H. W. Wilson Co., 1967. pp. 363-366.

2964 _____ . People, VIII (December 12, 1977), 63-66.

2965 _____ : "He Was There." Broadcasting, XCIII (September 12, 1977), 32-34.

2966 Hickey, Neil. "Neil Hickey Interviews Eric Sevareid." TV Guide, XVIII (March 14, 1970), 7-11.

2967 Keerdoja, E. "A Life of Leisure." Newsweek, XCII (October 9, 1978), 26-27.
2968 Kitman, Michael. "Eric Severalsides Signs Off." New Leader, LXI (January 16, 1978), 22-23.
2969 Maddocks, N. "Sermonets and Stoicism." Time, CVIII (August 30, 1976), 69.
2970 Robertson, N. "Sevareid: Days of Reflection." New York Times Biographical Service, X (May 1979), 702-702.
2971 Sevareid, Eric. "CBS's Sevareid Rebutts, Myths About Television." Broadcasting, XCII (May 30, 1977), 47.
2972 _____. Conversations with Eric Sevareid: Interviews with Notable Americans. New York: Public Affairs Press, 1976.
2973 _____. "In Defense of Television, Part 1: 'A Little Less Hypocrisy, Please.'" TV Guide, XV (December 30, 1967.
2974 _____. "Eric Sevareid on Today's Morals, TV, War or Peace, Prosperity: An Interview." U.S. News and World Report, LXXXIII (December 26, 1977), 60-62.
2975 _____. "Final Commentary: Transcript of CBS Broadcast, November 30, 1977." Congressional Record, CXXIII (December 1, 1977), 38249-38250.
2976 _____. "A Free Press for a Free People: Excerpts from an Address, March 28, 1977." Society, XV (November 1977), 11+.
2977 _____. Not So Wild a Dream. New York: Alfred A. Knopf, 1946. 516p.
2978 _____. "A Return to God's Country." Audubon, LXXXIII (September 1981), 44-59.
2979 _____. "Sevareid Criticizes the TV Critics." Broadcasting, XC (June 7, 1976), 23-24.
2980 _____. "The State of Television, Part 4: 'The Big Rock Candy Mountain.'" TV Guide, VII (April 4, 1959) 5-8.
2981 _____. "Take Heaven, Take Peace, Take Joy." McCall's, CIV (December 1976), 96-97.
2982 _____. This Is Eric Sevareid. New York: McGraw-Hill, 1964. 306p.
2983 "Sevareid Goes Gently into That Good-bye." Broadcasting, XCIII (December 5, 1977), 53.
2984 "Sign Off for Sevareid." Time, CX (December 12, 1977), 111.
2985 Stroud, K. "Poor Little Rich Boy." Biographical News, 1 (August 1974), 951.
2986 "A Truly Great Man." McCall's, C (March 1973), 30+.
2987 "Voice of Reason." Time, XCVI (November 2, 1970), 9.

SHERR, LYNN

2988 Bauer, Douglas. "Typecast for Television News." TV Guide, XXVIII (August 2, 1980), 26-28.

SMALL, WILLIAM

2989 Nobile, Philip. "The Man Who Took Daniel Schorr Off the Air." More, VI (October 1976), 42+.

SMITH, HOWARD K.

2990 Efron, Edith. "Howard K. Smith Views Network News." TV Guide, XVIII (February 28, 1970), 6-11.
2991 Harding, Henry. "Howard K. Smith Parts Company with CBS." TV Guide, IX (November 11, 1961), A-1.
2992 Hendrickson, Paul C. "Washington Profile: Howard K. Smith." Holiday, LVI (September 1975), 32-33+.
2993 Hickey, Neil. "'I'm Not Running a Sunday School Platform.'" TV Guide, XXIII (July 26, 1975), 20-24.
2994 Hilts, Philip J. "Howard K. Smith and the Rise of ABC News." Washington Post Potomac, (August 11, 1974), passim.
2995 "Howard K. Smith." In: Current Biography Yearbook 1976. New York: H. W. Wilson Co., 1976. pp. 376-380.
2996 "Howard K. Smith Steps Back from Anchorman Role." Broadcasting, LXXXVIII (May 19, 1975), 31.
2997 McDowell, E. "The State of Howard K. Smith." National Review, XIII (December 31, 1962), 511-512+.
2998 Smith, Howard K. "Howard K. Smith Tells of Departure from ABC and CBS." Broadcasting, XCVI (June 25, 1979), 60-62.

SPIVAK, LAWRENCE E.

2999 "A Durable Interrogator: Lawrence Spivak of Meet-the Press." Time, C (November 6, 1972), 71.
3000 Dusha, Julius. "'This is Lawrence Spivak and I'm Not Afraid of Anybody.'" Washingtonian, VI (December 1970), 61-62.
3001 Efron, Edith. "Stalking Lawrence Spivak." TV Guide, XIII (March 27, 1965), 14-17.
3002 "Lawrence E. Spivak." In: Current Biography Yearbook 1956. New York: H. W. Wilson Co., 1957. pp. 597-599.
3003 "Lawrence Spivak, Washington Gadfly." TV Guide, II (October 2, 1954), 16-17.

STAHL, LESLEY

3004 Cimons, Marlene. "Lesley Stahl of CBS News." TV Guide, XXII (May 4, 1974), 14-15.

STANTON, FRANK

3005 Davidson, Bill. "Frank Stanton of CBS." TV Guide, XI (January 12, 1963), 10-13.
3006 "Frank Stanton." In: Current Biography Yearbook 1965. New York: H. W. Wilson Co., 1966. pp. 402-404.

STERN, CARL

3007 "NBC's Stern Again Breathes Down the Back of the FBI's
      Neck." Broadcasting, XCI (December 6, 1976), 61.

STEWART, BILL

3008 Dudman, Richard. "Lessons from Bill Stewart's Murder."
      Washington Journalism Review, 1 (September-October 1979),
      36-37.
3009   Koslow, M. "Death in a Family." Newsweek, XCIV
      (July 16, 1979), 14.
3010 Lee, H. "Stewart Murdered for Telling Real Story."
      Editor and Publisher, CXII (July 21, 1979), 15-16.
3011 "Murder in Managua." Time, CXIV (July 1, 1979), 60.
3012 "TV Newsman Murdered on Camera in Nicaragua." Broad-
      casting, XCVI (June 25, 1979), 27-28.

THOMAS, LOWELL

3013 Gallagher, R. S. "Good Evening Everybody: An Inter-
      view with Lowell Thomas." American Heritage, XXXI (Sep-
      tember-October 1980), 32-45.
3014 Lerch, John H. "The Broadcasting Career of Lowell
      Thomas: A Historical and Critical Evaluation of His Pro-
      fessional Life." Unpublished PhD Dissertation, Ohio State
      University, 1965.
3015 Thomas, Lowell J. Good Evening Everybody: From Cripple
      Creek to Samarkand. New York: William Morrow, 1976.
      349p.
3016 _____ . So Long Until Tomorrow: From Quaker Hill to
      Kathmandu. New York: Morrow, 1977. 617p.

TROTTA, LIZ

3017 Trotta, Liz. "Hey Fellows: Chet and Dave Sent a Woman."
      TV Guide, XXI (April 19, 1969), 6-10.

TROUT, ROBERT

3018 "Robert Trout." In: Current Biography Yearbook 1965.
      New York: H. W. Wilson Co., 1966. pp. 424-427.

VALERIANI, RICHARD

3019 Valeriani, Richard. "'Didn't You Sell Me a Pair of Shoes
      Once?'" TV Guide, XXV (August 6, 1977), 8-9.
3020 Weisman, John. "At Home on the Street." TV Guide,
      XXVIII (January 5, 1980), 14-15.

VANOCUR, SANDER

3021 Bohr, Peter. "Singing the Blues at ABC News." Washing-
      ton Journalism Review, 1 (April-May 1978), 8-9.

3022 Efron, Edith. "Sander Vanocur: Fox in a Hair Shirt."
TV Guide, XVIII (July 4, 1970), 34-37.
3023 "Sander Vanocur." In: Current Biography Yearbook
1963. New York: H. W. Wilson Co., 1964. pp 439-441.
3024 Vanocur, Sander. "How the Media Managed Me: My 15
Years of Conditioning by Network News." Esquire, LXVII
(January 1972), 82-85+.

WALLACE, CHRIS

3025 Bedell, Sally. "The Kid Did It." TV Guide, XXVIII
(December 20, 1980), 18-20.
3026 Smilgis, Martha. "To the Top." People, XII (July 30,
1979), 37-38.

WALLACE, MIKE

3027 Efron, Edith. "Mike Wallace: Boon or Bane?" TV Guide,
XII (August 8, 1964), 25-28.
3028 "Jugular Journalism." Time, CIX (May 2, 1977), 60.
3029 Kieffer, E. "Lion or Lamb?: Which is the Real Mike
Wallace?" Good Housekeeping, CLXXXVI (May 1978), 98+.
3030 "The Mellowing of Mike Wallace." Time, XCV (January
19, 1970), 57.
3031 "Mike Wallace." In: Current Biography Yearbook 1957.
New York: H. W. Wilson Co., 1958. pp. 577-579.
3032 _____. In: Current Biography Yearbook 1977. New
York: H. W. Wilson Co., 1978. pp. 417-420.
3033 "Mike Wallace: Devil's Advocate?" TV Guide, VI (June
28, 1958), 6-7.
3034 Powers, Ron. "Behind Mike Wallace: The Story of His
Secret Weapon." TV Guide, XXIX (December 19, 1981),
4-6.
3035 _____. "The Outside Groups That Help Mike Wallace."
TV Guide, XXIX (December 10, 1981), 4-10.
3036 Wallace, Mike. "For a Change, I Get Interviewed." Dial,
2 (October 1981), 8-9.
3037 _____. "Mike Wallace Takes on His Toughest Subject:
An Interview." TV Guide, XXVII (November 24, 1979),
14-18.
3038 _____. "My Side: An Interview." Working Woman,
V (June 1980), 88.

WALTERS, BARBARA

3039 "Barbara Walters." In: Current Biography Yearbook
1971. New York: H. W. Wilson Co., 1972. pp. 432-434.
3040 "Barbara Walters--The $5 Million Woman." Senior Scholastic,
CIX (October 7, 1976), 4-7.
3041 Barnard, Charles. "Barbara Walters Answers Questions."
TV Guide, XX (December 30, 1972), 26-30.
3042 Berman, S. "Mother and Daughter: The Very Private
World of Barbara Walters." Parent's Magazine, LIV (July
1979), 57-61.

3043   Chan. C. "The First Lady of Talk." Life, LXXIII (July 14, 1972), 51-52+.

3044   Chase, Chevy. "The Plot to Get Barbara Walters: An Interview." Ladies Home Journal, XCIV (October 1977), 84+.

3045   Cockburn, Alexander. "What Barbara Walters' Deal Tells Us About the Future of TV News." New York, IX (May 10, 1976, 34-35.

3046   Conaway, Jane. "How to Talk with Barbara Walters About Practically Anything." New York Times Magazine, (September 10, 1972), 40+.

3047   Diamonstein, Barbaralee. "Barbara Walters." In: her Open Secrets. New York: Viking Press, 1972. 422-425.

3048   "Early to Rise, Wealthy and Wise." Life, LX (February 18, 1965), 49-50+.

3049   Edison, Robert. "How Does Barbara Rate?" Viva, IV (May 1977), 56-60.

3050   Efron, Edith. "Barbara Walters: Scapegoat for TV News' Sins." TV Guide, XXV (January 29, 1977), A5-A6.

3051   _____. "Today's Barbara Walters." TV Guide, XV (August 5, 1967), 15-19.

3052   Fox, Mary V. Barbara Walters, the News Her Way. Minneapolis, Minn.: Dillon Press, 1980. 47p.

3053   Goldsmith, B. "Happy Tenth Anniversary, Barbara Walters." Harper's Bazaar, CV (September 1972), 162+.

3054   Grenier, Richard. "The Prime of Ms. Barbara Walters." Cosmopolitan, CLXXXIII (October 1977), 226+.

3055   Huston, M. "Barbara Walters: Today's Woman." In: Barbara Mykoruk, ed. Authors in the News. 2 vols. Detroit, Mich.: Gale Research Co., 1976. II. 275-276.

3056   Lewis, Barbara and Dan. Barbara Walters: TV's Superlady. New York: Pinnacle Books, 1976. 217p.

3057   McKean, W. "For Today's Barbara Walters, It's All Uphill Before the Dawn's Early Light." Look, XXXV (February 9, 1971), 56-63.

3058   Musel, Robert. "Doing It Up Royally." TV Guide, XXIII (September 20, 1975), 2-5.

3059   "Not for Women Only." Time, XCIX (February 21, 1972), 66.

3060   Peer, Elizabeth. "Barbara Walters--Star of the Morning." Newsweek, LXXXIII (May 6, 1974), 56-60. Abridged in Reader's Digest, CV (August 1974), 88-92.

3061   Quinn, Sally. "Why Are People Mad at Barbara Walters for Earning a Million Dollars a Year?" Family Circle, LXXXIX (October 1976), 44+.

3062   Robinson, J. "The Real Barbara Walters." Vogue, CLXVIII (September 1978), 456-459.

3063   Rosenblatt, R. "One More Piece on Barbara Walters." New Republic, CLXXV (October 23, 1976), 31-33.

3064   Shalit, Gene. "Barbara Walters." Ladies Home Journal, XCVIII (June 1981), 20+.

3065   Simon, John. "Verbal Barbarians: How Miss Walters Talks with Practically Anybody." More, VII (February 1977), 42-49.

3066   Stout, Bill. "An Open Letter to Harry Reasoner: About
       Your New Partner." Los Angeles, XXI (June 1976), 63-66.
3067   "Supersalaried Superstar: Eyebrows are Up Everywhere
       Over Walter's High Price Tag." Broadcasting, XC (May 3,
       1976), 30-31.
3068   Swertlow, Frank. "Barbara Walters and ABC: Is the
       Marriage Working?" TV Guide, XXV (February 5, 1977),
       21-26.
3069   _____. "Barbara Walters and ABC: Which is She--
       Journalist or Cher?" TV Guide, XXV (February 12, 1977),
       15-18.
3070   "Today's Woman." Newsweek, LXXIII (May 19, 1969), 73.
3071   Vail, Thomas. "Will Evening News Suit Barbara?" Re-
       printed from the Cleveland Plain Dealer, May 2, 1976."
       Congressional Record, CXXII (May 4, 1978), 12518.
3072   Walters, Barbara. "Barbara Walters: An Interview."
       Ladies Home Journal, XCIII (September 1976), 26+.
3073   _____. "My Side: Excerpt from an Interview." Working
       Woman, III (July 1978), 80.
3074   _____. "Waiting for Those Unguarded Moments: An
       Interview." TV Guide, XXI (December 1, 1979), 31-35.
3075   _____. "Where TV Fails Us: An Interview." U.S.
       News and World Report, LXXXI (October 11, 1976), 43-44.
3076   Waters, Harry F. "$5 Million Woman: Barbara Walters."
       Newsweek, LXXVII (May 3, 1976), 78-80.
3077   _____. "How Barbara Tuned Up." Newsweek, LXXXVIII
       (October 11, 1976), 70.
3078   "Will the Morning Star Shine at Night?: Barbara Walters'
       Move to ABC News." Time, CVII (May 3, 1976), 51-52.
3079   Zoglin, Richard. "Can Bob Save Barbara?" More, VI
       (September 1976), 36+.

WOODRUFF, JUDY

3080   Cimons, Marlene. "She's a Better Reporter Than Softball
       Reporter." TV Guide, XXV (November 5, 1977), 12-13.

ADDENDA

The citations in this section were produced or uncovered too late for inclusion in the main body of the text. All are, however, noted in the Author and Subject indexes.

3081   Adams, William C., ed. Television Coverage of International Affairs. Norwood, N.J.: Ablex, 1982. 253p.
3082   Allen, Jennifer. "First the Good News--Linda Ellerbee." New York, XVI (May 30, 1983), 14+.
3083   Annon, Robert S. "Behind the Lines in the Network News War." Playboy, XXIX (September 1982), 132+.
3084   Arlen, Michael J. "The Falklands, Vietnam, and Our Collective Memory." New Yorker, LVIII (August 16, 1982), 70+.
3085   ATAS/UCLA Television Archives Catalog: Holdings in the Study Collection of the Academy of Television Arts and Sciences/University of California, Los Angeles, Television Archives. Pleasantville, N.Y.: Redgrave, 1981. 196p.
3086   Atlheide, David L. "Three-in-One News: Network Coverage of Iran." Journalism Quarterly, LIX (Autumn 1982), 482-487.
3087   Barnouw, Erik. Tube of Plenty: The Evolution of American Television. Rev. ed. New York: Oxford University Press, 1982. 560p.
3088   Barrett, Mary E. "Keeping Up with Barbara Walters." Cosmopolitan, XCII (June 1982), 212+.
3089   Barthel, Joan. "Network Newswomen: Do the Barriers Still Remain?" TV Guide, XXXI (August 6-13, 1983) 4-11, 8-11.
3090   Barton, Richard L. and Richard S. Gregg. "Middle East Conflict as a TV News Scenario: A Formal Analysis." Journal of Communications, XXXII (Spring 1982), 172-185.
3091   Battista, Mary. "Lesley Stahl." Washington Journalism Review, IV (October 1982), 42-46.
3092   Benjamin, Gerald, ed. The Communications Revolution in Politics. Montpelier, VT.: Capitol City Press, 1982. 205p. Also issued as the Fall 1982 (Vol. XXXIV) issue of The Proceedings of the American Academy of Political Science.
3093   Blomquist, David. Elections and the Mass Media. Washington, D.C.: American Political Science Association, 1982. 65p.
3094   Bormann, Ernest G. "Fantasy Theme Analysis of the Television Coverage of the Hostage Release and the Reagan Inaugural." Quarterly Journal of Speech, LXVIII (May 1982), 133-145.

3095 "Both Sides Fire Volleys in CBS-Westmorland Case." Broad-
      casting, CIII (October 11, 1982), 32+.
3096 Boyer, Peter J. "The '60 Minutes' Hour of Reckoning."
      Washington Journalism Review, V (July-August 1983), 13.
      Galloway case.
3097 Breen, Myles P. "Kangaroo Coverage: Is News from Au-
      stralia News from Nowhere?" Washington Journalism Review,
      IV (May 1982), 39-41.
3098 Brennan, James C. A Qualitative Analysis, 1973-1974/
      1978-1979. Vol. 1 of TV Coverage of the Oil Crisis: How
Well Was the Public Served? Washington, D.C.: Media Institute,
1982.
3099 "Brief Encounter [with Diane Sawyer]." Esquire, XCVIII
      (July 1982), 68-70.
3100 Brinkley, David. "The View from the Trenches: An Inter-
      view." Broadcasting, CIII (November 15, 1982), 95-99.
3101 Brokaw, Tom. "Why Should TV Save the Environment?"
      Backpacker, X (May 1982), 12-14.
3102 Carter, Bill. "Sunday-at-7 Showdown: Can ABC and NBC
      Challenge '60 Minutes'?" Washington Journalism Review, V
      (September 1983), 20-22.
3103   . "Whatever Happened to TV Documentaries?"
      Washington Journalism Review, V (June 1983), 43-47.
3104 "'CBS Morning News' Getting Ready for Prime-Time Player:
      The Class Act of Diane Sawyer." Broadcasting, CIII (No-
      vember 22, 1982), 37-38+.
3105 Chancelor, John. "These Presidential Press Conferences:
      How to Improve Them." TV Guide, XXXI (May 14, 1983),
      4-7.
3106   . and Walter R. Moore. The News Business. New
      York: Harper & Row, 1983, 181p.
3107 Cockburn, Alexander. "Fact Shortage [in Falklands War]
      No Problem, Analysts Say." Harpers, CCLXV (July 1982),
      27-31.
3108   . "The Tedium Twins [MacNeil/Lehrer]." Harpers,
      CCLXV (August 1982) 24-27.
3109 Cohen, Ron. "Dan Rather: Better with a Sweater." W,
      XII (March 26, 1982), 16-17.
3110 Cross, Donna W. Mediaspeak; How Television Makes Up
      Your Mind. New York: Coward McCann Geoghegan, 1983.
      254p.
3111 DeParle, Jason. "CBS News: Dressing Down the [Wash-
      ington] Bureau." Washington Journalism Review, V (Janu-
      ary-February 1983), 9-10.
3112 Devol, Kenneth S. Mass Media and the Supreme Court.
      3rd. ed., rev. and enl. New York: Hastings House, 1983.
      464p.
3113 Diamond, Edwin. "The Trouble with TV News: 'To Err
      Is Human, to Correct Is Like Pulling Teeth.'" TV Guide,
      XXXI (January 29, 1983), 28-29.
3114   , and Jack Link. "The Truth About TV's Morning
      Shows." TV Guide, XXXI (May 21, 1983), 4-7.
3115 Downs, Howard and Karen Karpen. "The Equal Time and
      Fairness Doctrines: Outdated or Crucial to American Poli-

tics in the 1980's?" Communications/Entertainment Law Journal, IV (Spring 1982), 67-90.

3116 Dreifus, C. "Talking with Jessica Savitch." Redbook, CLX (January 1983), 12+.

3117 Erlick, June C. "Women as the New War Correspondents [in El Salvador]." Washington Journalism Review, IV (June 1982), 42-44.

3118 Ferrell, Robert H., ed. The Diary of James C. Haggerty: Eisenhower in Midcourse, 1954-1955. Bloomington: Indiana University Press, 1983. 288p.

3119 "A Fifth Estate Glossary." Broadcasting, CIV (January 1, 1983), 75-76.

3120 "Final MASH Note [:Robert Pierpoint Reports from Korea, 1953]." Washington Journalism Review, V (April 1983), 15.

3121 Frady, Marshall. "Filming an ABC Documentary ['Closeup'] in South Africa." TV Guide, XXXI (March 19, 1983), 2-7.

3122 "Frank Reynolds: ABC Newsman Dead at 59." Broadcasting, CV (July 25, 1983), 97.

3123 Frankel, Haskel. "Douglas Edwards." Connecticut, XLV (March 1982), 29+.

3124 Friedman, David. "Hugh Downs of '20/20.'" TV Guide, XXX (September 4, 1982), 20-23.

3125 Gerbner, George, et al. "Charting the Mainstream: Television's Contribution to Political Orientation." Journal of Communications, XXXII (Spring 1982), 100-127.

3126 "Getting There: An Interview with Dan Rather." Broadcasting, CIV (March 7, 1983), 54-64.

3127 Gibney, James. "Live from the West Wing, It's the White House Press Corps." Washington Monthly, XV (June 1983), 26-27.

3128 Gilbert, Robert E. "Television Debates and Presidential Elections: The United States and France." Journal of Social, Political, and Economic Studies, VII (Winter 1982), 411-429.

3129 Goldberg, Carey. "TV Coverage of Controversial Medical Issues." TV Guide, XXX (November 27,1982), 43-46.

3130 Greenfield, Jeff. "Does TV Ruin the Election Process?" TV Guide, XXXI (January 1, 1983), 24-26.

3131 _____. "The Myth of the Media's Political Power." Channels of Communication, II (June-July 1982), 18+.

3132 Greer, Herb. "Terrorism and the Media." Encounter, XXIX (August 1982), 67-74.

3133 Guidry, Vernon. "How Television Covered the [Economic] Recovery." Washington Journalism Review, V (July-August 1983), 41-49.

3134 Hammer, J. "Newscaster Robert MacNeil Is Happy to Take a Firm Stand on Both Sides of the Issue." People Weekly, XVIII (September 20, 1982), 119-120.

3135 Henry, William A., 3rd. "Weighing Network Anchors." Time, CXXII (August 8, 1983), 56.

3136 Hersh, Seymour M. The Price of Power: Kissinger in the Nixon White House. New York: Simon & Schuster, 1983. 698p.

3137 Hickey, Neil. "Henry Kissinger on Politics and TV Journalism." TV Guide, XXXI (April 2, 1983), 2-9.

3138 Higgins, Chester A. "[The Civil] Rights Struggle Opened the Doors--and in Walked [Bryant] Gumbel." Crisis, LXXXIX (April 1982), 38-39.

3139 Hill, Doug. "ABC Anchorman Peter Jennings." TV Guide, XXXI (February 26, 1983), 40-45.

3140 Hofstetter, C. Richard and David W. Moore. "Television News Coverage of Presidential Primaries." Journalism Quarterly, LIX (Winter 1982/1983). 651-654.

3141 Hulteng, John L. Fourth Estate: An Informal Appraisal of the News and Opinion Media. 2nd ed. New York: Harper & Row, 1983. 483p.

3142 Jamieson, Kathleen H. Interplay of Influence: Mass Media and Their Politics in News, Advertising, Politics. Belmont, Calif.: Wadsworth, 1983. 287p.

3143 Jenkins, Loren. "Singing the [El] Salvador Blues." Channels of Communication, I (August-September 1981), 19+.

3144 Johnson, W. O. "Van Gordon Sauter." People Weekly, XIX (May 30, 1983), 67-70.

3145 Kahn, Ely, J., Jr. "'The Candy Factory.'" New Yorker, LVIII (July 19-26, 1982), 40-61, 38-55. "60 Minutes."

3146 _____. "Profiles: Dan Rather." New Yorker, LVIII (July 19,1982), 40-42+.

3147 Kaiser, Charles. "Dan Rather for the Defense [in the Galloway case]." Newsweek, CI (June 6, 1983), 89.

3148 _____. "Unhappy Days at ABC News." Newsweek, CII (August 1, 1983), 48-49.

3149 Karp, Walter. "Subliminal Politics in the Evening News." Channels of Communication, II (April-May 1982), 23+.

3150 Kasum, Eric. "Big Bucks for Newscasters--That's Show Biz." Emmy, IV (September-October 1982), 10+.

3151 Kaufman, I. R. "Reassessing the Fairness Doctrine." New York Times Magazine, (June 19,1983), 16-19.

3152 Kepplinger, Hans M. "Visual Biases in Television Campaign Coverage." Communications Research, IX (July 1982), 432-446.

3153 Kitman, Marvin. "Another Day, Another Million: Are the Network Stars Worth Their Weight in Gold?" Washington Journalism Review, V (September 1983), 38-42, 58.

3154 Knightly, Phillip. "The Falklands: How Britannia Ruled the News." Columbia Journalism Review, XX (September-October 1982), 51-53.

3155 Kohn, Howard. "TV Coverage of Nuclear Issues." TV Guide, XXXI (January 15, 1983), 4-10.

3156 Kuralt, Charles. "The Soul of America." Family Circle, XCV (July 1, 1982), 12+.

3157 Laqueur, Walter. "Foreign News Coverage: From Bad to Worse." Washington Journalism Review, V (June 1983), 32-42.

3158 Ledeen, Michael. "The Bulgarian Connection [in Pope John Paul II Assassination Attempt] and the Media." Commentary, LXXV (June 1983), 45-50.

3159 Lesher, Stephen. Media Unbound: The Impact of Television Journalism on the Public. Boston, Mass.: Houghton, Mifflin, 1982. 285p.

3160 Lipton, Michael A. "How Americans Rate TV News." TV Guide, XXX (September-25-October 2, 1982), 6-12, 15-18.

3161 Lower, Elmer W. "Violence in Northern Ireland: Is Media Coverage Tinged by Partisanship and Sensationalism?" Television/Radio Age, XXX (September 20, 1982) 44-48.

3162 McCavitt, William E. Radio and Television: A Selected, Annotated Bibliography--Supplement One, 1977-1981. Metuchen, N.J.: The Scarecrow Press, 1982. 167p.

3163 MacDougall, William L. and Daniel K. Levine. "TV News Gets Bigger, But Is It Better?" U.S. News and World Report, XCIV (February 21, 1983), 49-50.

3164 MacNeil, Robert and Jim Lehrer. "At Large: An Interview." Broadcasting, CIII (November 8, 1982), 85-89.

3165 Matusow, Barbara. The Evening [News] Stars. Boston, Mass.: Houghton, Mifflin, 1983. 287p.

3166 _____. "How Frank Reynolds Viewed the News, Networks, and Notoriety." Washington Journalism Review, V (September 1983), 26-28, 58.

3167 _____. "Intrigue at NBC: John Chancellor and the Struggle Over the Voice of 'Nightly News.'" Washington Journalism Review, V (July-August 1983), 50-62.

3168 Meeske, Milan D. and Mohamad H. Javaheri. "Network Television Coverage of the Iranian Hostage Crisis." Journalism Quarterly, LII (Winter 1982/1983), 641-645.

3170 "NBC Drops Mudd from Anchor Slot." Broadcasting, CV (August 1, 1983), 54-55.

3171 "The Networks and Foreign News Coverage: Interviews with Correspondents." Current, no. 245 (September 1982), 9-24.

3172 Nimmo, Dan, ed. Government and the News Media: Comparative Dimensions. Waco, TX.: Baylor University Press, 1982. 303p.

3173 "1983 Field Guide to the Electronic Media." Channels of Communicaton, II (November-December 1982), 1-68.

3174 Pappas, Ike. "Reporting from the Pentagon." TV Guide, XXXI (February 5, 1983), 14-22.

3175 Patterson, Thomas E. "Television and Election Strategy." American Political Science Proceedings, XXXIV (Fall 1982), 24-35.

3176 Polskin, Howard. "A Guide to Late-Night News Programs." TV Guide, XXXI (July 16, 1983), 12-15.

3177 _____. "Nothing Stops [CNN's] Sandy Freeman for Long." TV Guide, XXXI (June 25, 1983), 18-22.

3178 _____. "Reporter's Dilemma: Save a Life or Get the Story?" TV Guide, XXXI (July 23, 1983), 4-9.

3179 Rather, Dan. "Pressure: How to Keep Going When the Going Gets Tough." Ladies Home Journal, C (April 1983), 52+.

3180 Ribowsky, Mark. "Who Are TV's Best Investigative Reporters?" TV Guide, XXXI (January 22, 1983), 4-10.

3181 Rohrer, Stuart. "Profile: Connie Chung." Washington Journalism Review, V (September 1983), 32-36.

3182 Rosenbaum, Ron. "The Man [Van Gordon Sauter] Who Married Dan Rather." Esquire, XCVIII (November 1982), 53-56+.

3183   Sanders, Marlene. "My Side." Working Woman, VII (November 1982), 230-231.

3184   Savitch, Jessica. Anchorwoman. New York: G. P. Putnam, 1982. 191p.

3185   Schmid, Alex P. and Janny de Graaf. Violence as Communication: Insurgent Terrorism and the Western News Media. Beverly Hills, Calif.: Sage Publications, 1982. 283p.

3186   Schreibaum, Jay C. Television News Resources: A Guide to Collections. Washington, D.C.: Television News Study Center, George Washington University, 1981. 27p.

3187   Shaw, David. "Dan Rather: CBS's $8 Million Anchorman." TV Guide, XXXI (February 19, 1983), 4-8.

3188   Shields, Mitchell J. "Profile: Ted Turner." Washington Journalism Review, V (March 1983) 24-28.

3189   Singleton, Loy and Stephanie L. Cook. "Television News Reporting by Female Correspondents: An Update." Journal of Broadcasting, XXV (Winter 1981/1982), 487-491.

3190   Smith, Desmond. "The Third Man [of NBC Nightly News]." New York, XVI (January 31, 1983), 27-31.

3191   Smith, Myron J., Jr. Watergate: An Annotated Bibliography of Sources in English, 1972-1982. Metuchen, N.J.: Scarecrow Press, 1983. 329p.

3192   "State of the Art: Journalism." Broadcasting, CIII (September 27, 1982), 43-71.

3193   Tannenbaum, Percy H. Turned-on TV/Turned-off Voters: Policy Options for Election Projections. Beverly Hills, Calif.: Sage Publications, 1983. 245p.

3194   Thompson, Kenneth W., ed. Ten Presidents and the Press. Washington, D.C.: University Press of America, 1983. 128p.

3195   Tobias, Andrew. "The Bottom Line in TV's Business Reporting." TV Guide, XXX (November 20, 1982), 4-10.

3196   Tornabene, Lynn. "Tom Brokaw: Aloft in a Space of His Own." Cosmopolitan, CXCIII (August 1982), 189+.

3197   Townley, Rod. "Does the Specter of Vietnam Affect El Salvador Coverage?" TV Guide, XXXI (July 9, 1983), 2-6.

3198   _____. "Weatherman Willard Scott of 'Today.'" TV Guide, XXX (December 11, 1982), 22-25.

3199   United States. Department of Commerce. National Telecommunications and Information Administration. Print and Electronic Media: The Case for First Amendment Parity. Washington, D.C.: U.S. Government Printing Office, 1983. 115p. Printed as Senate Print 98-50 for use of the Committee on Commerce, Science, and Transportation, U.S. Senate.

3200   Viorst, Milton. "The Media Front: Where Israel Lost in Lebanon." Channels of Communications, II (November-December 1982), 89-92.

3201   Von Hoffman, Nicholas. "The White House News Hole." New Republic, CLXXXVII (September 6, 1982), 19-23.

3202   Wade, Richard C. "How the Media Seduced and Captured American Politics." American Heritage, XXXIV (February-March 1983), 46-53.

3203   Watson, Richard A. The Politics of the Presidency. New York: John Wiley, 1983. 496p.

3204   Weisman, John. "Covering International News: The Haz-
       ards of Inexperience." TV Guide, XXXI (May 28, 1983),
       2-8.
3205   _____. "How Good is '60 Minutes?'" TV Guide, XXXI
       (April 16, 1983), 4-14.
3206   _____. "Intimidation: How Reporters Abroad Are
       Scared off Stories." TV Guide, XXX (October 23-30,
       1982), 4-10, 48-52.
3207   _____. "NBC Anchorman Roger Mudd." TV Guide, XXX
       (December 4, 1982), 28-35.
3208   _____. "Network Coverage of the White House: Who's
       Toughest?" TV Guide, XXXI (August 27, 1983), 4-15.
       Answer: CBS News.
3209   _____. "White House Reporter Andrea Mitchell." TV
       Guide, XXXI (January 1, 1983), 14-17.
3210   Westin, Av. "Inside the Evening News." New York, XV
       (October 18, 1982). 48-54+. Reprinted in Reader's Digest,
       CXXII (February 1983), 128-132.
3211   _____. Newswatch: How TV Decides the News. New
       York: Simon and Schuster, 1982. 274p.
3212   Wimmer, Roger D. Mass Media Research: An Introduction.
       Belmont, Calif.: Wadsworth, 1983. 397p.
3213   Woodruff, Judy. This is Judy Woodruff at the White House.
       Boston, Mass.: Addison-Wesley, 1982. 229p.
3214   Wren, Christopher S. "Reporting from China: Cracking
       the Great Wall of Silence." TV Guide, XXX (December 18,
       1982), 4-10.
3215   Zoglin, Richard. "News in the [Late] Night." Washington
       Journalism Review, IV (September 1982), 22+.

AUTHOR INDEX

SUBJECT INDEX

ABC *see* American Broadcasting Company
ABC Evening News/World News Tonight 340–346, 2696; *see also* Jennings, Peter; Reasoner, Harry; Reynolds, Frank; Robinson, Max; Smith, Howard K.; Walters, Barbara
ABC News Brief 347
Abstracts and Indexes 73–112
Access *see* Fairness Doctrine
Agnew, Spiro T. 437, 1003–1005, 1007, 1009, 1011, 1014–1015, 1018–1019, 1022–1033, 1037, 1039–1040, 1044, 1047, 1049–1050, 1056–1058, 1061, 1065, 1069, 1072–1074, 1079, 1083–1084, 1086, 1095–1097, 1099, 1102–1103, 1121–1123, 1580, 1964; *see also* Distortion and Bias; Government Attacks on the Media
Agronsky, Martin 2478–2480
American Broadcasting Company 139–142, 144–153, 156–161, 168, 266–279, 324, 335, 340–347, 3148
Anchormen *see* News Management and Production; Reporting
Annuals and Dictionaries 113–133, 3119
Anti-war Movement 1260, 1267, 1269; *see also* Vietnam Conflict, Coverage of
Arab-Israeli Wars, Coverage of 2247, 2252, 2257, 2259, 2261, 2269, 2280, 2284; *see also* Middle East, Coverage of
Arledge, Roone 270, 273, 335, 2481–2487
Audiences, News 146, 222–265
Australia, Coverage of 3097

Bergman, Jules 2488
Bias *see* Distortion and Bias
Bibliographies 1–72, 3085, 3162, 3186, 3191, 3211
Bill Moyer's Journal 524; *see also* Moyers, Bill
Biography, Collective 2443–2477, 3150, 3153, 3165
Bitterman, Jim 2489
Blacks 1124–1137, 2464, 3138
Bradley, Ed 2493–2496; *see also* Sixty Minutes
Blair, Frank 2490–2492; *see also* Today
Brinkley, David 363–372, 380, 526, 531, 636, 2497–2518, 3100; *see also* Huntley/Brinkley Report
Britain, Coverage of 2209–2211, 2214, 3161; *see also* Falklands War, Coverage of; Terrorism, Coverage of
Brokaw, Tom 378, 381, 2519–2526, 3101, 3196; *see also* NBC Nightly News; Today
Broun, Heywood Hale 2527–2529
Business and Industry, Coverage of 1138–1158, 2031, 3138, 3195; *see also* Sixty Minutes

Cable News Network 145, 294–308; *see also* Turner, Ted
Campaigns and Politics, Coverage of 22, 29–36, 41, 53, 55, 59, 542, 646, 737, 751, 1271–1335, 1709–2044, 3092, 3125, 3149, 3152, 3175, 3193, 3202–3203
Careers in Network News 688–693
Carter, Hodding, 3rd 2142, 2173; *see also* Foreign Affairs, Coverage of; Iran Hostage Crisis, Coverage of

227

Face the Nation 523, 527–528, 532
Fairness Doctrine 825–826, 829, 842, 845, 850–851, 854–855, 858–859, 862, 865–868, 870–872, 874–877, 879–880, 882, 884, 887, 889–892, 894–895, 897–902, 911, 913–914, 918–919, 923–925, 930–933, 935, 939–941, 943–944, 946–952, 954–956, 958, 966, 968–970, 976–979, 981, 984–992, 995–998, 1000–1002, 3115, 3151
Falklands War, Coverage of 226, 2236–2237, 3084, 3107, 3154
Fenton, Tom 2641
Fetter, Diana 2642
First Amendment 823–824, 827, 830–832, 836, 841, 846, 849, 851–852, 860–861, 864, 866, 873, 878, 881, 885–886, 899, 903–906, 908–910, 912, 915–916, 920, 922, 927, 929, 934, 936–937, 942, 945, 957–965, 971–973, 975, 980, 993, 3199
Foreign Affairs, Coverage of 2135–2442, 2696, 2698–2700, 3081, 3136–3137, 3157, 3171, 3203, 3205
Frank, Reuven 2643–2644
Frederick, Pauline 2645–2649
Freed, Fred 387
Freedom of Information Act 6, 777, 812, 814, 816, 819
Freedom of the Press see First Amendment
Freeman, Sandy 3177
Friendly, Fred 2650–2660

Garroway, Dave 2661; see also Today
Good Morning America 325–326, 332, 334, 520–530, 540, 2667–2668, 2672–2673, 3114; see also Hartman, David
Government Attacks on the Media 1003–1123; see also Agnew, Spiro T.; First Amendment; Government Control and Censorship; Intelligence, Coverage of; Watergate, Coverage of
Government Control and Censorship 766–822, 828, 831, 841; see also Fairness Doctrine; First Amendment; U.S. Federal Communications Commission

Graham, Fred 2662
Greene, Bob 2663
Gumbel, Bryant 2664–2665, 3138; see also Today

Hart, John 2666
Hartman, David 2667–2668; see also Good Morning America
Hartz, Jim 2669–2670; see also Today
Hearst, Patty 1179, 1202, 1226; see also Terrorism, Coverage of
Herbert, Anthony B. 498; see also Sixty Minutes
Hewitt, Don 505, 517, 2671; see also Sixty Minutes
Hill, Sandy 2672–2673; see also Good Morning America
Huntley, Chet 363–372, 2448, 2674–2695; see also Huntley/Brinkley Report, 363–372; see also Brinkley, David; Huntley, Chet
Huston Plan see Political Surveillance

Inauguration Coverage 2067–2073, 3094
Indexes see Abstracts and Indexes
Instant Analysis see Commentators and Commentary
Intelligence, Coverage of 56, 766, 768–773, 775–776, 782, 786, 791, 795, 809, 818, 820–821, 2100–2134, 2922–2957, 3007, 3158; see also Government Attacks on the Media; Political Surveillance; Watergate, Coverage of
Interviewing see Reporting
Investigative Reporting see Reporting
Iran Hostage Crisis, Coverage of the 2021, 2249–2251, 2256, 2258, 2262–2263, 2267–2268, 2271, 2273–2278, 2282, 2285–2288, 3086, 3094, 3168
Israeli/Egyptian Peace Talks, Coverage of 2248, 2253–2254, 2260, 2265, 2267, 2282, 2289, 2291; see also Middle East, Coverage of
Issues and Answers 546–547
Italy, Coverage of 2217–2218; see also Terrorism, Coverage of